ROSES

To

BETTY CATHERINE HARKNESS
I met her in 1946, had the extraordinary
sagacity to marry her in 1947;
and we have lived happily ever after, thanks mainly to her.

Roses

JACK HARKNESS

J M DENT & SONS LTD

LONDON   TORONTO   MELBOURNE

First published 1978
© Jack Harkness 1978

Made in Great Britain by
William Clowes & Sons Limited
London, Beccles and Colchester
for J. M. Dent & Sons Ltd
Aldine House, Albemarle Street, London

This book is set in 9 on 10½pt Times New Roman

British Library Cataloguing in Publication Data
Harkness, Jack Leigh
  Roses.
  1. Roses
  I. Title
  583'.372   SB411

  ISBN 0–460–04328–5

Contents

LIST OF COLOUR PLATES

LIST OF DRAWINGS

1 What Is a Rose?   9
   Its place among plants; its credentials; its sub-divisions

2 How Roses Are Made and Grown   16
   By rose breeders, nurserymen and gardeners

3 Introducing What Follows   23
   And about rose books

4 Simplicifoliae and Hybrids   29
   The simple-leafed rose which is not a rose

5 Hesperrhodos   33
   The primitive western roses of the United States

6 Platyrhodon and Hybrids   35
   The rose with flaky bark

7 Eurosa   38
   The 'real' roses

8 Banksianae and Hybrid   39
   Mu-hsiang: the wood-smoke rose of China

9 Laevigatae and Hybrids   42
   America's Cherokee Rose; but it came from China

10 Bracteatae and Hybrids   44
   Lord Macartney's rose

11 Indicae and Hybrids   47
   The mystery behind modern roses. Chinas, Noisettes, Teas, Hybrid Teas, Floribundas, Hybrid Musks, Miniatures, Climbing Hybrid Teas, Climbing Floribundas, Climbing Miniatures

12 Synstylae and Hybrids   149
   The Field Rose, the Musk Rose, Polyanthas, Climbing Polyanthas, Wichuraiana Hybrids, Kordesii Hybrids

13 Gallicanae and Hybrids   172
   The old roses of the west. Gallicas, Damasks, Centifolias, Moss Roses, Portlands, Bourbons, Hybrid Perpetuals

14 Pimpinellifoliae and Hybrids 197
    Wild yellow roses, Austrian Briars, Scotch Roses

15 Caninae and Hybrids 214
    Why Dog Roses are unique. Albas, Macranthas, Sweet Briars

16 Carolinae and Hybrid 224
    American beauties

17 Cinnamomeae and Hybrids 227
    Fruit in flagons, leaves in lace, the shadow of roses to come

18 The Heights 241
    From shortest to tallest. Climbers and trailers

19 The Colours 248
    From white to dark red

20 The Flowering Times 256
    From Late Spring onwards

21 The Perfume 259
    The most fragrant roses

22 The Hips 262
    A selection

23 The Stars 264
    A table of recommendation

24 Classification of Species 271

INDEX 275

Colour Plates

Between pages 96 and 97

1 *Hulthemia persica* (Photo by Betty Harkness)
2 X *Hulthemosa hardii* (Photo by Betty Harkness)
3 *R. roxburghii normalis* (Photo by Betty Harkness)
4 *R. banksiae lutea* (Photo by Betty Harkness)
5 'Ramona' (Photo by R. C. Balfour)
6 'Mermaid' (Photo by Bertram Park, courtesy RNRS)
7 *R. chinensis mutabilis* (Photo by Peter Harkness)
8 'Hermosa' (Photo by Peter Harkness)
9 'Lady Hillingdon' (Photo by Betty Harkness)
10 'Alexander' (Photo by Betty Harkness)
11 'Escapade' (Photo by Betty Harkness)
12 'Cornelia' (Photo by R. C. Balfour)
13 'Rosina' (Photo by Peter Harkness)
14 'Allen Chandler' (Photo by Betty Harkness)
15 *R. arvensis* (Photo by Peter Harkness)
16 'Yesterday' (Photo by Peter Harkness)

Between pages 192 and 193
17 'Dr W. van Fleet' (Photo by Betty Harkness)
18 *R. kordesii* (Photo by Peter Harkness)
19 *R. gallica versicolor* (Photo by Peter Harkness)
20 'Madame Hardy' (Photo by Peter Harkness)
21 'Chapeau de Napoleon' (Photo by Peter Harkness)
22 'Common Moss' (Photo by Peter Harkness)
23 'Zéphirine Drouhin' (Photo by R. C. Balfour)
24 'Roger Lambelin' (Photo by Peter Harkness)
25 'Golden Chersonese' (Photo by Peter Harkness)
26 *R. foetida bicolor* (Photo by Betty Harkness)
27 'Marguerite Hilling' (Photo by Betty Harkness)
28 'Celestial' (Photo by Betty Harkness)
29 'Complicata' (Photo by Betty Harkness)
30 *R. foliolosa* (Photo by Peter Harkness)
31 *R. moyesii* (Photo by Bertram Park, courtesy RNRS)
32 'Scabrosa' (Photo by Betty Harkness)

Drawings

Between pages 10 and 20

1 Diagram of a rose, showing the parts of the flower
2 The calyx (or veil) opens into sepals
3 A pinnate (or compound) leaf
4 The simple leaf of *Hulthemia persica*
5 Stipules free from the leaf stalk
6 Stipules joined to the leaf stalk for most of their length
7 Smooth hips
8 Prickly hips
9 Straight thorns
10 Hooked thorns
11 The large winged thorns of *R. sericea pteracantha*
12 Pruning

Drawings by Betty Harkness

1. What Is a Rose?

Let us imagine that we survey the world as strangers; and that after some time of savouring its beauties, we make a more particular inspection of its obvious plants, and ask how roses may be identified from all the others.

The first great division is between plants which bear flowers, and those which have none. The flowerless such as ferns and mushrooms and mosses, are known as cryptogams, which means secret sex works. We can set them aside, and study the flowering plants, which are the phanerogams, or in a rough translation those with visible sex works; well, that is one way of describing a flower.

The second great division slices the flowering plants into two parts, according to whether their seeds are uncovered, as in the cones of a fir tree, or whether the seeds are protected by some kind of pod or hip, as with roses. The names are again descriptive, for gymnosperms means naked seeds, and angiosperms means seeds in a receptacle. We pass by those with naked seeds, for roses clearly belong to the angiosperms.

The third great division cuts the angiosperms into two, according to whether one or two primary leaves emerge from the seed as it germinates. Grasses and lilies have one, and are therefore monocotyledons, which indicates one seed leaf. Roses are among the dicotyledons, having two seed leaves.

No simple fourth division offers itself, because the further one goes in classifying, the more similar becomes the unclassified residue, and the more detailed must the comparisons be to separate its components. The dicotyledons are divided into hundreds of families, identified in the main by the structure of their flowers. We therefore take a short cut to the family of interest to us; it is called the Rosaceae, which means its members are like roses. To qualify as a member, a plant needs certain credentials, but of a fairly elastic nature. The rules of admission prefer the word 'usually' to the more prohibitive 'always'. Thus the nonconformists in nature are admitted to their correct families, instead of being cast out like erring Victorian daughters.

Rosaceous flowers contain in the one bloom all four essential parts, namely calyx, corolla, stamens and pistils. Calyx means veil; it surrounds and protects the bud, and opens into leafy segments when its duty is done. The segments are called sepals, which means the covers.

A corolla is a little crown, and refers to the petals. The stamens, from a word meaning threads, are the male fertilizing organs, and the pistils the female. The pistil gets its name from a pestle because of its shape, for in addition to its visible part, its lower end is a rounded ovary deep in the flower. (Pestles are not so common as they used to be; they are shaped like a short fat drumstick bone, the rounded end being used to pound ingredients in a bowl. The old name for the bowl was a mortar.)

These four organs are arranged in concentric circles, the protective calyx outermost, the petals next, then the stamens, with the female in the centre.

Such flowers are called perfect, because they contain within themselves all that is

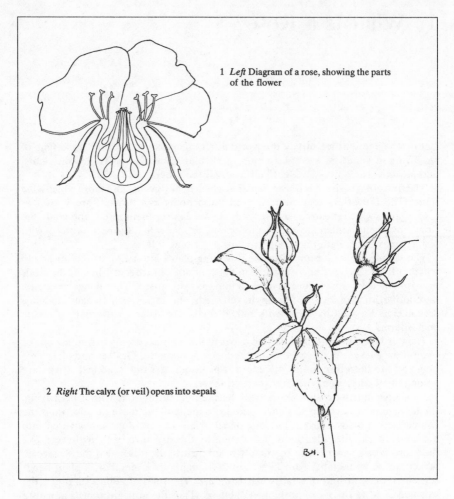

1 *Left* Diagram of a rose, showing the parts
of the flower

2 *Right* The calyx (or veil) opens into sepals

needed for reproduction, including both sexes in the same body, unlike some plants and all human beings; who might incidentally contemplate what peace of mind a rose must have. A rosaceous flower is also regular, that is to say the petals that form it are all much the same size; and the same uniformity applies to the sepals, stamens and pistils. The converse of this is to be seen in flowers like snapdragons, lupins and orchids.

Numbers play a part in plant recognition, and the natural rosaceous number is five; wild rosaceous plants normally have five petals and five sepals.

The leaves are placed alternately; if one grows on the left of the stem, the next is higher up and towards the other side. The converse of this is to be seen in many plants whose leaves are opposite one another.

Under those credentials, and one or two others which are less obvious, the family Rosaceae emerges as a distinguished one, being both useful and beautiful. It includes delicious fruits and charming plants: almonds, apples, apricots, blackberries, cherries, cotoneaster, geums, hawthorn, medlars, mountain ash, peaches, pears, plums, potentillas, quinces, raspberries, roses, sloes and strawberries; in all about ninety sorts.

Obviously it is necessary to take another step to separate these ninety from one another. Each is called a genus, which implies being generated, or born; and each genus has its own description, in addition to the family rules. We may ignore the other genera, and cite the recipe for roses thus.

Roses are shrubs or climbers, generally with prickly stems. Their leaf stalks do not bear a single entire leaf, but several leaflets, in an odd number, arranged two by two with one at the top. Where the leaf stalk meets the stem, it has a pair of rudimentary green growths known as stipules. (That word comes from the Latin for straws.) Roses have many stamens and pistils, and form a fleshy seed pod. Their seeds are like little nuts, with a woody shell, and an interior skin about the kernel.

Thus from all the plants upon the surface of the earth, roses may be recognized, placed in their own genus and given the international identification, *ROSA*.

A rose of five petals, which is the natural number in the wild, is termed single; and those with more petals are semi-double or double. It is important to understand that single means five petals; a great many intelligent people suppose it to mean that the stems bear one flower, a quite different conception, which could end in considerable annoyance. The intelligent people can justly plead to have been misled by botanists saying that flowers are borne singly, by which they mean one to a stem. But being single and being borne singly are completely different. Compare the case of a single man: he might be the only one upon a lonely shore, having let his wife and children go home; or he could equally be a merry bachelor roaring a rude chorus as he paints the town red with his friends. Between single and semi-double lies an uncertain area, for roses of seven or nine petals qualify on neither account. Some genius used the term

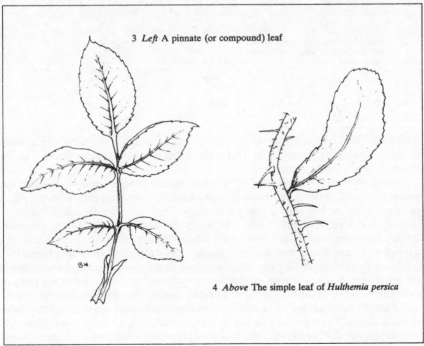

3 *Left* A pinnate (or compound) leaf

4 *Above* The simple leaf of *Hulthemia persica*

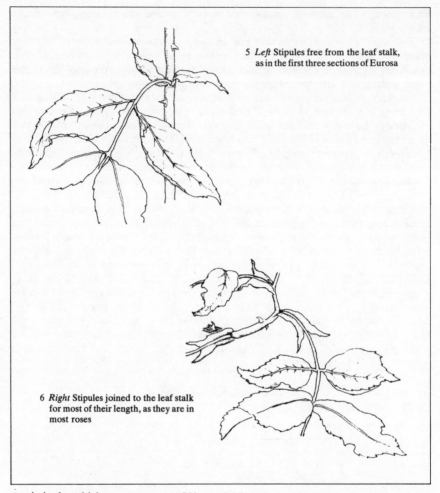

5 *Left* Stipules free from the leaf stalk, as in the first three sections of Eurosa

6 *Right* Stipules joined to the leaf stalk for most of their length, as they are in most roses

semi-single, which to me suggests 2½ petals! I suppose that if we had a logical term for roses having between 6 and 11 petals, it ought to be quarter-double; in its absence, semi-double must serve.

Having isolated the genus *ROSA,* we immediately observe that we have by no means escaped from diversity, because many kinds of roses were created in the wild, as clearly different from one another as cats from lions. Each kind is called a species; to qualify as such, it ought to have characteristics distinguishing it from all other species, and reproduce those characteristics faithfully from generation to generation; a rough test being that it should breed true from seed fertilized and borne by itself.

It is at this point that order and precision break down. Hard as it may be to believe, the exact identification of rose species has not yet been achieved. Botanists protest that the rose is one of the most difficult genera in nature to determine; and the reason may possibly be that it is yet in a state of evolution, far behind the more settled state of most plants. The best we can say is that about 130 rose species are generally acknowledged; and the likelihood is that about two-thirds of them would truly prove to be species, if only the proper tests could be made. It is not difficult to explain why this ignorance exists.

It was not until the twentieth century that all the wild roses of the world had been discovered for the benefit of western civilization; assuming they have all been found, for who knows if there may not be some more? They were described by their finders, and sent home to botanical gardens or botanists or gardeners in various parts of the world in the form either of seeds, or plants, or dried or pressed specimens. In some cases there was nothing but the description.

The botanists grew them, each in his own environment, and gave them specific names and descriptions in Latin. From this situation grew the following faults: the same species was sent to, and announced by more than one authority; the variability of roses was under-estimated, accentuated by the different environments, and as a result the Latin descriptions were not as exact as they should have been; if seeds were sent, they were apt to have fathers of another species, and to vary from the plant on which they grew; if seeds were grown from the plants sent, the same thing could happen, for roses happily set seed to pollen from a different rose. The result is fairly chaotic, and the only way to sort it out is to visit all the places in the world where wild roses grow, and fetch back plants of every one for a more careful examination. Unfortunately this option was only open for a brief period in the twentieth century, because the most important countries are China and the Soviet Union, neither of whom holds open their door and says 'Make yourselves at home, boys'. I can well imagine the reception of our rose explorers, upon asking the sentry at the Russian atomic testing grounds for permission to dig up a rose inside the fence!

If we do not know all we should about rose species, at least we know a reasonable

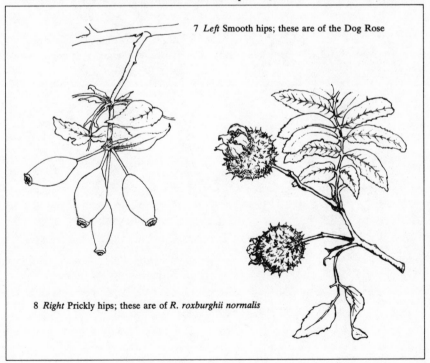

7 *Left* Smooth hips; these are of the Dog Rose

8 *Right* Prickly hips; these are of *R. roxburghii normalis*

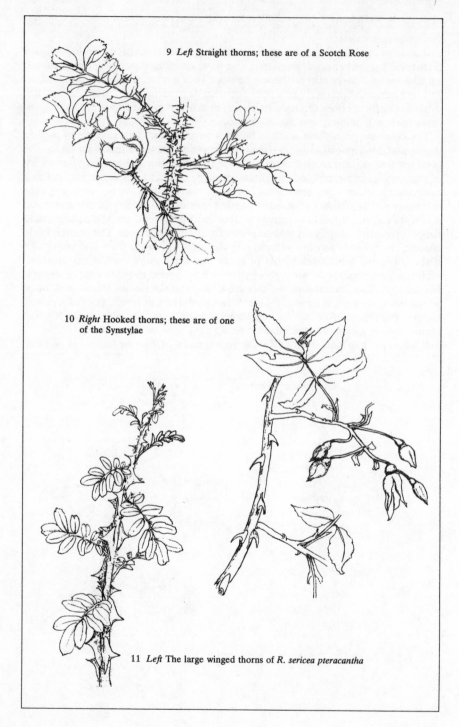

9 *Left* Straight thorns; these are of a Scotch Rose

10 *Right* Hooked thorns; these are of one of the Synstylae

11 *Left* The large winged thorns of *R. sericea pteracantha*

amount. A botanist named A. Rehder was particularly helpful in devising a classification for them. He divided the wild roses into four sub-genera, of which the first two and possibly the third appear to be primitive manifestations of the rose. Those three account for only a few wild roses; and as the fourth sub-genus contains most of them, it is divided into ten sections. You may follow Rehder's work in this book from Chapters 4 to 17. The first sub-genus was disqualified from being a rose after Rehder's time, owing to its leaves failing to conform to rosaceous fashion; but I have retained it, as it is most interesting, and experience shows that botanists are as likely as not to change their minds again in the future.

The final act of recognition among pure species is to distinguish plants which although plainly different are clearly only a variation from the species. For these the word variety is used; and the simplest example is to imagine a white variety of a pink species. There are two senses of the word variety, whether it is botanical or cultivated. The question is uniquely complicated in roses, due to their high rate of hybridity in nature, and their long history of cultivation. We can say with confidence that some are botanical, many are cultivated; but some plus many does not equal all, and we are left with a great number of hybrids and varieties whose origin cannot be ascertained. The convention is to refer to cultivated varieties as cultivars, which I described in the *Rose Annual 1974* as a graceless word, offensive in almost any context, sounding as it does like a grunt and a belch. Fortunately the rose's lack of precision absolves us from using that word in this book; or at least that is my story. I wonder why they didn't go the whole hog, and call the botanical varieties botivars?

Mankind's interest in roses has taken the genus far from its original wild state. In addition to the species and varieties, many classes of roses have been raised, some containing thousands of varieties of similar appearance. These are the roses which have delighted mankind through the ages. It is not easy to fit them into the genus at their correct place, but the effort is worthwhile, because it reveals to us much of the development, history and relativity of the rose.

I first tried to write this book chronologically, starting from creation, and proceeding to the present day. Unfortunately this does not work. It assumes that one completed development leads to another, like runners in a relay race handing over the batons. Roses, presumably, have never heard of time, and the whole wide genus is capable of advancing; nowhere is the development complete; also, the work done thousands of years ago can be repeated at will.

I have, therefore, inserted into Rehder's classification those hybrids and varieties we might wish to grow or know of. They follow that species which family likeness, tradition or common sense suggest. A human timetable has been thrown away in favour of describing the genus as it really is, an array of beautiful individuals each carrying her own jewels, and careless of time as immortals should be. The jewels are their progeny and history; it is better, I think, to insert the history into the roses, rather than the roses into a history. The result, to me, has been a panorama of the genus *ROSA* as living and evolving, its past, present and future all more vivid through forgetting time. I hope you may find it as exhilarating as I did. I could truly claim that this story has no end, an obscure beginning and a heroine who is for ever changing. That is to say, it is true to life.

2. How Roses Are Made and Grown

This is not a technical chapter aimed at the expert. My purpose is to ensure that a person who knows nothing about roses receives enough understanding to enjoy the rest of the book. In any case, I owe the experts a grudge for an old grievance.

Many years ago, I was puzzled as to why apparently healthy stems should allow their flower buds to wither, and the flower stalks to die. I therefore consulted an expert, who diagnosed the problem as Pedicel Necrosis. He had no more to offer in the way of cause and cure than the little I already knew, but it was grand to have the proper name of the blight. When people asked me what made their flower stalks die, I was pat with the answer: Pedicel Necrosis. It earned me many admiring looks. Then, one day, I saw the word necropolis, which I hadn't come across for some time, and I remembered its meaning, the city of the dead. It was used by some cemeteries, to provide the classical touch. My mind joined the necros together as meaning dead, and I idly looked towards pedicel. Why of course, a pedicel is a flower stalk. So when respectable citizens had been asking me why their flower stalks died, all I had told them was 'Death of the Flower Stalk'.

Turning from the death of stalks to what the journalists call 'The Birth of a New Rose', I remember many instances of explaining it to visitors in our breeding house, step by step, with the utmost clarity as I thought, down into the cells of the plant, its chromosomes and genes; and then some simple question revealed that the listener had been stranded from the outset by not realizing that new roses are made from seed. The exception admittedly exists of sports, which are dealt with later on; pray forget about them while we find our way to that vital element, the seed, the starting point of a new rose. 'Peace', 'Queen Elizabeth', 'Allgold' and company each started life as one seed.

The sexual organs of a rose, and for that matter of flowers in general, are the stamens and pistils. The stamen is the male, and consists of a stem, called the filament, on top of which is a head called the anther. Upon maturity the anther splits open and sheds the pollen grains. Both stamens and filament are words that mean thread; anther means flowering; and pollen comes from a Latin word for finely ground flour.

The pistil consists of an ovary down in the seed pod, and a long stem called the style, connecting the ovary to the head, which is called the stigma. Upon readiness for mating, the stigma covers itself with a fluid to which the pollen grains will stick. The word style means a thin post; and stigma is a mark such as might be made by a nail or by branding. Have a close look at the mature stigmas, and the reason for their name will be obvious.

When pollen grains fall on the stigmas, they have a race down the style, and the winner fuses with the egg-cell in the ovary. An embryo is formed, and grows into a seed. The number of seeds is variable, probably about twenty per flower on average; but I had a hip from 'Queen Elizabeth' with over a hundred in it.

If pollen and egg-cell are from the same true species, then the fusion is of male and female containing the same characteristics, and the seeds grow into identical reproductions of that species.

There are exceptions without which there would be no rose breeding at all. They started with wild roses, the only roses nature gave us. The stigmas of many roses are ready for mating before their stamens shed pollen. That interval gives time for pollen to arrive from other sources. The odds are that it will come from another flower on the same bush, or from other plants of the same species, because wild roses usually grow in colonies or thickets by spreading from the original plant by suckers or seeds.

However, wind or insects can bring pollen from a different species. Then the fusion is of male and female whose characteristics are different. The seeds, when they grow, are not reproductions of either parent, but are most probably a mixture of the two; and with some exceptions, the seedlings of a first generation cross between two species look more or less the same. A hybrid has been born. Instead of two complementary sets of characteristics, it bears within itself two different sets.

When the hybrid becomes fertile, which does not always happen, for many are as sterile as mules, there is the possibility of it fertilizing itself, or mating with other roses. Its characteristics, then become still more mixed, and they are legion. Pollen grains and egg-cells carry within themselves all the plans for their future child, down to the smallest hairs under its leaves. The easiest parallel to imagine is a kaleidoscope, in which new patterns are formed at every shake. New genetic patterns are likewise formed among hybrid roses when the male and female elements fuse into an embryo. Small as pollen grain and egg-cell may be, they contain more generative atoms than the kaleidoscope has pieces of coloured glass. Nobody knows how many, nor has anyone proved how many different roses can be raised from the same two hybrid parents; but one brave soul risked a guess that it could be 250,000,000. This is no cause of wonder. Go to a crowded place, watch the people pass, and marvel at the infinity of designs to be seen in the narrow compass of a human head.

What was begun in the wild was accelerated in cultivation, because gardens bring together roses which might never meet in nature; eventually it dawned on mankind that nature could be aided and abetted by transferring the pollen manually. The result may be seen by comparing a wild rose in the countryside with a bunch of roses in a flower shop; and any rose breeder will proclaim from the bottom of his optimistic heart, that we ain't seen nothing yet to compare with the beauty to come!

Rose breeders perform their task by growing their plants in an environment which will ripen the seed. That may perfectly well be out of doors, but in cooler countries, and for better control, a greenhouse is usually preferred. The mechanics are simple. The plant chosen to bear the seed is brought into flower, and before its stamens are ready to shed pollen, they are removed. Its stigmas, as soon as they are receptive, are covered with pollen brought from the chosen father. Thus a planned mating occurs, and much of the rose breeder's art lies in his vision in choosing which roses to marry. The seeds are taken from the mother in due time, and are sown. The seedlings grow quickly, and are normally flowering three months after the spring time of germination, given good growing conditions. They prove to be all different, identical twins being as rare as in the human race. Remembering the bold guess of 250,000,000 different seedlings from the same two parents, the breeder will be lucky if any of his seedlings happen to combine the qualities he wants; because most of the 250,000,000 are sure to be distinguished mainly by their glaring faults. It is at this stage that the rose breeder's experience tells him how to select the sheep from the goats. We will suppose that from the cross he made, he has selected one seedling as a glorious rose; let us see what happens to it next.

That glorious rose, risen from a seed in a few months, is the one and only plant of its kind in the whole world. The breeder hopes it may become a popular variety. If it should die, it cannot be replaced, except at odds of 250,000,000:1. Therefore it must be propagated. It is no use propagating it from seed, because the kaleidoscope will form different patterns in every seed of a hybrid rose. Therefore it must be propagated vegetatively, of which the simplest example known to everyone is taking cuttings. Cuttings, however, are too risky and too slow for the rose breeder. He has quicker methods, namely grafting or budding. These consist of taking parts from his rose, and splicing them on to the root of another kind of rose; in the case of grafting, a short piece of stem is used, and for budding a small piece of bark, so long as it contains an eye. The glorious rose, even though it is a young seedling, probably possesses enough growth to provide twenty or thirty eyes, most of which will have grown into flowering plants in twelve months.

From that point, propagation is no problem. Given the necessity, twenty-five plants can be turned into fifty thousand in another twelve months, although such a course is rare and expensive. The rose breeder prefers to study and assess his rose for a few years, in order to ensure that it is good; when he is so convinced, he will send it to various trial gardens, and offer it for sale to nurserymen, and through them to the public. Repeated propagation by the nurserymen add up to many millions of plants of that glorious rose eventually growing in the world; but their source all goes back to the solitary and unique seedling plant, which the rose breeder had originally selected, and which he might very easily have missed or lost.

The nurseryman who receives a new variety does so under terms agreed with the rose breeder. Usually the two will agree that the nurseryman pays an annual royalty. The new variety is normally supplied in the form of budding eyes; which means sufficient stems of the new rose to provide the number of eyes the nurseryman wishes to propagate. An average stem bears five eyes, and in case you do not know what an eye looks like, it may be seen in the summer by pulling a leaf stalk down, and looking for the eye on the bark of the stem immediately above the leaf stalk. The nurseryman plants wild roses, usually 'Laxa' or *R. canina* or *R. multiflora,* although several others are also used. These are the roots of his future stock in trade, and they are known as stocks, rootstocks or understocks. In the summer he propagates, by making a cut like a T in the neck of his rootstocks, deep enough to cut the bark in order to lift it slightly from the white wood within. The neck is the part between the roots and the stems, and has the nature of root, not of stem; it is usually at or near ground level. He slices the eye from the rose stem, so that it is roughly at the centre of a piece of bark about 2.5 cm long; he cuts it thinly and may flip out the wood inside, although some growers do not trouble with this. The sliver of bark slides into the top of the T, and is enclosed by the stem of the T. The wound is bound, to press together the parts which must heal. At a later stage, usually in the following spring, the neck of the understock is cut through, so as to remove all the top growth, and to leave nothing but the roots in the ground, and the rose eye on top of them, ready to receive their strength. By summer the eyes have grown and flowered, and by autumn they have turned into plants which may be dug up and sold. The whole process, from planting the understocks to digging up the roses, takes approximately eighteen months; but in some climates, given long growing seasons and fast growing understocks, it may be done within a year. Once the nurseryman has a new variety, he need never return to the rose breeder for more supplies; he obtains his propagating wood annually from the plants he propagated a year before.

In most countries, nurseries have three ways of selling their roses to the public:

they sell their own produce by mail order or from their premises; they sell their roses to other retail outlets, most commonly garden centres, landscape gardeners, or nurseries who sell roses they have not grown; the largest retail outlet is through shops and stores, for whom the roses are packed in containers designed to protect the plants from desiccation, and to tempt the customers to part with their money.

The rose breeder and the nurseryman depend entirely on the ability of their lovely products to delight the gardener. In a sense it can be said that the gardener has more problems than either of his suppliers. They are continually parting with young plants, which the gardener tends into their dotage. Fortunately roses are easy plants to grow, the most essential points being as follow.

Most roses like to see the sun; so do not plant them where it rarely shines. Their taste in soil is catholic, and the only time they shudder at soil quality is if their roots are drowned in water; beware therefore of low places near rivers, where the water-table may be unexpectedly high; a point which may be checked with no more trouble than digging a hole. On the other hand, they do not want to be permanently dry, and in dry places irrigation is a great help. Obviously a healthy, fertile, well-managed soil should pay dividends for the care that made it so; but it is surprising how well roses do in poor soils. They are usually unhappy in soils of extreme acidity, which as often as not are too wet for them anyway. They don't like the salt from the sea, but even a low wall between them and the sea will give sufficient protection. Wind reduces their stature, and although it blows some of their lushness and beauty away, they still bloom. There is a common belief that they need a clay soil, but this is untrue; all they need from the soil is anchorage, minerals and water.

When you plant a rose, remember that it absorbs water through pores on its root skin; and that any form of sucking or drinking is gravely interrupted by air locks. This teaches you to press fine soil very firmly around the roots, without leaving air pockets. The plant's need of anchorage ought to re-affirm that lesson. It is common sense to plant so that the stems are not buried, nor any portions of the roots exposed to the air. There's a knack in planting and potting which only comes with practice: after a while you know whether you have made a plant comfortable or not.

Pruning is considered by some to be a mysterious art; just remind yourself that nature did it for countless years with the crudest of tools, namely frost, fire and the teeth of animals. Frost froze immature growth; fire burnt old wood; animals ate tender shoots, causing them to break into several growths where otherwise there was only one, and that probably a lanky one. A blunt pair of secateurs will not make as clean a job as nature's three agents, so it is as well to keep a good pair for pruning. Do not cut your plants down to some pre-conceived height, but let each enjoy its natural stature. Pruning consists primarily of removing the wood which is of no use. If all the wood is good, why cut any of it? Before the new growing season starts, imitate frost, and remove all the frozen and the soft wood. You may recognize both by making a trial cut high on the stem, and looking at the pith. Frozen wood has brown pith instead of white. Soft wood has crumbly pith, usually in a wide ring, to indicate that the process of turning into wood was not achieved.

Study the old wood carefully in your role as fire before you cut it out. The old wood that ought to go is that from which no significant younger wood is arising. Mature plants with much growth benefit greatly by losing large sections of old wood. Finally, after the style of a deer, you may shorten the shoots that remain, so that they are not tempted to spend their strength growing from their thin ends, which can bear none but thinner wood still; oblige them to grow from wood thick enough to provide you with a good stem for a cut flower. Some types of roses need special pruning, which is described later on, and may be located by use of the index.

If you have planted new bush roses, prune them fairly short, so that they start their new lives in your garden with growth near the ground.

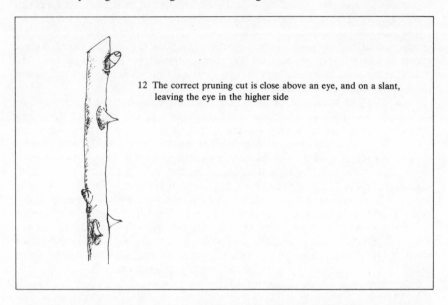

12 The correct pruning cut is close above an eye, and on a slant, leaving the eye in the higher side

Pruning cuts should be made just above an eye, with the cut on the slant, leaving the eye on the higher side. I often advise people not to bother too much about looking for eyes. In a few weeks the plants will grow, and then it will be easy to trim off any stubs, probably in warmer and more pleasant conditions.

Roses are food for insects and fungi, both of whom must be deeply grateful to mankind for planting so many larders for them. The chemical industry provides specifics to deal with them; and, as they are apt to improve their products one after the other, like bell ringers waiting their turn on the rope, there is a strong chance that between my writing and your reading X will be withdrawn and Y sold instead. Learn to recognize the more important troubles you are likely to meet; and then obtain from your garden shop the appropriate specific. Apply it promptly, because propagation in the world of insects and fungi occurs as fast as a bush fire. The most common troubles are greenfly, mildew, blackspot and rust, and the best way to get to know them is not by reading a book, but by asking an experienced rosarian to point them out to you. Caterpillars can be a pest in the spring, especially if there are trees nearby. Red spider is a pest both in greenhouses, and in warm, dry conditions outdoors. Its presence should be suspected if there are pale dots on the leaves, when an examination of the underside may reveal little creatures like red lice, and their downy webs. If you have no specific to hand, plain water is better than nothing, especially for insects and mildew. Roses are extremely lively plants, and usually recover from the depredations of their parasites.

There's a wealth of difference between roses which are fed and watered, and those which are neglected. A good rose fertilizer should be applied in moderation three times a year: after pruning; when the first buds form; and after the first flowering. Do not apply any towards the end of the season, otherwise you invite soft wood for the winter to bite. Fertilizers can be applied not only to the soil, but also to the leaves, in which case they are called foliar feeds, and give quick and excellent results, as the leaves are even more important than the roots in supplying the plant when growth is in full swing.

I wonder how many people in the world grow roses? No census can tell us, but there are so many millions in so many countries that rose growing cannot be a difficult art. The methods and duties of breeder, nurseryman and gardener have been indicated in essence in this chapter, in order to show how the rose moves in the modern world. Many fascinating details could be added to this brief outline; for example, the breeder must study the genetic components of the plant cell, and learn something of chromosomes and genes, although we know so little of the latter, that my kaleidoscope may leave a clearer picture in the layman's mind than a lengthy study of genes.

Underlying every operation is that miracle of growth, the living cell's power to divide itself into two, thus starting the progression through four, eight, sixteen and thirty-two, which as every enquiring child discovered, leads to unexpected and indeed disconcerting mental arithmetic, with a million up at the twentieth step.

We rosarians are also witnesses of the miracle of life, which crams into the microscopic cell the instructions for making the entire organism; not only the instructions, but the power to switch them on and off, so that a leaf, an ear, a flower or a finger-nail grow when and where they ought to be.

Those who find this book a means of meeting the rose, or of knowing it more truly than before, and my prayer is that they may be many, should certainly take the next step to more particular knowledge and friendship by joining their rose society. By that means the advice appropriate to one's area and requirements may always be to hand. The leading national rose societies are:

Argentina Rose Society of Argentina, Solis 1348, Hurlingham, Buenos Aires.
Australia National Rose Society of Australia, 271 Belmore Road, North Balwyn, Victoria 3104.
Belgium Société Royale Nationale Les Amis de la Rose, Vrijheidslaan 28, B-9000 Gent.
Bermuda Bermuda Rose Society, PO Box 162, Paget.
Britain The Royal National Rose Society, Bone Hill, Chiswell Green Lane, St Albans, Hertfordshire, AL2 3NR.
Canada The Canadian Rose Society, 12 Castlegrove Boulevard, Apartment 18, Don Mills, Ontario M3A 1K8.
France La Société Française des Roses, Parc de la Tête-d'Or, 69459 Lyon.
Germany Verein Deutscher Rosenfreunde, 7570 Baden-Baden, Postfach 1011.
India The Rose Society of India, A-267 Defence Colony, New Delhi 17.
Israel The Israel Rose Society, Ganot-Hadar, PO Natania.
Italy Associazione Italiana Della Rosa, Villa Reale, 20052 Monza.
Japan The Japan Rose Society, 8-28-12 Okuzawa, Setagata-Ku, Tokyo.
New Zealand The National Rose Society of New Zealand, 11 Donald Street, Karori, Wellington 5.
Poland Polish Rose Society, Warszawa 86, Browiewskiego 19M7.
South Africa The Rose Society of South Africa, PO Box 65217, Benmore, Transvaal 2010.

Switzerland Gesellschaft Schweizerischer Rosenfreunde, Haus Engelfried, 8158 Regensberg.
United States The American Rose Society, PO Box 30000, Shreveport, Louisiana 71130.

I am grateful to Mr Len Turner for the addresses of the above societies at the time of writing. Mr Turner is Secretary of the Royal National Rose Society, a component of the World Federation of Rose Societies, which has an International Rose Conference normally held every two years.

3. Introducing What Follows

In the following chapters we shall meet the more interesting members of the genus *ROSA* one by one, in logical sequence of their relation to one another. The four sub-genera receive a chapter each, followed similarly by the ten sections of the fourth sub-genus.

Each begins with a short appreciation, including its means of identification; and continues with the true species and their varieties in alphabetical order, as for example *R. chinensis* and *R. chinensis minima*. As *R. chinensis* has hybrids which associate better with it than with any other species, they next intrude under the heading CHINENSIS HYBRIDS. And as some of those hybrids have developed into classes, they are dealt with under such sub-headings as NOISETTES, HYBRID TEAS, MINIATURES. All the Chinensis Hybrids having been dealt with, the species continue, in this case with *R. gigantea*.

The varieties of most of the classes are described not alphabetically, but in the order they developed. This enables items of rose history and culture to be appropriately inserted, and traces the rise and fall of various types of roses. The story of a particular class, say Miniatures or Floribundas, can therefore be read as an individual item if so desired.

For ease of reference, the headline of each rose described has some condensed information, except in cases where reliable news is not available. The headlines refer as follows, with an example underneath:

Name of rose	Height	Colour	Flowering Time	Perfume	Hips	Recommendation
'Queen Elizabeth'	*Taller*	*Pink*	*Remontant*	*P2*	*H4*	*****

HEIGHT

Roses are generally variable in height according to their environment. One cannot safely put measurements to them, and must therefore resort to comparisons. Even these are not fool-proof, especially in respect of those kinds which are kept low in colder countries through frost damage, but have no such check in warmer places. The comparisons used for bushes are:

Shortest	Tall
Shorter	Taller
Short	Tallest
Medium	

And for Climbers:
Climber
Trailer
For any that are betwixt and between, a plus or minus sign has been used.

COLOUR
The main impression of the colour is conveyed in one word if possible. It is usually described more fully in the text.

FLOWERING TIME
The terms used are:

Late spring	Summer +
Early summer	Late summer
Midsummer	Remontant
Summer	

In the cooler temperate regions, the first four should normally flower for about three weeks, centred on the time stated. In countries with a short winter, or scarcely any at all, this entry is of value not so much as a timetable, but for comparisons. *Summer +* means that a few flowers are also likely to appear in the autumn. The *late summer* varieties usually flower for four or five weeks.

Remontant has been preferred as a better word than *perpetual, recurrent* or *repeat-flowering.* Its Oxford English Dictionary meaning is precisely what we wish to say: 'Of roses: blooming a second time or oftener in a season.' It has the advantage of being understood in the same sense by the French, from whom we got it. It is truer than *perpetual,* has a sweeter sound than the cloddish *repeat-flowering,* and is more precise in meaning than *recurrent,* which is probably the best alternative. For some vague reasons English speaking rosarians are shy of *remontant,* but as they have nothing as good to put in its place they should accept this gift from France.

PERFUME
I have never known much agreement between people as to the fragrance of roses, but I cordially agree with myself, and have marked perfume on an ascending scale of merit from P1 up to P10.

HIPS
The seed pods can be one of the great beauties of roses in late summer and autumn. They are marked on an ascending scale of merit from H1 to H10.

RECOMMENDATION
Each to his taste; I can only give you mine, with the five-star roses as my favourites, down to the one-star roses, many of which are specialist items of interest. The standard has deliberately been set high, and many well-known roses are not dignified with a star at all.

BIBLIOGRAPHY
When supplying information, one should identify the authority, so that suspicious readers may check for themselves, the trusting may know in what they trust, and the enthusiastic may explore the same sources for their further edification. This is usually done by a list of books somewhere at the back, under the heading bibliography; but I have more love for my rose books than to consign them to a dull list.

Rose literature is an extraordinary hodge-podge of dutiful instruction, earnest research, hopeful fictions, sloppy sentimentality, confident autobiography, bad poetry and well-intended moralizing. I think it may be said that out of the hundreds of rose books, only a few were truly worthy of being published. And the influence of those few can be seen in the lesser ones, distorted like the bottom of a swimming pool seen through well-used water.

There is an imprecision of information which almost passes belief, until we remember that most of the people concerned with roses were more likely to file facts in their heads than commit them to paper: and those cheerful sons of the soil are less to be blamed than the scribes, who constructed a hypothesis upon a hint, and copied it one from the other as a fact. I cannot offhand point to any rose book in which I have failed to find an error; and I know many in which the errors could justly be called howlers. When you write of something which comes not from your own experience you need to be careful indeed.

Even the masters are not free from error; but I forgive them as I hope for pardon in my turn, and gladly acknowledge my debt to them as follows.

Thomas Rivers   The Rose Amateur's Guide

Published in 1832, this little book appeared in eleven editions, the last one in 1877. I have referred to the second edition, dated 1840, since that is the copy I possess. The author was a nurseryman in Sawbridgeworth, Hertfordshire, where the firm still exists. Rivers' observations were nearly always from practical experience, but he had imagination too. He rarely wasted words; his short and sweet descriptions of the roses and cultural practices of his time enable us to form a clear picture of his rose world. And he must have been a good man, for he won this posthumous tribute from Dean Hole: 'His portrait has a conspicuous place in the long galleries through which my memory roams, and I rejoice in its genial smile. I know that he helped to make my life brighter and better, and there are times, when I think of him or read his books, in which I pray and hope that when I am gone, I may be remembered . . . with something of the affectionate, brotherly regard which I cherish always for Thomas Rivers.' That quotation is from *The Memories of Dean Hole*.

William Paul   The Rose Garden

Published in 1848, this book ran into its tenth edition in 1903. How strange that the author should also be a Hertfordshire nurseryman, in this case from Cheshunt. I have referred to the 1848 edition, by courtesy of the Royal National Rose Society, and have been surprised at the excellence of the colour plates. This edition contains a list of subscribers, one of whom was Thomas Rivers. The outstanding feature of Paul's book is thoroughness. He sweeps up every crumb of fact, and if the result is somewhat ponderous, it is a very touchstone of authority. He was only twenty-five years old when it was published.

Dean Hole   A Book about Roses

This is the rose book nearest to a literary work of art. It was published in 1869, and is still going strong. To be honest I have scarcely referred to it at all, because it is not a mine of facts; but I think no rosarian can read it and remain uncoloured by its influence. Abounding in anecdotes, love, morality and instruction, it is like a breath of Victorian life, which the Dean of Rochester, first President of the National Rose Society, friend of Thackeray, lived to the full. From it comes the Dean's famous sentence: 'He who would have beautiful Roses in his garden must have beautiful Roses *in his heart.*'

Rev. A. Foster-Melliar   The Book of the Rose

Published in 1894, this book went into four editions, the last in 1910. I have referred to the third edition, 1905. The writer was Rector of Sproughton, Suffolk, and his interest in roses was to exhibit them. I have found him very useful for his accounts of those Teas and Hybrid Perpetuals which, famous in his day, have not survived to ours. Frequently he gives a long account of the rose, with no mention of its colour, presumably taking that to be common knowledge to his readers. His book is sound in cultural instruction, the chapter on pruning being a small masterpiece. He had no idea of treating roses as garden plants. Straight rows in parallelogrammatic beds; that was his style.

Rev. Joseph H. Pemberton   Roses – Their History, Development and Cultivation
Published in 1908, with a second edition in 1920. I have referred to the first edition. The clergy were well to the fore in the earlier days of the National Rose Society, and Pemberton was not only full of rose knowledge, but also extremely perceptive. This book contains useful observations on many types of roses, and carefully written cultural instructions. I found Pemberton's articles in the *Rose Annuals* of the period 1918–26 most helpful.

Ellen Willmott   The Genus Rosa
I am indebted to the Royal National Rose Society for being allowed to consult the two volumes of this large and valuable work. It was produced in parts from 1910, and completed in 1914. Its object was to illustrate in colour all the wild roses of the world, to furnish their exact botanical descriptions in both Latin and English, and to render an account of their discovery and history. Alfred Parsons distinguished himself by the accuracy and beauty of his illustrations; *R. moyesii* flowers on the page as if on the bush. For the researcher, *The Genus Rosa* contains many a pitfall among its benefits, because the names and identity of some of its roses are no longer valid. Miss Willmott's text is rich in old lore, which she records without committing herself to its factual exactitude. Unfortunately others have assumed that everything in a work of such authority must be true, and passed it on as gospel.

Dr J. Horace McFarland   Modern Roses
Dr McFarland was a master printer from Harrisburg, Pennsylvania; he was also Editor of the *American Rose Annual* for some years, and eventually President of the American Rose Society. The purpose of *Modern Roses* was to provide an international check list of roses. The first edition came out in 1930, containing 2511 roses; the seventh, known as *Modern Roses 7*, was published in 1969, and contains on my rough estimate about 12,000 entries. The raiser, date of introduction and parentage are generally included, with the result that *Modern Roses* to the rosarian is what *Wisden* is to the cricketer. Dr McFarland died in 1948; and the last few editions have been printed by his company, in association with the International Registration Authority for Roses and the American Rose Society.

August Jäger   Rosenlexikon
This is an extraordinary directory, compiled under the aegis of the German Rose Society in the 1930s. It lists by my estimate some eighteen thousand roses, none more recent than the year 1936. Most of the printed sheets were stored away unbound, until a department of the East German Government intervened; my copy is dated 1970. August Jäger procedures requires some patience to follow, but we owe him a debt for preserving records of many old roses, which were lost from human memory apart from his writing. The Zentralantiquariat der Deutschen Demokratischen Republik probably made no profit from rescuing this book, and we should be thankful for their action.

Dr C. C. Hurst   Notes on the Origin and Evolution of our Garden Roses
Dr Hurst studied genetics, and unlike most scientists he chose the rose as his special subject. His particular aim was to deduce from genetic evidence the way in which roses had evolved. This work he performed at Trinity College, Cambridge, and it could fairly be said that he had no rivals in his particular sphere. His *Notes* were published in the *Journal of the Royal Horticultural Society* in March, July and August 1941; and they were republished in *The Old Shrub Roses* by Graham Thomas. Dr Hurst was a bold and imaginative pioneer, who set an example to all scientists by the lucidity of his prose and his avoidance of technical terms. In these *Notes*, he outlined the development of the rose like a visionary who knows the answer whether the evidence is complete or not. We may gulp as we swallow some of his assumptions, we may doubt some of his statements. But his work stands like that of a good teacher, who has switched on the light of understanding in the minds of his pupils.

André Leroy   History of Roses
I might never have come across this book, had not the author kindly sent me a copy after I had met him in Paris. It was published in 1954, the pictures and type very handsome, the leaves not bound together, but presented in a folder and box. It is a short book, written with easy grace, not at first sight a promising source of research and instruction. However, it did two things for me: it gave me a better understanding of how a Frenchman sees roses, and introduced me to some useful grains of information; for although the book is so short as to make a serious history impossible, the author collects his nuggets of news, and issues them in a sentence where anyone else would need a page. He is like a doctor pouring soothing syrup down the patient's throat, his medicine for the most part bland, but containing the vital elements.

Roy E. Shepherd   History of the Rose
This masterly book was published in the United States in 1954, and is a landmark in rose literature. Its purpose is clearly stated in its title; and although the book wavers between being a history and a botanical guide, the author crams so much information into it either way as to earn our gratitude. Roy Shepherd lived in Medina, Ohio; he was a prominent member of the American Rose Society, a devoted and painstaking student of the rose, and also a rose breeder who will long be remembered for his best variety, 'Golden Wings'.

Ann P. Wylie   The History of Garden Roses
Miss Wylie was working in the Department of Botany at Manchester University when she read this paper to the Royal Horticultural Society as the Masters Memorial Lecture in 1954. It was printed in the *Royal Horticultural Society's Journal* in December 1954, and in January and February 1955. It derives much from the work of Dr C. C. Hurst, but goes into greater detail, especially about modern roses, and the genetic factors involved in breeding. Miss Wylie eventually went to the University of Otago, New Zealand, and contributed generously to our knowledge with *Why the Caninae Roses are Different* in the *New Zealand Rose Annual, 1976*.

Graham Stuart Thomas   The Old Shrub Roses
Shrub Roses of Today
Climbing Roses Old and New
These three books, published respectively in 1955, 1962 and 1965, mark Graham Thomas as a powerful influence in the rose world. He swam ahead, and others have

jumped in behind him, helping themselves to his superior knowledge, and disguising it all too thinly. I do not know of any guide half so good to those parts of the genus *ROSA* discussed in these books. Graham's work is discussed at greater length in the chapter on Gallicanae.

E. B. Le Grice   Rose Growing Complete
There are many excellent books explaining how to grow roses; and had my purpose been to write a cultural handbook, I should have consulted them. Edward Le Grice's book goes beyond the how-to-do-it stage, for the author was in love with roses, and happily explored by-roads which others do not usually see. It was published in 1965.

Wing-Commander Norman Young   The Complete Rosarian
With a bold, enquiring mind, and strong powers of disbelief, Norman Young smashed some dearly treasured fables about roses, and unearthed some delightful items from the past. I much enjoy this book, for it invites one to think, and points to the road which researchers should take. They may need a pinch of salt on the way. Wing-Commander Young died in 1967, and his typescript was edited by L. Arthur Wyatt, and published in 1971.

Rose Annuals
Last but by no means least are the publications of societies. The Royal National Rose Society issued the *Rosarian's Year-Book* from 1881 to 1902; and the *Rose Annual* from 1907 up to the present time. The *American Rose Annual* started in 1916; and valuable publications come from many other rose societies, especially those of Australia, Canada, France, Germany and New Zealand. The Royal Horticultural Society's *Dictionary of Gardening*, published in 1951, contains a useful guide to rose species.

These publications are a gold-mine; from them one could construct an encyclopedia of the roses of the past century. If nothing else justified the existence of a rose society, this preservation of knowledge would be enough. That is not to say that every statement in a rose annual is the gospel truth; fallacies grow in them like weeds in a flower bed, and the researcher's task is to know which are which. I have referred to other sources also, but those mentioned above are the significant ones.

4. Simplicifoliae and Hybrids

The genus *ROSA* is divided into parts known as sub-genera. Formerly there were four, of which Simplicifoliae was the first, and although officially this category has ceased to exist, I make no apology for calling it back into being, because it introduces a plant which simply cannot be omitted.

The name Simplicifoliae means simple leaves; it describes those leaves made in one piece instead of being split into leaflets. The simple leaves set this sub-genus completely apart from all roses, and it is further uniquely distinguished by having no stipules, which are the pair of leafy growths, attached one each side of a leaf stalk near where it joins a branch. Here the leaves sit almost directly upon the branches, with no leaf stalk to speak of, and consequently no stipules. A third distinguishing character, shared with the next two sub-genera, is hips which are armed with prickles.

SPECIES

Hulthemia persica *Shorter Yellow, red eye Early summer* P4 H2 *
The most remarkable feature of this fascinating plant is a red eye at the centre of its vivid yellow flowers. No such dark eye exists in any species of rose, and the genetic potential of the Persian Rose is therefore crystal clear. It is named in memory of a botanist of the Netherlands, Van Hulthem.

A native of Iran and the neighbouring areas of Afghanistan and Russia, *H. persica* was brought from Iran to France in about 1788. It has had a rich assortment of names, as one botanist after another wondered what it was, and between them christened it *R. simplicifolia, R. persica, R. berberifolia, Lowea berberifolia, Hulthemia berberifolia* and finally *Hulthemia persica*. To add to the roll-call, people have also used the spelling berberidifolia, and it will come as no surprise when we add that in France it is termed the Barberry Rose.

The plant is a xerophyte, that is, adapted to live in dry conditions by its small, firm, grey-green, almost veinless leaves and its long roots. Young seedling plants waste no time in sinking their roots deep into the soil, and a young plant only as high as your finger may have a root 45 cm long. The stems are thin and lax, with sharp prickles; in time the plants form a loose ball of undergrowth, which is used as kindling by the people of its native regions. The stems are bicoloured, except the very young or very old; a strip of brown goes up from each eye, and a strip of white downwards.

The flowers are small, fragrant and extremely beautiful, mainly due to their vivid colour and regular parts. The petals fall at a touch, and if we pick one up for a close look, we see that the red eye is formed by a mushroom-shaped blotch covering the inward third of each petal's length. Presumably the red eye is a landing mark for insects, made to stand out in the bright light of its semi-desert home. The hips are small, with sharp prickles of vicious aspect; but they do not become attractive like most hips, they merely mark their maturity by withering.

H. persica has a reputation of being difficult to keep in cultivation, but I do not believe it, despite the following from John Lindley in 1829: 'It resists cultivation in a remarkable manner, submitting permanently neither to budding, nor grafting, nor laying, nor striking from cuttings; nor in short to any of those operations, one or other of which succeed with other plants. Drought does not suit it, it does not thrive in wet; heat has no beneficial effect, cold no prejudicial influence; care does not improve it, neglect does not injure it.'

I have grown dozens of plants of *H. persica* in Hertfordshire, some of them being now over twelve years old, and I think its chief enemy is probably nothing more than water. The answer therefore is to plant it under glass where the water-table is not high; then the watering can be easily controlled. Its native soil is alkaline. I agree that it does not look very easy to propagate vegetatively, apart from the occasional runner; but it grows easily from seed, the main danger being mildew when the seedlings are a few weeks old. It is a plant of such rare character that I have marked it with a star, to encourage people to grow it under glass, although I fear they will not easily locate supplies. That is not surprising. Even the French write it off as too tender, and an expert in 1955 could locate only one decent plant in the whole of Britain.

This plant invites a look to both the past and the future. From the past, it perhaps exhibits characteristics of primitive roses which do not survive elsewhere; no evidence supports that suggestion, apart from the apparent sense of simple leaves preceding compound leaves in evolution; but it is an attractive plausibility which at least invites some speculative thought. For the future, this is surely a species with its children yet to come, and they should be famous when they are finally produced. It is a shame, I think, to have taken it out of the genus *ROSA*, and I wish it was still *R. persica*.

PERSICA HYBRIDS

No code of identity exists for hybrids; in Persica Hybrids one should expect the colour in the centre of the flower to show relationship to *H. persica*. All the hybrids I have seen are more roses than hulthemias, because they have pinnate leaves, stipules and smooth hips. Pinnate leaves are the type normal to roses; the word means 'feathered', and illustrates the leaflets arranged two by two along a leaf stalk, with one at the terminus.

About 1941, a hybrid genus was constituted to accept the hybrids between hulthemias and roses, under the title × HULTHEMOSA. The × indicates hybridity.

× **Hulthemosa hardii**   *Short   Yellow, red eye   Early summer*   P3   H1   *

The rose that proved *H. persica* could breed, and in doing so pass on its red eye. It was named after the Curator of the Luxembourg Gardens in Paris, M. Eugène Hardy, under whose authority it was raised.

Some books claim that *H. persica* was the pollen parent of 'Hardii'. But I believe the truth is the other way round, that the seeds and not the pollen came from *H. persica* around 1832. When this seedling flowered it was clearly seen to be a hybrid; a point that can be checked as soon as a seedling from *H. persica* grows a pinnate leaf. An effort was made to guess at the identity of the pollen parent, and opinions fixed upon a nearby plant alleged to be *R. clinophylla*. That guess has become a fact in certain records, and *R. clinophylla* if firmly marked as the mate, whether mother or father. All I can say is that some people are easily convinced! In those days, it was believed that propinquity was the recipe to make plants fertilize one another, and speculation would therefore focus upon the nearest neighbours; but an establishment which contained two roses as rare as these must surely have had a formidable list of possible fathers within range; and presumably all the compatible roses of Paris were eligible suitors. I do not accept the published parentage as anything but a guess, reconstructed some years after the event.

When introduced about 1836, this rose caused great interest, its flowers being most spectacular, light yellow with a large red eye. Those who had never seen *H. persica* now saw something completely strange in roses, and naturally the breeders fastened upon it in the hopes of raising stranger roses still. But it has proved completely sterile and defeated everyone, cruelly flaunting round hips which are full of hope until found empty of viable seed. Alas for human hopes! In 1840, Thomas Rivers forecast: 'It will probably be the parent of an entirely new group.'

The flowers are larger and paler than those of *H. persica*. The leaves are pinnate, if irregular, and furnished with stipules. The hips are smooth. This is a beautiful rose to grow, and flowers two or three weeks later than *H. persica*. It can be budded quite easily, and is best grown as a pot plant under cool greenhouse conditions in colder climates. The main drawback is mildew, but that is not difficult to control under glass.

I do not feel happy at the clumsy name, and in bowing to authority can only say I would prefer plain 'Hardii'. Chaos will be the result of everyone using the names he fancies, so where I have written 'Hardii', will you please assume it is really × *Hulthemosa hardii?*

Harkness Seedlings

It appears that one rose breeder after another suffered disappointment from 'Hardii'. but that few thought of going back to *H. persica*, which was considered difficult to grow and hard to find. The erroneous reports of the parentage of 'Hardii' had moreover concealed the vital fact that *H. persica* was the source of seed. About 1964, Alexander Cocker of Aberdeen resolved to obtain *H. persica* and to breed with it, all for the sake of its pretty red eye. After searching Britain in vain, he was obliged to commission the collection of seed from Iran.

On a visit to the present author in Hitchin, Mr Cocker observed the soil under his feet was of a kind likely to appeal to *H. persica*. He therefore gave me half his seed, a decision as wise as it was generous, because I got along very well with *H. persica* and soon raised the first hybrids from it, so far as either of us is aware, since 'Hardii'. In fact I now have over one hundred, some of them of great beauty, and it is plain that the red eye is a dominant feature.

We do not wish to introduce first generation hybrids, because they flower only in early summer; the purpose of breeding them is to get a fertile one, a difficult task. The hybrids I have at present are all from the seed of *H. persica* with pollen of 'Ballerina', 'Buff Beauty', 'Canary Bird', *R. chinensis mutabilis*, 'Cornelia', 'Frau Dagmar Hartopp', 'Margo Koster', 'Mermaid', 'Perla de Alcanada', 'Phyllis Bide', 'Roseraie de l'Haÿ' and 'Trier'.

Russian Hybrids

In Komarov's Flora of the USSR, descriptions are given of two × *HULTHEMOSAS* found growing wild, but subsequently lost. The descriptions tally with the hybrids I am now well used to seeing, and there is no doubt that where *H. persica* grows in reach of compatible rose pollen, hybrids may result. Unfortunately they cannot be counted on to be fertile; and unless they can produce runners, they are likely to become extinct. Observers in relevant areas should look out for hybrids. The two lost

Russian ones were × *H. guzarica* and × *H. kopetdaghensis*. There is no reason why hybrids should be confined to Russia. Miss Nancy Lindsay reported one growing wild in Iran. She took it to be 'Hardii' and gave a rave notice about it, conveying enthusiasm rather than botanical conviction for her 'Golden Star' rose.

The only other Persica Hybrid I have heard of is in the possession of Dr de Vries at Wageningen, Holland.

But they keep turning up, for since writing the above, I hear one has been found in the garden of the late Edward Hyam, who was a skilled horticulturist, and a sensitive writer.

5. Hesperrhodos

The name of this sub-genus means Western Roses; and it has another name, sometimes used: Minutifoliae, which means little leaves. Now that we have left the Simplicifoliae, all roses thenceforth have pinnate leaves and stipules. The chief distinguishing mark of the Hesperrhodos is prickly hips which remain on the plants a long time.

SPECIES & VARIETY

R. minutifolia
A species from Lower California, little known in Europe, where few people have seen it. It apparently has a restricted habitat, and its discovery is put at the surprisingly late date of 1882. It is very rare in cultivation and generally sounds as if its existence could be precarious. It is interesting that the two species forming this sub-genus appear in the same region of the world, albeit separated by several hundred miles; they may be primitive forms of the rose.

R. stellata *Shorter*   *Rose purple*   *Early summer*   P4   H2
Known as the Gooseberry Rose, because its leaves and thorns both imitate those of that familiar fruit bush. The leaves look very much like a stepping stone between *Hulthemia persica* and more sophisticated roses. The name 'stellata' sounds appropriate does it not? Star-shaped flowers are quite romantic. But in fact it was applied to the hairs on the bark, which is not nearly so exciting.

This rose is a native of southern New Mexico; note the word 'New', which is often omitted, with the result that *R. stellata* is shifted down the Rio Grande to the south. The records state that it was first collected in the Organ Mountains by E. O. Wooton in 1897; it is well-nigh incredible that our knowledge is of such recent origin. A name briefly used for it was *R. vernonii*.

The rose-purple flowers are deep and brilliant, and are much enhanced by numerous stamens standing in a dusty yellow ring. Such brightness seems to be a requirement for flowers in arid regions, to ensure visibility when the sun's glare reflects light harshly from every object. The interesting leaves are normally of three leaflets to the top of the shoots, or five lower down; and anyone who has handled hybrids of *H. persica* will see something familiar about the leaflets of *R. stellata*. This is not a difficult plant to grow, provided one remembers it comes from a dry region. It is used to cool weather, for it grows at a fairly high altitude. It is worth growing for the abruptly brilliant flowers, starting cactus-like from a stunted plant; but perhaps it is safer to plant the following variety, as it is a little stronger.

R. stellata mirifica *Shorter +*   *Rose purple*   *Early summer*   P4   H2   *
The differences between this and *R. stellata* may not be obvious. There should be an increase in vigour in this variety, reflected in a tendency for more of the leaves to

have five leaflets and fewer to have three; and (one hopes) for the plants to grow a little taller and stronger. For these improvements it is named in Latin 'the wonderful star-shaped rose', but in fact it has lost most of the hairs which earned the name 'stellata', in the first place.

Otherwise it is similar to *R. stellata*. In the United States it is called the Sacramento Rose, from having been found in the mountains of that name in New Mexico about 1910. It has quite often been recorded in rose books as *R. mirifica*.

HYBRIDS

To my knowledge, there are unfortunately no Stellata Hybrids, although it could be supposed to offer three major prospects. Possibly it has a close affinity to *H. persica*, and may assist in the search for fertile hybrids from that source. Secondly it has remarkable brightness, and the instinct of a desert plant to show a contrast in its flower (the stamens against the petals in this case) can benefit gardens. Thirdly it has strange thorns, like pale short needles. *R. stellata* has a reputation of not setting seed freely; I have never had enough of them to test the point, which is of little moment to breeders, because the pollen is ample.

6. Platyrhodon and Hybrids

Platyrhodon means the Flaky Rose; and the sub-genus is named thus because it contains the only known species of rose whose bark peels off the stems. There is an alternative name, Microphyllae, which means little leaves in Greek (it was Latin in the last chapter); but it is a misnomer, because many roses have smaller leaves. The main distinguishing feature of the Platyrhodon is prickly hips which drop off the plants early.

SPECIES & VARIETY

R. roxburghii *Medium* *Pink* *Midsummer* P2 H2 *
This is the double pink variety; not the single pink which ought to be the true species, and is obliged to lurk under the name *R. roxburghii normalis.* It would really be more sensible to add the word 'plena' to this one, and take 'normalis' off the other. The reason a variety bears the title of a species is almost laughable: because a rule of priority in nomenclature applies. The cultivated roses from Chinese gardens were seen and named in some cases before the wild ones from the hinterland. Any reasonable person corrects an error instead of perpetuating it, but that simple step is apparently too long for the legs of the world's botanists. We shall find several examples, and having made our point here, we will let it pass in the other cases.

   R. roxburghii has a bent for collecting nicknames, usually a sign that a notable character is about. The Chestnut Rose describes its hips, which have a skin not unlike the seed cases of chestnuts. This title is adapted in the United States to a local species of *Castanea* as the Chinquapin Rose. The English name, Burr Rose, is not nearly so convincing, as the hips are not like burrs at all, unless they become shrivelled. The French call it Rose Châtaigne, which is chestnut again; and in his *History of the Rose* Roy Shepherd tells us that generations of Chinese have called it Hoi-tong-hong. I hesitate to suggest to the botanists that this is obviously a case of an earliest known use, and that the species should promptly be renamed *R. hoitonghongii.*

   The flaky bark is unusual in roses, but I would not say it is attractive. The foliage is quite spectacular. The leaves are formed of a great many leaflets, up to fifteen quite commonly, sprucely arranged in a brushed and combed style which once seen is not readily forgotten. The spreading nature of the plant, and its relative shortness enable these leaves to be effectively displayed. The hips stay green, and fall off without waiting for autumn. They are scarce; *R. roxburghii normalis,* which follows, is the one to prove why the Chestnut Rose is so called.

   We assume the Chinese discovered this variety, and most probably improved it by selection; although it is not impossible that the Japanese or some other oriental race may have been responsible. There is every likelihood it is a very old garden variety, but we have no means of knowing how long it had been cultivated before Europeans first took note of it around the start of the nineteenth century. The records state it came from Canton to the Calcutta Botanic Garden, where Dr Roxburgh was stationed; and it was sent on to England about 1820. It was generally known as *R. microphylla;* and the botanist Rehder thoroughly wins my approval with his name *R. roxburghii plena.*

R. roxburghii normalis *Medium Pink Midsummer* P2 H6 **

The true species. We shall observe that where it failed to receive the specific name, a species is usually indicated by the word 'normalis' or 'spontanea'.

This rose is similar to *R. roxburghii* in all respects save three: it bears plenty of hips, it has single flowers instead of double, and it is rather an easier grower. The flowers of these Chestnut Roses are fairly large as wild roses go, but transient, and borne close to the leaves.

Gardeners in general have followed the Chinese example of preferring the double to the single Chestnut Rose, although they may not thereby have given themselves the more handsome bushes. From what we have reported, it is obvious that both double and single forms are shrubs of interest and beauty, which anyone may plant and enjoy in the garden. There is also a variety collected in Japan about 1860, and known as *R. roxburghii hirtula,* which differs because it has more hairs on the underside of its leaves, especially on the veins. It would be interesting to know why these roses are in such a hurry to drop their hips, and no doubt there is an answer connected with their environment and evolution.

ROXBURGHII HYBRIDS

No code of identity exists for hybrids; we should expect the leaves to show a relationship to *R. roxburghii.* Hips like chestnut cases, and bark that peels would be strong qualifications.

The species has not been greatly explored by breeders, despite its unique characteristics and handsome foliage. One can appreciate a reluctance to seek after peeling bark, surely no advantage in a rose bed. On the other hand, hips that fall off promptly might save some deadheading; a circuitous way to achieve that economy I fear. But in addition there is always the unexpected transmutation of qualities that may occur in breeding; what seemed curious or of little use may turn into something useful, beautiful, and quite unforeseen.

The French breeder, Guillot, of Lyon, most active and constructive from about the middle of the nineteenth century, introduced some hybrids in about 1872, of which 'Ma Surprise' and 'Triomphe de la Guillotière' achieved some note. Both were blush pink to white.

R. × coryana *Taller Pink Summer* P2 H4

The official name is R. × *coryana,* but I would prefer it to be 'Coryana'. For those who wonder where 'official' names come from, our check list is *Modern Roses,* published from time to time by the International Rose Registration Authority in consultation with the American Rose Society and the McFarland Company. The latter are publishers, and have performed what one imagines to be a labour of love in the world of book production, largely because a former principal was J. Horace McFarland, a President of the American Rose Society, and a rosarian of good influence.

'Coryana' was raised by Dr C. C. Hurst at Cambridge in about 1926, and the parentage has been understood to be *R. roxburghii* × *R. macrophylla;* this however is reversed in *Modern Roses,* and the order is relevant, because the first named is the seed parent, the second the pollen parent. A further confusion arises from referring to this rose as 'R. microphylla coryana'. Whether this is an error for 'macrophylla' or whether it harks back to the old name 'microphylla' for *R. roxburghii,* we are unclear, and so we imagine is everyone else. 'Coryana' is a hybrid, and clearly cannot be expressed as a variety of a species.

We do not take this rose to be high on anyone's list of garden plants, but it has some interest in breeding, because it was introduced by Sam McGredy into his 'Picasso' strain. It has some family likeness to *R. roxburghii,* but without the same charm. It is a tough sort of plant, at home in the undergrowth.

R. × **micrugosa**   *Medium* +   *Pink*   *Midsummer*   P2   H5

This is an interesting hybrid assumed to be between *R. roxburghii* and *R. rugosa;* and once more we find the leading authorities nominating either one or the other as the seed parent. The plant has characteristics of both parents especially conjoined in the foliage, of which a copious inheritance was available from either side, and generously given. The result is a dense shrub, rather wide; and when it grows flat at the top, which it often does, it is quite an interesting sight. The flowers are single, light pink, and quite large. The bark does not peel, it is more like rugosa's bark; and the hips are very bristly but not prickly. This originated by chance in the Institut Botanique de Strasbourg, we do not know precisely when; it suddenly appears in the records in 1905.

7. Eurosa

Before enjoying the Banksian Roses, we ought to explain that they constitute the first section of the fourth and last sub-genus, the Eurosa. We have dealt with the other three (one of which admittedly might be called a past sub-genus) but that does not mean we have travelled 75 per cent of our journey. Nearly all roses belong to the Eurosa, which is divided into ten sections. Eurosa does not mean anything to do with Europe; the sense of it is roses which would readily be recognized as such; 'true roses' gives the idea.

The distinguishing mark for species of Eurosa is smooth hips; whereas the previous three sub-genera have had species with prickly hips, those of the Eurosa do not run to anything more than hairs or bristles. Please do not forget that hybrids are exempt from distinguishing marks. Hybrids have been placed next to the species they most closely belong to, in order to keep before us a picture of the genus *ROSA* as a living, related and progressing entity. It helps us to dissociate the development of roses from the limits of history and time; for it is possible for us to repeat the breeding of the ancients, more likely by accident than design, because we do not know precisely what they did. But we know that in the beginning, there were only the wild roses to work on, they are the patriarchs, and still able to breed. It is quite different in the animal world: we cannot make our ancestors breed again.

One cannot resist hoping that a new rose will sometime receive the highest honours and awards, even though it would have been instantly recognized as a familiar by rosarians in the reign of Nebuchadnezzar. Perhaps it has already occurred?

8. Banksianae and Hybrid

This is the first of ten sections of the sub-genus Eurosa, and therefore marked by smooth hips. The stipules provide a distinction within Eurosa by being joined to the leaf stalk only by their base in the first three sections, but by being joined their entire length or mostly so in the latter seven. In this section, the stipules are narrow, pointed, and soon drop off, so that one might think these roses had no stipules at all at some times of the year. The Banksianae have many small flowers close together in rounded clusters. Their name pays a compliment to Lady Banks, whose husband Sir Joseph Banks was a keen English horticulturist, a companion of Captain Cook, and a founder of the Royal Horticultural Society.

In order to avoid repeating under each heading the news common to all the Banksian Roses, I will now say that they are climbers of great vigour, regularly the objects of wonder that plants should grow so far. They do not respond well to budding, but grow easily from cuttings. They require a kind climate, and cannot be guaranteed to live through hard frosts. To grow them in colder climates one might try in pots brought under glass for the winter and flowering period. If the plants are kept in check by repeated trimming, they settle to their restrictions after a while, and provide flowers each spring to the great satisfaction of their owner. The double varieties in particular are delightful, and the form of the little flowers, something like double primroses, has a power to charm that none but a basilisk could resist.

The leaves are composed usually of three or five leaflets, and are clean cut round the edges compared with most roses. They are a fresh and lively green, both above and below. The plants have so few thorns that it is possible to find thornless shoots as long as oneself. The flowers are borne most readily from fairly old sections of the plant. For this reason advice is often given not to prune these roses, in order to prevent us from ignorantly cutting away their flowering wood, which we should do if we followed the normally recommended procedures. However we have already mentioned that they can be kept trimmed in pots, so pruning is obviously possible, and the thing to remember is that flowering shoots are apt to come from older wood. We should not therefore remove old wood for any reasons apart from its superfluity or deterioration; and in the matter of young wood, we must remember as we shorten it that we are taking away future footholds for flowers, and the question to ask before each cut, is 'Why should flowers *not* appear along here?' If no reason answers, don't cut.

SPECIES & VARIETIES

R. banksiae alba-plena   *Climber   White   Late spring*   P3   H1   *
The double white Banksian Rose was grown in Chinese gardens, having presumably been selected or developed from wild forms by the Chinese in the past. The first specimen recorded in the west was brought from Canton to England by William Kerr in 1807. This pretty rose has neat double flowers, and its scent is like a suggestion of

violets. We have ventured to use the name 'alba-plena', although *Modern Roses 7* prefers *R. banksiae banksiae* which is the proper name at present. This is very far from a natural species, being incapable of propagating itself, for it sets no seed. A plant of this variety at Tombstone, Arizona, was credited with being 'the largest rose bush in the world'. Its girth at the base was reputed to be 58 in. (147 cm) and its branches covered 4,620 square feet.

R. banksiae lutea   *Climber   Yellow   Late spring*   P1   H1   ***
Generally known as Yellow Banksian or Banksian Yellow, without heeding the equal but later claim of the single variety to the descriptive title; this is the double one, assured of its place among roses for distinction and beauty. The soft primrose colour is very pleasant, the flower form enchanting; it has little scent. This is one of the world's choicest plants. The Royal Horticultural Society of London, to their eternal credit, sent John Parks to China to collect various plants, and he returned with this among others in 1824. It is certain that various forms existed in China, and have turned up also in cultivation in other countries; but until we have a proper study of them, they are all lumped together under this name.

R. banksiae lutescens   *Climber   Yellow   Late spring*   P3   H3
This is the single yellow variety. We assume it came as a variation from the wild white one, through creamy whites. No doubt a number of colour variations exist in the wild. Unlike the two double varieties, this and the next one have many small hips. The accounts of its discovery are not entirely convincing; it seems to have been the best part of fifty years behind the double yellow in reaching Europe.

R. banksiae normalis   *Climber   White   Late spring*   P4   H3
This is the true species, single white, fragrant, with plenty of small, round hips. It is a native of central and southern China, where it trails along the ground, and having made a mound of itself, ascends into trees for a considerable height. Roy Shepherd gives the pleasing information that this rose is Mu-hsiang to the Chinese, whose fishermen use the bark of its roots to dye their nets. It was identified and sent to Europe about 1877; there is a story that it went to Scotland in 1796, and was never seen in flower because it was cut down by the frost every year. That tale depends on the correct identification in 1905 of a rose planted in 1796. It may be true, but in my experience gardeners can confuse their plants in one season, let alone one hundred and nine.

   Mu-hsiang, we are told, denotes wood-smoke; it is said to refer to the scent, which may be true. But if we imagine a hillside white with blossom, might it not be likened to a cloud of white smoke?

BANKSIAE HYBRID

Little or no breeding has been attempted with Banksian Roses in recent years, but I must point out that it was no mean achievement by the Chinese of the past to obtain the double white and double yellow forms. To wait for flowers until plants are comparatively old does not suit modern gardeners; and that quality would deter most breeders from working upon Banksians, but that is the wrong way to consider the matter; it would be better to ask whether Banksians could not improve the flowering capacity of old plants of other kinds of roses. The reply might suggest that if their lack of hardiness was also inherited, none of the plants of the future would so much as grow old! But then we remember the entrancing shape of the little double flowers, and see another gift there. I have never see any hope of fertility in the double Banksians, and I presume *R. banksiae lutescens* would be the most hopeful variety to breed with.

R. × fortuniana   *Climber*   *White*   *Late spring*   P3   H1
Discovered in a Chinese garden about 1850 by Robert Fortune, this is thought to be a natural hybrid between a Banksian Rose and *R. laevigata*. It is double, white, fragrant; and has been grown and sold in error for *R. banksiae alba-plena;* but it has larger flowers. For some years it was used as a rootstock in Southern Europe. Mr Fortune described the trellises and pergolas upon which the Chinese grew this hybrid; and they apparently valued it more highly than we do. It is only worth growing in warm climates.

SPECIES continued

R. cymosa   *Climber*   *White*   *Early summer*
Formerly known as *R. microcarpa,* because it has very small hips. It has had at least five other names too. Very few western rosarians have seen it, for although it is a common wild rose in China, it has not apparently had any appeal in cultivation. I regret I have no first-hand knowledge of it; but it is right to note its existence here.

9. Laevigatae and Hybrids

The second section of the sub-genus Eurosa, and therefore marked by smooth hips, apart from some bristles. The stipules are joined to the leaf stalk only at their base; variations from the Banksianae are that the stipules are toothed, the flowers are larger, and are not borne in rounded heads, but individually or in small clusters. The name means polished smooth, in reference to the glossy leaves.

SPECIES

R. laevigata *Climber* *White* *Midsummer* P5 H5

A common wild rose in China, this has become perfectly naturalized in the southern part of the United States; indeed it has been taken for an American species, because people cannot believe that a rose imported into America in the eighteenth century could have spread so far and so fast. And the question has been raised whether *R. laevigata* was brought to the United States by some previous visitors from the orient, before ever the traffic from China was opened up by way of Europe. It is so much a native that the Americans call it the Cherokee Rose, and the state of Georgia has it for an emblem. It has at least seven other Latin names, of which *R. sinica* and *R. ternata* were the most used. In France it is known as the Camellia Rose.

The Cherokee Rose is a handsome wild plant, with single flowers of pure white, embellished by golden stamens. The flowers are quite spectacular, about 6 cm across, and they are backed by handsome glossy leaves nearly always of three leaflets. The hips are orange red, and bristly. The plant is vigorous and sends out climbing shoots. The waxy white flowers and highly polished leaves would appear to offer splendid promises of handsome progeny. But we must conclude that the right mates have not yet been introduced to it, for there are few hybrids to show. We note that it prefers the southern USA to north, where it does not flower so freely, and this sounds a warning to breeders, who are concerned that roses should flourish in colder climates. This one does not; it is a wonderful rose for warm climates only.

LAEVIGATA HYBRIDS

R. × anemonoides *Climber* *Pink* *Late spring* P3 H1

Known as the Anemone Rose, the Pink Cherokee, Sinica Anemone; and in France, 'Rosier Camellia à fleurs d'anémones roses'. This rose came from J. C. Schmidt of Erfurt, Germany, in about 1896, as a seedling from *R. laevigata;* the pollen was thought to be from a Tea. It has large single flowers of soft pink, very silky and perfect. It is fairly hardy, if a little less so than average, and for a brief time before many other roses are out it is a cheerful sight upon a warm wall. Unfortunately it appears to be sterile, and so closes one avenue of breeding progress from the Cherokee Rose.

'Ramona'   *Climber*   *Red*   *Late spring*   P3   H1

A deeper coloured sport from *R.* × *anemonoides,* which it resembles except for its colour. It is known as the Red Cherokee, and was introduced in 1913 by Dietrich & Turner of Montebello, California.

'Silver Moon'   *Climber*   *White*   *Summer*   P4   H2

One of the most vigorous climbing roses; it will grow for yards. But it brings with it an adverse factor from *R. laevigata,* a reluctance to flower freely in cooler areas. There is no question so far as I know about its hardiness; but there is a question as to whether some factor of light or temperature causes it to miss a season in flower from time to time. Considering the space it takes, this will disqualify it from most small gardens. Where it flowers freely, in the more equable climates, it is spectacular, and the name describes the large white flowers very well. A little later in flower than many climbers, it was for years used at Hitchin as an indicator to judge the readiness of other varieties for the Summer National Rose Show, because in those years it decided to bloom, 'Silver Moon' did so with unfailing regularity one week after midsummer day. This rose was bred by a distinguished American rose breeder, Dr Walter van Fleet, of Glenn Dale, Maryland. The published parentage records are not consistent; it is frequently said to be a cross between *R. wichuraiana* and *R. laevigata,* which is not impossible; I prefer the other version, which reads for *R. wichuraiana* one of van Fleet's hybrids of that species.

10. Bracteatae and Hybrids

'The roses with bracts' are our third section of the Eurosa. Bracts are leafy growths near to the flower, and they are usually imperfectly formed, as if the plant was misfiring as it changes from producing ordinary leaves, and starts upon the complex parts of the flower. Sometimes bracts are sophisticated, and take over the task of petals, as in *Bougainvillaea*. Bracts are the distinguishing mark here, for they surround the flowers unusually closely for roses; the stipules are joined to the leaf stalk near its base, and are indented, like the teeth of a comb, but there may only be one or two teeth per stipule.

Bracts are by no means unique to *R. bracteata;* it would be misleading to think so. This section, however, out of those in which the stipules are only partially joined to the leaf stalk, is the one most noticeably possessing bracts; many roses in the sections yet to follow also have them.

SPECIES & VARIETIES

R. bracteata   *Climber*   *White*   *Summer*   P4   H2

The Macartney Rose, so named because it was collected in the course of a diplomatic mission to China led by Lord Macartney, was brought back to England in about 1793. A few years later, about 1799, it was sent to the United States, and it has become naturalized in the south-eastern part of that country. In warmer climates it can grow into a nuisance because it can layer itself by rooting where its shoots touch the soil. Where there is frost, it is not very easy to grow, and may prove more of a shrub than a climber.

The flowers are large, single, fragrant and white, with golden stamens; the leaves are most attractive, dark, glossy and persistent; they have rounded ends, instead of the points of most rose leaves. In warm climates, they are retained so long that *R. bracteata* can almost claim to be an evergreen. It has often been said that this rose is immune to blackspot, but we should take a pinch of salt with that statement. In the past, it has been called both *R. macartnea* and *R. lucida*.

BRACTEATA HYBRIDS

The obvious relationships one would expect to see are large flowers with the type of leaf of *R. bracteata*. If the hybrids had prominent bracts, it would set the seal on their affinity. Lack of hardiness is an obvious deterrent to breeders, but one famous hybrid is so good that it is a wonder more have not been raised from *R. bracteata*.

'Marie Leonida'

I include this rose to illustrate that plants are not easily recognized, recorded and retained: it serves as a warning.

'Marie Leonida' is first heard of in France in 1832. By 1840, one of England's most expert and trustworthy rosarians, Thomas Rivers, declares it 'is now an established favourite; its fine bell-shaped flowers of the purest white, sometimes slightly tinged with pink towards their centre, and its bright red anthers peeping from among its central petals, give it an elegant and pleasing character . . . a few plants soon cover a bed, or clump, with a dense mass of foliage and flowers, ornamenting the flower garden from three to four months . . .'

Even before Rivers, warnings were coming from the Continent about the risk of confusing three double Bracteata Hybrids. One of them, it was explained, had anthers which stayed yellow, instead of turning red like those of 'Marie Leonida'. Another would not open its flowers properly. It surprises me that nobody noted that a double Bracteata Hybrid would more likely be touched cream than pink.

With those facts in mind, see the result: by 1969, 'Marie Leonida' is officially 'yellowish-white' or 'cream'; no longer white tinged pink. It is no longer grown in Britain, because its flowers do not open properly. Anyone who cares to read again what Thomas Rivers said is free to draw his own conclusions. This unfortunate variety, having apparently lost its individuality and its life, was finally robbed of its name too, by receiving the official title *R.* × *leonida.*

'Mermaid' *Climber Creamy yellow Remontant* P3 H1 *******
Here is our first 'five-star' rose, a most beautiful climber, introduced by the firm of William Paul, of Waltham Cross in England in 1918. It was immediately recognized as a winner, the great width of the single flowers attracting awed comment from the rosarians of the time. Never, in their eyes, had five rose petals covered so much space, and conveyed so much beauty. Almost at once it fell under a cloud, because the plants which had been propagated failed to grow, and 'Mermaid' was assumed to be too tender. With a lifetime's experience of 'Mermaid', we know that it is not compatible with certain rootstocks, especially *R. canina,* and no doubt that was the whole of the trouble. It was investigated by the Secretary of the National Rose Society, Mr Courtney Page, who went with the famous rose breeder Mr Sam McGredy, to the nurseries in Waltham Cross from which 'Mermaid' had come. This they did in September 1919, and were entirely satisfied, as the following report from Mr Page beautifully testifies:

> 'Unexpectedly we came upon a large breadth of cutbacks of Mermaid, and what a sight it was! The sun had only recently broken through the autumn mist, and the beautiful shining foliage was still wet with dew. There were blooms by the thousand, enormous ones, too, many being five or six inches across. We stood admiring them for some considerable time, when suddenly Mr McGredy turned to Mr Paul and said, "I have seen the sight of my life, it's simply magnificent. I would not have missed it on any account." Surely a very graceful tribute from one raiser to another!'

Arthur Paul is reported to have said that 'Mermaid' was one of about a dozen seedlings from *R. bracteata,* pollinated by a double yellow Tea Rose. One of its sisters was introduced in 1919 as 'Sea Foam', but had a short lease of life, and that name was used again for a different rose in 1964.

'Mermaid' is well known as a thorny brute, best not pruned very much, and with brittle stems which easily snap; worse still, it is liable to be damaged beyond recovery by frost. The answer to all these troubles is to put up with them, and buy another 'Mermaid' if the old one is lost. The single flowers in light primrose are made alive by the crown of amber stamens, and this pleasure may be had for months every year. Unfortunately 'Mermaid' is not easy to breed with. Occasionally it produces a seed, but not one which is likely to germinate, and we may wonder where some writers found the notion that it sets plenty of seed. Its pollen has a low fertility rate, but sufficient to obtain seedlings, if applied to a fertile mother. Some two or three dozen have been raised at Hitchin, but have not shown as yet the promise I believe will one day be kept.

SPECIES continued

R. clinophylla   *Climber   White   Summer*

A rarity in Europe, I have never seen it. I believe it may not be a distinct species from *R. bracteata,* and it would be interesting to examine it. One of the few roses which is a native to India, where it occurs in several different areas, also in Bangladesh, Burma and China. It is referred to in older records as *R. involucrata,* and was the species guessed to be one of the parents of 'Hardii'. It has also been called *R. lyellii* and *R. lindleyana.* It is recorded in England early in the nineteenth century; and the name describes the tendency of the long, narrow leaflets to bend.

11. Indicae and Hybrids

This should prove to be the longest section in the book, for here we have the paradox of only two species, of which one is tender and the other apparently non-existent, proving to be the most important, and the most progenitive of all. Indeed it is scarcely an exaggeration to say that the familiar look of a garden rose is due to the family likeness inherited from the two elusive species of the section Indicae.

Leaves, hips and stipules have provided the main distinguishing marks hitherto. We have already left behind the roses with simple leaves and prickly hips; and at this point we pass also from those with stipules joined briefly at their base. Now and henceforward the stipules are joined to the leaf stalks for most, if not all, of their length. It is now the turn of the styles. The word 'style' is the same as for a stylus or pen, its sense being of a slender column. In a flower, the style is the column connecting the stigma with the ovary, and down it the pollen is destined to travel. In the Indicae and in the next section, the styles stick out of the tube they grow in, whereas thereafter they do not protrude in this manner. The difference between the Indicae and the next section is that here the styles are free from one another, but there they are fused together.

The name means Indian, but it was given under a misapprehension, as we shall see.

SPECIES & VARIETIES

R. chinensis
The China Rose. This is perhaps the most moving story of past achievements we expect to record in these pages. The China Rose more than any other is responsible for nearly all the popular roses of the present time. It is at once the rose world's greatest blessing and mystery.

The mystery comes of our being unable to identify any original species as the China Rose. *R. chinensis* itself is not a living entity, but a dried specimen in a herbarium collection of the Dutch botanist Gronovius. He labelled it 'Chineesche Eglantier Rosen' in 1733, and it now rests in the British Museum. It is most probably the same as a red China Rose brought to Europe later in the eighteenth century; but nobody is really sure what it is. The true, natural species is supposed to be *R. chinensis spontanea,* but my remarks upon that rose will show that it is even more elusive; there is not even so much as a dried specimen of that one.

The truth appears to be that the China Rose was developed many years ago in that country of ingenious and long-civilized people, and we simply have no evidence how they did it. In the eighteenth century Europeans saw China Roses on sale, the Fa Tee Nurseries in Canton being a celebrated source; and they bought them and sent them home. It is a pity they did not pump the proprietors dry of all the knowledge they had. In due time China Roses mated with Western roses, the Flower of East and West meeting one might say, despite Rudyard Kipling, and the rose was magnified far beyond what had been seen hitherto. This example of human co-operation comes along free of charge with the beauty of modern roses. In a flower of 'Peace' there is not only the work of the Frenchman who raised it, but the hands of men who prepared the way to it, old hands gnarled and buried a long time, Chinese, Persian, Chaldean, Mycenean, Greek, Roman and who knows what else, up to the new hands, Irish, English, American and French. All subscribed to the making of 'Peace'; and were we to take the generality of roses instead of that one variety, we should embrace nearly the whole of the nations in this peaceful and purely beneficial pursuit. 'Peace hath her victories no less renowned than war.'

I do not believe that we have, amongst the China Roses that came to the West, any true species, nor any botanic varieties. In my opinion they are all Chinese cultivated varieties, and the source material is unknown to us. I suppose the original was a hybrid of the second or a subsequent generation, and the nearest parallel to such an occurrence in modern experience is *R. kordesii.* I fear this theory may bring the hornets round my head, but it seems to fit the facts better than the accounts of *R. chinensis* written in the rose books.

Other names for the species have included *R. sinica* and *R. indica,* and on the latter hangs the explanation of the section name, Indicae: the Calcutta Botanic Garden was fairly active in collecting oriental roses, and it was also co-operative in accepting shipments of plants from Chinese ports, and holding them (or perhaps reviving them) until a ship sailed for Europe. For this reason, the French in particular assumed that the plants came from Calcutta, and they called them 'Bengal Roses', which is still the common name in France and Germany; the specific name in Latin for Indian Roses (*R. indica*) was therefore acceptable. I have often thought that botanists going to Calcutta in those days could hardly have believed their botanic fortune when they saw the plants of the Orient for the first time.

The chief blessing brought by China Roses was an extension of the flowering period from summer even up to the gates of winter. It is easy to let that statement pass, but to arrest it, and emphasize its importance, let us repeat it another way: until the China Rose came, nearly all European roses flowered for a few weeks like the cherry, the lilac, the hawthorn, the apple and the broom. The miracle of flowering again and again made the rose a very special plant.

The shape of flower which we take to be the traditional rose, is no more traditional than appearing about the middle of the nineteenth century; and it comes, so far as we can judge, from the stock in trade of the Fa Tee Nurseries. The types of leaves, stems and bushes crowded into millions of rose beds about the world have the family stamp of the China Roses upon them. We know much of modern rose breeders, among whom are good and great men, but the greatest of all may be from long ago and quite unknown; and may their bones rest with our blessing in the soil of Mother China.

R. chinensis minima

The China Rose had a miniature form, which is the chief progenitor of modern miniature roses. It would seem most likely that the original strain of this variety has suffered changes since it came to the west, and it would be a bold man who could produce a plant today, and swear it was this. We learn of no record of importation direct to Europe from China, nor even of any discovery there. One authority suggests that it came to England from Mauritius about 1810. This subject will be more fully discussed under Miniatures.

R. chinensis mutabilis   *Medium +   Cream to red   Remontant*   P3   H1   **
This remarkable shrub has large single flowers, which open from orange red buds to a colour between cream and pale sulphur, and gradually turn through pink to purple red. Fortunately they do not open all at once, and the extraordinary contrast of young and old is frequently before one's eyes.This rose needs warmth and shelter from the wind; and the plus sign, and even the medium in the headline, depend upon those wants being satisfied. Some people train it on a wall as a climber, but this is not its natural habit. The best way to grow it in colder countries is probably as a pot plant in a cool greenhouse, and it is worth doing. Presumably it is one of the varieties brought from China in the eighteenth century, for it is obviously the same as 'Tipo Ideale', painted by Redouté early in the nineteenth. But there is no record of its origin. The colour contrast is just as vivid and surprising as that with which 'Masquerade' amazed the rose world after the second world war. The disposition to change colour is clearly a genetic feature of China Roses, and surely capable of affording more surprises yet.

R. chinensis semperflorens   *Short   Red   Remontant*   P2   H1
This is 'Slater's Crimson China', one of the early imports, and possibly the same as the specimen alluded to under *R. chinensis*. Graham Thomas makes the important point in his *Shrub Roses of Today* that dark crimson like this was unknown in garden roses until this variety arrived. It follows that this is an ancestor of virtually all our modern dark red roses, so far as the evidence shows. It was brought home, so the story goes, by a ship's captain of the East India Company, and presented to Gilbert Slater, who was one of John Company's directors. Later, C. C. Hurst was to emphasize its importance by designating it one of the 'Four Stud Chinas' primarily responsible for the evolution of modern roses. From the regularity of its flowering, it was affectionately known as the Monthly Rose in Britain; but the Americans thought that was an understatement, and had a vogue of calling it the Daily Rose. Norman Young in his fascinating book *The Complete Rosarian* complains that the 'Monthly Rose' was an honourable title stolen from the Autumn Damask.

R. chinensis spontanea
This is the true official species seen by Dr Augustine Henry in 1885, and described by him in the *Gardeners' Chronicle* in June 1902. Dr Henry was serving the Chinese Maritime Customs, and his discovery was made near Ichang, which is in the middle of China, about 600 miles (1000 km) both west of Shanghai and north of Hong Kong. Unfortunately no specimens have ever been brought or sent out of China, and so Dr Henry is the only witness we have to the existence of this rose. Reading about it in rose literature, one would not suppose that to be the case, for it is described with the utmost confidence by writers who have never seen it. It is said to grow from four to twenty feet in height, that is roughly one metre to six; and its flowers are crimson, pink or white; such versatility presents a blurred picture to my mind, and although Dr Henry may have been perfectly right, it seems wrong to confer specific identity upon the evidence we have.

R. chinensis viridiflora   *Short   Green   Remontant*   P1   H1   *
An engaging monstrosity, the Green Rose; and as a plant is very easy to grow, the small space occupied is well repaid by the amusement afforded. The flowers are small, double, and imperfectly developed. Somewhere from the classroom comes an echo of a master's voice, saying 'flower parts are all modified leaves'. If we say, here the modification is incomplete, a fair idea of the Green Rose is imparted. The green 'flowers' at least have the advantage of an extremely long life.

It will be clear by now that China Roses are versatile, with such variations as *minima, mutabilis* and *viridiflora.* Indeed there was a variety *longifolia,* with leaflets very long and narrow, like a willow; it appears to be extinct, unless it is to be found somewhere in China.

Obscurity of origin no less than versatility is also a common factor, and it extends to the Green Rose, which we may doubt is a variety in the botanic sense. Reports of its origin in the most reputable authorities cover 113 years and two continents, which is really quite a remarkable feat. An English nursery named Bambridge and Harrison appears to have introduced the rose in 1855 or 1856, but there is a strong presumption it originated elsewhere: the United States about 1833 is as convincing a report as any we are likely to find.

CHINENSIS HYBRIDS

A long and complex list of hybrids must now swell the section Indicae, and it is necessary to begin with a simple signpost to show the road we are about to follow.

First we have an assortment of Hybrid Chinas, which include some of the original imports from China, and some later ones which are roughly similar to China Roses. Our criterion is general appearance; and it beckons us to follow with Noisettes, Teas, Hybrid Teas, Floribundas, Miniatures, Hybrid Musks and Modern Climbers.

But because their appearance seems more akin to that of the Gallicanae, we have put the Portlands, Bourbons and Hybrid Perpetuals into that side of the family. There is, in fact, no rule or law of classification to guide us, only our taste and common sense.

HYBRID CHINAS

This is an assortment of hybrids, as explained immediately above; but it used to be a well-defined class with a particular meaning, namely hybrids between the China Rose and the European roses. They were summer flowering only, and as Pemberton pointed out, would more accurately have been called Hybrid Centifolia or Hybrid Gallica. Any survivors of that class are now to be found in more appropriate classes, which leaves Hybrid China empty for use in its proper sense, once it is clearly understood that references to it in nineteenth- and twentieth-century books have separate meanings.

'Bloomfield Abundance'   *Tall   Light pink   Remontant*   P2   H1   **

Like a coarse growing 'Cécile Brunner', with huge heads of buds. The small light pink flowers, like miniature Hybrid Teas, will be familiar to everyone who loves 'Cécile Brunner'. This is a mass supplier of them. It has long been obvious to nurserymen, who see their stock of 'Cécile Brunner' suddenly change into 'Bloomfield Abundance', that the parentage in *Modern Roses* cannot possibly be right. It is credited to Capt. George Thomas of California, 1920; and whatever the books say, it is a sport of 'Cécile Brunner'.

'Cécile Brunner'   *Shorter   Light pink   Remontant*   P2   H1   ***

Restrained growth, attractive foliage, and perfect little roses in miniature have made this a favourite since its introduction by Pernet-Ducher of Lyon in 1881. The light pink buds are thumb-nail copies of perfect Hybrid Teas. If only the Miniatures invariably had flowers of this shape, they would more nearly fulfil expectations. 'Cécile Brunner', so far as we know, is a cross between a Polyantha and a Tea, and it is a pity there are not many more like it. Unfortunately it is very difficult to breed with. I have never found it set seed, nor can I see pollen-bearing stamens in it, although some people have apparently been more successful according to the records. As personal adornment, Madame could very well pin 'Cécile Brunner' on her breast, and leave her jewels at home. Was sold as the 'Sweetheart Rose' by some English speaking nurserymen, and as 'Mignon' by some French.

'Cécile Brunner Climbing' *Climber   Light pink   Summer*   P2   H1   **

I have used the word 'sport' several times, without keeping my intention to explain such terms as they arise. The word is used in three ways. A sport is said to occur when a part of a plant (or more rarely the whole plant) shows a healthy variation from its normal character. Secondly, upon the changed factor being successfully propagated and established as a new variety, that new variety is called a sport. The word may thirdly be used as a verb, to say that one rose sported from another. The most common sports among roses are changes of colour, and from bush to climbing growth. Sports occur because the growth control organisms have varied from normal; and that simple apology avoids a lengthy study in genetics. The variation may only be in the outer cells of the plant, in which case the sport is termed a 'chimera'; or it may be a total change; to test which, it is necessary to see if the reproductive material such as seed, formed out of the plant's inner tissue, will propagate true to the sport, or revert to the original. In the case of hybrid roses, which do not come true from seed, this means taking cuttings and waiting for suckers from their roots, those being formed of inner tissue. The word 'mutation' is commonly used as a synonym for sport, which is rather a pity, because a sport is a clearly defined type of change, whereas a mutation may be a change for other reasons too.

Reverting to 'Cécile Brunner Climbing', it is a very vigorous plant, with large leaves, and it is an agreeable provider of button-hole roses. If allowed to grow in the most favoured position, it will abuse its owner's hospitality by growing to an extraordinary size, and by making more greenery than flower. It is better to keep it starved and struggling, when it will not only give more flowers in the summer, but very possibly some later in the season as well. The sport first occurred in California, and was introduced by F. P. Hosp in 1894.

'Comtesse du Cayla'   *Short   Orange-red   Remontant*   P3   H1

During the nineteenth century, there were hundreds of different roses called Chinas or Hybrid Chinas, and most of them are now forgotten. It is not my purpose to make this book a dull list of roses, but rather to concentrate on the most interesting, even if extinct, and the best. I shall therefore give short notices of the others, as a matter of necessary reference, and in order to save space for the important ones. 'Comtesse du Cayla', from Pierre Guillot, introduced 1902, has orange-red flowers, with more yellow on the reverse side, turning towards salmon-pink with age. They are semi-double, rather loose, the effect bright, warm, and careless. Billed in some quarters to grow head high, it is usually quite short and fragrant. Walter Easlea was an old time expert who could not imagine why this should be classed as a China Rose. To him it was more of a Tea; and there was a time when people referred to a class of China Teas.

'Cramoisi Supérieur'   *Short   Crimson   Remontant*   P2   H1

From Coquereau, 1832; also named 'Agrippina'. Double, dark crimson flowers, rather small. Has thin stems, rather small leaves. There is also a climbing form which came from Couturier, 1885.

'Fabvier'   *Shorter   Crimson, marked white   Remontant*   P2   H2
Laffay, 1832; may be found as 'Mme Fabvier'. Short plants with bright crimson
flowers, small for a China; semi-double; the white lines are a well known feature, an
inheritance which can be found in many modern red roses.

'Fellemberg'   *Tall   Red   Remontant*   P2   H2
From Fellemberg 1857; this variety is also known as 'La Belle Marseillaise'. A
vigorous, rather open bush, with pinky-red flowers in random scattered array. Can
be used as a pillar rose as well as a shrub.

'Fortune's Double Yellow'   *Climber   Yellow & red   Early summer*   P4   H1   *
Robert Fortune, sent to China by the Royal Horticultural Society of London,
reported his visit in 1842 to Ningpo, where he visited nurseries and gardens: 'On
entering one of the gardens on a fine morning in May, I was struck by a mass of yellow
flowers which completely covered a distant part of the wall; the colour was not a
common yellow, but had something of buff in it, which gave the flower a striking and
uncommon appearance. I immediately ran up to the place, and to my surprise and
delight found that I had discovered a most beautiful new yellow climbing rose.' He
sent it to England, where it was growing in 1845.

This rose is indeed a striking colour, with more orange red in its yellow than
Fortune's description suggests. It is not perfectly hardy, and should be grown under
glass in frosty countries. It will prove an admirable pot plant in a cold greenhouse,
being interesting, beautiful, historic and unusual. The origin is unknown, and it is not
easy to say which class it belongs to; it has been called a Tea, a Noisette, a China, a
species, a variety of a species, and (by the crafty) just a climber. It differs from most of
this section by failing to repeat its flowers. I have traced eleven different names of this
rose, the best known being 'Beauty of Glazenwood', 'Gold of Ophir', 'San Rafael
Rose', and its present official name, *R.* × *odorata pseudindica*. It flowers from its old
wood, and does not need to be pruned very hard, which is one reason for growing it
out of the reach of the frost. The best way to prune it is just to trim off the old flowers
to a sound eye after it has bloomed.

'Gruss an Teplitz'   *Tall   Crimson   Remontant*   P4   H2
A tall rose, with open heads of small double crimson flowers. It has a loose and
scattered look. Some people grow it as a climber or a hedge, but it is scarcely worth
such prominence, and is best pruned, and kept in the bounds of a bush. It will flower
more freely that way. The leaves are small, dark when young. This rose has been
assigned to more classes than most, and some experts call it a Hybrid Tea, although it
is no more like one than is 'Paul's Scarlet Climber'. I think it should be considered a
Hybrid China, with Bourbon as the nearest runner-up.

The parents were ('Sir Joseph Paxton' × 'Fellemberg') × ('Papa Gontier' ×
'Gloire des Rosomanes'), a mixture of Bourbon, Hybrid China and Tea. Peter
Lambert, often referred to as the breeder, was the introducer. It was raised by G.
Geschwind of Karpona, Hungary, and introduced in 1897. It proved in due time a
useful parent, one of its more famous offspring being 'Hugh Dickson'.

'Hermosa'   *Short   Pink   Remontant*   P2   H1
From Marcheseau, 1840. Has also been 'Armosa', 'Mélanie Lemaire', 'Mme
Neumann' and 'Setina'. It has been 'Old Blush' too, due to nurserymen making
mistakes, for the two are alike, but this has double flowers. Bright rose pink. The

number of names occurred because the same or a very similar rose was produced by different breeders, as if it was a fairly natural development in China Roses. A climbing form was introduced about 1879, but this is only summer flowering.

'Hume's Blush Tea-scented China'

This rose was imported from China in 1809 by Sir Abraham Hume of Wormley Bury in Hertfordshire, having been purchased on his behalf along with other plants from the Fa Tee Nurseries near Canton. It flowered the following year (in King's Road, Chelsea) under the care of a nurseryman, James Colvill; and a portrait was promptly painted by Henry Andrews, a leading illustrator of flowers. It was given the name *R. indica odorata,* which over the years has become *R. × odorata,* and is a somewhat loosely used hybrid specific name for Tea Roses. *The Gentleman's Magazine* of 14 November 1811 notes that plants of this rose were taken to the Empress Joséphine, a transaction that involved safe conducts by the British and French Admiralties, who were otherwise at war.

In fact there is reason to believe that the nurseryman concerned, John Kennedy, had fairly regular journeys of this nature during the war; and *The Gentleman's Magazine* may have made a story out of one of them. Such is the way of journalists; and we may stretch a point for that particular magazine, because its publisher some seventy years or so previously had employed Samuel Johnson to write for it, thereby rescuing him from poverty. When it flowered in Joséphine's garden at Malmaison, the rose was painted by Pierre Joseph Redouté, under the name *R. indica fragrans* 'Hume's Blush'. It is in his Volume 1, Plate 61, and is quite regularly reproduced. The use of the word 'fragrans' is of course interesting.

C. C. Hurst confidently states that this rose is a hybrid derived from *R. gigantea* and *R. chinensis,* but we should be wary of accepting these reconstructions, while willing to agree that Hurst's theory is the best we have. 'Hume's Blush' is one of Hurst's 'Four Stud Chinas', that is four varieties which he took as the fountain-heads of modern roses; and its importance is that it is the ancestor of virtually all the Tea roses and consequently of the Hybrid Teas, not to mention other classes less exciting.

According to Hurst and to Norman Young, living material is no longer available, the West having typically used it and thrown it away; but Arthur Wyatt in the *Rose Annual 1975,* states that it has been preserved in the Rosarium at Sangerhausen in Germany since 1908, and that he obtained it from there. We should hope this is accurate, for those who preserve and identify old roses are sadly used to finding that the rose is not always what the label says it ought to be.

'Miss Lowe's Variety' *Shorter Crimson Remontant* P2 H1

More correctly known as 'Sanguinea'; but is it not ungentlemanly to ditch Miss Lowe? A single red sport from *R. chinensis semperflorens;* the colour deepens as the flowers age. An interesting possibility has been raised, that this may be not so much a sport as a reversion, in which case it would show us what one of the 'Four Stud Chinas' arose from. Has interesting quilled petals, so far an unexploited feature of China Roses.

'Mme Laurette Messimy' *Medium – Pink with yellow Remontant* P2 H2

A lively little rose; its salmon buds open into semi-double flowers, deep rose with yellow. Has the same look about it as 'Comtesse du Cayla'. From Guillot Fils, 1887. Given parentage: 'Rival de Paestum' × 'Mme Falcot'. May stay short. A bright coloured sport from this rose is 'Mme Eugène Résal', from P. Guillot, 1894.

'Old Blush'   *Medium − Pink Remontant*   P3   H2   ******
This is perhaps the most fertile of the 'Four Stud Chinas', partly from being the most
robust and thus growing in many different areas, partly because its pollen initiated
the Noisettes and the Bourbons, and thus played its generative role on both sides of
the Hybrid Tea family; and some authorities give it credit for the Miniatures also.
Such a remarkable chapter of rose history being available to be put in one's garden, it
seems almost heresy not to have it.

So far as we can be reasonably sure, this pink rose was one of the favourites in
eighteenth-century China, and was sent home by Europeans on several occasions.
There are reports of it coming to England from Sweden and from Holland, as well as
direct from China. And while the exact story of this rose can never be known for sure,
the first recorded import appears to have been to Upsala, Sweden in 1752, organized
by a man called Peter Osbeck, a friend of the great Linnaeus, and chaplain of the
Swedish ship 'Prince Charles'. Stock from Sweden went to England around 1759.
The rose appears to have arrived in France by 1798, and in the United States around
1800.

It was named 'Parson's Pink China', and shares with *R. chinensis semperflorens* the
names Monthly Rose and Daily Rose, sometimes with the adjective 'pink'. 'Common
Blush China' was another soubriquet. The rose pink flowers are small, semi-double,
and freely produced. The plants have great stamina, and if anything survives from an
old time overgrown rose garden, it is likely to be 'Old Blush'.

'Parks' Yellow Tea-scented China'
The Royal Horticultural Society of London deserves the credit for bringing this
important rose to the west; although the Society's main purpose in sending one of
their gardeners to China in 1823 was to find new chrysanthemums. John Parks
(Parkes in some versions) was the man, and he returned the next year with the
chrysanthemums; he also brought the Yellow Banksian Rose, which was no mean
discovery, and this yellow Tea-scented variety, the ancestor designate to many of our
modern roses, and responsible in particular for their delicacy in colouring. It is one of
Hurst's 'Four Stud Chinas'. The botanic name given is *R.* × *odorata ochroleuca;* the
latter word means yellowish-white. The Redouté plate names it *R. indica sulphurea*
'Parks's Yellow'.

According to Hurst, this rose very soon found its way to M. Eugène Hardy in Paris,
whom we have already met in connection with × *Hulthemosa hardii;* and it became a
popular pot plant in Paris, as Thomas Rivers records in his *Rose Amateur's Guide.*
Unfortunately it had disappeared in sixty years, for Hurst said no living material had
been available since 1882. Well, perhaps when it had played its part, there was no
point in keeping it; but one feels a sense of loss, and the nagging thought that perhaps
it had not reached the end of its script. Some of us would have liked to have seen it;
we must think of our own children, before we throw things away.

'Perle d'Or'   *Shorter   Light pink & yellow   Remontant*   P2   H1   *****
To modern eyes this rose is not very yellow; but it was the 'Yellow Cécile Brunner' to
past generations. Pretty flower form, short compact habit. Raised by Rambaud of
Lyon and introduced 1884. Parentage assumed to be a Polyantha and a Tea Rose.

'Serratipetala'   *Short   Red & pink   Remontant*   P2   H1
Two gifts for breeders to unwrap: the outer petals are red, the inner ones pink; the
petals are fringed like those of a carnation. This seems to have been found in France

in 1912, and was known there as 'Rose Oeillet de Saint Arquey'. A specialist's rose, mean with its blooms, gaunt in growth, but rich in promise.

NOISETTES

Noisettes originated from a hybrid raised in Charleston, South Carolina, on the premises of a rice growing farmer named John Champney, or Champneys in some versions. The class showed the West, for the first time, how the rose of the East could transfer its important power of repeating its blooms in the same season.

Mr Champney grew the summer flowering Musk Rose in his garden, that is to say the genuine *R. moschata,* which for a long time was the most attractive and fragrant of the very few climbing roses which were to be had. He also grew 'Old Blush', or 'Parson's Pink China' as it was then known; he received it most probably by way of France, for he was in touch with a French nurseryman named Philippe Noisette, who had settled in Charleston.

Early in the nineteenth century, he raised and introduced a seedling which was a climber like his Musk Rose, but pink instead of white. It flowered only in the summer, and it was fragrant. He named it *R. moschata hybrida,* but eventually it became known as 'Champney's Pink Cluster'. The dates given as a guide are 1802 for the time of raising it, and 1811 for its introduction. It gradually became popular, and by 1820 was known to rosarians in the United States, France and England.

So far we feel ourselves on safe ground; but we are told that Mr Champney himself transferred the pollen, which I consider unlikely, because deliberate pollination was not a general practice at that date; it was left to nature. Nor can we confidently say which parent supplied the pollen, and which the seed. Dr Hurst is quite sure the seed parent was *R. moschata,* to the pollen of 'Old Blush'; but most authorities put the parentage down as *R. chinensis* × *R. moschata.* I doubt if the issue can be proved one way or the other, and it is quite possible nobody ever knew for certain, although John Champney was clear at least as to its Musk affinities. I might point out that *R. chinensis* is not necessarily the same as 'Old Blush'. It is, and then was, so far as I am aware, a pressed specimen in the collection of a Dutch botanist, destined for the British Museum, and in no heart to commit adultery in South Carolina.

One of the first people to know 'Champney's Pink Cluster' was Philippe Noisette, the French nurseryman in Charleston. He sowed seeds of it, and provided a classic demonstration of a law of inheritance: **the mating of once flowering with Remontant gives once flowering children; in the grandchildren a Remontant line can be established.** It is a matter of which rose breeders must be aware, that the desired factor may skip one generation; or many. Musk and China had given a summer flowering climber; which in its turn gave a remontant rose.

The momentous seedling was a shrub; it was light pink, and it repeated its blooms in a manner it could inherit only from the China Rose, certainly not from the Musk. Philippe sent it to his brother Louis in Paris, and the speed of events from that point is the best evidence we have of the value in those days of a rose which would flower again the same year. We do not know the exact date it was sent to Paris, or rather we know several dates if we read enough books, but if we say around 1814, we find that it has already been introduced about 1819 and painted by Redouté by 1821. Louis is said to have received it bearing the terse title 'Blush'. He expanded that to 'Le Rosier de Philippe Noisette'. Redouté's plate is entitled *R. Noisettiana;* to which may be added the soubriquets 'Old Blush Noisette', 'French Noisette', and several others, French, Latin and English. It finally settled to 'Blush Noisette' in the vernacular tongue, and *R.* × *noisettiana* in the official.

The early Noisettes were overshadowed by the intrusion of 'Parks' Yellow Tea-scented China' into their bloodstream; crosses between that rose and 'Blush Noisette' initiated some of the most lovely yellow roses we have seen, and changed the character of Noisettes in a Tea-ward direction. The Noisettes are frequently dodging from Noisette to Tea and back again in rose literature, and it is charitable, and affords the greatest possible latitude, to follow tradition in classifying them. There are no hard and fast rules to classify hybrids, apart from appearance; that great rosarian the Rev. Joseph Pemberton once said, 'You can always tell a Noisette by the way the foot-stalks form on the centre stalks.' But you can't any more, if ever indeed you could.

The Noisettes were not destined for a long run. Many were not quite hardy enough; and their distinctive character became merged with other classes well before the end of the nineteenth century. But they did stand as ancestors of many other roses, in particular and most fortunately adding to the vigour of yellow Teas. And they have many splendid memorials about the world, for plants of some of these nineteenth-century varieties are giving pleasure to this day. Let us hope that 'Blush Noisette' may not be lost, for its parentage of Musk and China may yet cause some rose prospector's instincts to twitch, as if sensing an unexhausted mine.

'Aimée Vibert' *Climber White Remontant* P4 H2
From Vibert of Angers, France 1828. Said to be 'Champney's Pink Cluster' × a hybrid of *R. sempervirens;* a complicated ancestry if true, which we are not sure of, the Noisette element already diluted. Double white, fragrant flowers, backed by attractive dark leaves. It is rather a lax climber or shrub. Known also as 'Bouquet de la Mariée' and 'Nivea'. The effect of *R. sempervirens* is shown in the glossy dark leaves.

'Alister Stella Gray' *Climber Yellow Remontant* P6 H1 *
This was highly thought of, and came from a redoubtable amateur of roses, especially Teas, Mr Alexander Hill Gray of Bath; but how he raised it has eluded my researches. It was introduced by Paul & Sons in 1894, and is known in the United States as 'Golden Rambler'. It had the reputation of being a slow starter, and probably needed more warmth than it found in a British summer. The flowers have deep yellow centres, pale perimeters, and are very beautifully formed.

'Blush Noisette' *Taller Blush Remontant* P4 H2
The official name is *R. × noisettiana,* and we are at fault in not so listing it. But suppose Philippe Noisette had raised not one but a hundred different seedlings from 'Champney's Pink Cluster', which do you suppose would be called *R. × noisettianà?* Its story is told in the introduction to Noisettes. It is still in existence, a historic rose to be seen in some of the world's leading collections, including the Royal National Rose Society's garden at St Albans, England.

'Bouquet d'Or' *Climber Pink & yellow Remontant* P4 H1
From Ducher of Lyon, 1872, and said to be a seedling from 'Gloire de Dijon'. There's a lot of pink in the golden bouquet.

'Céline Forestier' *Climber Light yellow Remontant* P7 H1
Light yellow, apt to be white towards the perimeter; a beautiful double flower, with

the quartered style so admirable in old roses and abhorrent in the new, at fashion's whim. From Trouillard of Angers, 1842; a fragrant offering and vigorous, if a little tender.

'Chromatella'   *Climber   Yellow   Remontant*   P5   H1
More famous under its English name 'Cloth of Gold'. A seedling of 'Lamarque', said to be self-set, and therefore a descendant of 'Parks' Yellow Tea-scented China'. From Coquereau 1843. Somewhat tender, I have never seen a strong plant; but by repute an outstanding double yellow rose in its prime.

'Claire Jacquier'   *Climber   Yellow   Summer* +   P6   H1
From A. Bernaix, near Lyon, 1888. Vigorous yellow climber, finishes pale, sweetly scented.

'Desprez à Fleur Jaune'   *Climber   Pale yellow   Remontant*   P4   H1   *
'Desprez's Yellow Flowered' has always been looking rather white when I visited it; it is a splendid grower, with attractive healthy leaves. It is said to be shaded peach and apricot, no doubt just before I arrive. The double flowers are fairly large, give the impression of soaking up the sun's warmth, and paying it back in a sleepy scent. Parents are supposed to be 'Blush Noisette' × 'Fortune's Double Yellow', an interesting pair. Official name is 'Jaune Desprez', though we have honoured what we believe is the original French title. From Desprez of Yèbles, France, who is said to have sold the marketing rights for Frs 3000 (and kept his name on it). Various introduction dates are given, 1830 is probably about right. Also known as 'Noisette Desprez'.

'Gloire de Dijon'   *Climber   Buff yellow   Remontant*   P4   H1
'Old Glory' they used to call it on the nurseries in England. Dean Hole nominated it his favourite rose, saying, 'Were I condemned to have but one Rose for the rest of my life, I should ask, before leaving the dock, to be presented with a strong plant of Gloire de Dijon.' And George Paul said of its breeder, 'I hope M. Jacotot made his fortune by it!' But how are the mighty deteriorated! Today it cannot be a shadow of its former self, and should be good subject matter for the person who wants to find out why roses change. From Jacotot of Dijon (where else?) 1853.

'Lamarque'   *Climber   White   Remontant*   P6   H1
A historic rose, being from 'Blush Noisette' × 'Parks' Yellow Tea-scented China', and leading on to the Teas. It came from Maréchal of Angers in 1830; 'raised by a shoe-maker in Angers', said the Rev. Joseph Pemberton; he added that it was the sweetest scented of all, white with a lemon tint, but liable to be damaged by frost.

'L'Idéal'
This had much more red than normal in the class, and was praised for its qualities as a free standing shrub. I include it, though I have never seen it, and do not know that it still exists. It was later used to breed ramblers, and therefore has some importance. Its coppery pink made quite a stir, until the Pernetianas overhauled it. Raised by Gilbert Nabonnand of Golfe Juan, France; introduced 1887.

'Manettii'   *Tall   Pink   Summer*   P3   H1
The authorized name is *R.* × *noisettiana manettii*. This was used as a rootstock to bud roses on, and many were the debates about its reliability or treachery. It was raised

in the Botanic Garden of Monza, Milan, by Manetti, and first used commercially in England as a rootstock by Thomas Rivers in Sawbridgeworth, Herts, before 1850. By 1892, Mr Frank Cant, the famous rose grower from Colchester, wrote: 'To abolish its use altogether would almost ruin the Rose-growing world'; although he had in mind as much as anything its value for forced propagation. At all events, it disappeared with the rise of Hybrid Teas, because it had the reputation of not uniting with them. It was quite discredited in the *Rose Annual 1940:* 'This stock is not now used by the best Rose producers'. But we may wonder to what extent its disappearance hastened the adieux of some older types. It had the advantage of making the plants flower early, and was deliberately used by exhibitors in the north, who had to steal every day if they wished to show at the 'National' in London. It suckered with horrifying energy. I do not know whether it really should be included in the Noisettes, but that is an old tradition; equally old, we imagine, is the refusal of the rose nurserymen to pronounce, spell or even think of it bearing its final letter. 'Manetty', they said; who heard anything else?

'Maréchal Niel'   *Climber   Yellow   Remontant*   P6   H1
Had this rose the strength of former years, it would be garlanded with our stars of recommendation. Alas, it seems to have deteriorated, and its revival would be a public service. The great rosarians of its time were unanimous in praise; take the first two, consulted at random: 'Quite unapproachable,' wrote Foster-Melliar; 'The very best,' claimed Alfred Prince, and added that one could name it with closed eyes by its perfume. Imagine that, in a clear yellow flower of most beautiful form on a large climbing plant.

It really needed glass, if in a frosty climate, because it was one of the earliest roses to grow in the spring; so early that the normal pruning time was likely to be too late, and it could scarcely hope to escape all the frosts. If those first shoots were lost, no flowers for that season; but if they safely grew, 'Maréchal Niel' flowered almost as freely in the autumn as in the summer. It is becoming a beautiful memory, with its lovely colour, its scent, its clear smooth foliage. From Henri Pradel, Lyon, in 1864. The parentage is unfortunately a matter of speculation.

'Mme Alfred Carrière'   *Climber   White   Remontant*   P5   H1   **
From J. Schwartz of Lyon in 1879. This white rose has a flush of pink on the outer petals, and soft, light green foliage. A very successful and fragrant white climber.

'Rêve d'Or'   *Climber   Yellow   Remontant*   P3   H1
From the widow Ducher, 1869; a successful and popular climber, with some Tea character, which it is presumed to have got from 'Lamarque' via its seed parent 'Mme Schultz'. Quite a vigorous grower, with buff yellow flowers partly lighter, and going over paler.

'William Allen Richardson'   *Climber   Orange yellow   Remontant*   P4   H1   *
For some reason this variety evokes strong affections, perhaps because of the indefinable individuality of its neat, quartered blooms, with their deep egg-stained centres and paler perimeters. The author E. V. Lucas allowed the National Rose Society to print an essay of his in the *Rose Annual 1910,* enquiring who William Allen Richardson was; and the best reply he received made that gentleman a rosarian in Kentucky, in correspondence with the widow Ducher of Lyon. I have to report that nearly seventy years later, I have recently encountered two correspondents who are

quite convinced that W.A.R. is someone they know of, their William Allen. The rose was a deep coloured sport from 'Rêve d'Or', and came from the widow Ducher in 1878.

TEAS

For one of my generation to write about Teas demands an act of faith in the past. I have to believe my own grandfather, John, who wrote in 1890: 'If the Rose be the queen of flowers, the Tea-scented Rose may be regarded the queen of queens, for undoubtedly the "Teas", as they are familiarly called, are in refinement and delicate beauty superior to their robust and more highly coloured relatives.'

Similar high opinions of the Teas spring from the pages of great rosarians who lived when people knew and grew Teas. The Rev. A. Foster-Melliar called them 'the true aristocracy of the rose world'; and H. R. Darlington, a most learned English rosarian, wrote: 'The most beautiful forms in this group have perhaps most nearly attained perfection of form in the Rose'. The most compelling testimony of all was provided by a Scot, Alexander Hill Gray, who is said to have sold up his property in Scotland, and moved to Bath on purpose to grow Teas in the more suitable climate of the West of England.

They must have been beautiful. But where has all the beauty gone? The Teas which survived for my eyes to see had little in the way of growth or flower to compel one to take up a spade and go planting. Perhaps here is one reason why their history ought not to be forgotten: it has a nasty moral somewhere. So let us try to reconstruct it.

They were originally called 'Tea-scented China roses'; and very few people have been perfectly sure why their scent was compared with tea. The name goes back to the first import, 'Hume's Blush Tea-scented China'; and it is quite possible that no subsequent rose had exactly the same scent as that first one. Thomas Rivers, in 1840, stated that Mr Parks's Yellow had a very slight tea-like scent. The name may partly have been suggested by the Chinese nurseryman or intermediary concerned in the sale; in which case 'Tea-scented' might be a complete misunderstanding, even an outrageous Anglo-Chinese pun. But if the name was given in England upon sight of the bloom, it might help resolve the puzzle to remind ourselves that tea has as many different scents as roses. At all events, the name was shortened to Teas. In three chops off came the 'roses', the 'China' and the '-scented'. As for the third chop, the why-have-roses-lost-their-scent brigade took it as proof of their case; for they existed then, and no doubt always have existed, even in the days when (they say) roses had not lost their scent. In any case the scent was sure to be changed at once, because the first marriages of importance were with Noisettes, and admitted into the family the powerful scent of the Musk Rose.

The origin of Teas is speculated to be a mixture of *R. chinensis* and *R. gigantea,* resulting in the hybrid species *R. × odorata* which otherwise is 'Hume's Blush Tea-scented China'; and of its variety *R. × odorata ochroleuca,* which is otherwise 'Parks' Yellow Tea-scented China'. As I wrote in the Hybrid China part of this chapter, I am confident neither in the speculation, nor in the propriety of the hybrid specific names. But there is no doubt about the importance of those two roses, for between them they were ancestors of all the Teas, and in consequence of all the Hybrid Teas too.

Who the other ancestors were is not so certain; we have to use the reins of honesty to curb our desire for exact facts, and admit that the original breeders themselves were not sure. The parentage records started as intelligent estimates, which became facts by virtue of being repeated by one author after another. That is not what I call a fact, it remains an intelligent estimate. Well, then, on that understanding we can say that it is natural that the most popular roses of the period would be the mates of the two Tea-scented Chinas, provided they were compatible. Self-set seeds may have played an important part too.

Teas were first distinguished by their scent, and that delicacy of leaf and stem which cannot be understood until one has compared a China or a Tea with the normal European roses of old, such as the French or Damask. Where the one is thin, reddened and smooth, the other is thick, light green and bristly. The sight of the plants in full growth in the autumn was counted one of their beauties, quite apart from the flowers. The flower form was various, especially in the beginning, but it developed into an accepted style which we can see in the high centred rose of today; the focus of fashion upon a certain feature is a sure way to implant death in a family, unless fashion chances to run hand in hand with life and health, which is rarely.

The weak point about Teas was their willingness to grow. Not for them the sensible, early dormancy of a Scotch Rose, brought up in Siberia. No, the Teas grew as soon as a false spring tempted them, to be nipped in subsequent frosts; they innocently continued into the winter, and were slaughtered by the thousand in hard weather. John Harkness in the north of England ruefully recorded the prompt sequel to his exultation in his Teas in 1890: 'The winter, however, proved one of the severest experienced for many years, with the result that the dwarf "cutbacks" were most seriously crippled, whilst standards, and half standards – dormant buds, maidens and cutbacks alike – were completely destroyed; not one survived the general and melancholy catastrophe.' It was a few years later that he and his brother started a daughter nursery down south in Hitchin. But that sort of disaster did not stop people growing Teas. It was the Hybrid Teas which eventually ended the Teas, by offering something better. Until the something better was available, people in the cooler countries went to great trouble to grow the most beautiful roses they knew, even to covering the plants in winter with earth or leaves or straw. Says Thomas Rivers, 'I have found the branches of furze the best of all protectors.'

The Teas were terrors for hanging their heads, owing to their slender flower stalks. Hence came a practice of growing them on standards, to keep the blooms out of the mud, and give one a chance of seeing them. With standards, the problems of winter protection were rendered more difficult, though attempted by many, who thatched or otherwise coated their plants. Such devotion must have had a more worthy object than any Tea I ever saw.

The advice to grow Teas on standards was fairly usual, but for those who wished to have bushes, the trick was to use Dog Rose cuttings and not seedlings for the understock. I wondered why there should be a difference, and suppose it may be that the roots of a cutting are nearer the soil surface, and are prompted into growth earlier, due to temperature, than those of a seedling. If that is the case, the seedling might have suited the Teas better in the long run; but the advice was firmly believed in, and I can substantiate it as regards a Hybrid Tea 'Ena Harkness'. The best plants I ever saw of that rose were grown on Dog Rose cuttings, and many rosarians saw them for years, because they were planted near the entrance of the National Rose Society's Trial Ground when it was at Oaklands, St Albans; that was before the Society became Royal. So perhaps the significance of a cutting as against a seedling for understock is not fully known. The other popular understock of the time was 'Manettii', but it was no use for Teas, as there was no cohesion.

Such were the trials and toils of growing Teas in the colder countries; and the envy of the rosarians concerned must have been immense at the tales of Teas in the South of France, Bermuda and other fortunate sunkissed lands, where growth never stopped, and flowers were to be had by the hundreds. George Paul concluded that 'Tea Roses . . . are none of them perfectly hardy under all the possibilities of our English climate'; should anyone wish to revive them here, it would be sensible to grow them under glass.

The list that follows places on record some of the famous and significant Teas. I suppose that nobody in our time can see any of them through Victorian eyes. They have no qualities to excite those who are used to Hybrid Teas, no power to make us cry out with pleasure at cutting roses in the autumn. By what I have seen of them in England, France and Germany, they must be a poor pale shadow of their former selves. Some of them I have never seen, in common with most rosarians of my generation, and my fellow feeling for them came from talking to Ernest Barker, who was known as Tarter, a member of our nursery from 1902 for about fifty years. Tarter and I used to work together, and as we went along the rows of roses doing whatever job we were at, I heard about many roses and people who were before my time. Not all of them, of course. There were about 1400 Teas introduced in nearly a century, and Tarter had no time for a rose unless he could put its flowers in an exhibition box and cut budwood from it without having to search. Many of the 1400 never had a ghost of a chance of earning his approval.

'Mme Roussel'

The first Tea roses are no longer in existence for us to argue over whether they were Teas or not. This appears to be the first upon which there is general agreement. It came from the French raiser, Desprez, about 1830. It is white, with a rosy edge sometimes appearing and sometimes not. The flowers are large, with many small centre petals. Was also known as 'Eugénie Jovain'.

'Adam'

This was the first to make the rose world sit up and realize a new and significant class had arrived. Like most of them, it is French, the British having convinced themselves their climate prohibited the raising of Teas. It came from a raiser named Adam, of Rheims, in 1833. It has a globular bud, which opens to show many short rosy-salmon petals. *Modern Roses 7* says 'Adam' is semi-double and deep blush, but I have preferred to follow William Paul's 1848 description, which tallies with the existing stock reported by L. Arthur Wyatt in his brilliant article on Teas in the *Rose Annual 1975*.

'Safrano'

With the arrival of 'Safrano' in 1839, the Teas demonstrated their intention of bringing new colours into roses, as well as abundant flowers. Saffron was a fair name to give it, although the old colour plates made it look a brighter yellow. It had red flushes on the outer petals, a familiar sight to us, but so enthralling in those days that it was sold in the bud as a cut flower on the strength of that feature for many years, and must have kept many growers in the South of France happy, fed them, housed them, clothed them, sent their children to school, and pointed the way to the continuance of their industry in the region. Thousands of well-dressed men emerged from their mansions with 'Safrano' in their buttonhole.

Once out of the bud stage, 'Safrano' opens pale, with a poor centre of short petals. It had a great reputation for blooming freely; if only one rose was out in the garden in the nineteenth century, you expected it to be 'Safrano'. It is credited to a raiser with the appropriate name of Beauregard. And it was destined to play an important part in making the roses which should succeed the Teas.

'Devoniensis'

The rose from Devon marks the entry of a British raiser, who is something of a chameleon in the rose books, apt to come from Davenport, Devonport or Plymouth, and to be Mr Foster or Mr Forster. I should warn those who propose to follow their rose interests into libraries that such inconsistencies are rather the rule than the exception. If we satisfy ourselves by saying Foster of Devonport, we still have little knowledge of him, other than the best memorial a rose breeder can have, the continued life of his creation. 'Devoniensis' was introduced in 1841, and would most likely be extinct now, had not a climbing sport been introduced in 1858. There are still some plants of the climber in existence; it was known as the 'Magnolia Rose', presumably after *M. grandiflora*. Its creamy white flowers, perhaps blushing, are stuffed with petals in a roughly quartered design, and its breath is warm with fragrance.

'Niphetos'

'The purest of all white roses,' wrote Foster-Melliar of this beauty, so well named with the Greek for 'snowy'. It was a great market rose, for although it was easily spoilt by rain outdoors, its long buds of pure white were immaculate under glass, and it was for many years a standby of the cut rose growers. It is surprising that so thin a flower should have been successful in the markets, and I think we have to realize that cut roses were used for brief occasions, such as wedding bouquets, wreaths and buttonholes; the attraction of roses was the long buds, still a novelty in those days, with their promise of rosy openings in the future. The promise was not very well kept by 'Niphetos' to those who retained it after the party, because the centres were usually split, and the soft outside petals did not open so much as flop. Like most Teas, it bent its head towards the ground, and it had to be grown as a standard if one wanted clean blooms outdoors. The ultimate answer to that was offered in 1889 by a climbing sport, 'The most valuable introduction since Maréchal Niel was sent out' said Keynes, Williams & Co, as they advertised it at 7/6 each in 1890. I have always liked that advertisement, which proceeds to offer TEAS IN POTS. That firm was from Salisbury, and introduced some of the Sweet Briars. I doubt whether the Climbing version of 'Niphetos' was entirely satisfactory; if grown under glass, it required an enormous space, and the impression that remains with me from the time we grew it is that it was usually a bit stingy with its flowers for its size. The original bush rose came from Bougère in 1843.

'Mme Bravy'

A famous Tea, from Guillot about 1846. Its colour was so familiar that Foster-Melliar wrote twenty-one lines about 'Mme Bravy' without disclosing it. It was creamy white, warmly shaded blush. The flowers are globular, not very regular in form, having short, folded centre petals, and rather short outer petals. It was named 'Danzille' by the Guillot who raised it, 'Mme Bravy' by the Guillot who introduced it, and 'Mme de Sertot', 'Alba Rosea', 'Mme Denis' and 'Joséphine Maltot' by various French growers, much to the annoyance of other people by the time they had bought the same new rose five or six times. Its real claim to fame, not perfectly proved, is to have been one of the parents of the first Hybrid Tea, 'La France'.

'Souvenir d'un Ami'
This was one of the easier Teas to grow, and being very fragrant, with luminous flowers of light rose touched salmon, it obviously had a strong hold on rosarians of the day; until it faded off in its dirty way. It came from Bélot-Defougère in 1846, and was hardy above average. From it in 1889 came a white sport, also greatly treasured, issued by Prince of Oxford, and named French style 'Souvenir de S. A. Prince'. The first name is so delicate: In Memory of a Friend. One wonders who, and what happened. The second name is more explicit but more abrupt: In Memory of S. A. Prince. It tells more but expresses less feeling. Perhaps it helps to know that the S stood for Sarah.

'Souvenir d'Elise Vardon'
'Incomparable. Worthy of every care,' wrote Thomas Rivers. And Foster-Melliar declared, 'Nothing has been raised to surpass or even equal it.' Grunted H. R. Darlington, 'Shy bloomer.' And they were all right. It needed lots of care. It was a new flower form, leading into the Hybrid Teas, the first with the high centre we take to be traditional. It was an exhibition Tea, and started the division of Teas between decorative types to grow for pleasure in the garden, and exhibition roses to cajole show blooms from, and never mind what sort of a weed the plant was. It was a watershed, at the turn of the century, 1855, from Marest of Paris. The colour is pale rosy salmon on the outside of the petals, more cream inside, and paler as the petals expand.

'Duchesse de Brabant'
I should not have included this, except for Roy Shepherd's affirmation that this is the rose usually in the buttonhole of Theodore Roosevelt, President of the USA, should you see a picture of him. It was soft rose pink, very fragrant, with long buds like tulips, opening to show confused short petals inside. From Bernède, 1857. Also issued as 'Comtesse de Labarthe' and 'Comtesse Ouwaroff'; so the aristocracy were running neck and neck to put their names on this one.

'Mme Falcot' & 'Mme de Tartas'
These two came out in 1858 and 1859 respectively, were to figure prominently in parentage records subsequently, and for that reason should be remembered. A cross between the two of them is supposed to have produced 'Marie van Houtte', which was in turn a useful parent. The climax of their twin careers was achieved by 'Mme de Tartas', who produced a seed which grew into the famous (Mme) 'Caroline Testout', and laid the trail towards 'Ena Harkness' in 1946.

It is a possibility that 'Mme de Tartas', was the pollen parent of 'Mermaid'. My reasons for so suggesting are that we grew 'Mme de Tartas' at the nursery, and I know it fairly well; when I raised a number of seedlings by the pollen of 'Mermaid', there was a strong look of 'Mme de Tartas' about them. There cannot possibly be any proof of this, it is merely a rose grower's hunch, but I believe it is more nearly correct than the 'double yellow Tea rose' of the record books.

I should mention that 'Mme Falcot' came from Guillot in 1858, and it was something after the colour of 'Safrano', but not a good grower. 'Mme de Tartas' on the other hand is actually coarse in its growth and blowsy pink blooms, to a degree most unexpected in the supposedly refined Teas. It came from Bernède in 1859.

'Catherine Mermet'
One of the great Teas of the greenhouse industry, even into the twentieth century;

but a pain in the neck every time it rained, if you tried to grow it outdoors, because it damaged easily. It also lost its pink colour quickly, by fading away pale, and it would not have prospered, had it not been for exhibitors, the cut flower growers and its sports. A pure white sport was named 'The Bride', with an eye on the flower shops' wedding trade; it came from H. B. May of New Jersey in 1885, and had several advantages over its mother, such as a better form, and the fact that white can't fade. The Moore Nursery of Tyler, Texas made a bid for what was left of the wedding trade by calling their pink sport 'Bridesmaid' in 1893. There is nothing rose breeders like less than sports from a rose of theirs of the same colour; they supersede the original and the royalties. 'Bridesmaid' is said to have held its colour much better than the original 'Catherine Mermet', which came from Guillot in 1869.

'Comtesse de Nadaillac'
This was a famous exhibition Tea; although at least two leading showmen complained that one never knew which bud would grow into a superlative bloom; it was just as likely to be from a twig as on a strong shoot. It was not a good grower, but had a fine, high centred bloom in light apricot pink. It came from Guillot in 1871.

'Marie van Houtte'
Light yellow, with some carmine at the petal edges. Of the Teas I have never seen, this is the one I should first choose to resurrect. It could grow, it had form; and attractive foliage in Foster-Melliar's photograph; do I see some mildew there? He said 'It must take first prize among the Teas,' perhaps forgetting his remarks about 'Souvenir d'Elise Vardon'. From Ducher, 1871.

'Anna Olivier'
A Tea with superior powers of survival, for it is now in several collections about the world. In its day it had credit for avoiding damage from rain, always a critical point about Teas, because many of them had thin, soft petals. What sort of a mess would some of them have been in if they held their flowers up straight, instead of bending them down to the avoidance of rain and assistance of drainage? The exhibition Teas had larger flowers and more petals than decoratives such as 'Anna Olivier', and as the petals multiplied, so the reputation of Teas for spoiling in the rain increased. This rose is buff pink, and came from Ducher in 1872.

'Perle des Jardins'
A popular Tea in its time, partly because it was yellow, or we would probably say straw yellow, still a sought-after colour when Levet introduced this in 1874. It was a vigorous Tea, and was grown under glass for cut flowers. Foster-Melliar observed that it scarcely ever gave a show bloom until the autumn, all the summer flowers being malformed; and noting that in Australia and other countries warmer than Britain it was a valued show rose, he deduced that the summer flowers in England were spoilt by frost nipping the newly formed buds in the spring.

'Général Schablikine'   *Medium   Coppery red   Remontant*   P3   H2   *
From G. Nabonnand 1879 (some say 1878). This was perhaps the best of the many Teas raised by Clement, Gilbert and Paul Nabonnand in the South of France, and it certainly found favour with many gardeners, on account of its very good colour and performance. It was not so popular with exhibitors, because it had the quartered flower form so distressing to the judge's eye. Judges should not feel that pain, for if

quartering is natural to a particular variety, it is as estimable as the different form of another rose.

Exhibitors more than gardeners make a rose famous; which is a natural extension of saying that roses are loved for their flowers rather than as plants. But a careful balance must be maintained; if enthusiasm for one feature is excessive, the whole suffers, including the particularly cherished part.

An example lies to hand in the story of the Royal National Rose Society's shows, where exhibitors show extremely large flowers as a test of skill, and for the sheer excitement of competition. Roses were selected for the size and shape of their blooms, all other qualities of the variety being subservient and forgiveable, whether health, or vigour, or habit; some keen exhibitors were ready to propagate every year such varieties as gave their best blooms in the first year of their life, and had no worthy growth to follow. Then follows this sequence: the shows are supported by the public. The public start buying the roses they see at the shows. Their roses do not grow. They complain. Advice is given not to buy on the evidence of shows. The public stop ordering at the shows, and attendance falls. Trade growers reduce or stop exhibiting, for want of business. Result: the future of the shows is insecure. Basic reason: a part has been allowed to unbalance the whole.

All of which has little to do with 'Général Schablikine', except that if the decorative Teas had the care and attention concentrated upon the exhibition Teas, we might have more Teas in our gardens today; and this would be one of the first.

'Maman Cochet'

The folks at our nursery had a glint in their eyes whenever this pink rose was mentioned; for although it had been discarded some years before I came to join them, they well remembered the many times it had been star of their exhibits. It was generally considered one of the best of the Teas, both for vigour of growth and for quality of bloom. It came out near the end of their popularity from S. Cochet in 1893; and although it held its own against the Hybrid Teas for twenty years or so, they proved too good for it in the end, and saw that its life was shorter than it might have been. It was still a highly recommended show rose in Britain in the early 1920s.

In 1896, John Cook of Baltimore introduced 'White Maman Cochet', a sport of such excellence that it was generally recommended as the best white Tea, and exceeded its mother's popularity.

'Lady Hillingdon', 'Mrs Foley Hobbs' and 'Mrs Herbert Stevens'

The year 1910 saw a kind of rearguard action from the Teas, with the introduction of these three. 'Lady Hillingdon' came from Lowe & Shawyer, of Uxbridge, near London. They gave its parentage as pure Tea, 'Papa Gontier' × 'Mme Hoste', but this has been regarded as improbable by some, and I agree. The colour is a very beautiful apricot yellow; the flowers are not full, but elongated and handsome; and it is much hardier than Teas usually are.

'Mrs Foley Hobbs' was raised by Dicksons of Newtownards, and is purely an exhibition variety, in creamy white with some variable pink at the tips. It has magnificent flower form and substance, more than the stems can hold upright. Some of the most lovely illustrations of the British way of exhibiting in boxes feature this rose, as may be seen in the *Rose Annuals* of 1923 and 1927.

'Mrs Herbert Stevens' was from McGredy, a cross between 'Frau Karl Druschki' and 'Niphetos'. By parentage therefore, it should be a Hybrid Tea; but in appearance it is rightly associated with the Teas by most rosarians. The flowers are white, slim, prone to weather damage. Their main variation from Teas is the gift from their

German mother of a firmer flower stalk. A climbing sport came from Pernet-Ducher in 1922, and was widely grown for twenty or thirty years.

'Lady Hillingdon Climbing' *Climber   Apricot yellow   Remontant* P5   H2   *
Probably the most reliable representative of the Teas for those who live in frosty areas; this climbing sport came from Elisha Hicks in 1917. It has considerable charm in its individual blooms, which are produced a few at a time over a long period. I have never seen a plant of it which could be described as a mass of bloom, it does not seem to grow that way. Give her a reasonably sheltered wall or pillar, and enjoy her distinctive colour and pleasant scent.

Having traced the Teas from 1830 to 1917, I have no heart to record their swan song. 'Muriel Wilson' received a Gold Medal in London in 1921, and was the last Tea to do so. Its career was brief.

HYBRID TEAS

They are the most popular roses of our day; that large, high centred flower held up on a thorny stem is the modern idea, however false, of the traditional rose; the present climax of thousands of years of loving and growing roses. What a st.ange name they bear! It is often translated by the uninitiated as 'High bred Teas'. The Germans call them Edelrosen, which means Noble Roses, and describes them gratefully. But Hybrid Teas! Can it mean what it says?

A class composed of hybrids of the Tea-scented China Rose would simplify classification, by lumping nearly all the garden roses of the world under one heading. The Hybrid Teas began more narrowly than that, as hybrids between the Teas and only one other class, the Hybrid Perpetuals. It was seen that the Hybrid Perpetuals had given to the issue of that marriage something of their vigour, hardiness and firm flower stems, so noticeably inadequate in the Teas; but the Teas transmitted their elegant leaves, persistent growth (and therefore continued blossoming), and best of all their long petals formed into high centred flowers. The Hybrid Perpetuals had been deficient in those qualities. The first Hybrid Tea to be recognized as such was 'La France', introduced in 1867. As the class developed, the crosses very soon ceased to be Tea and Hybrid Perpetual in favour of between Hybrid Teas themselves. The introduction of other classes or species from time to time has brought fresh blood, without which the class would certainly have become enfeebled long ago.

The development of the Hybrid Teas will be told in the list of varieties, which is more or less in chronological order. I am sorry if that makes them a little more difficult to find; the index provides the ABC order, and I make the excuse that this is not a catalogue, but a survey of the genus as it has unfolded. You do not expect to read a history book with the monarchs of England beginning with Anne and ending with William; nor does the map of the United States conveniently contain towns beginning with 'A' in the north-western corner, and ending with 'Z' in the south-eastern. You would only be bored if you turned the page and found an alphabetical list.

There may have been other Hybrid Teas before 'La France'. Some people take 'Brown's Superb Blush' to have been the first; it was raised in Slough and introduced in 1815, a seedling of 'Hume's Blush Tea-scented China'; probably it looked and behaved nothing like a Hybrid Tea, but as it is not available for our inspection, it is really not worth arguing about.

The vigour of Hybrid Teas has been sustained because the policies of breeding changed from chance to purpose. For most of the nineteenth century, it was the practice of rose breeders to gather hips at random, sow the seed, and make a selection from the resulting seedlings. That is why the old breeders did not quote parentages; they had no means of knowing them; they gathered hips by the thousand, having left nature to do all the work of fertilizing. They trusted quantity to make sure of chance. In *The Rose Garden,* published in 1848, William Paul quotes the case of 'M. Laffay, who raises seedlings on an extensive scale, and has this year between 200,000 and 300,000'.

A more sophisticated method was to plant the roses one wished to mate in the same bed together, and trust proximity to achieve fertilization. Very few people thought it worth while to intervene and ensure the match they wanted, by stripping the mother flower of her stamens before they shed pollen, and dusting the pollen of the desired father upon her. The process was perfectly well known, and is described in Paul's book of 1848. A few French rose breeders applied it, notably those who had been taught by Jean Sisley of Lyon. Sisley's interests were not confined to roses; he was famous for his double zonal geraniums. Henry Bennett, an English cattle breeder, applied this simple science to roses, seeing its message very clearly from his experience with cows. He astounded the rose world with his claims and achievements in 1878. Anticipating the Englishman's intrusion into a French preserve, Jean Sisley, in the *Journal des Roses* in 1877, published his advice to breed deliberately. It was important advice, because it invited rose breeders to use their brains and imagination in conceiving crosses, in observing the results, and in applying the knowledge thus gained. Bennett and Sisley between them caused the rose breeders to follow the way shown at the very babyhood of the Hybrid Tea class. The timing ensured that Hybrid Teas received the full benefit of the improved methods.

Many thousands of Hybrid Teas have been introduced. Nearly every hybrid rose seedling is different, and it therefore follows that there is scarcely a limit to the number of varieties. The introduction of a variety does not prove anything about its virtue. Indeed a good breeder, whose standards are high, will have discarded roses far better than the introductions of a breeder who is a bad judge.

Nor does the introduction of a variety give any claim to permanence. Roses of complex hybridity appear to have a short period at their best, after which they change in some way. The change is invariably for the worse, and the process is called deterioration. It may be related to the formation of the generative atoms (as we may term the genes) and of the chromosomes (the coloured threads on which the genes are strung). If a variety is to remain stable, these governors of its character must advance in a stable condition at each cell division. The chromosomes are not always regularly formed in hybrids, and sometimes there are spare fragments or fractions of them. Irregularity must be a handicap in the involved dances which the chromosomes perform each time cells divide. But this is speculation; the causes of deterioration are not certainly known, nor has anyone found the means of arresting them. Experiments that might be worth trying are to root cuttings and take propagating wood from their suckers in due time; thus employing the plant's central tissue for propagation rather than its exterior tissue; or one might lengthen a variety's life by ridding it of virus by heat treatment. This consists of forcing a shoot to grow faster than the virus can ascend it, and then propagating from it. One does not have to be told that such shoots are not the best of propagating material.

I should mention that the chromosomes are called 'coloured threads' not because they are coloured, but because they can absorb colouring matter. By this means they are observed.

'La France'   *Medium*   *Pink*   *Remontant*   P2   H2

To the family of Guillot belongs the extraordinary double honour of having raised the first officially recognized members of two very important classes, 'La France' in the Hybrid Teas and 'Pâquerette' in the Polyanthas. It was common in France in those days for a nursery to be an individual's concern, with its name changing from generation to generation, rather than a company or a corporation. In France, the name changed with the proprietors. The Guillot family's first title as rose breeders was Guillot Père, from whom came a number of roses in the 1840s and 1850s, including the important Tea, 'Mme Bravy'. Guillot Père was succeeded, logically enough, by Guillot Fils (Jean-Baptiste Guillot), to whom we are indebted for 'La France', 'Pâquerette', and several other famous roses. After him came Pierre Guillot, whose best known variety was 'Comtesse du Cayla', in 1902. Marc Guillot was next, but his roses failed to scale the formidable heights to which the family was accustomed. Marc's firm reverted to the name Rosiers Pierre Guillot. And another Guillot started up as Henri Guillot, and introduced roses of other breeders in the 1930s; he brought out several of Charles Mallerin's roses, but not 'Mme Henri Guillot', which was one of Mallerin's best, an orange red Hybrid Tea distributed by Meilland just before the second world war. The Guillot family are credited with being the first nurserymen to use *R. canina* as an understock.

To go back to 1867, 'La France' is a pink rose in two shades, not all that gentle on the eye. The flowers are tight with petals, and of attractive form, without being very big. We grew it at Hitchin until quite recently, more for its history than its charm, and I had the pleasure of staging some of its blooms at the 1967 summer show of the Royal National Rose Society, my own tribute upon its centenary. It has rather a good way of bearing its flowers just the right distance above its leaves, so they float gracefully above the foliage, without standing on a long stilt of a stalk.

Naturally there has been speculation as to the parentage of such a rose; and the usual guesses involve 'Mme Victor Verdier', 'Mme Bravy' and 'Mme Falcot'; there was formerly a claim that it came from a Tea called 'Socrates' ('Socrate' in France). We have a very capable witness in the Rev. H. Honywood D'ombrain, for some years joint Secretary of the National Rose Society. He was also Editor of the *Rosarian's Year Book* (which he subsidized out of his own pocket) and he wrote as follows in the 1895 edition, admittedly some thirty years after the event:

> A year or two before it had been brought out I had visited Guillot's garden at Lyons, and there he pointed out to me the original plant of La France, saying to me, 'I think this is a commencement of a new race.' On my asking him how he had obtained it, he said that he did not know; that it came amongst his seedlings, and he could not trace its origin. This I could well believe, for at that time the hybridization of the Rose was not attempted by the French raiser, nor am I aware that there is much of it practised among them even now. I have seen some of their nurseries – beds of thousands of seedlings without a tally amongst them; the hips have been gathered promiscuously, and the seed sown without any reference to the plants from whence they have come, so that it was impossible that the assertion that La France is a seedling of Socrate can have any valid foundation.

Somebody, anxious that a new class should have botanic expression, ventured the name *R. indica odorata hybrida* for 'La France'. This is a prize example of the weakness of giving Latin names to hybrids, because there were soon to be hundreds of Hybrid Teas. There could be no justification, apart from the crippled plea of priority, to name 'La France' on any different system from her sisters.

'Cheshunt Hybrid'

It was years before the British National Rose Society agreed to the existence of Hybrid Teas. To them the new roses were either Teas or Hybrid Perpetuals. As we shall see, the French were the first to adopt Hybrid Teas; whereupon the perfidious English began to talk of 'Cheshunt Hybrid' as the first Hybrid Tea. An affront indeed to 'La France', as the English eventually had to acknowledge. All credit to the breeder, George Paul, who wrote in his 1872 catalogue when first announcing 'Cheshunt Hybrid': '. . . promising to be, like La France, the beginning of a new race'.

The Pauls are not quite as confusing as the Guillots, but it is not always realized there were two of them. The original firm was Paul & Son of Cheshunt, Hertfordshire. It was founded by Adam Paul in 1806, and was controlled in due course by George Paul. This was the firm which produced 'Cheshunt Hybrid' and some famous climbers, such as 'Paul's Lemon Pillar', 'Goldfinch' and 'Tea Rambler'. William Paul grew up in it, and wrote *The Rose Garden* in Cheshunt; but in 1860 he started his own nursery not far away at Waltham Cross, as William Paul & Son of Paul's Nursery. That nursery has to its credit 'Ophelia', 'Mermaid' and 'Paul's Scarlet Climber'. Wm Paul & Son had a foreman named Chaplin, who in 1922 took over the firm as Chaplin Brothers, of whom there were seven, including some quite remarkable characters, far too individual to remain in harness together for very long.

'Cheshunt Hybrid' was reckoned to be 'Mme de Tartas' × 'Prince Camille de Rohan', on the evidence of the latter growing over the former in Paul's greenhouse. It was a tall, straight, gawky plant, fit to be tied to a clothes post. It was the first red Hybrid Tea, but was virtually sterile, and little use to breeders.

'Captain Christy'

Introduced in 1873, by François Lacharme of Lyon who gave its parents as 'Victor Verdier' × 'Safrano'. Lacharme bred some of the best Hybrid Perpetuals, and was also responsible for a Moss Rose with the unexpected name 'L'Obscurité'. 'Captain Christy' is pink, and it marks the importance of 'Victor Verdier', another of Lacharme's roses.

'Victor Verdier' came from 'Jules Margottin' × 'Safrano', and was thus a Hybrid Tea by parentage not by appearance. It was a parent of 'Lady Mary Fitzwilliam', and therefore grandparent of 'Mme Caroline Testout' and ancestor of many modern roses. Speculation affiliates 'La France' to 'Victor Verdier'.

There is also a rose called 'Mme Victor Verdier'. I assume they cover a husband and wife, in which case it was inconvenient of Eugène Verdier to issue 'Mme Victor' four years after Lacharme had so generously perpetuated Victor's memory.

'Beauty of Stapleford'	**'Duchess of Connaught'**	**'Duchess of Westminster'**
'Duke of Connaught'	**'Hon. George Bancroft'**	**'Jean Sisley'**
'Nancy Lee'	**'Pearl'**	**'Viscountess Falmouth'**
'Michael Saunders'		

These ten roses are individually gone, forgotten and not grown, apart from a report a few years ago of the rediscovery of 'Beauty of Stapleford' and 'Duchess of Westminster'. Collectively they are a solid paragraph in the history of the rose.

In 1879, a Wiltshire farmer named Henry Bennett amazed the rose world by introducing ten 'Pedigree Hybrids of the Tea Rose'. His claim to have bred a 'pedigree' line was opposed, but he was able to prove it by the records he had kept.

Bennett was a cattle breeder; knowing for sure the mother and the father of his beasts was as natural to him as eating his dinner. The word 'pedigree' came straight from the cattle ring, and its brilliant use was as good as a goad in the flanks of every rose breeder in the world. The British, all too apt to leave rose breeding to the sun-favoured continentals, were taught that the only hindrance to breeding roses in Britain was laziness. Bennett has been called the father of the Hybrid Teas, which may be an exaggeration. He should certainly be taken as patron saint by all British rose breeders.

Some of these ten roses were shown in 1878. The presentation of the whole set created a great sensation in 1879. George Paul wrote of Bennett: '. . . he made for himself a name as a successful and original raiser of roses by a process involving method and skill'. The pedigree ten were from the seed of Tea roses, seven from 'Adam', two from 'Mme Bravy' and one from 'Mme de St Joseph', a buff pink variety which I did not mention in our list of Teas. The pollen was provided by Hybrid Perpetuals in eight cases, a China and a Moss serving the other two. The names of the ten varieties show that the Connaughts were well favoured; what's more, there had been a 'Duke of Connaught' from Paul's only four years previously. We also notice that Bennett had some association with Jean Sisley, who had just advocated in France the kind of breeding that Bennett had now demonstrated in England.

In the spring of 1880, the Horticultural Society of Lyon invited Bennett to an important meeting, at which the status of Hybrid Teas was discussed. Without waiting for international agreement, or any other authority beyond their common sense and good judgement, the French announced that the new class should be called Hybrides de Thé. From that time French breeders and growers began to list Hybrid Teas, not always in perfect unanimity regarding the composition of their lists. Their example was copied in Britain; Hugh Dickson's catalogue of 1884 was one of the earliest to have a section for Hybrid Teas. But the National Rose Society in London objected to the new class, thinking it an artificial device, which is true of all classification; and claiming there was no necessity for it. After arguing about it for thirteen years, they recognized Hybrid Teas officially in 1893. There can be no doubt that Henry Bennett's achievements of 1879 were the chief evidence to convince the meeting in France that a new class had arrived.

In 1880, Henry Bennett made some small capital of his reputation as a breeder by selling exclusive rights on a red Hybrid Tea called 'William Francis Bennett' to an American grower for $5000. This rose also came from 'Adam' seed, crossed this time with 'Xavier Olibo'. We shall return to Bennett's roses; one bore Hybrid Tea pollen far more valuable than gold dust, and the other is to me the most beautiful of all the Hybrid Perpetuals. Let us record here that Bennett died in 1890, only eleven years after his triumph; and at the date of his death, Hybrid Teas were still not an official class in England.

'Camoëns'

Joseph Schwartz of Lyon is a little known breeder, which is quite unfair to the originator of 'Mme Alfred Carrière', 'Mme Ernst Calvat' and 'Roger Lambelin'. He was succeeded by his widow, in whose name stand some of the firm's later introductions. 'Camoëns' is of interest as being one of the early Hybrid Teas of no earthly use to exhibitors, but indicating that for gardeners the class was to be the most valuable of all roses. This was achieved almost under the noses of the experts, not noticed by them, because they were fixed on exhibition roses. 'Camoëns' was bright pink, with a generous supply of flowers little more than semi-double. The logical extension of this was Floribundas, via single Hybrid Teas; the latter came along in due time, but surely would never have been heard of had there been Floribundas in those days. 'Camoëns' came out in 1881.

'Lady Mary Fitzwilliam'
Henry Bennett introduced this light pink rose in 1882, and its importance lay in its pollen. There's a study in the *Rose Annual 1956* by James Alexander Gamble of Maryland, in which the author had industriously examined the contemporary edition of *Modern Roses,* and found that of 3575 varieties whose parentage was stated, no fewer than 1300 could be traced back to 'Lady Mary Fitzwilliam'.

To the rosarians who grew it, 'Lady Mary Fitzwilliam' was known as a feeble plant with perfect flowers. D'ombrain remarked that 'a weaker and more unsatisfactory grower than Lady Mary Fitzwilliam it would be difficult to find'. The exhibitors consoled themselves by accepting that there were worse things than a rose which put all its strength into its flowers, and they nursed it on standard stems, in the belief it was a little better grown that way.

We can only note with surprise that such powers of procreation lay within such weakly loins. Through its pollen it had three particularly significant children, 'Mme Caroline Testout', 'Mrs W. J. Grant' and 'Antoine Rivoire', through which it became ancestor of very many Hybrid Teas. Its own parentage was 'Devoniensis' × 'Victor Verdier'.

If C. C. Hurst could point to four 'stud Chinas', this rose could be taken as a 'stud Hybrid Tea'. It is no wonder that a consequence of its debility was its disappearance, which set modern rosarians searching for it. Gordon Rowley, then of the John Innes Horticultural Institution in Bayfordbury, Hertford, England, received from two different sources a rose alleged to be 'Lady Mary Fitzwilliam'. The coincidence that both sources submitted the same variety convinced the rose world that it was the true variety. I received stock of it by Mr Rowley's generosity, and it certainly appeared to be a lavish provider of pollen, and a mean supplier of seed, bearing out its recorded breeding history. The colour was deeper than I expected, and although the growth was feeble by modern standards, it was not beyond forgiveness. I was surprised at the irregular formation of the sexual organs, my experience being that successful parents are more likely to be sweetly formed in that respect; although it is not an immutable rule. Alas for all this endeavour and goodwill! It now appears someone has located the same rose, and identified it as 'Mrs Wakefield Christie-Miller', introduced by McGredy in 1909.

'Mme Caroline Testout' *Medium Pink Remontant* P3 H4
In 1890, Joseph Pernet-Ducher introduced 'Mme Caroline Testout', which established the Hybrid Tea not only as the leading bedding rose, but as a serious alternative to other kinds of plants. In the nineteenth century, gardeners used bedding plants to supply most of their summer flowers; a middle class home would employ a gardener to raise a succession of plants to follow one another in the same bed, and some of the summer plantings might be quite tender, begonias, or calceolarias for example. Geraniums were a great favourite, or rather pelargoniums as we are taught to call them now. The place for roses was away from the centre of things, because of their long period out of bloom. But the Chinas, the Teas and the Polyanthas were beginning to suggest that roses might be bedding plants: and if one rose proved the claim, it was 'Caroline Testout' as she was generally known, for in England only the pedants called her Madame. This rose more than any other brought

roses into the central and choicest positions in gardens, to be grown where they could actually be seen, instead of being enclosed in a rose garden. From the lessons 'Caroline Testout' taught, the world was only too happy to learn, because in the twentieth century, gardeners and elaborate bedding schemes began to strain previously untroubled purses. When the owners of those purses discovered that in addition to their undoubted beauty, roses were also the cheapest way of filling flower beds, they went cheerfully to the rose growers. Thus began the amazing twentieth-century rose industry, which reached its peak in 1955 to 1967. For a time in Britain in that period, a rose bush was being propagated annually for every man, woman and child in the population.

'Mme Caroline Testout' is bright pink, an uncompromising colour, yet not at all disagreeable, as bright pinks sometimes are. It was a seedling from 'Mme de Tartas' × 'Lady Mary Fitzwilliam', and its well-formed blooms brought memories of the Teas to the delighted rosarians of the day, who received a vision of supreme beauty and virtuous utility united. To Joseph Pernet-Ducher, then aged thirty-two, it was the first major success of a career which earned him the title 'The Wizard of Lyon'.

Joseph Pernet's father was a rose grower in Lyon. Nursery families are notorious for teaching their children young; indeed it is a part of the life surrounding them that the youngsters absorb. My own two sons, Robert and Philip, began to help quite efficiently and for long periods on our nursery at the age of six. Joseph Pernet most probably did so too, and he was formally apprenticed when he was twelve. For all the modern theories of education, some people are happier to learn in nurseries than in schools, to read green leaves rather than printed ones.

He became rose foreman to the firm of Ducher in Lyon. The Duchers had only sixteen years as raisers and introducers of roses, during which Antoine Ducher died and his widow carried on; but they had six varieties which ought to ring a bell with most students of the rose a century later: 'Anna Olivier', 'Bouquet d'Or', 'Cécile Brunner', 'Marie van Houtte', 'Rêve d'Or' and 'William Allen Richardson'. It is therefore clear that the Duchers had skill and good judgment.

In 1880, Joseph Pernet attended the meeting in Lyon, which was recounted a few pages back under 'Beauty of Stapleford' etc. It is clear from his future that thereafter he practised deliberate hybridization as advocated by Sisley and Bennett; whether he knew much of it beforehand, we have no means of knowing, but the chances are that his environment in the Ducher nursery had not left him ignorant. He was twenty-two at the time of that meeting, ten years since the premature start of his career, while Henry Bennett was ten years from the premature end of his. When in later life the Wizard of Lyon was asked to give a paper at the International Rose Conference in 1912, he spoke most of Henry Bennett and his roses, without which foundation, he said, he would not have had the bases to work from.

A year or two after the meeting of 1880, Joseph Pernet took over the firm from the widow Ducher, and married her daughter. He changed his name to Pernet-Ducher. So far as we know, it was exactly as it appears from those brief facts, an arrangement to satisfy the dearest wishes of all three persons concerned.

The original Caroline Testout was engaged in selling Parisian fashions through a London showroom. She bought the name of the rose as an advertisement, being not only wise in her generation, but considerably in advance of it. It is usually hinted or assumed that Pernet-Ducher was quite taken in by the sharp lady, and sold her a rose he had little expectation from; but I do not know the evidence of this. In fact it is difficult to evaluate a rose until it has been on the market three or four years, and most breeders are content to share the risks with those who buy varieties or names from them. How many millions of 'Caroline Testout' were grown, nobody knows; it used to be said that an astronomic number were planted in Portland, Oregon, where the municipality used roses along the roadways, to the great benefit of that place. Portland's example has been followed in recent years by Aberdeen, where even the ring roads are bordered and divided by roses, certainly to the delight of visitors to that great city. However, there will be no 'Mme Caroline Testout' in Aberdeen's miles of roses, nor I suppose in Portland today. If you planted it in the old days, you were repaid more than a hundred-fold. There's a picture in the *Rose Annual 1947* of a standard, forty years old, and bearing over 150 open blooms.

'Gustave Régis'

Although this rose is little known, it was obviously a distinct and interesting variety. It came from Pernet-Ducher in 1890, the same year as 'Mme Caroline Testout'. Foster-Melliar writes: 'It is in the very early bud stage that this Rose is at its best, for the shape is long and pointed, and the three colours, red, yellow, and white, are present together in a more charming combination than I am aware of in any other Rose.'

High praise indeed, especially for a flower with few petals, of little use to the arch-exhibitor who wrote those words. It was generally found to be the ideal buttonhole rose, a vigorous garden variety, and a good autumnal rose.

'Kaiserin Auguste Viktoria' *Medium White Remontant* P4 H3 *

An early German Hybrid Tea, introduced by Peter Lambert of Trier in 1891, and raised from 'Coquette de Lyon' × 'Lady Mary Fitzwilliam'. One of the best white Hybrid Teas ever raised, although it has for long been more appreciated in the United States and Australia than in northern Europe. It is quite remarkable that it is still widely grown in America today, surely the oldest Hybrid Tea to have any commercial significance.

'Mme Abel Chatenay' *Medium – Bicolour pink Remontant* P3 H3

Joseph Pernet-Ducher introduced this in 1895, and it was soon recognized as one of the finest garden roses, and very good in the autumn. Its two or three pink colours blended in so distinctive a manner that the colour was known as 'Chatenay pink'. Those are agreeable reports for a breeder to hear of his variety, but they were not the last, because the growers of cut flowers took 'Mme Abel Chatenay' into their hearts, or at least into their greenhouses.

One does not often see bushes of Chatenay about now, but the climber is quite common in England. Its carmine – rose – buff mixture is still as distinctive a 'Chatenay pink' as ever.

'Antoine Rivoire'

Pale creamy buff; or if you looked hard in the centre at the base of the petals, you could convince yourself you saw yellow. And plenty of people were ready to be convinced that the yellow Hybrid Tea they longed for had come, even though dressed in an off-white cloak.

This rose came from Pernet-Ducher, a cross from 'Dr Grill' × 'Lady Mary Fitzwilliam', introduced in 1895.

'Mrs W. J. Grant'

From 'La France' × 'Lady Mary Fitzwilliam', two distinguished parents, and like them it could scarcely escape being pink. Ireland has been the home of most of the daffodils and roses recently bred in the British Isles, and the two Ulster families,

Dickson and McGredy, have been responsible for the roses. Both families have been rose breeders for some generations, the McGredys favouring the name Samuel, and the Dicksons calling their sons Alexander, although the present Dickson uses his second Christian name, Patrick.

'Mrs W. J. Grant' had received the National Rose Society's Gold Medal in 1892, being the first Hybrid Tea to do so. The available stock was sold to an American nursery, and it was not until 1895 that Dicksons could introduce it in England. It was sold in the United States as 'Belle Siebrecht'.

This rose was known chiefly for its immaculate shape, taken to be the standard of elegance among roses. The growth was not much good, in fact Foster-Melliar cheerfully said it was best as a maiden, which means you throw it away every year, and grow it afresh. This is no great recommendation for purchasing a rose, because the maiden period is spent in the nursery before ever the customer receives his plant. But in those days exhibitors were willing to propagate their own plants annually, in the hope of show blooms to confound their competitors. Such practices have died out, mainly because modern roses are judged in the soil instead of in the vase; and poor growers are rarely introduced.

The Gold Medal won by 'Mrs W. J. Grant' was instituted by the National Rose Society in 1883, as the mark of an outstanding new rose. It has been awarded ever since in bursts of generosity or fits of parsimony, according to the mood and judgment of the times. In H. R. Darlington's view, it was not an award of general merit, but merely marked those roses worth a trial; but he was pleading an excuse for some of the sad selections made. Of course it was intended to be the Society's commendation to the world at large of the best roses.

For much of the period the great prize was decided on the evidence of a few flowers at a show, a challenge the exhibitors welcomed and enjoyed. They did not stop to think of the purpose of the award, to acquaint the world of merit, but cheerfully disguised every shortcoming, and left the mildewed branches at home. The disappointments which this policy was certain of inciting were to a great extent responsible for the establishment of a trial ground in 1928 in Haywards Heath, Sussex. But the judging was not totally divorced from the show bench until 1963, when the Society's third trial ground, at Bone Hill, St Albans, Hertfordshire, became the only place where a new rose could qualify for awards. Starting in 1930 Trial Ground Certificates had been issued to new roses which proved to be reliable growers; the first year saw a generous rush of 61 certificated varieties, including 'Mrs Sam McGredy', leading to the conclusion that roses grew well in Haywards Heath. A Certificate of Merit had previously been instituted for roses which just missed the Gold Medal; in 1952, and with the intention of identifying the best roses from time to time, the Society awarded its President's International Trophy. The first winner was a scarlet Floribunda from Meilland, 'Moulin Rouge'. After the death in 1964 of their Secretary, Harry Edland, the Society issued a medal in his name for the most fragrant new rose each year. I well remember the inception of that award, for it took place in my sitting room one winter evening in front of the fire. My wife and I loved the Edlands, and Bess Edland was with us. She said, 'What do you think would be the best way to commemorate Harry's memory?' And within a minute or two, the conversation had minted the Harry Edland Medal, although its eventual title was the more formal Henry Edland Memorial Medal.

The first variety to win it was 'Charm of Paris', a small flowered pink rose from Tantau. I had the pleasure of winning it with a lilac Floribunda in 1975, and I named that rose 'Harry Edland'.

'Mme Ravary'

A few minutes ago, we had hopeful rosarians looking for yellow in 'Antoine Rivoire'. With 'Mme Ravary' they thought they had it. 'It is a real yellow H.T.,' exulted Foster-Melliar. 'Orange-yellow', hoped Pemberton. I can remember this rose very well; a kind of light chamois pink colour I would call it. It came from Pernet-Ducher in 1899, and was popular for about thirty years.

'Liberty'

The best red Hybrid Tea to date, by quite a long way, arrived in 1900. It was raised by Alexander Dickson from 'Mrs W. J. Grant' × 'Charles J. Grahame'. The pollen parent, 'Charles J. Grahame' (for these parentages should always be expressed 'Seed Parent' × 'Pollen Parent') was a vigorous red rose, which Dickson's apparently kept for breeding for some time, because it was not introduced until 1905.

'Liberty' had a cold hearted reception in Britain, receiving no Gold Medal, owing to its slim flowers being small beside the coloured cabbages preferred by the exhibitors. Its value was correctly estimated by the Americans. The E. G. Hill Company, of Richmond, Indiana, were even in those days famous growers, particularly of cut roses, and they introduced 'Liberty' in the States, and made it one of the best loved roses there. It had, of course, a very good name for them.

In due course it was used by many of the world's rose breeders, who found it an important parent of red Hybrid Teas.

'Soleil d'Or'

The patient work of Joseph Pernet-Ducher, initiated we may suppose at the meeting of the Horticultural Society of Lyon in 1880, had been rewarded, as we have seen, by several of the leading Hybrid Teas since 1890. His greatest achievement had now flowered, and most appropriately was put before the world in the year 1900.

Yellow Hybrid Teas were greatly desired; but for some reason the yellow from the original 'Parks' Yellow Tea-scented China', which had shone so beautifully in the Noisettes, was only palely transmitted to the Teas, and even more diluted in the Hybrid Teas. Pernet-Ducher's answer was to find another source of yellow in the genus *ROSA,* and he chose 'Persian Yellow', which is *R. foetida persiana.*

The yellow colour in the Teas is pale, and fades quickly to cream or white. 'Persian Yellow', on the contrary, is a bold, golden yellow, still deep when the flowers are old. Against the advantages of its colour, one had to set 'Persian Yellow's' bad habits. It flowered in the summer and stopped. It grew into a gaunt shrub, nothing like the bedding roses of the twentieth century. Nor were its flowers to be compared in form with the Teas and Hybrid Teas, for they were small, with a confusion of narrow, folded petals enclosed by the outer five. Joseph Pernet-Ducher was about to discover some of the difficulties of breeding between two widely different types of roses. Others had tried 'Persian Yellow', and given it up as a bad job. And no wonder, for this yellow rose shoots two bolts to bar the breeder's entry: it is reluctant to bear seed, and most of its pollen is infertile. It is almost a mule of a rose; but not quite.

Pernet-Ducher reported that he began to breed with 'Persian Yellow' in 1883, and after making hundreds of crosses, the first seeds he germinated were a few from 'Antoine Ducher' × *R. foetida persiana* in 1888. 'Antoine Ducher' was a red Hybrid Perpetual raised by his father-in-law and predecessor, and introduced in 1866; there's a sentimental little family story if one cared to weave it.

Most modern roses flower a second time, or even more often in the season. We carelessly say 'perpetual' and the French more accurately 'remontant'. When you cross two such roses and sow the resultant seeds, the little seedlings immediately produce a flowering shoot, and bear their first flowers when they are only about three months old. But it is different if you cross two roses of which one is a sort that only flowers once in the year. In that case all the seedlings take after the summer flowering parent, whether it was mother or father, and they bear no flowers at all in their first year. The exceptions to that rule are few. Pernet-Ducher may not have had exact knowledge of this, although I imagine he had a good idea of it, for he must have had a working knowledge of the behaviour of summer flowering roses. It meant that his seedlings from 'Antoine Ducher' would initially be a disappointment, for they would bear no blooms in their first year.

He planted the seedlings outdoors, and noticed in 1891 that one of them had semi-double flowers, pink and yellow. It appears that these plants remained in situ until 1893, when an extraordinary stroke of luck crowned his work, almost as if nature had resolved to give him the yellow rose he had asked for so intelligently. A friend, Ernest Viviand-Morel, caused Joseph to show him this seedling with 'Persian Yellow' blood in it. When they arrived at it, they found close by a little seedling with small, double flowers, orange-yellow and red. No rosarian midwife attended the birth of this seedling, whose origin rests upon the deduction that one of the 'Antoine Ducher' × *R. foetida persiana* hybrids had set seed, which fell and germinated. It was of course promptly cared for, and was first shown in Lyon in 1898 as 'Soleil d'Or'. Although it was not pure yellow, its colour was sufficient to make it a sensation.

As one who is used to the ways of nurseries, I have often thought how easy it would have been for some scrupulous worker to hoe that border clean of everything bar what had been planted in it, 'Soleil d'Or' and all.

'Pharisäer'

Introduced in 1903 or possibly a year or two earlier by Wilhelm Hinner, who raised it in Trier, Germany. This was easily his most successful rose, although his 'Georg Arends' outlived it in the rose catalogues. 'Pharisäer' was light pink with some salmon shading, like a paler 'Mme Abel Chatenay'. It had quite a vogue as a successful bedding rose, especially as it had pleasant stems and flowers to cut for the house. A seedling of 'Mrs W. J. Grant'.

'Radiance'   *Medium   Pink   Remontant*   P5   H2

This was also called 'Pink Radiance', and for many years was the favourite pink Hybrid Tea in the United States. Indeed we can say that plants of 'Radiance' did much to make roses popular in that country. Why it had so little favour in Europe is hard to say, for it adapted itself to most of the diverse weather conditions in the States; it was rich pink, fragrant, and opened easily to show a good expanse of colour, not having too many petals.

The breeder was John Cook of Baltimore, raiser of twenty-five varieties, of which this was the most successful. It was bred from two other roses of his, 'Enchanter' × 'Cardinal'. Mr Cook produced it in 1904, and it was taken up by Peter Henderson of New York, who introduced it in 1908.

'General MacArthur'   *Medium   Light red   Remontant*   P4   H4

A good constitution is a great help to a rose, and so is a memorable name. Those two assets must have helped 'General MacArthur' to its forty years in favour, because it was not a remarkable rose in other respects. The colour is cherry red, the flowers are thin, open quickly, and possess no great charm in form. But it was healthy, it grew well, and flowered freely. It was usually considered a red rose, but I fear some disappointments may have come to those who assumed it was dark red. Raised by the E. G. Hill Company of Richmond, Indiana, and introduced in 1905.

'Irish Elegance'

The innocent beauty of a natural rose consists of five petals honestly revealing the reproductive system in the centre; which is what we term a single rose. The flower's colour and scent are for the delectation of insects, to guide them to pollen and stigmas, not for men. Rosarians of the time we are now considering can have grown very few single roses; and I have no doubt that singles were scrapped as a matter of course by most breeders, whenever one dared to open its five petals in the seedling bed. 'Single' was another way of going back to the wild, quite opposed to the instincts of the generations which believed in the inevitability of man's progress from barbarity to the golden age of the future; an excellent belief, which could be true given faith in it. Who likes the twentieth century's barbarity?

The delicacy of the Teas, not only in colour but also in the texture and size of their petals, was bound to be reflected in single as well as in double roses. 'Irish Elegance' showed the first notable evidence of this beauty, given upon its five large petals in a medley of apricot, pink and orange-red; there had been other singles, 'Irish Beauty', and 'Irish Modesty' from 1900; and 'Irish Brightness', 'Irish Engineer', 'Irish Harmony', 'Irish Pride' and 'Irish Star' all introduced in 1904. But 'Irish Elegance' in 1905 was the first to make a reputation, aided by the Gold Medal it won from the National Rose Society. A similar rose, more vivid in colour, was 'Irish Fireflame' in 1914.

The breeder responsible for all these was Alexander Dickson of Newtownards, Ireland. It was his good taste that taught rosarians to appreciate the single rose, and in no small measure prepared the way for the Poulsen roses to be accepted in the 1930s. Whether we should ever call a single rose a Hybrid Tea today, I very much doubt, it would be a Floribunda straightaway.

'Richmond'

Named for the home town of the E. G. Hill Company, who had lost no time in putting 'Liberty' to good use, by pollinating 'Lady Battersea' to raise this valuable red rose. H. R. Darlington said that 'This Rose is more constantly in flower than any Rose in the garden'; and in America it had the nickname Everblooming Jack. It was for many years a mainstay of the cut rose industry, upon whose agenda a red rose has usually been the first item. The smooth stems and long slim buds of 'Richmond' live in my memory, although it is many years now since we grew it. Its only trouble as a garden rose was the way the colour burned in hot sun.

'Marquise de Sinéty'

This is a little piece of France's rose history, because it was the first rose to win the Gold Medal in the Bagatelle Rose Trials, in 1907. The Bagatelle Trials are conducted just outside the city of Paris, in the Bois de Boulogne. For most of the nineteenth century, Bagatelle was owned by English families, including Sir Richard Wallace of the famous Wallace Collection of Art. It was sold to the city in 1904, and opened to the public.

The man responsible for the rose gardens and trials at Bagatelle was Jules Gravereaux, and it is due to his knowledge and skill, as well as to the intelligence of the municipal authorities of Paris, that France has the credit of the first rose trial ground in the world.

'Marquise de Sinéty' has no other claim on our attention; it was yellow and red, raised by Pernet-Ducher, and introduced in 1906.

'Lyon Rose'

In 1907, exactly seven years after the introduction of 'Soleil d'Or', Joseph Pernet-Ducher introduced the next significant rose in that breeding line. He had descendants of 'Soleil d'Or' of course, and one of them provided the pollen which fertilized the Tea, 'Mélanie Soupert' to produce 'Lyon Rose'. 'Mélanie Soupert' was a white seedling of 'Gloire de Dijon'. 'Lyon Rose' was a striking variety in those days, shrimp pink with some orange yellow at the base of the petals. It had a handsome flower, fit to please exhibitors, but the plant revealed some of the weaknesses which were the heritage of 'Persian Yellow' through 'Soleil d'Or'. It lost its leaves early in the autumn, often from blackspot, but also because it just naturally dropped them. The shoots had a habit of growing sideways. Those faults did not prevent it from being grown and admired, nor from winning the Bagatelle Gold Medal in 1909.

'Château de Clos Vougeot'

The darkest red, black as night, to be stroked with the eyes, velvet and voluptuous; so run the images of desire for a red rose. Unfortunately nature has never been too ready to oblige with a respectable plant to carry these hedonistic dreams. I think she disapproves, because such a colour defeats her objects of attracting insects. Dark red roses, therefore, are usually weak in growth, with nodding flowers and mildew; the colour is rarely true past the midway stage of the flower; either it goes purple, or burns brown in the sun.

Having said all that, neither I nor any other breeder will give up hope of finding a dark, dusky 'Peace', nor will people cease to say that red is their chosen colour in a rose. Robert Burns, always a matter-of-fact poet, was not being fanciful when he likened his love to a red, red rose (not ordinary red, but double red you notice); it was a natural, straightforward simile, in which highest beauty equals highest beauty.

For many years after its introduction in 1908, Joseph Pernet-Ducher's 'Château de Clos Vougeot' was the dark red rose of our dreams, despite its spindly, sprawling growth.

'Lady Pirrie'

This rose came from Hugh Dickson of Belfast, a raiser whose greatest success was a Hybrid Perpetual bearing his own name. 'Lady Pirrie', introduced in 1910, was much loved on account of its distinctive colour. On reading contemporary descriptions, one might suppose it was like some rich brocade in copper and apricot; but catalogue descriptions are not always successful in projecting an accurate image into the reader's brain. 'Lady Pirrie' was quite pale, but subtly coloured, the outside of the petals fawn to salmon (which the catalogue writers took to be deep coppery reddish salmon) and the inside fawn to palest apricot. This combination proved so charming that the deficiencies of the plant were excused by many, and it was loyally persevered with, and blanketed with manure like the invalid it so often was. In the 1930s, when rose rust was more generally experienced, it became obvious that 'Lady Pirrie' was one of rust's favourite roses, and so she ceased to enjoy the favour of being purchased again after she had faded away. She had had a long run in very high favour as a garden rose.

'Rayon d'Or'

The year 1910 is marked in rose history by the introduction of Pernet-Ducher's 'Rayon d'Or', the first golden yellow Hybrid Tea. Let us say at once that 'Rayon d'Or' had a short life. It was sure to get blackspot, it died back in the winter, and within ten years most knowledgeable rosarians in England had turned it out of their gardens. Its importance lies solely in bringing the yellow from *R. foetida persiana* into a Hybrid Tea, as Pernet-Ducher had intended when he began this breeding line twenty-seven years previously. Other hands were to take it, and raise better yellow Hybrid Teas from it, but Joseph Pernet-Ducher is the father of the yellow roses in our gardens today. Take his work away, and you wipe nearly all the yellow out.

The National Society of Horticulture in France, recognizing the distinctive roses coming from Pernet-Ducher, had recently instituted a separate class to distinguish them from Hybrid Teas, and honoured the breeder in the best of all possible ways, by naming it Pernetiana. We are apt to think it was an unnecessary class, but it did not appear so in those days. In fact many nurserymen were not calling them Hybrid Teas at all, but listed them along with the Austrian Briars, those being the archetypal yellow roses, then known as Lutea, to which 'Persian Yellow' belonged. Even the yellow Scotch Roses spent years as Lutea hybrids in the catalogues. In rose lists of the time may be seen the initials HAB for Hybrid Austrian Briar, against roses such as 'Mme Edouard Herriot' and 'Christine'. The National Rose Society of Britain adopted the Pernetiana class in 1914, reluctantly I would say, for on 23 June 1914, their President, Charles E. Shea, rebuked a speaker who had used the word: 'If it is decided to group the Pernet Roses,' he said, 'they cannot for botanical reasons be called Pernetiana.' I see Pernetiana was used once in the 1916 *Rose Annual,* but not until the 1917 *Annual* did it replace Hybrid Austrian Briar. The National Rose Society has the British quality of going by the book (whether this is a virtue or a vice may vary) and is well known for caution in accepting new class titles. The sequel is easy to guess. The Pernetianas were rapidly bred with Hybrid Teas, so that in the 1930s the two had in effect become one; and the word Pernetiana has by common consent virtually disappeared. This is one of many lessons of the drastic changes in our roses, not noticed because they occur by imperceptible steps year by year.

In respect of Pernet-Ducher's achievement, we can honestly say that in so far as men can judge one another's work, he appears to be the most brilliant of all rose breeders. Who can we put anywhere near him? Francis Meilland, if his life had not been so short; Wilhelm Kordes of Germany and Samuel Darragh McGredy of New Zealand (formerly of Northern Ireland) might complete one's game of assembling the four great ones of the recorded history of rose breeding; like picking a World Cricket Team, anyone may play it.

When man seeks to develop nature, he discovers faults to set against his successes. In the case of the Pernetiana Roses, the faults were clearly shown by 'Rayon d'Or' and many of its successors: those villains blackspot and die-back. It is no surprise that a rose such as 'Persian Yellow' from the dry climate of Iran, might breed in its children (by an outlandish mate) foliage unable to resist the fungus of humidity. Similarly we may wonder whether the softness of the wood was related to climatic differences, because it is the sun which ripens wood. These are the factors in the background; there's explanation enough without them, in the chance alignment of the generative atoms upon fertilization between two diverse parents, to make combinations different from either parent. Whatever the reason, the success of one breeder usually includes problems for his successors to solve. The die-back problem has been well solved, and the blackspot trouble is at least ameliorated. In our gratitude to Pernet-Ducher, we should not be blind to the truth, which is that we had to accept a good deal of blackspot with his gifts to us.

'Rayon d'Or' was raised from 'Mme Mélanie Soupert' × 'Soleil d'Or'. It had heavy red flushes on the outer petals, a trait common in yellow roses to this day; and I am glad to say that, unlike 'Soleil d'Or', this rose did receive the National Rose Society's Gold Medal. I like to think that Joseph Pernet-Ducher showed that medal to his family at home, to his sons Claudius and Georges, now taking an interest in the roses, especially Claude, in the house and high walled gardens just half a mile from the dusty village square of Vennissieux, as Rose Kingsley described it in the *Rose Annual 1910*.

'Mme Jules Bouché'   *Medium   White   Remontant*   P4   H1
Both in Europe and America, plenty of surviving plants may still be seen of this 1911 introduction. It is a white rose, very slightly creamy, with slim flowers on slightly purple stems, the leaves light green. The flowers are easily spoilt by damp weather, and it survived that disadvantage by producing many of them. Bred by J. Croibier et Fils, Saint-Tous, Rhône, from 'Pharisäer' × seedling. There's more than a hint of Tea Rose about it.

'George Dickson'
I used to be amazed that this ugly plant could be admired by anybody, let alone achieve its high reputation. It won the National Rose Society's Gold Medal, and was regarded as a really fine rose, supreme for exhibition, 'the most successful of our period', according to H. R. Darlington. I saw it differently.

Its long shoots, more like a Hybrid Perpetual than a Hybrid Tea, were covered with dull green leaves, which appeared to open on purpose to prepare a bed for mildew. On top of each over-extended shoot grew probably three buds, of which it was advisable to remove two, otherwise they were too close to open properly. The survivor swelled, overwhelming its flower stalk, and bloomed in a pendulous position looking dolefully to the ground. Well trained in exhibition lore, you bent it upwards, as being preferable to lying down on the ground and looking up, expecting to see a medal bloom. And as like as not, it was quartered, with mildew beginning to grow on the petals. Ugh! Someone wrote that this rose hung its head owing to the weight of the flower, a neat way of diverting the attention from the weakness of the stem. Sometimes it gave a wonderful dark crimson flower, which on being seen in an exhibition box set people admiring it for another few years. I grew it for seven years, and never had that luck. My apologies to the Dicksons, who got away with it in 1912. Even in the *Rose Annual 1952* it had a supporter calling it 'supreme' and 'grand', but wondering why his best flowers every year were on shoots six feet long in late autumn.

'Ophelia'   *Medium   Light pink   Remontant*   P8   H4   ***
The mystery and the glory of roses in 1912. It was introduced by Wm Paul & Son of Waltham Cross, with the honourable admission that they didn't know where it came from. They had bought 'Antoine Rivoire' from Pernet-Ducher, and supposed that this may have been a stray plant in that consignment. We shall not find proof of the matter now.

'Ophelia' looks almost white from a distance; its beauty is to be appreciated on close inspection, both by nose and eye. The delicate touches of blush pink, a suggestion of yellow at the petal's foot, the clean, trim shape of the petals around a simple and upright heart; all these points show why this rose is the epitome of the decorative Hybrid Tea. Its growth is free, the foliage functional but handsome. Often it produces a stem bearing twenty buds or more, prompting modern owners to ask 'what Floribunda is this?'

For many years 'Ophelia' was grown in greenhouses by the cut flower nurserymen, which is a certain way of sports being discovered. In this respect, 'Ophelia' is unique among roses. Twenty-three of its sports have been introduced, and those sports have proved sportive in turn, to bring the total to thirty-six. Ann Wylie has traced 'Ophelia's' sports further still, asking whether the tendency may have been passed genetically to her progeny, notably 'Columbia', 'Talisman', 'Premier', 'Joanna Hill' and 'Golden Ophelia'. Miss Wylie found a total of 206 sports from them, which was just over half of all Hybrid Tea sports she could discover in a twenty-five year period. These interesting statistics may be seen in the Royal Horticultural Society's *Journal* for January, 1955. The name 'Joanna Hill' instructs us that 'Ophelia' was a maternal forbear of 'Peace'. And 'Golden Ophelia' gave the sport 'Roselandia', for years the leading yellow in the flower markets. Of these sports, two have been especially popular: 'Mme Butterfly', from the E. G. Hill Company in 1918, in which 'Ophelia's' colours are more pronounced; and 'Lady Sylvia', a sport from 'Mme Butterfly', found by another greenhouse grower, Walter Stevens of Hoddesdon, Hertfordshire. 'Sylvia', as it has been known in the flower markets for years, is a clear fresh pink, as pleasing a pink Hybrid Tea, I think, as there has ever been. It was introduced in 1926. Both 'Mme Butterfly' and 'Lady Sylvia' are as worthy of being grown today as is 'Ophelia'. All three have one small failing, that the buds open in such a way as to admit thunderflies, also known as thrips. Should these scurrying little insects be about, they enter the buds and deform the petals. They may be deterred by a suitable insecticide.

'Mme Edouard Herriot'

The London *Daily Mail* in 1912 was young and roaring with energy coming out with schemes to impress its name upon the public by associating itself with the more newsworthy aspects of human progress. Had the newspaper's policies not been modified, I am quite sure the first duty Mr Armstrong would have performed upon the moon would have been to open an envelope and accept the *Daily Mail's* cheque for £100,000. Certainly some of the early aviators received generous rewards from this newspaper. Incentives and publicity may indeed accelerate progress, or at least circulation. So at any rate the *Daily Mail* firmly believed. Turning their attention to roses, they offered a cup and a cheque of £1000 to the best new rose. A condition of the competition was that the winning entry should be called 'The Daily Mail Rose'.

A page or two back, I wrote something about the British doing things by the book, and here is a wonderful warning to my fellow countrymen. I cannot suppose that any British grower would have let an entry go forward in this competition, having already named it contrary to the rules. It takes a Frenchman to do a thing like that *and get away with it*. The best entry beyond any shadow of doubt was 'Mme Edouard Herriot' from Joseph Pernet-Ducher. But of course Monsieur will change the name? Ah, I regret that is not possible, for it honours the wife of a respected Frenchman.

In the end, the *Daily Mail* backed down before the quiet courtesy of a rose grower from a French village, gave him the cup and the thousand pounds, and accepted the name 'Mme Edouard Herriot or the Daily Mail Rose'. And all the British entrants obeyed the rules and went empty away. Naturally the awkward mouthful of a name did not last five minutes. Pernet-Ducher was perfectly happy with it, for it made no difference in France at all. The *Daily Mail* was fairly happy, for it supposed that of the two names, the familiar English one would stick. But there they reckoned without British rose growers. The proper name of a variety is that first given; and 'Mme Edouard Herriot' it became, strictly according to the book. Game, set and match to Pernet-Ducher.

The rose was a very good one, a garden favourite for many years. Its garish colour was novel, and to write all its colours down on paper is like a shopping list for an artist's palette. Imagine a film pan through coral from light to dark, with yellow illuminations, and you are somewhere on the way. The thorns were quite remarkable, large, flat and close together, rather handsome. The flowers were thin, but very freely produced. It was a seedling from 'Mme Caroline Testout', the pollen parent not known, and it was introduced in 1913.

'Mrs Wemyss Quin'

The future of yellow roses had now passed from Pernet-Ducher's exclusive control, as his varieties had reached other breeders. The almost metallic golden colour of the yellow Pernetianas was preserved by 'Mrs Wemyss Quin', 'Golden Emblem', 'Christine', 'Mabel Morse', 'Marcelle Gret' and 'Spek's Yellow' (or 'Golden Scepter' in the United States). It appeared in other varieties of a transient nature; but please note that the latest introduction I have mentioned is in 1947. Has the pure metallic gold been impossible to divorce from the blackspot and poor growth? Have breeders been like Canutes, failing to stop waves of red and pink sweeping into their yellow sand? I expect I shall have yellow roses pointed out to me, perhaps 'Peer Gynt' or 'King's Ransom' or 'Gold Crown' or 'Summer Sunshine', and told 'There they are! Open your eyes, Jack.' But does anyone really think that the raiser of 'Rayon d'Or' would see in any of those the pure golden rose of his imagining? It is my contention that in this respect, the high water mark was 'Mrs Wemyss Quin'. And it was introduced by Alexander Dickson in 1914. The alert French gave it a Gold Medal at Bagatelle in 1916.

A prickly rose, blessed (or cursed?) with big spines, strong growth, grassy green leaves and stems, flowers as yellow as a golden guinea. The guard petals (the outer ring of five, in other words) had the usual red splash. It was tough and long lived, unlike many yellow roses; or to put it another way, it was hardy, withstanding the winters. The parentage is unknown, for in 1921 Dicksons had a fire in their office and lost their records.

'Los Angeles'

Fred Howard, of Howard & Smith, Montebello, California was a successful breeder of Hybrid Teas. His 'Los Angeles' had a great run, due to a pleasing colour like pale shot silk, and to the great number of flowers it carried. It became a favourite in Europe, especially with the help of its Gold Medal from Bagatelle; if it was introduced today it would look very much like one of those double Floribundas with flowers all at the top of the bush. Introduced in the States in 1916, it received its Bagatelle award in 1918, and soon spread across Europe at the end of the war. It began to lose favour in the 1930s by getting rust.

'Golden Emblem'

Raised by Sam McGredy. straight from the Pernet-Ducher line, namely 'Mme Mélanie Soupert' × 'Constance', the latter being one of Joseph Pernet-Ducher's own seedlings from 'Rayon d'Or'. This brilliant yellow came on a stubby, thorny plant, with some of 'Rayon d'Or's' die-back trouble. Its flowers were lustrous, so beautiful that the plant *had* to be grown. It was introduced in 1917.

'K. of K.'
A semi-double rose of beautiful scarlet colour. The name was for Lord Kitchener of Khartoum, a British general who was known by those initials. Alexander Dickson was still interested in single or semi-double roses, and had produced 'Irish Fireflame' and 'Red Letter Day' in 1914. This one came out in 1917, and it was a favourite on our nursery into the 1930s, as being the most attractive red variety to include in our exhibits.

'Christine'
McGredy continued his yellow line with this in 1918. The flowers were smaller than 'Golden Emblem' but the growth better, and the colour similar; perhaps a trifle less lustrous.

'Emma Wright'
The buds of this rose are a most attractive orange. It has proved difficult enough to produce a one coloured Hybrid Tea in golden yellow, but it is even more so in orange. The influence of the old China Rose is strongly in favour of mixed and changing colours. About this time we see the orange colours develop; McGredy's had this charming rose in 1918, its buds perfectly set against dark leaves, its flowers unfortunately opening pale and semi-double. Also in 1918, Walter Easlea (who at one time worked for Paul's) had an apricot orange variety called 'Lamia', an interesting colour. Now that I have unintentionally linked McGredy and Easlea, I remember a strange remark the latter made when writing of McGredy's 'Golden Emblem' to the effect that if the raiser could produce it on a really good plant, and with one or two more improvements, 'he may be sure of lasting fame, if that is any good to him'.

'Etoile de Hollande'
One of the most popular red roses of the 1920s and 1930s. The colour was dark, the scent rich, the growth clean-cut, healthy, good to see. The only disappointment was that the buds opened too quickly. Raised by H. A. Verschuren & Sons of Haps, Holland, from 'General MacArthur' × 'Hadley', and introduced in 1919.

'Souvenir de Claudius Pernet'
This rose was introduced in 1920, and was followed the next year by 'Souvenir de Georges Pernet'. The Wizard of Lyon had remembered his two sons, who went to the war, but never returned to Vennissieux.

Claudius's rose was yellow, from the seed of 'Constance'; it proved a good parent, and is an ancestor of most modern yellow Hybrid Teas, as well as some Floribundas. Georges's rose, from pollen of 'Mme Edouard Herriot', had a large orange pink flower. Joseph Pernet-Ducher continued a successful rose breeder, and we shall return to his roses, but it may be appropriate to state here that the death of his sons ended his immediate family succession, which no doubt had been the dearest wish of his heart. However, the same problem had been overcome for the Ducher family, and it was to be resolved again by the succession of Jean Gaujard to this wonderful rose business under similar circumstances, for he married Pernet-Ducher's daughter Gabrielle.

Joseph Pernet-Ducher died in 1928, leaving Jean Gaujard in charge at the age of twenty-five. Jean and I should have some fellow feeling, for our portraits are side by side on a page of *Modern Roses 7*. He moved the business to Feyzin, Isère in 1930, and it is now entitled Roseraies Gaujard.

'Betty Uprichard'   *Medium   Pink & red   Remontant*   P3   H4   **

An excellent rose raised by Alexander Dickson and introduced in 1922. The outside of the petals is carmine and the inside pink, the two colours happily contrasted. Although the flowers are not very large, the plants grow so well and bloom so freely that 'Betty Uprichard' was a leading garden rose for nearly thirty years. From the nurseryman's point of view, the plants easily branch from the union and grow fairly upright; these qualities are much appreciated, because not only are nearly all the plants fit to sell, but they are also easy to pack. This latter factor ensured that 'Betty Uprichard' was on the shelves in the big stores long after it had been abandoned by the general nursery trade.

'Mabel Morse'

Raised by Sam McGredy, and introduced in 1922, 'Mabel Morse' extended the golden thread of bright yellow roses. It had a pure and brilliant colour, and although it gave the initial impression of vigour and hardiness sufficiently well to merit a fair run in favour, it eventually proved a bush with a fairly short life. The Samuel McGredy of the day was an exhilarating character, very outspoken, ebullient and enthusiastic. His advertisement for 'Mabel Morse' begins 'We stake our reputation on this being the finest yellow Rose'; and that sort of confidence and certainty was perfectly sincere. He meant it.

At the National Rose Society's show in the summer of 1920, when both 'Mabel Morse' and 'Betty Uprichard' received a Certificate of Merit, the American raiser E. G. Hill was a guest member of the committee of judges. Both these varieties received their Gold Medals the following year.

'Sensation'

The most careless study of the Hybrid Teas of the 1930s will reveal 'Sensation' appearing as a parent with impressive frequency. The sensation has died down, for now the rose is scarcely known, rarely referred to, and I cannot remember that I ever saw it.

We should not forget 'Sensation', however. It was raised by the Joseph H. Hill Co. of Richmond, Indiana from 'Hoosier Beauty' × 'Premier'; and introduced in 1922. It was a parent of 'Talisman', 'President Herbert Hoover', 'Signora Piero Puricelli' and 'Violinista Costa'. It should have been a great rose to breed with for perfume, both 'Ophelia' and 'Château de Clos Vougeot' being forbears. Although red itself, it was apparently very co-operative in the direction of orange. It was also the pollen parent of 'Cathrine Kordes', and therefore involved in 'Crimson Glory' and 'Ena Harkness'.

'Shot Silk'   *Medium − Orange pink   Remontant*   P5   H3   *

One of the most beautiful and successful of all Hybrid Teas. The name is a good description of its lively colour; and the light green sparkling foliage set the flowers off perfectly. Never was there a rose which looked so fresh and clean. It has now perhaps lost some of its former vigour, but there are still thousands of plants of 'Shot Silk' in the gardens of Britain. It was a disappointing parent, although it appeared to be full of promise. Raised by Alexander Dickson from 'Hugh Dickson' seedling × 'Sunstar', and introduced in 1924. In Britain, this and 'Betty Uprichard' were considered practically indispensable in any scheme requiring rose beds for the next twenty years.

'Angèle Pernet'

One of the roses nearest to pure orange we have ever seen. The flowers were small but the colour was rare. I believe more should have been developed from it. Raised by Joseph Pernet-Ducher from 'Bénédicte Seguin' × a Hybrid Tea, and introduced in 1924. It won Gold Medals in England and France. Unfortunately we know practically nothing about the seed parent, apart from its orange-yellow colour, and that it was a 1918 introduction from Pernet-Ducher.

'Dainty Bess' *Medium Light pink Remontant* P3 H4 *

The unforgettable single rose. Five big petals, silky and light pink, are the backdrop for the dusty heads and purple legs of its chorus of stamens. Raised by W. E. B. Archer & Daughter of Sellindge, Ashford, Kent, from 'Ophelia' × 'K. of K.' Introduced in 1925. They used to advertise it as THE ARTISTIC ROSE.

'Mev. G. A. van Rossem'

One of the most beautiful roses of the 1920s, the orange-yellow petals run through by red veins. It was a rose one knew at once, there being none so similar as to be confused with it. 'Mrs G.A.' as we invariably called her, had excellent firm flower stems. When I began to work in the 1930s, it was our practice before leaving for a rose show, to support every Hybrid Tea flower by a piece of stub wire pushed into its ovary, and wound two or three times around the stem about a handsbreadth below. If there was one variety in those days which did not need its wire, it was 'Mrs G.A.' Thirty years later, by which time more and more varieties had been excused wiring, I discontinued it completely; and to me that proved the progress made in breeding firm flower stems over the period. We are now far removed from the nodding heads of the Teas.

The veining of 'Mrs G.A.' was potentially a very beautiful feature. Something of the same character was shown by 'Signora Piero Puricelli' (usually known as 'Signora') and its pollen child, 'Mojave'. 'Mrs G. A. van Rossem' does not appear to have been used to breed those two. Her parentage is given as 'Souvenir de Claudius Pernet' × 'Gorgeous'. The veining could well have come from 'Gorgeous'. The breeder was G. A. van Rossem of Naarden, Holland, and the rose was introduced in 1926 (1929 in USA).

'Margaret McGredy'

In 1927, McGredy introduced a highly individual rose, marked by hard leaves of unusual texture and form. Despite its Gold Medal at the Autumn Show in London in 1925, it never became wildly popular, although the McGredy's did their best by describing its carmine and yellow colours as orange scarlet. This was not the public's favourite colour, being neither clear nor bold enough. The most distinctive part of 'Margaret McGredy' was her foliage.

This was perceived quite clearly in the *Rose Annual 1926,* where it was shrewdly described editorially as 'quite a new break; though undoubtedly of Pernetiana origin, the Pernetiana blood has been quite eliminated.' It is a pity that 'Margaret McGredy' is one of a minority of McGredy's roses to be introduced with parentage unknown.

The influence of its leaves is distributed all over the world, because Francis Meilland used this rose in breeding 'Peace', and the eye instructs us that the beautiful leaves of 'Peace' owe much to 'Margaret McGredy'. Even before then, the lesson was clear in 'Condesa de Sastago', healthiest of the red and yellow bicolours, from Pedro Dot of Spain in 1930. He bred it from 'Margaret McGredy's' pollen.

In April 1926, before this variety was introduced, its breeder died suddenly. He was the second of the four Sam McGredys, the one to put the family name near the head of the profession. His first of many Gold Medals had been for 'Countess of Gosford' in 1905. The *Rose Annual 1927* described him as 'one of the finest, most straightforward and conscientious Rosarians that ever walked'. Unhappily the next Sam McGredy died only eight years later, at the age of thirty-seven, when his son, the fourth Sam, was three.

'Polly' *Medium – Blush Remontant* P9 H2 *

With iron resolution I have cut out many old friends, in order that this list be confined to the main stepping stones which mark the descent of roses, either genetically or in man's awareness, decade by decade. But I am only human, and cannot be unfaithful to 'Polly'.

This lovely thing is like a well-filled 'Ophelia', plump bottomed but comely, sea-shell pale and full of sweet odours. If this sounds like one writing of his mistress, I may add that her limbs are smooth, and she ought to be well fed and cared for, being a tender thing. She must be kept in order, for she will spend herself in a multitude of buds, and lose her beauty unless they are reduced in number. From an 'Ophelia' seedling × 'Mme Colette Martinet'; introduced 1927 by G. Beckwith & Son, Hoddesdon, Hertfordshire.

'Golden Dawn' *Medium Yellow Remontant* P3 H2 **

Patrick Grant of Macksville, New South Wales, Australia set an example to all rose breeders by his modest total of three introductions, of which two were great successes; it is not necessary to be the most senior of rosarians to remember with pleasure 'Golden Dawn' and 'Salmon Spray'. His third was 'Midnight Sun', quite unfamiliar to me, indeed I asked myself whatever colour could it be? Black as night or yellow as sun? Or a combination of both, like a poached egg on burnt toast? The answer turns out to be dark crimson, and it was an introduction of 1921. Thirty odd years later, the Brownells of Little Compton, Rhode Island, were apparently grieved to see the name wasted, and they used it for a yellow rose with a red edge, with the spelling altered to 'Midnite Sun'.

'Golden Dawn' is an interesting yellow Hybrid Tea, one of the most reliable growers of that colour, and with handsome and unusual leaves. I have always felt there was something very interesting for the breeder here, but I got no reward for the work I put into it. The parentage tells us very little, 'Elegante' × 'Ethel Somerset'; for those two came from Pernet-Ducher and Alexander Dickson without a hint of their antecedents.

The soft yellow flowers are large, and tend to look at their best when other Hybrid Teas are taking a rest, particularly in the autumn. By the time they are wide open, one usually notices a 'split', in other words the petals are not folded around the centre in a perfect cone, but are tucked back among themselves. When 'Peace' became available, few people could see any reason to keep 'Golden Dawn', but it is still a good rose. Introduced by Hazlewood Bros., Epping, NSW; and in Britain in 1929.

'Mrs Sam McGredy' *Medium – Salmon to red Remontant* P2 H4

There has never been another rose quite the same as 'Mrs Sam'; which is not only a familiar abbreviation of the name, but also a rose grower's description of the coppery red colour of its buds. The flowers opened all too soon to a kind of stale salmon, quite uninteresting, but while they were young there was no rose their equal in colour before or since.

'Mrs Sam McGredy' is no longer sufficiently robust to plant, except as a climber; bushes of it seem to issue an irresistible invitation to blackspot, although there are still many surviving. It was found remarkable for the purple red of its young leaves. One of the beauties of a rose nursery is seen by its staff and few others: the colours of the leaves at first growth, block by block, variety by variety, green, olive, red, purple, few exactly the same, and the whole winking in the sun like the newly minted treasures they are. Purple leaves lose some charm by turning green as they age; then the contrast on the same plant of purple red above and green below may not be handsome.

'Mrs Sam' has flower shoots which are usually thin, and the plant is very often a floppy affair. It was introduced in 1929, and raised from ('Donald Macdonald' × 'Golden Emblem') × (seedling × 'The Queen Alexandra Rose'). The story goes that when Mrs McGredy knew of the intention to use her name for a rose, she chose this one, and insisted on it against the advice of the men. She could not have found a much more famous rose from the whole of McGredy's output up to 1950.

The great seed pods of 'Mrs Sam' make promises without keeping them, and I never heard of any breeder finding much therein, or fixing that colour in a better plant, or for the flower's full life.

'Talisman'

The Montgomery Company of Hadley, Massachusetts, did not breed a long list of roses, but they had a widely grown red Hybrid Tea, 'Hadley', and one of the most important varieties for the cut flower market in 'Talisman'. This came from 'Ophelia' × 'Souvenir de Claudius Pernet', and was introduced in 1929.

'Talisman' was notable for its even height, every shoot apparently deciding to produce a bloom upon the same level; many shoots were produced, and therefore the number of blooms per plant was high, an important consideration for a market rose. Indeed before anyone will plant his valuable greenhouse with a fresh variety, he expects to arrive at an exact idea of how many flowers it should yield per square metre per annum. The flowers were surprisingly small and thin for a successful market rose. They were yellow with flushes of pink and red, quite variable; this rose produced thirty-nine sports, in continuance of the family tendency of 'Ophelia'. One of the prettiest was the red 'Mary Hart', from George B. Hart of Rochester, New York, in 1931.

It is to be remembered that when a variety is prone to sport, it may do so in several different places, with the result of different growers proudly introducing varieties which are indistinguishable. We have seen this very clearly in the Royal National Rose Society's Trials. I remember two or three white 'Queen Elizabeth' sports; three yellowish 'Mischief' sports; and a few from 'Whisky Mac'. To my certain knowledge at least two of each were named and introduced; and very likely similar sports were also being introduced in other countries.

'President Herbert Hoover' *Tall   Pink & yellow   Remontant* P7 H3   *

A gaunt bush, which stretched up without quite enough leaves. But at least it grew bigger than most Hybrid Teas, and with very little trouble from diseases. Everyone forgave it for its bright buds, the guard petals orange red, and the tips of the centre petals rings of yellow within them. When the flowers opened, the brightness faded to a more modest yellow and pink, spiced with a lively scent. The flower stems were long and straight; like 'Mrs G. A. van Rossem' there was no need to wire it.

'President Hoover' as it was invariably called in Britain, is still worth growing today if you can obtain it. Nurserymen are not too keen on growing it, as it is one of those roses of which most of the nursery crop is plants of one or two stems, hardly any of three or four. Such roses are malignant influences on nurserymens' balance sheets; an efficient producer aims to convert his labour and materials into a production yield of 100 per cent as nearly as he can. An acceptable yield in British rose nurseries out of a hundred rootstocks planted is sixty first quality plants; but this depends on the ruthless exclusion of such roses as 'President Hoover', which would give about thirty. Although sixty does not sound very high, it is in fact a very good field of roses that yields it, and it does not need many errors and weak patches to bring the figure below fifty. You hear growers talking of 'a good nurseryman's rose', by which they mean one that will yield eighty good plants from a hundred rootstocks planted, given the best of conditions and skill. A wise grower reduces the worries in his life by growing such roses as the major part of his stock. The grower who seeks to make a speciality of the rare and difficult roses is treading a path well known in the rose trade as directed towards bankruptcy. He needs a business economy different from the normal rose nursery.

'President Herbert Hoover' was raised by L. B. Coddington, Murray Hill, New Jersey, from 'Sensation' × 'Souvenir de Claudius Pernet'. It was introduced in 1930 by the Charles H. Totty Co., Madison, New Jersey.

'Picture'

One of the best loved pink roses from its introduction in 1932, until it began to lose its constitution around 1960. 'Picture' was one of the first salvage operations which were to occur in the National Rose Society's Trial Ground. Sam McGredy, having entered it in the trials, subsequently judged it a failure by its performance at home in Portadown; when the judges approved it he had none left, but had to apply to Haywards Heath for stock from his trial plants. This is by no means a rare occurrence, proving that two expert opinions may be at variance, in this case those of breeder and judges. I have to confess that I have been obliged to follow Mr McGredy's example on three occasions, for 'Seven Seas', 'Harry Edland' and 'Lysbeth-Victoria'.

'Picture' was a neat little flower, rose pink, with fairly short petals, a perfect buttonhole rose. It was an excellent bedding rose from its compact and even growth, and its tendency to flower early.

'Geheimrat Duisberg'

This yellow rose was an important cut flower variety; but it is also of interest as the first Hybrid Tea we record here from Wilhelm Kordes of Sparrieshoop, Holstein, Germany. Let us admit that Herr Kordes had already introduced 'Cathrine Kordes' in 1929; and two varieties of fascinating nasturtium colours, 'Heinrich Wendland' in 1930 and 'Hinrich Gaede' in 1931. These three might well have qualified for mention, had their life in commerce not been short.

Wilhelm Kordes was an imaginative breeder, who was to provide groundwork for most of his rivals. It will be proved in these pages that his imagination and energy searched widely within the genus. 'Searching widely' gives a poor idea of the vast amount of work it requires; it is a euphemism for 'raising millions of rose seedlings, selecting the few significant, and burning the rest'; it hides the ceaseless work of the brain and the eye which has to complete that of the hands.

Kordes had started a nursery in Witley, Surrey in 1913, and was mercifully taken out of the war, so avoiding any risk of the waste that struck the Pernet-Ducher family. He spent it in internment in the Isle of Man. Any idea he might have had of working in England was lost in those events, and he returned to run the family business in Holstein, with his brother Hermann. They made it one of the largest in Europe, and made no bones of their confidence: as witness their slogan, 'The most beautiful Roses in the World'. Wilhelm Kordes was one of the least frivolous men I ever met, serious, courteous, a student not only of roses, not only of horticulture, but of the whole of nature. One felt that his time was too precious to be frittered away; and although it was highly unlikely one had anything to contribute to his store of knowledge, the only reason in his mind for converse is what is nowadays entitled meaningful debate. He was a great man, and died in 1976 at the age of eighty-five.

'Geheimrat Duisberg' was one of the better yellow roses upon its introduction in 1933. It had shiny foliage, easy growth and handsome flowers. They were yellow, apart from the early blooms, which in common with many yellow varieties of the period, came white. The parents were 'Rapture' × 'Julien Potin'. 'Rapture' was one of the deepest pink sports on the 'Ophelia' line, from 'Mme Butterfly' in fact. It provided a means for the American introducers to escape the awkward German name, and substitute for 'Geheimrat Duisberg' the more familiar 'Golden Rapture'.

'McGredy's Yellow' *Medium Yellow Remontant* P2 H3
I have seen few things in this world more beautiful than flowers of 'McGredy's Yellow'. Upon our nursery, when cutting roses for a show, we would start as early in the morning as the light and the moisture permitted, for it might be prudent to allow a time for the dew to disperse. One would know how many flowers of each variety were needed, and in each case one's task was to walk every row, so that if seventy blooms were needed, the best seventy were taken. By hook or by crook I took 'McGredy's Yellow' as part of my beat whenever I could. I well remember the feeling of intense joy in the early morning sunlight, as one accumulated seventy blooms as near perfection as one could hope to see. Alas for the beauty of this variety, it is gone for ever. Whereas each bloom was then high in the centre, all the lovely form has gone, in as tragic a case of deterioration as I know. It is no use planting 'McGredy's Yellow' any more, nor is there any rose to replace its particular beauty.

Our early morning cutting expeditions were governed by the need to collect some thousands of selected blooms. In the days of old, when the finished exhibit was of seventy-two blooms, each one of a different variety, our people used to cut them in the evening. They were marked in the day with white ties, so that they could be found in the dark. There was a belief that this was the time when the flower's chemistry was most favourably inclined to encourage growth after being cut. Like many of these beliefs, nobody stated the proof, and I am sure it depended on other factors, from the growing and feeding before cutting, to the handling and storage after cutting. I am glad that for my generation it was 'McGredy's Yellow' in the early morning. It was introduced by McGredy in 1933, and raised from 'Mrs Charles Lamplough' × ('The Queen Alexandra Rose' × 'J. B. Clark'). Once again it was a case of the raiser being short of stock, for it had its Gold Medal in 1930; and our firm had to supply stock back to Mr McGredy, whose hesitancy about this obvious winner was quite strange. He claimed to have been growing it for twelve years before he got round to selling it.

'Crimson Glory' *Medium Dark red Remontant* P8 H1
Introduced in 1935, the dark colour, rich fragrance and elegant form made this the finest red Hybrid Tea ever raised at that time. More than any rose, it made Wilhelm

Kordes his reputation as a rose breeder. The parentage was 'Cathrine Kordes' seedling × 'W. E. Chaplin', and 'Cathrine Kordes' establishes a direct line back to 'Lady Mary Fitzwilliam', being ('Mme Caroline Testout' × 'Willowmere') × 'Sensation'. Quite a lot of the story is in the dark, however, because we do not know what fertilized the seedling of 'Cathrine Kordes', nor do we know the parents of 'W. E. Chaplin'.

No matter where roses were grown, from Europe to New Zealand, 'Crimson Glory' became the great favourite. The National Rose Society has solicited votes for roses in order of merit, in order to publish the resultant opinions in its 'Rose Analysis'; in one form or another, these tables have appeared in their *Annuals* since 1909. Before then, it was done annually by the *Journal of Horticulture*. In the Annual for 1948, 'Crimson Glory' arrived at the top of each appropriate table: best exhibition rose, best garden rose, best dual purpose rose. It was similarly successful in other countries. Yet its fall when it came was sudden, due to an increasing liability to mildew, and usurpation by one of its own seedlings, 'Ena Harkness'. Although like all other Hybrid Teas, it had its few years and faded away, 'Crimson Glory' has left important seedlings for the rose's future.

'Eclipse'
One of the areas of misunderstanding between British and American rose breeders, is that the Americans tell us that our roses do not have enough petals for their climate, and then proceed to make best sellers out of their roses with even fewer, of which we may take 'Eclipse' and 'Fandango' as examples. In fairness I must own that 'Eclipse' did very well in Europe by earning Gold Medals from Bagatelle and Rome, but not in England. It looked unhappy with us. Raised by J. H. Nicolas of the Jackson & Perkins Co., then of Newark, New York. Bred from 'Joanna Hill' × 'Federico Casas', 'Eclipse' was introduced in 1935, and is still being grown and sold in the United States.

The books tell us that it earned its name by flowering for the first time on the day of an eclipse in August 1932. I have not checked the almanac for that eclipse, but I am quite certain of two things, that most Hybrid Teas in North America are in bloom a little earlier than the end of August, and that nobody seeing the first bloom at that time could possibly introduce the rose three years later, complete with Plant Patent and all. The average time is seven years.

'Phyllis Gold' and 'Christopher Stone'
The British rose world was woken up in 1935 by a form of salesmanship quite new to it: Wheatcroft Brothers were introducing these two roses. It is a measure of his personality, and I suppose a sign of our times, that Harry Wheatcroft's name comes to mind before that of the breeder. So let us put that right, as we remember him banging the drum for 'Phyllis Gold' and 'Christopher Stone'.

Herbert Robinson, of Hinckley, Leicester, was born to be a plant breeder, and more's the pity he could not spend all of his long life at it; he passed his ninetieth year, and in that time interested himself in sweet peas, pyrethrums, delphiniums, roses, tomatoes and apples, to name some that I happen to know of. His pyrethrums were widely grown; his tomatoes and apples were kept at home for his own amusement, and Herbert could not be pushed into 'doing anything with them'. He was a gardener at heart, and indeed began his career working in private gardens. He was happy with plants and pots in his hands, and his attitude towards business decisions was like that of the stream and the logs: wait for the current to detach a log and send it downstream. Several of us in the trade had his tomato seed free of charge for our private use, and very good the tomatoes were.

In the Wheatcroft Brothers, Herbert Robinson had found a powerful current; but the partnership did not achieve its potential, which ought to have been Herbert free to spend his time breeding, and the Wheatcrofts never short of good new roses. I suppose it was like mixing mercury and oak; the one could do little for the other; the fast and slow trains could not adjust to a communicating speed. Wheatcrofts had only four more varieties from Herbert Robinson, 'Nottingham', 'Percy Izzard' and 'Walter Bentley' before the war, none of them top class; and 'Mary Wheatcroft', which they kept until 1945, after which their energies became fixed on Meilland's varieties. 'Mary Wheatcroft' was one of the best roses out of a reluctant mother: 'Mrs Sam McGredy' × 'Princess Marina'; that is, if Herbert's memory was right, for it was in his head that his parentages were filed, and I would not bet very heavily on factual accuracy down to the finer points.

Herbert's son, Harold, was of much the same mould; they don't change too fast in Leicestershire. Britain's rose growers were sad when young Harold died in 1976 while old Herbert was still alive. His funeral was fixed on the day of the Autumn Rose Show in London, which meant that most of us could not attend. By a spontaneous understanding, at the time of the funeral a group of rose nurserymen sat in St Stephen's Church just near the show, and remembered Harold. It was a moving occasion, especially as most of those present were not noted for religious observance.

'Phyllis Gold' was a fine yellow rose. According to Herbert it was bred from 'Lady Florence Stronge' × 'Julien Potin'. It had the familiar habit of the first flowers being nearly white. But thereafter it was a splendid yellow, the petals long and the flower shapely. 'Christopher Stone' was a brilliant red rose, dark but flashing, its petals rather short. Herbert was stumped to remember its parents. He thought perhaps 'Etoile de Hollande' and 'Hortulanus Budde'. The details of parentage are important to breeders, but we may well wonder how many guesses, mistakes and lies are enshrined in them. At least Herbert Robinson made no secret of his limitations as a keeper of records.

'Signora' *Medium Orange red Remontant* P2 H3

One of the most beautifully coloured roses, a medley of orange red with some apricot, some carmine pink, some yellow in varying degrees: it came out in 1936. Its full name was 'Signora Piero Puricelli', and it was raised by Domenico Aicardi, from San Remo, Italy. His 'Rome Glory', as it was known in the United States, was a successful exhibition rose, sold under 'Gloria di Roma', or close translations, in Italy, France and Britain.

'Signora' was bred from 'Julien Potin' × 'Sensation', and gave much of her character to 'Mojave' in due course. Although she began to succumb to blackspot, I remember her with affection for straight stems, firm little thorns, and most attractive colour.

'The Doctor' *Medium – Pink Remontant* P10 H3

A wonderful pink rose, with plenty of colour and none of it harsh, which is not always the way of pink roses. The petals were huge, forming a deep, high centred flower, from which the perfume was issued beautifully. It was introduced in 1936 in the United States, but the British distributor, Laxton Brothers, hesitated to release it, much to our impatience. Then a grower in Kent advertised it in one of the Trade journals, and my firm with Walter Bentley of Leicester promptly bought all he had.

This forced the British distributor to agree to introduction in 1939, but he was not well pleased. In those days there were no rights in a plant variety in Britain other than a monopoly of the supply, which was gone the minute a plant or a bloom was sold or strayed away; thereafter the goodwill among some nurserymen upheld a system of royalty payments for two or three years. The United States was far ahead of Britain with their Plant Patent Act of 1930, against the British Plant Variety and Seeds Act of 1965. In 1939, the British had not begun to appreciate that rose breeders were people who needed to be paid.

'The Doctor' was greatly loved in Britain, both as a garden and exhibition rose, until it was discovered that he could not heal himself of blackspot and rust. His flower stems were on the weak side, but could be forgiven, because the flowers rose well above the leaves. A pleasing rose, which leaves pleasant memories; although somebody's memory was short indeed: six plants of 'The Doctor' were sent to the Royal National Rose Society to grow in its trials of new roses in 1973. In some ways one can regard 'The Doctor' as the climax of the type of pink Hybrid Tea ushered in during the 1890s. After him came the tougher look of 'Peace's' children.

The breeder was Fred H. Howard of Montebello, California; the parents were 'Mrs J. D. Eisele' × 'Los Angeles', two more of Mr Howard's roses.

'Violinista Costa'   *Short   Coral & rose   Remontant*   P3   H1   ******
For many years the *American Rose Annual* has contained a feature called *Proof of the Pudding,* in which the new roses of the past few years were criticized and assessed by members of the American Rose Society. The average points over five years, expressed for example as 7.8 out of 10, hold in the future as the Society's assessment of the rose. Provided the assessments are reasonably reliable, it is exactly this sort of recommendation that members of a rose society most need. Few things are more galling in one's gardening career than to resolve to plant some unfamiliar subject. The handful of varieties in the catalogue become a cipher, the descriptions baffle, and we probably choose the wrong variety unless we make a determined attempt to discover the information we need. *Proof of the Pudding* used to fill up pages with brief comments, in which the compliments were often sickly ('It even wowed Fido') the condemnations witty ('Save time – plant straight on bonfire') and the general reading value low. It is more concisely edited now. However the National Rose Society in Britain tried once or twice to copy their go-ahead cousins across the Atlantic, not to the extent of course of a vernacular title like *Proof of the Pudding*. No, they preferred the more snappy *A Summary of Remarks on Some of the Newer Roses.* And in featuring 'Violinista Costa' they neatly exposed the shortcomings of this type of rose journalism.

Eight replies from selected experts inform the bewildered enquirer that 'Violinista Costa' is healthy, were it not easily afflicted by blackspot. It has not been found free blooming, although the plants are always in bloom. A quite ordinary rose, which is one of the best bedding varieties of recent times; or to put it more plainly, the rose world could dispense with it but it will please in any garden.

'Violinista Costa' is a strange colour, pink and orange red, glowing well against its background of dark foliage. Probably it will need some medicine for mildew and blackspot, and it is one of the roses which persuades people not to grudge it that trouble. It was introduced in 1936 by Carlos Camprubi Nadal, having been bred from 'Sensation' × 'Shot Silk'.

'Charlotte Armstrong'   *Medium   Rose red   Remontant*   P2   H2   *****
This rose significantly influenced Hybrid Teas in the 1950s, and transmitted its long

and graceful shape to the future. It is surely the most important American contribution to modern roses. If you remember it, the petals were long, the heart perfectly regular, each petal around it slightly parted in an expectant way; a very handsome Hybrid Tea flower, in that typical but not very popular rose colour which may be deep pink or light red at the speaker's whim. If 'Peace' was husky, 'Charlotte Armstrong' was refined; and those qualities may be seen in some of their children; compare for example, 'Eden Rose' and 'Karl Herbst' of the 'Peace' family with 'First Love' and 'Sutter's Gold' from 'Charlotte's'. Her good points were given to the Floribundas via 'Pink Parfait', and she also has the credit of the seed which grew into 'Queen Elizabeth'.

'Charlotte Armstrong' was introduced in 1940 by Armstrong Nurseries of Ontario, California. That date ensured that Europeans did not know her well until nearly 1950; and it reserved her breeding capacity almost exclusively to Americans. One may ask what was lost through this failure to mix a valuable stud rose into the strains of European breeders. The breeder was Dr W. E. Lammerts of Livermore, California, who was a serious student of the science, endeavouring to ascertain the course of heredity by careful observation. The parents were 'Soeur Thérèse' × 'Crimson Glory', and these two brought together two classic Hybrid Tea lines, 'Souvenir de Claudius Pernet' on the one side, and 'Mme Caroline Testout' on the other. Dr Lammerts won practically every Gold Medal in the United States, and eventually, in 1950, one from the National Rose Society too. My firm had the pleasure of showing it for its Gold in Wolverhampton, an unusual venue for the Provincial Show. We had accepted the task of introducing Armstrong's roses in Britain.

'Peace' *Tall Yellow & pink Remontant* P2 H3 ***
In 1935, a young man of twenty-three was pollinating his roses, and when he laid his work aside one evening, a pollen brush had made its master stroke; his career, although he did not know it, was heading to an early climax.

Books have been written about Francis Meilland and 'Peace', and it is not my purpose to repeat at length what may be read in a hundred other places. I think it was in some ways sad that a variety like 'Peace' should have arrived at the start of his career. Lightning does not strike the same place twice, or at least one should not count on it, and who is to tell how much the pressure of his early success shortened his life? He died in 1958, aged only forty-six.

A connection exists between Joseph Pernet-Ducher and the Meillands, because Antoine Meilland, the father of Francis, was employed by Pernet-Ducher. Antoine is the 'Papa Meilland' of that glorious but mildewed dark red rose. He was a splendid looking man, with a calm and kindly face which looked as if it had been pointed at good and beautiful things all through its life. No false professional pride affected the Meilland family. Francis had been to learn about rose breeding not from one of the world's leading establishments, not from some erudite professors, but from a retired railwayman named Charles Mallerin. This remarkable amateur won a Gold Medal from Bagatelle in 1929 for a yellow rose which still looks good in France, if not in England, by name 'Mrs Pierre S. du Pont'. I never understood why it was 'Mrs' instead of 'Mme' and suppose it may have been an adjustment by the American introducer, the Conard-Pyle Co. Mallerin evolved a series of breeding precepts, and endeavoured to find logical reasons for the observations he had made, particularly to trace which characteristics are dominant, a difficult task in hybrid roses. His intelligence and industry were rewarded by such success as perhaps no other amateur ever attained; and his goodwill is proved by his willingness to take pupils and teach them well. His qualifications will be recognized from some of his roses: 'Beauté', 'Danse des Sylphes', 'Danse du Feu' (which is 'Spectacular' in the United States), 'Guinée', 'Mme Henri Guillot', and 'Virgo'. His pupil, Francis Meilland, proceeded to give him the best testimonial a teacher may have: his pupil's successes.

Francis has described from the pages of his note book 'already yellowing' that 55 flowers of 'Joanna Hill' were fertilized with pollen of his seedling 103-32-A, which was 'Charles P. Kilham' × 'Margaret McGredy'. The first of these crosses was done on 15 June 1935. From them came 52 hips, and the following year 800 seedlings, which is a very high proportion, and makes one wonder if that was the number of seeds sown, rather than seedlings grown.

Of them, fifty were propagated in 1936 for further trial, of which the future 'Peace' was the fortieth, designated 3-35-40. That code tells the breeder where to look for the parentage (number 3), the year of the cross (1935) and the number of the seedling of that cross (40). He is quite specific about these details, but we shall see that he is to have second thoughts about the parentage. Like all breeders, he is not committed to the seedlings as yet. We do not believe anything we see at that stage; we wait to see the plants grown on.

If one propagates roses by budding, it is usually done in the summer, in the expectation that the new plant will grow the following spring. But a minority do not wait so long. They grow away in a few weeks, and flower in the autumn. Thus in the autumn of 1936, Francis and Antoine Meilland saw for the first time what a flower of 'Peace' could be. One of those to see it, later on during its trial period at Meilland's nursery in Antibes, was the Duke of Windsor, who was quoted in the words that people all over the world were to echo, 'I have never seen another Rose like it. It is certainly the most beautiful Rose in the whole world.'

During the summer of 1939, propagating wood was sent to Germany, Italy and the United States, according to Francis Meilland in the *Rose Annual 1953*. It is often said that the wood for the United States was got out in a diplomatic bag, almost under the boots of the advancing German Army. Considering that Francis Meilland said 1939, when the German Army was nowhere near Antibes in the South of France, we must suspect some element of romance in that story. It might wear if the year of despatch had been 1940. No stock of 'Peace' was sent to England, because Meilland had no distributor there. When I took charge of our business in 1960 I found out why. In my uncle's desk was an old letter from Francis Meilland, asking Harkness to be his distributor, and the war had interrupted that correspondence.

Francis and his father agreed that their new rose should be named 'Mme A. Meilland', in memory of his mother, and it has always had that name in France, where it was introduced in 1942. The German distributor introduced it as 'Gloria Dei' and the Italian as 'Gioia'.

The American distributor was the Conard-Pyle Co., whose principal was a single-minded Quaker named Robert Pyle, a decisive, determined and kindly man. Conard-Pyle had been looking at Meilland's seedling during the war, and determined to name it 'Peace' at the kind of ceremony they manage very well over there due to everyone's courtesy, and which puts pictures of people shaking hands or giving one another things in all the papers. You know: the sort of thing we English find fearfully embarrassing and pseudo, and make the most fearful hash of when we try it, because we haven't the sense to appreciate it is all a play, as Americans and Continental Europeans do quite naturally. Having arranged this ceremony, they found on the morning of it that Berlin had fallen, and the war in Europe was virtually over. If fate was taking his hand, Robert Pyle was ready to respond, and the news of the 'Peace' rose went all over the world, because he caused a bloom and a message to be placed in the apartment of each chief delegate to the San Francisco Conference which set up the United Nations. With such a rose upon the American market, and a US Plant Patent for it, 'Peace' was all set to earn more royalties for Francis Meilland than anybody earned from a garden rose in history. Which was as well, for he cannot have seen much from Europe.

He appointed Wheatcroft Brothers as his agents in Britain. I fear Mr Harkness was too independent to sign contracts very freely, and in any case he had his hands full with the productions of a British amateur named Albert Norman. The first 'Peace' I saw was two plants sent to William E. Harkness by Robert Pyle, with a flattering message to the effect that three such gifts were despatched to England's great men – Winston Churchill, Bill Harkness and I forget who the third one was. We endeavoured to buy stock from Wheatcrofts, but they could not spare it, so those two plants came in handy. When Harry Wheatcroft came to see us I made a point of letting him see our stock of 'Peace', ready for sale at the same time as his, in 1947. There was no question of royalties to be paid; but we felt that the holder of a new variety had some obligation to distribute it to his fellow rose growers, whether he charged for the stock, or charged royalties. All too often it turned out there was not enough; or propagating wood arrived so late it was three-quarters doomed.

Of the future career of 'Peace' I could write at length, but think it better to concentrate on its importance as a holder of genetic particles. It was much more vigorous than any other Hybrid Tea, its foliage was dark, its flowers were sumptuously large. All these factors began very soon to change Hybrid Teas into more bushy plants, and to hasten the farewells of older varieties. Where did 'Peace' get its extraordinary character from? Francis Meilland's account of its parentage was simple: 'Joanna Hill × ('Charles P. Kilham' × 'Margaret McGredy'). And although he had just referred to his note book with its yellowing pages, we must accept that the note book is not necessarily the parentage book, and will not hold him too closely to what he declared. At a meeting in Williamsburg, USA, Francis had apparently given the parentage differently, and included *R. foetida bicolor* ('Austrian Copper') in it. He confirmed this by letter to the American Rose Society in January 1949.

But after Francis' death, the secretary of his firm said that the records did not mention *R. foetida bicolour. Modern Roses 6* put it in and *Modern Roses 7* left it out. And a friend named Henri Fessel gave another parentage in 1966, also claimed to be based on Meilland's records. We find ourselves thrown back on our own common sense. Those who believed in 'Austrian Copper's' involvement are looking for some influx of new blood as the reason for 'Peace's' strength. The pedigree, based on Meilland's letter, would be in these steps:

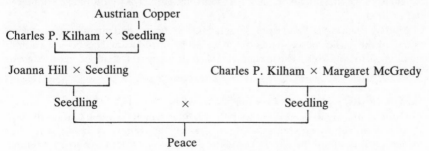

This, according to Francis Meilland 'will allow your giving out information absolutely in conformity with the truth'. And if we take him at his word, let us see what follows. (The *Rose Annual 1963* has these details, but unfortunately interprets them erroneously in a diagram intended to make them clear.)

The 'Austrian Copper' seedling should be summer flowering, therefore the seedling which mated 'Joanna Hill' is the first remontant seedling on this line. It has taken three generations to travel from a summer flowering seedling of 'Austrian Copper' to 'Peace'. There is no hint of 'Austrian Copper' about 'Peace'; I have seen no trace in the progeny I have raised from it, nor have I heard it reported by others. I think that the balance of probability is against there being any 'Austrian Copper' in it at all; it seems to me that reference to Francis Meilland's records was not always made without error.

The parentage to stand so far as we can be sure of any, has to be that of Henri Fessel, which is as follows:

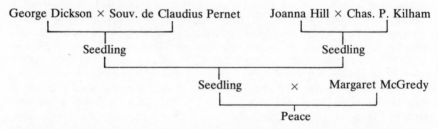

This appeals a good deal to one's sense of appearances. 'Peace' has some of the Hybrid Perpetual vigour of 'George Dickson'; it is the kind of rose that 'Souvenir de Claudius Pernet' and 'Joanna Hill' could sponsor, and it has the look of 'Margaret McGredy' in its foliage and flowers. We should remember that Francis Meilland was twenty-three at the Seedling × 'Margaret McGredy' stage, and as for those records, it is my guess they were some of Antoine's and some of Francis's, and not too easy to follow by any third parties, nor apparently by the first and second parties either. Whatever cloud of doubt shades 'Peace's' origin, the whole world is grateful to the breeder of this revelation of how yellow and pink may be perfectly mingled in a large and lustrous rose.

'Michèle Meilland'   *Medium   Light pink   Remontant*   P3   H3   **

Everyone who admires delicacy and grace ought to see 'Michèle Meilland', which is lovely in its dark smooth stems, its leaves, and its slim blooms. The colour varies greatly, from a ghostly pallor to a jolly flush; and I believe when one's back is turned, 'Michèle' makes herself up on the sly, and favours a touch of yellow or even orange in her powder.

Bred by Francis Meilland from 'Joanna Hill' × 'Peace', and introduced in 1945, it is one of the earlier descendants of 'Peace' to be introduced. This brings a double helping of 'Joanna Hill', whose character is accordingly well stamped upon 'Michèle Meilland'.

'Ena Harkness'   *Medium   Crimson   Remontant*   P5   H2   **

My firm has reason to be grateful to this rose, for our name became famous through it, at least to rosarians. One is aware of these things without knowing what they mean; it was not until the 1960s, travelling down muddy tracks to nurseries remote

1 *Hulthemia persica, showing its unique red eye, and the simple leaves which place it in the Simplicifoliae*

2 *X Hulthemosa hardii, the chance hybrid between Hulthemia persica and a rose; introduced 1836*

3 *R. roxburghii normalis, the single Chestnut Rose, from the sub-genus Platyrhodon; note its many leaflets*

4 *R. banksiae lutea, or Banksian Yellow, from the section Banksianae. A vigorous climber, with charming little flowers*

5 Ramona, the Red Cherokee, from the chapter Laevigatae. It is a charming climber, flowering in late spring

6 Mermaid, the glorious climber from the chapter Bracteatae. 'The sight of my life,' said Mr McGredy

7 R. chinensis mutabilis, from the section Indicae. The old flowers will finish purple red

8 Hermosa, a Hybrid China, from the section Indicae. Raised in 1840, it is like a double Old Blush

9 Lady Hillingdon, a Tea, from the chapter Indicae. This flower was growing on the climbing form

10 Alexander, a Hybrid Tea, from the chapter Indicae. A vigorous and popular variety, introduced in 1972

11 Escapade, a Floribunda, from the chapter Indicae. A fragrant and unusual variety, introduced in 1967

12 Cornelia, a Hybrid Musk, from the chapter Indicae, taken in late autumn (6th November)

13 Rosina, a Miniature, from the chapter Indicae. The whole plant is about 30 cm high

14 Allen Chandler, a Climbing Hybrid Tea, from the chapter Indicae. It was introduced in 1923

15 *R. arvensis, the Field Rose.*
A close look at the pistils will
show the fused styles of the
section Synstylae

16 *Yesterday, a modern*
Polyantha, from the chapter
Synstylae. It was introduced in
1974, is fragrant and charming

from the road around Steinfurth in Germany, that I fully appreciated what Ena had done for the Harkness name. The Steinfurth area is noted for having some hundreds of rose nurseries, most of them small; and as my host introduced me upon one holding after another, I received broader smiles and heartier hand clasps than my presence earned. Ena was being greeted; and to make it worse, we did not even raise the rose. We only introduced it. The raiser was an amateur.

Albert Norman worked in Hatton Garden as a diamond setter, and he lived in a little Surrey village appropriately named Normandy, near Guildford. Besides gardening, his hobby was studying insects, which often enough he was obliged to track to their lair upon roses. After a while, he took note of the roses as being preferable to the bugs upon them. He joined the National Rose Society, of which he eventually became President. His enquiring mind made of him the most interesting companion, it was not enough for him to know that something happened, he had also to know why, and knowing the reason taught him how the occurrence might be induced, improved, delayed or prevented. His visits to Hitchin went by in a flash, for one was so much absorbed in discussion that the time passed without ticking. Only once did I find it pass slowly in his company: I accepted a lift home from London in his car. He appeared to set his eyes on a distant objective half a mile down the street, and put his foot hard down until he reached it, chatting about the problems of rooting standard stems, while all the other users of the road dodged out of his path, accumulating miracle upon miracle. I often wondered if he never saw something strange about the roadway in his wake when he looked in the driving mirror, scenes like the retreat from Moscow done by the Keystone Cops, and large men shaking their fists. Or perhaps it was an off day, for I never heard of him having an accident. Nor did I let him drive me again.

In a tiny home greenhouse, Albert Norman put his enquiring mind to breeding roses; the first question he would ask was what colour? To which the answer was red. The next, what parents? He took the best dark red variety to seed, and the best bright red colour to pollen, which gave him a cross of 'Crimson Glory' × 'Southport'. Often this is shown in reverse order in the books, but my information was checked carefully with Albert Norman. I never discovered how many seedpods he had of the cross, but I suspect from something he said it was only one. It yielded 'Ena Harkness', 'Red Ensign' and 'William Harvey', and thus an amateur gave a classic but deceptive example of how easy rose breeding might appear.

It is a compliment to my teacher and predecessor, William Ernest Harkness, that Norman selected him to distribute his roses; because, knowing Norman, I am sure he gave it much thought. I am told the approach was a request to try the seedlings and to introduce any of sufficient merit, coupled with a proposal to name one of them W. E. Harkness. I understand they arrived on our nursery in Hitchin in 1943. At that time we grew more vegetables than roses, for during the war it was the rule that 90 per cent of ornamental horticulture must cease, but a tenth could continue to preserve stock for the peaceful future. I was invited to join His Majesty's armed forces, and often thanked heaven I was not at home growing onions, carrots, brussels sprouts and potatoes in our sticky soil, scarcely the happiest medium for market garden crops. To relieve the tedium, our few remaining rose growers used to bud roses on the wild briars in the hedge. Souvenirs of that amusement have only recently become difficult to find.

When Norman's seedlings flowered in 1944, they were like day-dreams come true. Out of that batch came 'Ena Harkness' and 'Frensham', destined to run for some years as Britain's best red Hybrid Tea and Floribunda. Willie Harkness brushed aside the proposal to use his name, and suggested his wife's instead. In fact he was much troubled to exercise the privilege given him, as to which rose to name after her, the Hybrid Tea or the Floribunda? And a few years afterwards, he said to me when we were looking at 'Frensham', that the laugh would be on him if it turned out the better of the two. Norman thought it was. When asked to nominate his 'Masterpiece' for the *Rose Annual 1953,* he put it down as 'Frensham'. He added his thanks to Wilhelm Kordes, without whose 'Crimson Glory' there would have been no 'Frensham', no 'Ena Harkness', nor a great many other roses. That is a very proper tribute; some breeders give one the idea that they did it all by themselves.

'Ena Harkness' was introduced in 1946, the year before 'Peace' in Britain, and it had the kind of success one would expect, remembering the circumstances. The nation was starved of peace and beauty, even denied the habitation of its own homes. We waved in its face the most beautiful red roses ever seen, and the result could be foreseen without any need for a strong prophetic gift.

Over the years we introduced Norman's roses, the most pleasant of relationships was sustained. We learned to love Mrs Norman, who was commemorated in 'Charlotte Elizabeth'. Their daughter had the excellent rose 'Vera Dalton', and a grand-daughter was 'Ann Elizabeth'. William and Ena Harkness travelled often to Normandy, and the Normans to Hitchin. After the rose had run its three years in which royalties were paid to him, Norman set down on paper his pleasure in the business, and presented Ena with a brooch.

We learned that 'Ena Harkness' had her favourite places in the world. I am told that she liked Portland, Oregon even better than Hitchin, Herts. In Tasmania, a rose growing nun may have grown the biggest and best 'Ena Harkness' in the world; apparently Tasmania was real Ena Harknessland, other varieties had no chance. There had been a similar case with the pink 'Dame Edith Helen' in Queensland, where it grew so well that it was confined to special classes in the show of a society there, on the grounds that there was no competition between it and others. I was tempted to include 'Dame Edith Helen' in this list of Hybrid Teas, because it was a superb flower, clear rose pink, full of petals, and as fragrant as any. It came from Alexander Dickson in 1926. But it was of little use to anyone who was not an exhibitor or a Queenslander, because of its reluctance to grow.

I have often thought 'Ena Harkness' was almost the last of a certain type of Hybrid Tea. It inherited so much of the Tea from the late nineteenth century, and was about to encounter the fresh influx of vigour, and may we say loss of refined beauty at the middle of the twentieth. 'Ena Harkness' is not quite vigorous enough, and her flower stalks always have been too weak. Now we have stronger red roses, with brighter leaves, and necks like the Brigade of Guards. But if you can find one of them with a flower one half as good as Ena's in colour and shape, I should be glad to see it.

'Charles Mallerin'   *Medium   Dark red   Remontant*   P6   H1
Francis Meilland paid his old tutor the compliment of naming this dark red rose after him. It was the kind Charles Mallerin might himself have raised, the quality of colour extended to its deepest expression, while the rest of the plant was less admirable. It had a habit of growing straight up on one or two shoots, and the only reason to grow it was for the velvet red flowers that sought to be black. Raised from ('Glory of Rome' × 'Congo') × 'Tassin', and introduced in 1947. The books usually say 1951, which was the date in the United States.

'Spek's Yellow'   *Medium   Yellow   Remontant*   P2   H4
The European name for 'Golden Scepter'. This rose came from Jac Verschuren-

Pechtold, of Haps, Holland. It was bought by Jan Spek, a nurseryman in Boskoop, indeed an exporter, which is a great cachet in Holland, for one cannot start an export nursery there without qualifications. The rose was introduced in Europe as 'Spek's Yellow' in 1948, and in the United States as 'Golden Scepter' in 1950. The seed parent was 'Geheimrat Duisberg', otherwise known as 'Golden Rapture'. Surely a tendency to have one's name changed cannot be hereditary?

This rose is brilliant yellow. It is an ugly, leggy grower, but a good survivor, for I see many plants doing well after twenty years. The leaves are sparse, and the flower buds too numerous. When it blooms nicely, the colour and form are pleasing.

'Josephine Bruce' *Short Dark red Remontant* P6 H2 **

The British attempt at a blackish red rose, and probably the best of the period, for it is still widely grown. This came from Bees of Chester, a very large nursery engaged not only in roses, but seeds and many other plants. It supplies one of the large chain stores with horticultural produce, and has recently named a rose for this prominent customer, 'Wonder of Woolies'.

'Josephine Bruce' seems to produce its best flowers at the start of the summer. They are not only dark, but large and regularly formed. The ensuing blooms are apt to be ragged, and in the autumn another handsome crop arrives, threatened however by mildew. Lest these factors constitute discouragement, I add that this is the best blackish red rose; the fact is that dark red roses are most difficult to raise. The remarks applied to 'Château de Clos Vougeot' of 1908 hold good for 'Josephine Bruce' in 1949, and today.

The parents of 'Josephine Bruce' are usually given as 'Crimson Glory' × 'Madge Whipp'. I was told this was wrong by Eric Shreeves, who used to be responsible for Bees' rose department. He maintained that it should have read 'Crimson Glory' × 'Jane Thornton'.

Other dark red roses were raised, notably two by Dr W. E. Lammerts. 'Mirandy' was from 'Night' × 'Charlotte Armstrong', introduced 1945; and 'Chrysler Imperial' was from 'Charlotte Armstrong' × 'Mirandy', introduced in 1952.

'Karl Herbst' *Medium Red Remontant* P1 H1

A vigorous red rose, bred from 'Independence' × 'Peace' by Wilhelm Kordes, and introduced in 1950. I remember my reply on being asked whether we should grow it, that a dull red rose with no scent was not likely to be sold. And it certainly proved difficult. It was somewhat ugly except when its flush coincided with hot weather, in which case the blooms were one and all large and shapely. But it never was the rose the ordinary gardener wanted.

For breeders, it was an important variety, for it proved an effective pollen parent. It was said that one could not go wrong by putting its pollen on a yellow variety. All I can say is it never worked for me, but I admit I was late in the field. 'Karl Herbst' was vigorous and healthy, and future rosarians may perhaps point to him as a significant breeding rose.

'Sutter's Gold' *Medium Yellow & pink Remontant* P7 H2 ***

One of the most charming roses I know. The buds deserve the name, being a ruddy golden colour. They open to light yellow, in which pink is mixed, and the perfume is pleasant, like a kind of soap. The stems are smooth, inviting to cut, although it is not a very long lasting flower either in vase or on bush. It flowers early, in magnificent profusion, and is never quite so good the rest of the year, although its blooms are always welcome for their beauty. It grows into a good plant, usually after a slow beginning.

Armstrong Nurseries engaged a man who was to prove one of the world's great hybridists as their Director of Research in 1940. He was Herbert Swim, who followed Dr Lammerts and his 'Charlotte Armstrong' line. 'Sutter's Gold' came from 'Charlotte Armstrong' × 'Signora', and was introduced in 1950. It was named to mark the centenary of the discovery of gold in Sutter's Creek. The miners were 'forty-niners', and Armstrong's had introduced another of Swim's roses in the previous year, the red and yellow 'Forty-niner'.

'First Love' *Medium   Pink   Remontant*   P2   H2   **

One of the most appealing and graceful pink roses ever raised. Its flowers are slim and long, and the petals have points of distinction upon them. The stems are smooth and wiry; you can grasp a full hand of blooms without a scratch. If only it grew a little more freely, it would be nearly the perfect rose.

'First Love' was raised by Herbert C. Swim from 'Charlotte Armstrong' × 'Show Girl', and introduced by Armstrong Nurseries in 1951. Its breeder was born in Stillwater, Oklahoma, in 1906, and after periods at Oklahoma and Iowa State Universities, he spent eleven years gaining experience of nursery work, before accepting Armstrong's appointment. He is a quiet man of mild manners, not very tall, rather short of hair; most courteous, gentle. He believed rose breeders should breed roses to grow where they cannot grow at present, in order that more people should be able to enjoy growing them. His nursery training had made him most keenly aware what the characteristics of a plant must be; this is one aspect of rose breeding which is second nature to a nurseryman, but may have to be learnt at great difficulty by amateurs. Herbert Swim's eye was obviously attracted to roses of good form; the cone of a heart at the centre, the petals lapped evenly and respectfully around it: these things were consistently seen in his roses.

Armstrongs received a succession of wonderful roses from their Director of Research until 1955, when he left them in order to form a partnership with O. L. Weeks. Interruptions rarely favour rose breeders, and if they have to leave their breeding stock behind as being the property of an employer, they must expect a hiatus in production. I wished at the time that Armstrongs had showered honours and gold to keep Herbert Swim. To me there is an element of tragedy in reading two lists of roses, the one raised by Swim as Director of Research for Armstrongs, the other what he and his previous employer accomplished apart. Herbert Swim returned to Armstrongs in 1967.

'Baccara' *Medium + Vermilion Remontant*   P1   H1   *

The famous rose of the flower shops, with scarlet vermilion flowers. Sometimes they seem to be on stems as long as walking sticks. It is a little past its zenith, because it is not considered by the greenhouse men to be sufficiently generous in supplying blooms when they compare it with roses which have been introduced since. This will stop neither the florists nor the public from asking for 'Baccara' for years to come. In fact the breeder has pointed out that all his investment in making the name so famous, and the pleasure the public have in it, ought to be preserved by using Baccara Mark 2, or Baccara 1980 or some such device upon the improved one when he finds it.

'Baccara' needs greenhouse conditions to be worth growing in a cold climate. It is a waste of time to grow it out of doors in Britain, except in some exceptionally well favoured spot. The only good 'Baccara' I ever saw in the open in England were growing between two greenhouses. I have often said that if we had raised it at Hitchin, it would have ended its first year's field trial leading the race to the bonfire by several lengths. Yet this rose may have earned for Meilland even more money than 'Peace' did.

It was raised by Francis Meilland from 'Happiness' × 'Independence', according to the record given, and introduced in 1954. The world of cut roses is quite separate from that of garden roses: the investment is high, the income is at the risk of market prices, which may respond to abundance or scarcity more than to quality. The breeder of a cut flower variety must prove it by growing and marketing it. He must know how it yields, travels and sells. When he can place convincing evidence before the trade, people will begin to plant his rose in their greenhouses. Some years ago I was in Holland in the winter, and watched part of an order for 1,300,000 plants of 'Baccara' being grafted. This was at one nursery, in the evening, when all sorts of people from the village, having finished their ordinary work came to earn some extra money by grafting. I was informed that the royalty payment equalled just under a shilling, which lasted for the life of the plant, an average probably of seven years or a little over. All the same, if I was correctly informed, a royalty of about £60,000 was involved in that contract.

You may have noticed that the roses which come out of a flower shop are not strongly scented. There is a reason for this, as we may see by considering perfume.

Perfume starts in the green parts of the plant, and its ingredients are light from the sun, carbon dioxide from the air, and the plant's own water. The energy is supplied by the sun, which causes the tiny granules of green colouring matter within the plant to move. The substance from which the green granules are made is called chlorophyll, which means green leaf. Movement of itself promotes impulses and a chain of consequences; and the result of this solar energy is to form compounds of water and carbon, known as carbo-hydrates, of which the most important to the plant are starches and sugars. The process is called photosynthesis, which means making things with light.

The carbo-hydrate needed for perfume is a kind of sugar, which is transported from the leaves and other green parts of the plant, via the inside of the bark, up into the petals, while they are still in the bud. Chiefly on the inner side of the petals, the sugary substance undergoes a series of transformations, so rapidly that the precise sequence has been most difficult to trace. It appears that enzymes are first used to ferment it, and then oxygen and water change it into an oily compound of glucose and alcohol. At this stage there is little scent, until more oxygen is brought to bear on the compound, which magically turns into highly scented substances. These are completed and stored near the petal surface. The manufactories are tiny projections upon the surface of the petals called 'papillae', which means 'nipples', and from which the droplets of perfumed plant can readily burst out upon the correct stimulus, then to float in the air.

The workings of the plant's perfumery in making sufficient raw materials in its green parts, conveying them to the petals on schedule, and conducting an intricate laboratory process within a swiftly growing and fragile material are marvellous indeed. The perfumery is only one industry within the green skin of a plant, for also in the making are colours and pollen and ovules, to name but a few, all to be initiated and placed in working order at precise times and places.

From this it will be noted that the petal surface of a fragrant rose is broached by nipples; and the skin of the petal must be elastic to admit of the storage of the perfume as it is manufactured. Such petal surfaces are susceptible of damage; they do not travel; they have a fairly high transpiration rate; they are chemically active. For a cut flower variety, we need a thick skin on the petal, a tough skin, which will take no damage, which will not transpire, bruise, rot, nor be heated with alcohol. Such petals are unlikely to contain any perfume at all.

'La Jolla' *Medium – Pink Remontant* P3 H1
From the commercially important 'Baccara' to a rose which I suppose hardly earned anyone a halfpenny. It is self-indulgence to mention it, but there you are, I cannot be untrue to my great loves. 'La Jolla' is my idea of the perfect Hybrid Tea flower, a substantial bloom well rounded at the base, with the point of the centre high, yet admitting the eye to the folds of the petals. I can imagine Herbert Swim falling in love with this one, the colours so beautifully flushed and creamed together. The only trouble was that every blessed flower leaned down and looked at the soil. O what might have been! It was raised from 'Charlotte Armstrong' × 'Contrast' by Herbert Swim, and introduced in 1954.

'Mojave' *Medium Orange red Remontant* P2 H2 **
One of the best orange Hybrid Teas, so long as one agrees to a lot of red or pink in it. The flowers are rather too thin, but are attractively formed in the bud. The plants are upright, and bloom freely and evenly. As usual with Swim's roses, the stems are smooth and wiry. The name is to suggest the fiery sunsets in the Mojave desert. Raised from 'Charlotte Armstrong' × 'Signora' by Herbert Swim, and introduced in 1954.

'Montezuma' *Medium + Salmon red Remontant* P1 H1 *
A strange and interesting rose. As Armstrong's representatives in Britain, we kept in touch with our fellows in other countries. Wilhelm Kordes wrote of 'Montezuma' that it was the best yet; but he was wrong, we were all wrong about it. One felt it was full of promise, bound to be a mother of a rich future. But precious little has it given.

The plants knew how to grow, indeed few modern varieties are more vigorous, long lived and free flowering. The colour was strange, bright plum red in the bud, changing to rather a dull salmon red as the flower opened, and with a metallic gleam lying in the outside of the petals. Of all the flowers it gave, none would escape white spots of damage wherever the rain drops hit them; and if you thought of cutting them to save them from damage, they would sit in the vase unmoved for days, and then collapse without expanding.

Indeed a strange rose. I still think it has something to give. We have not looked far enough. Raised by Herbert Swim from 'Fandango' × 'Floradora', and introduced in 1955. 'Floradora' was the reason no doubt for 'Montezuma's' individuality, for it was a rose of strange breeding, and pollen parent of 'Queen Elizabeth'.

'Pink Favourite' *Medium Bright pink Remontant* P2 H2 **
The 1950s marked the greatest dominance which American rose breeders had ever known; I have tried to pick out the most significant Hybrid Teas of the decade, and about half of them come from the United States. Perhaps I should add here that the American growers gave us free with their roses the unwanted gift of a virus called rose mosaic, which they knew perfectly well inhabited pretty well their entire stocks. Their view was that it appeared to have no detrimental effects on the roses, and was therefore not worth worrying about; indeed some went so far as to advance

the possibility that it might be beneficial. This mosaic may be recognized as yellow tracery upon the leaves, and it always adopts a symmetrical pattern, and may thereby be identified. It is most likely to be seen in very hot weather; although if it cannot be seen, one should not conclude that it is absent. It lies within, latent, ready to do its stuff when conditions invite, just like countless other organisms which inhabit living bodies, including yours and mine. It lives in the sap of the plant, and may be transmitted by intrusions of the sap, which occur mainly through the bites of insects or the tools of rose growers. The great means of transference in America was through the roots they grew their roses on. In Europe, these were supplied by rootstocks grown from seed, through which mosaic is rarely passed. But in America, they grew them from cuttings, and once the stocks from which cuttings were taken were infected, then every rose granted on them was infected too. After much complaint from Europe, the Americans began some cleaning up, but I don't know that they have much heart in it. Well, when you consider that every plant of 'Queen Elizabeth' most probably has rose mosaic, you can understand their scepticism.

'Pink Favourite' has been kept waiting, and it is an important rose because of its strong and healthy foliage. It shows a breeder (in this case Gordon J. von Abrams of Davis, California) acting in a manner calculated to bring fresh blood into Hybrid Teas. He had a seedling from 'Georg Arends' × 'New Dawn'. Now 'Georg Arends' was a Hybrid Perpetual from 'Frau Karl Druschki' × 'La France', introduced in 1910 by Wilhelm Hinner, whom we have already met as the raiser of 'Pharisäer'. 'New Dawn' is a well-known climbing rose. He put the pollen of that seedling on to 'Juno', and the result was 'Pink Favourite'. We must pause to think of 'Juno'. It was an odd rose from Herbert Swim, the purest and prettiest pink you could wish to see, on a stumpy little plant with lovely shiny leaves. It was difficult to find a rootstock on which it would grow without signs of incompatibility.

'Pink Favourite' is a splendid, healthy rose to grow, and we may hope it will breed some still better. The bright pink flowers are large, but I fear they have missed the ethereal touch of 'Juno'.

'Kordes' Perfecta' *Medium Cream & pink Remontant* P2 H1 **

From a squat and ugly bud, which the more aesthetic gardeners objected to, this rose produces a massive bloom of stately form. It is so beautiful that one has full sympathy with Herr Kordes when he exclaimed 'My perfect rose!' Under similar stimulus many years ago, another discoverer uttered 'Eureka!' 'Perfecta', as it is usually known in Britain, has a creamy flower with pink and red in it, especially at the edges. The cream varies in its degree of yellow, and the pink and red vary in response to the weather. Anyone who wishes to grow a rose of exemplary size and shape should plant 'Perfecta', and although it will respond perfectly well outdoors, it is even more magnificent under glass. One objection to it in the garden is that if a strong wind blows when the flowers are swelling, it can blow them off.

The parents were 'Spek's Yellow' × 'Karl Herbst', and the rose was introduced in Britain in 1957. It was a useful object lesson for the young Sam McGredy, who brought it home from Germany, and enthused so lustily that the British rose trade immediately grew it in great quantity. Sam McGredy said subsequently that it taught him how to sell a new variety. In 1963, Kordes introduced a deeper coloured sport, 'Kordes' Perfecta Superior'.

'Rose Gaujard' *Medium Pink & white Remontant* P1 H1 ***

One of the easiest Hybrid Teas to grow, not that they are a difficult class; this one normally makes a bush of superior proportions, and produces more flowers than most. The blooms are bicoloured, the inside of the petals mostly pink, but white towards the base; and the outside off-white. From the buds, one would think it a well formed rose, but before they open very far, each bloom shows a split centre. This is regarded as a serious defect in a rose bloom at exhibitions, but it is perfectly natural and typical of 'Rose Gaujard'.

In the course of these pages, I have made some references to exhibitors in a mood of amused tolerance, but that is a shallow and unworthy attitude. We should understand both what they have given to the rose, and what they have taken away. Exhibitors are a tiny minority of the rose growing fraternity, and like the yeast in the dough, their contribution is not to be measured by their volume. In effect, they have taken the rose as the subject for a game of skill, and the rose shows are their playing fields. Nearly every rose society in the world owes its inception and continued existence to exhibitors, and much of the dissemination of knowledge of the rose has arisen from their work. Not only is a rose show a competitive game, it is also an exhibition, in which there is an element of sharing with others the beauty that would otherwise be for a few eyes only. Far be it from me to underestimate the pleasures of this game, for I have spent many a day and night playing it myself, with great enjoyment; and with my companions from our nursery, I have seen the Nurserymens' Championship come home more often than anyone else, alive or dead, except for our senior rose grower, Herbert Larman, who joined us in 1927, and retired fifty years later.

We should also see what shows have cost the rose. The great cost is in the exaltation of varieties which have only one virtue, that of a prize winning bloom; and vices everywhere else. It is, I submit, a mockery of rose growing to so exalt them, and thereby commend them to the public. And the remedy clearly lies in the standards by which exhibits are judged. We have in Britain at the moment a wonderful exhibition rose named 'Admiral Rodney', light pink with a suggestion of lilac; very large, very beautiful, sweetly scented, and let me say, not so weakly as some I could mention. Now suppose a plate-sized flower of 'Admiral Rodney' should be shown, with its perfect heart, and against it poor little 'Rose Gaujard' with its split centre: the judges will think they had an easy task, as they stick the First Prize ticket on 'Admiral Rodney', and we will admit they have chosen the more beautiful flower. But let them think again. The one is naturally large, the other naturally smaller. The comparison should not be between those two blooms, but between each and what is usual for its variety. It may then be thought that the huge 'Admiral Rodney' is in reality only normal, and the smaller 'Rose Gaujard' actually unusually big for that rose. Then, on size, 'Rose Gaujard' ought to win. Consider the shape of each flower: if the straight heart and the split heart are each typical, then one cannot be better than the other, except in relation to what is typical of the relevant variety. The rules for judging everywhere condemn split centres in exhibition roses, and I really do not know why, apart from it having been accepted from the past as an ideal. I agree that the straight centre is more beautiful; but it is not 'Rose Gaujard'; and in this instance we are exhibiting that rose as it truly exists. In some old roses, the hearts are quartered or incurved, and delightful to see. In modern roses, a preconceived standard is set up as a barrier to such developments.

Similar comparisons apply to the other qualities for which roses are judged at shows, of which the most important are the colour and the freshness. One cannot blame the exhibitors for playing their game to win, but I think the game would be much better for the rose if its rules were such that there was no longer a division between 'exhibition' and 'garden' roses.

'Rose Gaujard' was introduced in 1957, and came from Jean Gaujard, the successor to Pernet-Ducher. It was raised from the seed of 'Peace', fertilized by a seedling of 'Opera'; M. Gaujard stated that the breeding line which led him to 'Opera' was a continuation of work he inherited from Joseph Pernet-Ducher and in which 'Austrian Copper' was involved.

'Wendy Cussons' *Medium + Carmine Remontant* P6 H2 *****
I first saw this rose some years before its introduction in 1959, because its raiser, Walter Gregory, let us have it on trial. When we saw how strong and clean its growth was, how well formed the flowers, and when we discovered its pleasant scent, we immediately advised him that we would be more than delighted to have a licence to grow it. This involved giving it a complete absolution for its colour, something between light red when young and deep pink when open, and considered unpopular. When the rose was introduced it won the highest British award, the President's International Trophy, and elicited a comment from another and more famous breeder that he regularly pulled out any seedling of that colour and threw it away.

Now, about twenty years later, I have not changed my mind at all. It is my idea of the perfect rose for England, and I doubt whether any more reliable Hybrid Tea for our country has been bred in modern times. Mr Gregory is a practical rose grower who is modest about his breeding, and has never adopted any posture of doing it as a research or a mission in life. His attitude was very simple. He liked to introduce new roses in the way of his rose growing business, and thought he might have a shot at raising his own. He therefore planted up a greenhouse with reliable roses, and fertilized them with the pollen of others of similar character, without going to the uneconomic bother of recording and labelling his crosses. When he visits other breeders he surveys their work in wonder, with every expression of respect for their expertise, which he makes no claim to share. In 1971 he received the Queen Mary Medal of the Royal National Rose Society, their award to outstanding British rose breeders. And his response to it appeared to be compounded half of gratitude and half of surprise.

Hence he was never quite sure of the parentage of 'Wendy Cussons', and in response to repeated requests did his best to reconstruct it. It is usually quoted as 'Independence' × 'Eden Rose'; when we were sharing the back of a car on a journey in Holland, I quizzed him about it at length, and he frankly said it could as easily have been something different. At any rate, it is a splendid rose, and its birth a tribute to the practical common sense of one of the most shrewd and kindly of British rose nurserymen.

'Piccadilly' *Medium − Red & yellow Remontant* P2 H2 ***
This is the masterpiece in red and yellow; a typical bicoloured Hybrid Tea, in which the red is on the inside of the petal, the yellow on the outside. It may be held that this is the archetypal Hybrid Tea colour, for Joseph Pernet-Ducher's original seedling from 'Antoine Ducher' × *R. foetida persiana* was pink and yellow. The prototype of 'Piccadilly' and its kind was 'Juliet', from Wm Paul & Son in 1910; and among others through the years had been 'The Queen Alexandra Rose' from McGredy in 1918, 'Condesa de Sastago' from Pedro Dot in 1930, 'Gay Crusader' from Herbert Robinson in 1948 and 'Tzigane' from Meilland in 1951.

'Piccadilly' was raised by Sam McGredy from 'McGredy's Yellow' × 'Karl Herbst' and introduced in 1960. It immediately became popular, for its bright colours and attractive bedding habit. One of the earliest Hybrid Teas to bloom, it is notable both for its freedom of flower, and for the number of sports it has given; but most of them are minor variations.

When 'Piccadilly' came before the National Rose Society's judges, it was in competition with another rose named after a place in London, namely 'Westminster'. The two as shown were similar in colour, and the Gold Medal went to Herbert Robinson's 'Westminster'; we may say the judges met their Waterloo on that occasion, and their mistake reinforced the decision to transfer all the judging of new roses to the Trial Ground two years later.

'Super Star'   *Medium* +   *Coral orange*   *Remontant*   P2   H2   *

Most people would agree that this was the finest rose introduced in the 1960s. Its colour was a revelation, a vermilion kind of coral inside the petals, the outside similar, but touched with salmon pink. It introduces to us a remarkable German, Mathias Tantau, whose successes in the 1960s were almost as overwhelming to his competitors as had been Pernet-Ducher's fifty years previously.

Herr Tantau is rarely seen in those meetings, exhibitions, conferences and trial grounds which can so easily seduce rose growers from their premises in the summer months. He prefers to stay at home and breed roses the world cannot ignore. I visited him only once, some years ago, when he received four of us from Britain with every courtesy. The order on his nursery astonished me. I never saw one so clean and tidy. As he was escorting us from one of his greenhouses, he stepped back, and stared at the ground as if a serpent was in his path. Following his line of vision, I saw that he had been affronted by a small piece of string some employee had dropped there. I fear we in Britain were happy-go-lucky in comparison.

The origin of 'Super Star' is not exactly clear. Mathias Tantau does not publish all the parents of his roses. He has said that the strain which led to 'Super Star' began in 1937 from experiments with *R. multibracteata.* If so, it has caught that rose's habit of flowering late, for it is noticeable that 'Super Star' is one of the last Hybrid Teas to show a flower. Another statement from Tantau, made verbally I believe, was that 'Super Star' was ten generations away from the first admission of *R. multibracteata.* The parentage given is (Seedling × 'Peace') × (Seedling × 'Alpine Glow'), and that leaves out all the interesting bits about *R. multibracteata.* However, it starts a surprising line of thought, which one would have thought even more worthy of mention, for 'Alpine Glow' is supposed to have been born of three roses, all of which had *R. roxburghii* as pollen parent. Obviously that cannot be so; the parentage quoted is either wrong, or else given in the form of a short cut. So even as with 'Peace', we are in doubt as to the origin of this, its great successor.

'Super Star' was introduced in 1960 in Britain, and in 1962 in the United States. Harry Wheatcroft made a great job of it in London. The first time it was shown, the name had not been agreed, and he exhibited it under the label 'The Great Unnamed Seedling'. It looked great, and everyone wanted it. But they did not all get it, the demand was beyond fulfilling. My nursery reduced its order to a thousand eyes for propagation, in order to relieve the pressure on the Wheatcrofts. We were not so pleased to receive them weeks after propagation was finished, and in such quality as to yield a poor quarter of the plants we had expected. British rose nurseries then turned to the cut flower markets, for 'Super Star' was being grown on the Continent for that purpose; and they stocked up with all the 'Super Star' they wanted by buying bunches of roses from Covent Garden.

Harry Wheatcroft secured the rights to introduce into Britain four out of the five most successful garden roses of the past thirty-five years: 'Peace', 'Queen Elizabeth',

'Super Star' and 'Fragrant Cloud'. I would say the other was 'Ena Harkness'. It sounds easy enough to tie them up with the breeders in France, or Germany or the United States; but that is not the whole of it. You have to recognize them before anyone else from your country does so. It required more than entrepreneurial skills, it needed energy and good rose judgement. Those same qualities were allied in Harry Wheatcroft to abounding optimism and a strongly competitive spirit. He would therefore concentrate on stocking up Wheatcrofts to secure a head lead over his rivals, whom he saw no sense in feeding. They, on their part, were perfectly willing to pay a proper price for being fed, and when they considered their supplies inadequate, they immediately fended for themselves. No Plant Breeders' Rights were in force, and a race for new roses developed, the Dutch leading it. It is a fact that out of the four wonderful varieties I have quoted, I myself was obliged to furnish my firm's stock of three of them by methods other than that I should have preferred, namely a straightforward purchase or licence from Wheatcrofts. We did not harbour any grudge about it. Our relations were not like that; Harry Wheatcroft was an attractive man, with a personality that crackled; he would wipe away small minded things and substitute his present excitements for them. If he thought about it at all, he probably took credit for teaching us all to stand on our own feet. I loved his own comment about his world wide travels in search of new roses: 'Full many a flower is born to blush unseen, and waste its sweetness on the desert air, but not if I can help it.'

In the United States, the Jackson & Perkins Company decided to change the rose's name to 'Tropicana'. I am told that this was in consideration of the fact that one of their main rivals, the Conard-Pyle Company, traded their plants as 'Star Roses'; and it seemed over-generous to present them with 'Super Star'. Maybe they foresaw an argument about proprietorial rights in the name.

'Super Star' marked a climax in the use of the rose as a garden plant. Since 1945, and more in Britain than anywhere else, the population had been planting roses with the profligacy of Roman Emperors. In one year the British Rose Trade was propagating enough roses to plant a ring of them all the way round the equator, were planting conditions more suitable in those parts. It is almost incredible that the gardens of the British Isles could hold the roses produced year after year; remembering that some roses live longer than their owners. Like all statistics, there is a trick in that one, because all that were propagated were not eventually planted; but the likeness illumines the facts like a floodlight. The rose had leaped from Victorian obscurity to become the chief ornament of suburbia. And it was noticeable that persons of sensitive taste were beginning to turn away from Hybrid Teas and Floribundas. They were surfeited.

Along with that feeling came the presence of diseases. There is nothing new about rose diseases, but there was something new about their breeding grounds. The three main diseases are fungi, which live mainly on rose leaves. Mildew is a familiar grey mould; blackspot is a descriptive title which ought to make recognition fairly sure; rust, the least obvious but most damaging, may first be seen on the lower leaves of the plant. It grows on their underside as groups of orange red pustules, which later turn black. A sign of it on the upper surface of the leaf is small yellow dots.

The reproductive powers granted to these fungi are beyond belief. Their equivalent to seeds is spores, which being very light are easily airborne. I do not know how many spores might be produced in a year on one plant which was host to all three of these fungi; but I should not be surprised if it is some millions. It therefore follows that the reserves of spores in the atmosphere of the British Isles could reach the sort of figures astronomers deal in; their hosts had been planted in multitudes. Moreover, that same atmosphere had changed. Where before it had been sulphurous, the British Parliament had for once done something sensible, and enforced a Clean Air Act. The sulphur had been a free fungicide to rose growers, and death to the fungi, which could now float over Britain with impunity.

Rosarians who had never seen any need to spray a rose in their lives now had to do it. I can quote from experience here. The first time in my career that my firm sprayed their roses was in 1951 or 1952, I am not sure which. I know that in the autumn of 1950 I noticed some black spots, and took one to our oldest hand, Ernest Barker, who then had forty-eight years service with us. He looked at it, shrugged his shoulders and said 'I shouldn't think that's anything to worry about'. I was as ignorant myself, but not for much longer. Just think of it, growing all those plants, year after year, and never even knowing what diseases looked like!

Noting the popularity of roses, which was far in excess of any plant in Britain, except possibly grass, the chemical companies turned their attention to curing their diseases. This, I should say, they have done with great success; but cure is not prevention. It was natural that in order to sell their products, the chemical companies advertised; and because they were selling to rosarians, they chiefly featured pictures of diseased roses in their advertisements. This, of course, was a self-defeating manoeuvre, because it discouraged people from planting roses.

Suburbia discovered that the plants it had set for a lifetime of no more trouble now required the expense and the work of spraying. And this was not received kindly at all; the great incentives to plant roses had been economy and convenience. Both quivered at the need to spray.

One might say that only healthy varieties should be grown, and in general such will be found marked with four or five stars in this book. But it is not a complete answer. Diseases appear to change, or at least to have different forms, like the flu viruses which cross the world. A variety may start life healthy, and attract a disease later. 'Super Star' itself is an example of this, for after several years of growing to the general wonder and delight, it has now become susceptible to mildew.

The position at present is that the rose has lost some of its universal appeal; and this may not be a bad thing. People who grow roses must be prepared to spray them, and the roses they grow will be more beautiful than any previous age has known. There are a few roses which need no spraying, but not many. An ecological change has taken place; the air has been cleaned, and we have a race of roses which suffer thereby, a fact one did not foresee. The breeders are the people who must change the roses to suit the new conditions, and without doubt they will succeed in time. That is an example of their office and of their importance.

When I realized these trends, about 1967, I concentrated my energies almost exclusively upon the breeding department of our own business. But it was obvious to me that the task required some co-ordination between breeders, if it was to be achieved with sufficient speed to produce 'no spray' roses before the public turned to other plants. I was therefore delighted when Sam McGredy told me, shortly before he went to New Zealand, that he would welcome co-operation with other breeders in Britain. Even better was a letter from Pat Dickson, upon which he and I conferred with Alec Cocker for a few days in Alec's home in Aberdeen. The result of that conference was the British Association of Rose Breeders, familiarly known as BARB. Its members now include nearly all the most famous breeders, not only in Britain but abroad.

I certainly hoped that BARB should promptly be able to start co-operative breeding of 'no spray' roses, and one of our first acts was to take scientific advice, and recruit assistance on this subject. But I had reckoned without the feelings of the rose nurserymen who are licensees of the breeders. Nearly all of them came into BARB with a sense of relief, because now they had one licence instead of many different ones, and they could see that a properly constituted association gave them greater assurance of fair treatment. But we had some objectors, and much of our initial energy was diverted into defending our being. Next, we had the problem of nurseries who were determined to grow new roses without paying any commission, or by paying less than they should. This may appear short sighted, for on those funds depends their own future; but it is a fact that evasion has robbed us of time and money we ought to have spent on research. One has to see it from the viewpoint of those growers; they are independent of spirit, they are not convinced of the ethics of rights being held in plant varieties, and there is a long tradition that anything that grows should be as free as air. The last thing BARB wants is to spend its time maintaining its members' rights, but such a situation has been forced upon us, because if Tom can get away with it, Dick and Harry will justly complain of unfair competition. I have been secretary of BARB since its foundation on 6 April 1973, and I am very proud of the work that has been done, both for its volume, and its usefulness. It rests upon voluntary work by busy men, of whom Pat Dickson, John Mattock, Roger Pawsey of Cants, and Michael O'Dell of the Meilland organization have been outstanding.

'Mischief' *Medium Pink Remontant* P4 H2 ***

We must turn back from BARB and the present day, to remember one of Sam McGredy's great successes in the years when everything in the rose garden was lovely. He bred 'Mischief' from 'Peace' × 'Spartan', and introduced it in 1961. It can be the most beautiful of roses when the bushes are full of expanding blooms; the regular form of the flowers is apparently repeated in every single one of them, a marvellous sight. The colour is salmon pink, without much of the red one associates with salmon. In the autumn it looks like another variety, due to an increase in orange. The story goes that when Sam was staging it at a show, Major-General Frank Naylor asked what he was calling it. Sam told him it had no name. 'Why don't you call it Mischief?' says the General. Later on, after Sam had accepted that suggestion, he discovered he had named it after the General's dog. Frank Naylor was one of Britain's most enthusiastic amateur rosarians, the only one in the last thirty years to serve for two terms as President of the National Rose Society.

'Dr A. J. Verhage' *Short Yellow Remontant* P5 H3 ***

This is not a great garden rose, but it is one of the most rewarding to grow under glass, and it is more than useful as a parent. The colour is not plain yellow, but a rich yellow with the slightest suggestion of bronze. The form of the flowers, and the scent cannot fail to please. It was raised by G. Verbeek & Zn. of Aalsmeer, Holland, a breeder whose speciality is roses for growers of cut flowers; of that trade Aalsmeer is an important centre, a small Dutch town in which there are more roses in greenhouses than in the whole of Britain. Verbeek's 'Ilona' is at present a popular red variety.

'Dr A. J. Verhage' was raised from 'Tawny Gold' × ('Baccara' × seedling) and introduced in 1962. It is also known as 'Golden Wave'.

'Fragrant Cloud' *Medium – Red Remontant* P9 H2 ***

The name is translated from its original German name, 'Duftwolke'. The French call it 'Nuage Parfumé'. It was raised by Mathias Tantau from Seedling × 'Prima

Ballerina', and introduced in 1963. For some years it was the most popular rose in Britain according to the number sold, and that must show how fragrance is esteemed, because the colour is not remarkable. It starts scarlet, but no sooner is it open than the clouds of dullness overshadow it, and it ends its life with a touch of purple far from royal. If you wonder why it was so popular, well so do I. Its moments of youthful glory were apparently sufficient to redeem it.

'Pascali' *Medium White Remontant* P2 H2 *****
Some psychologist might do worse than transfer his attention from sex, and enquire into the healing properties of flowers in the home. I am sure they soothe man's spirit, and quietly direct his mind to the betterment of life. What influence might they exert upon children? It is not just for gaudy gardens that we rose growers practise our profession.

Much as I admire the meticulous lines and cunning marriages of colour achieved by expert flower arrangers, I prefer the flowers in my house to be arranged without art, as if a little bit of nature had jumped off its bush and into the vase without pausing to dress itself. Roses can easily satisfy both the floral expert and myself and 'Pascali' is one of the best to do this. It is a slim and graceful white rose, with a lovely cone for its heart, which it holds in good shape longer than most. It was raised by Louis Lens of Wavre-Notre-Dame, Belgium from 'Queen Elizabeth' × 'White Butterfly', and introduced in 1963. In spite of its name, 'White Butterfly' is not a sport from 'Mme Butterfly', but a seedling of 'Ophelia' × 'Curly White'. The latter rose was raised by Frank Spanbauer, a greenhouse rose nurseryman from Decatur, Illinois. When he produced 'White Butterfly' from it, he discontinued 'Curly White' as having been clearly superseded. His contribution towards 'Pascali' may be rewarded by the eclipse of his 'White Butterfly', good as that rose is. That is the best of back handed compliments to a breeder.

'Blue Moon' *Medium Lilac pink Remontant* P7 H2 **
Well-meaning people, charged with the social duty of igniting conversation with a rosarian, normally infuriate him by asking when he will produce either a black or a blue rose, neither of which, they hasten to add, they would be seen dead with. We can forget about black roses after one quick vision of a black climber draping the walls of Dracula's castle; along of which the well-meaning persons would undoubtedly be dead. But blue roses remain an intriguing possibility. Blue flowers are beautiful, and there is every reason to suppose that a blue rose would share that beauty. The colour of roses is made by the chemical works of the plant, and although at present the ingredients necessary to form blue are not part of the rose's chemistry, it is not beyond possibility that they may be acquired. A very small interior change can cause a revolutionary outward one. It may come in an unexpected way. I have raised many thousands of seedlings which I thought might improve the lilac pink and purple colours in roses, but I have to confess I am baffled to know how to proceed to make them more blue than they are.

The generative atoms (or genes) which govern colour are responsible for some of the plant's most intricate work. Colour in roses is made chiefly of sugar, which is brought under the influence of complex chemical substances within the plant called enzymes, a word which means fermenters. Enzymes ferment other materials, and in this case they alter the sugar until a compound which will be the colour directed by the gene is obtained. This is not done all in one step, but by a series of reactions, in each of which an enzyme is employed, until the dye is mixed to its proper hue.

Only the surfaces of the petal are coloured, as may be tested by tearing a red petal, and seeing its white interior. The process is beautiful in its placing and timing, being complete on schedule when the petals expand.

All the so-called blue roses are in truth failed reds or pinks. We are kidding ourselves they are blue, just like the early rosarians thought 'Mme Ravary' was yellow. Some of these colours can be quite pleasant, especially if yellow stamens enliven them, but the fairest description of them is some word such as 'different', or 'interesting'. Either of these fit 'Blue Moon', the best Hybrid Tea of this type. It has also the advantage of being exceptionally fragrant. For the best view of it, grow it under glass.

It was raised by Mathias Tantau from seedlings of his own, in which no doubt he had incorporated the lilac pink roses of other breeders, and almost certainly including 'Sterling Silver'. It was introduced in 1964. The original German name is 'Mainzer Fastnacht', and in France it is 'Sissi'.

'Grandpa Dickson' *Medium − Yellow Remontant* P3 H1 ****
A good yellow rose, with quite a lot of red flushes as the flowers open, especially in hot weather. It is not the most lusty of growers, but it does provide flowers of exceptional quality. Although it is primarily a garden rose, anyone with a greenhouse would be rewarded by blooms of exceptional beauty by taking a few plants of 'Grandpa' inside. The colour is fairly light, with a suggestion of lime.

This is one of Pat Dickson's most successful Hybrid Teas, and won him the President's International Trophy. It was raised from ('Kordes' Perfecta' × 'Governador Braga da Cruz') × 'Piccadilly', and introduced in 1966. The name was changed in the United States to 'Irish Gold'.

'Red Devil' *Tall Light red Remontant* P5 H2 *****
The perfect exhibition rose, because it grows with great vigour, and gives the most inexpert gardener the opportunity to grow flowers as good as those which win prizes. Expect it to match 'Peace' as a plant, if not to outgrow it. 'Red Devil' is a superb variety, almost a shrub, an asset to any gardener whose heart leaps when he sees a wonderful flower he has grown himself. The colour is perhaps a little disappointing, because we always like our reds to be dark. If all exhibition varieties were also garden roses as great as this, my previous strictures on the subject, inserted under 'Rose Gaujard's' name, would be pointless.

Raised by Pat Dickson from 'Silver Lining' × a seedling from a 'Prima Ballerina' line; it was introduced in 1967. In France it goes under the name 'Coeur d'Amour', a marked reformation of a 'Red Devil'.

'Whisky Mac' *Medium − Apricot Remontant* P7 H2 *
A triumph of colour over common sense, because the popular 'Whisky Mac' is quite frankly an unreliable grower with poor foliage, and plenty of mildew. After its maiden year it is somewhat stingy with its blooms. The flowers are so beautiful in their apricot yellow colour, their form and their scent, that the penalties of the plant are counted a light cost. It is the sort of rose whose flower hangs in the memory so sweetly that one looks lovingly at the empty bush. It may prove a useful parent if anyone succeeds in divorcing its beauty from its weaknesses.

Raised by Mathias Tantau, and introduced in 1967. Unfortunately we do not know the parentage which led to this valuable colour.

'Elizabeth Harkness'   *Medium   Ivory   Remontant*   P4   H2   ****
The nearer we approach the present day, the more difficult it becomes to distinguish
the momentous roses from the ephemeral. History has sorted them out for me so far,
but now I have to guess what history will do next; and I must be wary of supposing my
own varieties are entitled to a high place.

'Elizabeth Harkness' shows that a rose can be supremely beautiful with a slightly
unconventional flower form. Her central petals at the heart are a little shorter than
the outer petals, whereas fashion decrees they should be as long, if not longer. She
confounds this criticism by two tricks, of spreading the outer petals into an
uncommonly wide circle, and of blushing innocently on the tips at the centre. This
blush on the ivory or slightly buff paleness of the flower is charming. She has a
pleasant scent to reinforce her good looks. Like most pale roses, she needs
reasonably dry weather.

Two more of her virtues are those of flowering early, and producing (like
'Mischief') nearly every flower to a high degree of perfection. She annoyed me
considerably at the Trial Ground by reaching her perfection before the visits of the
judges were scheduled. I treasure two comments among many: the catalogue of Fred
Edmunds in Wilsonville, Oregon referred to her 'haunting beauty'. And Margaret
Powell, in *The Rose Annual 1973*, looking for paler coloured Hybrid Teas, because
when she got home from work in the evenings they looked so well, took 'Elizabeth
Harkness' as her top favourite: 'An aggressively healthy bush, that will produce
simultaneously twelve to fifteen blooms eight inches in diameter, is quite hard for
other varieties to compete with.' (For our metric readers, eight inches is twenty
centimetres.)

I raised Elizabeth from 'Red Dandy' × 'Piccadilly', which may indicate that the
result was not the target; and introduced it in 1969. It is named after my daughter,
and by a delightful coincidence *Amateur Gardening* issued a glamorous front cover of
'Elizabeth Harkness', bearing the date of her wedding day.

'Alec's Red'   *Medium   Crimson   Remontant*   P9   H2   ***
By the year 1970, the best red roses of former years were looking out of date, partly
from deterioration, partly because the vigour of the newer varieties had outstripped
them; for which 'Peace' was in the main responsible. Since 'Ena Harkness' in 1946,
only one deep crimson Hybrid Tea had impressed gardeners in Britain, 'Ernest H.
Morse' from Kordes in 1964. And that variety was more likely to be marked
meritorious than superb. The year 1970 brought three of note, 'Alec's Red', 'John
Waterer' and 'National Trust'.

'Alec's Red' has a large, globular flower of many petals and rich scent. It was
obvious upon trial in our nursery that it excelled the other red roses we then had, in
growth, size, perfume and in holding its colour in the old flowers. I could have wished
it had a deeper and richer colour to hold. I will not forget those trials in a hurry, for
when we had only a few plants of 'Alec's Red', the soil around them was compressed
to a smooth, hard surface by the feet of the rose nurserymen who clustered around it.
The raiser, Alexander Cocker of Aberdeen, allowed several growers to have it on
trial, and while he was wondering what attractive name to bestow on the rose, they
called it 'Alec's Red' and the name stuck. It became very popular in Britain, and won
the Royal National Rose Society's premier awards for merit and fragrance.

It was raised from 'Fragrant Cloud' × 'Dame de Coeur', and introduced in 1970.
Subsequently Mr Cocker repeated that cross in greater quantity, but whereas his first

trial of it had yielded about fifteen seedlings of promise, the second and much larger endeavour produced nothing of merit at all.

'John Waterer' *Medium + Deep crimson   Remontant* P2 H1 **
A deep crimson rose of upright growth. The colour is usually marked, but not spoilt, by going black towards the edges, really a collapse of the crimson in the sun. If the deep colour of 'John Waterer' and the scent of 'Alec's Red' could come together, we should have a red rose indeed. Raised by Sam McGredy from 'King of Hearts' × 'Hanne'. Introduced 1970.

'National Trust' *Short   Bright crimson   Remontant* P2 H2 ***
The third of the fine red roses of 1970, very brilliant, but with little scent. It is a sparkling red rose for the front of the border, or where a fairly short grower is required. The foliage is bright and clean. Raised by Sam McGredy from 'Evelyn Fison' × 'King of Hearts'. In Germany it is named 'Bad Nauheim'.

'Alexander' *Tall   Vermilion   Remontant* P3 H3 ****
The colour of 'Super Star' had appeared to be something quite new in 1960, and in 1972 it was taken some stages further by 'Alexander'. The difference can best be appreciated by setting a flower of each rose side by side, when the luminous vermilion of 'Alexander' reveals how much pink underlies 'Super Star'. Probably some influence from the yellow pollen parent contributes to 'Alexander's' brilliance. It was bred from 'Super Star' × ('Ann Elizabeth' × 'Allgold').

'Alexander' is a tall and vigorous plant, with gleaming dark leaves and long flower stems. It can grow as a stalwart hedge, provided it is pruned each year; and will bear most of its flowers about chest high in the British climate. The flowers are well formed, but not of such substance as those of 'Super Star'. They open from an attractive bud form into wide blooms of about twenty-two petals. Sometimes the petals have scalloped edges, and always the flowers gleam in the sun in quite astonishing brilliance.

I named this rose in memory of Earl Alexander of Tunis, who was the outstanding British General of the Second World War. He had been Honorary Colonel of the 3/2 Punjab Regiment, in which I spent most of my six years in the Army. The idea came to me when Major-General Naylor took me to see Alexander's grave in his church at Ridge in Hertfordshire, and it was enthusiastically supported by my old friends in the Regiment.

'Just Joey' *Medium −   Coppery buff   Remontant* P3 H2 ***
I find it impossible to choose two words that tell this rose's colour. And I fear that a longer description will only cloud your understanding of it. It is unique among roses, rich coppery orange; but areas of the petals are unreached by that gorgeous colour, being left light, and buff pink. It was raised by Roger Pawsey of Cants of Colchester, one of Britain's famous and most respected names in roses. The parents were 'Fragrant Cloud' × 'Dr A. J. Verhage'. Introduced in 1972, 'Just Joey' bears its name in affectionate reference to the breeder's wife.

In growth, 'Just Joey' is not typical of modern Hybrid Teas; it lacks the normal height and heavy foliage, and resembles a rose of 'Ena Harkness' vintage. It may need more favourable treatment than most other roses of the 1970s, and in return will give flowers which attract attention no matter what competitors may blossom around it.

'Sonia Meilland'   *Medium   Rosy salmon   Remontant*   P2   H2   *****
Known in Britain as 'Sweet Promise' and in the cut flower markets of the world as
'Sonia'.

This is a highly successful rose for the growers of cut blooms, but it is also one of the
finest garden roses for cutting. It needs a good British summer, which suggests that in
warmer countries it will be even better than with us. A rose for the flower markets
must produce plenty of flowers to sell, and in this respect 'Sonia' is superb. The long,
smooth stems are topped by an elegant bloom on the salmon side of pink. If you buy a
Hybrid Tea in that colour from a flower shop, it is most likely 'Sonia'. It was bred by
Alain Meilland, the son of Francis, and introduced in 1973, bearing his daughter's
name.

This rose had the dubious honour of being the subject of a case in a court at
Cambridge, where the British Plant Variety Rights Office proceeded against a
grower for selling it as 'Sonia' instead of 'Sweet Promise'. Under the latter name it
holds a grant of Plant Breeders' Rights. The offender was fined £20. This introduces
us to the difficulties of rose names, and I cannot explain it more clearly than quoting
an article I wrote for the *Rose Annual 1977:*

The idea of having one name for each type of plant was put into practice in the
eighteenth century by Linnaeus, who promptly got two names himself in the
process, for his native name was Carl von Linné.

An example of the fruit of his labours is that no matter what people might call
the Dog Rose in their own language, they can speak to one another with
certainty about it across their borders by using the words *Rosa canina.* Thus
students of nature were better able to comprehend one another, and to identify
the strange plants which they so gladly welcomed from the awakening trade
routes of the world in those days.

And the system left to ordinary people the full use of some of the most
beautiful words in their languages, such as daffodil, daisy and dandelion.

Some years after Linnaeus, it was suggested that his successful identification
of wild plants should also be applied to cultivated varieties in some degree; it
took 106 years for those suggestions to mature, which they did in 1953, as an
International Code of Nomenclature for Cultivated Plants.

The International Code, in the minds of its devisers, was intended to clean
away confusion like a windscreen wiper, so that varieties with several names
would henceforth have one, a great gain in clarity of understanding. One variety,
one name, was in effect principle number one. And it entirely missed the point of
Linnaeus' work, that he had left all the common names in natural use.

Unlike the swamps of legislation issued by governments, the International
Code had no force of law, though I daresay it was no more faulty than the
average Act, and would have done less harm than many. The American Rose
Society promised to preside over the regulation of rose names, and was
appointed the International Rose Registration Authority; other Societies, such
as our own, fed it with applications from their home territories, and accepted its
decisions as morally worthy of support. Indeed one might note that great efforts
were made to achieve the ideal of one rose, one name, and the Australians and
New Zealanders tried harder than anyone, perhaps because they were prime
victims, and a little tired of buying from British or American catalogues
gorgeous new roses which they had actually got in their gardens already.

In human affairs, the truth is what happens, and I found it in an American catalogue in 1975. That catalogue contained twenty European roses, all with names different from their originals, and I had to admit that even with the benefit of professional experience, coloured pictures and expressive descriptions, I was quite ignorant of the European identity of fourteen of those roses. I began to wonder how far from the ideal we were, and examined the Rose Analysis in the current *Rose Annual*.

Out of the forty-eight most popular Hybrid Teas and Floribundas, I knew twelve had more than one name, an impressive 25 per cent. I heard a report of an American store, which was unwittingly selling the same rose under three different names. I studied French and German catalogues, and realized that beside them the Americans were strict conformists. I was obliged to conclude that the ideal of one rose one name was not a reality of life, and no convincing evidence was found from the past, present or conjectured future to make it so.

Why not? We took that question to a BARB meeting, and a discussion revealed three main reasons, linguistic, social and commercial.

Linguistic, because people fight shy of trying to use unfamiliar tongues. The German names were especially singled out as unpopular in France and the USA, because their unfamiliarity bred feelings of inferiority, putting customers off the rose.

Social, because roses are a source of pleasure. To ordinary people in most societies, the pleasure is enhanced by a familiar, happy name; especially if it has some significance in regard to the variety. Such people are, after all, those whom the industry exists to serve.

Commercial, because if the industry is to survive to carry out its services, it needs to sell the best varieties in such a manner as will result in their being bought. The almost universal opinion of nurserymen internationally, to the best of our belief, is that a name which appeals to the customer is essential. For the breeder, this means that unless he defers to that opinion, and allows nurserymen in various countries to alter his rose names to local requirements, he will forgo any hope of earning royalties from them, with in consequence a disastrous reduction of the funds by which he hopes to continue his research.

These are the facts of the case, and they suggest that we should all grow up to accept facts for what they are, instead of wishing they were different; in which case, of course, they cease to be facts. Nobody could be very pleased about them; not the breeder, for he could lose control of his varieties. Not the nurseryman, for he could import a rose he already had, to the confusion of his customers and the wrath of the Plant Variety Rights Office. Not the gardener, who in his travels sees 'Oregold', and goes blue in the face looking for it at home, where it lurks under another name. Not the Royal National Rose Society, intent on recording the progress of the rose for its members and posterity.

The only people to offer a realistic answer are the French. They have advocated for many years that roses should have a permanent and positive denomination in the form of a code, which stands as the actual variety name; and that so long as the code is always there as a reference, people around the world can use what common names come natural to them.

This French scheme has been scoffed at, long and hard, from our side of the Channel; but in the face of difficulties, including commercial disadvantages, Meilland and others have persisted, with the obstinacy of men who know they are right.

Their codes normally begin with the first three letters of the breeder's name;

thus 'Meipuma' is clearly a Meilland variety (it is 'Scherzo') and 'Korp' comes from Kordes (it is 'Prominent'). All that Meilland asks, is that everyone around the world, when putting 'Scherzo' in his catalogue under that or any other name, prints also the word 'Meipuma'.

Then all the confusion is resolved, and in exactly the same way as Linnaeus did it two centuries ago, by providing an international reference for the students, and leaving the common name to the pleasure of the people.

'Precious Platinum'   *Medium +   Bright crimson   Remontant*   P2   H2   ****
A bold rose in brilliant deep red, vigorous, and generously adorned with glossy leaves. It was raised by Pat Dickson from 'Red Planet' × 'Franklin Englemann', and introduced in 1974. (Note: Englemann is the correct spelling, but the rose was wrongly registered as Engelmann.)

The development of red Hybrid Teas on plants very different from those they had previously inhabited has been Pat Dickson's brilliant contribution to modern roses. Breeders in the past could not separate from the dark red colour, weaknesses of flower stems and leaves; it is assumed that the generative atoms which govern these characters are so closely linked that they have never been separated. Pat Dickson's breeding line was exemplified by 'Red Planet', a rose of handsome growth and glowing crimson, although I always thought its flowers came good too seldom. 'Precious Platinum' shares the family likeness, but with much better flowers. The final hurdles remain, of darker colour and more scent, and if Pat can clear them, he will put us all very deeply in his debt. His present achievements are a great boon, because his red roses up to date are healthy.

'Silver Jubilee'   *Medium −   Pink blend   Remontant*   P2   H1   *****
The Hybrid Tea has had a fairly long life, especially considering the limitations imposed upon it by the beautiful but unnatural form of flower it must bear. Unnatural it is without a doubt, for the reproductive organs are swathed in petals, instead of being open to the air and the insects. Hybrid Teas cannot continue unless breeders invigorate them from time to time from other sources. An early instance of this was Joseph Pernet-Ducher's success with 'Persian Yellow'. Through the Floribundas as they were mated with Hybrid Teas, came something from *R. multiflora*. We have some doubts about *R. foetida bicolor* entering 'Peace', and whether it was *R. roxburghii* or *R. multibracteata* or both which assisted 'Super Star'. We shall see the work of Wilhelm Kordes as we study the Floribundas, for he brought to them the peculiar gifts of his 'Baby Château' and of his work with Sweet Briars, and these have passed into Hybrid Teas. More *R. roxburghii* came with Tantau's 'Floradora'. Finally we have Alec Cocker and his 'Silver Jubilee'.

These efforts, upon which the continuation of Hybrid Teas entirely depend, are not made without much experiment and cost, most of it wasted. Success comes from perseverance with seedlings which you or I might throw away as useless, but in which are hidden the genes of their parents. The breeder hopes these genes will come out of hiding in some future generation.

Alexander Cocker started to breed roses in 1963, and enjoyed his first triumph with 'Alec's Red' only seven years later. He was deeply conscious of the need to breed healthy roses, and he thought of a way to do it, by using some of the climbers which Wilhelm Kordes had bred from *R. kordesii*. With *R. rugosa* and *R. wichuraiana* as parents, *R. kordesii* has a fine promise of foliage upon which fungi do not feed.

Mr Cocker chose a scarlet climber, 'Parkdirektor Riggers', and made it a mother by the pollen of 'Piccadilly'. He was not much interested in the seedlings which were climbers, which one would expect most of them to be, on account of the dominance of the climbing habit over the bush when the two are mated. He was seeking a seedling which was a bush and remontant. He found one, and ugly it was, a dull red flower with thick petals, and the kindest word you could use about its form was crimped. He gave me this fruit of his research for my own use, and when he saw the shocked look I gave it, he impressed upon me its potential value.

That seedling in its turn became a mother, and the pollen came from another of Mr Cocker's seedlings, 'Highlight' × 'Colour Wonder'. The fruit of that union was a blazing scarlet rose with seven petals, nothing like a Hybrid Tea, but handsome in its vigour and glossy foliage, and the picture of health. In due course its pollen went on to 'Mischief', and that was how 'Silver Jubilee' was born.

'Silver Jubilee' has long petals, not too many of them, but they hold together to make a handsome flower. The colour is complex to describe, pink and cream with a dash of the red from a peach skin may give the idea. When Mr Cocker showed it to Her Majesty the Queen Mother at a rose show, she suggested it was a confection of pink, and that is a good description. The plants are compact, with so many leaves they look almost squared off, and the production of flowers is well above average.

In closing our section of Hybrid Teas with this introduction of 1978, I hope we have imitated the writers of serial stories, by leaving off with the stage set for thrilling developments in the next instalment; and with 'Silver Jubilee' one of the likely heroes.

And the sense of transmitting our work to the future is all the more poignant; for a few hours after I laid down my pen on finishing the previous paragraph, my dear friend, the breeder of 'Silver Jubilee', died at his home. God rest you, Alec Cocker.

FLORIBUNDAS

Many wild roses have much smaller flowers than those of the countryside of Europe and North America. Some of them, if one can describe it this way, go in for quantity rather than size, and their small flowers are crammed together in a flowering head, so that if one tries to count how many there are, one will probably lose count and be obliged to start again. Of such are many of the Synstylae, which form the next section of this book, and among them is the prototype of the Floribundas, *R. multiflora*.

From *R. multiflora* came the Polyantha Roses, short growing plants with an abundance of small flowers, very attractive at the time when it was being realized that roses were not only shrubs or providers of cut blooms, but also bedding plants. It was not long before the Polyanthas were crossed with other roses, so that the flowers became larger, and the plants more like members of the Indicae than of the Synstylae. The trick was to enlarge the flowers, without losing their abundance. As we shall see in the ensuing pages, the breeders who were the conjurers-in-chief were a Dane and an American. Poulsen of Denmark introduced 'Else Poulsen' and 'Kirsten Poulsen' in 1924, and established a new class, which the National Rose Society acknowledged in 1932 as Hybrid Polyantha. Boerner of the United States was the most successful, although not the first, of several breeders in turning the plain flowers of the Hybrid Polyanthas into something like small Hybrid Teas. His roses of 1947 and 1949 included 'Goldilocks' and 'Fashion'. American nurserymen, anxious for a more attractive name than Hybrid Polyantha, and aware that the class had undergone a considerable change since 1924, invented the name

Floribunda. As we noticed in the case of the Pernetiana roses nearly forty years before, there were objections to the new name as being botanically unsound. Very sensibly, the Americans took no notice, but started using it, and in 1951 the British followed suit. It soon became obvious that as providers of colour, Floribundas had many advantages over Hybrid Teas. Their heads of bloom occupied a larger area; and because all the buds did not open at once, they were in flower for a longer period. This is particularly useful in bad weather, which can spoil the best blooms of a Hybrid Tea, but cannot affect the unopened buds of a Floribunda, even though it may spoil the open flowers. Moreover, the flowers of a Floribunda weigh less, and on those shoots which grow sideways they can be borne more elegantly than Hybrid Teas; thus the best Floribundas could clothe in bloom not only the top of the plants, but also the sides. A further advantage in favour of the Floribundas was an acceptance of a wide range of flower forms. A Hybrid Tea without its straight, high centre is in the popular view a failed Hybrid Tea; but a Floribunda may be single, semi-double, double, shaped like a rosette or a Hybrid Tea or anything in between, so long as it is beautiful. All we ask of Floribundas, and we have to watch carefully in case it be withheld, is that they grow away at once to flower a second or a third time in the season. Those which flower once, and then wait a long time, are failed Floribundas.

The course of their development may be traced through the archetypal or outstanding varieties as follows.

'Mlle Bertha Ludi'
This rose is now so extinct it is not in *Modern Roses*. However, Jäger's *Rosenlexikon* preserves the record for us. It may be considered the first of the class, being raised by Pernet-Ducher and introduced in 1891. Its parents were 'Mignonette' × 'Jules Margottin', that is a Polyantha and a Hybrid Perpetual. According to Jäger, it was white, flushed carmine rose and blush.

'Gruss an Aachen' *Short Creamy pink Remontant* P3 H1 *
Introduced in 1908, and still grown by a few people, this agreeable little rose has smaller flowers than we expect in a Floribunda. The colour is pale and changeable, light pink soon going towards white. It was raised by Philipp Geduldig of Kohlscheid bei Aachen in Germany. The parents are said to be 'Frau Karl Druschki' × 'Franz Deegen', at first sight an unlikely story. We all know 'Frau Karl Druschki', the snow white Hybrid Perpetual; but 'Franz Deegen' is a stranger. It was a Hybrid Tea, also called 'Yellow Kaiserin Auguste Viktoria', and that parentage would suggest that 'Gruss an Aachen' was the first of many roses which on failing to turn out as Hybrid Teas, were introduced under the umbrella of the Polyantha or Floribunda classes. It still happens, as may be seen from Sanday's 'Sugar Sweet', a Floribunda of 1973 bred from two Hybrid Teas, 'Wendy Cussons' × 'Prima Ballerina'.

'Yvonne Rabier' *Short White Remontant* P5 H1 ***
An excellent white rose, well worth growing today. The flowers are double, rather small, borne close together on compact plants; they have a pleasant scent, and keep on appearing through the season. Try it near the front of a border, or in a little area of a terrace. It was introduced in 1910, and raised from a Wichuraiana and a Polyantha, neither named in the records. The breeder was E. Turbat & Co., of Orléans, France.

'Rödhätte'
Dines Poulsen now enters the story with this important rose, which he introduced in 1912. The name means Red Riding Hood, and probably it was the first rose which we

should take to be a Floribunda. It was semi-double, with light red flowers. The parents were 'Mme Norbert Levavasseur' × 'Richmond'; that is a red Polyantha crossed with a red Hybrid Tea.

Dines Poulsen lived in Kvistgaard, Denmark, and his interest was to breed roses of sufficient hardiness for Scandinavia. The Hybrid Teas were chancy, the Pernetianas even more so. Hence he crossed them with Polyanthas which he knew to be hardy. The Poulsen family is a little confusing, and perhaps we may identify its members as follows.

The firm was begun by Dorus Theus Poulsen as a market garden about 1878. Two of his sons started breeding roses, Dines Poulsen up to about the time of the Great War of 1914–1918, and subsequently Svend Poulsen. It is the latter who was responsible for Else, Kirsten and Karen; his career as a breeder was unusually long, for his 'Rumba' came out in 1969. Svend's son is Niels Dines Poulsen, a large and popular figure among rosarians, who began working with his father, and raised 'Chinatown', 'Troika' (otherwise known as 'Royal Dane') and the valuable red cut flower rose, 'Nordia'.

Their founder accumulated some of his experience in London, and the inspiration of their breeding was probably Peter Lambert of Trier in Germany, for whom Dines Poulsen worked for a period.

'Nathalie Nypels' *Short Pink Remontant* P2 H2 **

This excellent pink rose is one of the best for continuous flower, although its blooms are rather small and thin. It has quite the touch of the China Roses about it, and some people class it with them. The parentage is given as 'Orléans Rose' × ('Comtesse du Cayla' × *R. foetida bicolor*), an interesting amalgamation of Polyantha, China and Austrian Briar. It was raised by M. Leenders & Co of Tegelen, Holland, and introduced in 1919 as 'Mevrouw Nathalie Nypels'.

'Joseph Guy'

Light red, but bright red, this rose came of an extra influx of Hybrid Tea into 'Rödhätte', for the breeder used that rose's own Hybrid Tea parent upon it again, in the cross 'Rödhätte' × 'Richmond'. It was introduced in 1921, having been raised by Auguste Nonin & Fils of Chatillon near Paris. It was popular in Continental Europe, and in the United States, where it was named 'Lafayette', and introduced in 1924. But it failed to cross the English Channel in any force.

'Else Poulsen' and 'Kirsten Poulsen'

1924 was the year of introduction of these two historic roses from Svend Poulsen. They were both fairly tall and upright, and 'Else Poulsen' in particular insisted on carrying all her flowers on top of the plant. She was semi-double, brash rose pink; 'Kirsten Poulsen' was single, rosy carmine, and much the better looking plant. They are not really worth growing now, because 'Else Poulsen' is sure to get mildew, and there are many more interesting roses than 'Kirsten Poulsen'. But in their day they proved that the rose had the capability of challenging any plant to make a more colourful bed; and they won. The National Rose Society was puzzled as to which class to put them in, and for a few years described them as Hybrid Teas. They came from the same cross, 'Orléans Rose' × 'Red Star', which is pink Polyantha crossed semi-double red Hybrid Tea. Little credit has gone to 'Red Star' in that marriage. It came from a Dutch breeder, H. A. Verschuren & Sons, of Haps.

'Karen Poulsen'　*Short　Scarlet　Remontant*　P2　H4

It took ten years to make perceptible improvements on Else and Kirsten, which is proof of the startling advance they had made. 'Karen Poulsen' came from Svend Poulsen in 1933, a lovely single rose, with heads of velvet scarlet flowers illuminated by their stamens. It was an improvement only in colour, for the plants were liable to put up one flowering shoot at a time, not the hallmark of a successful Floribunda. It was shorter than its sisters. The parents were 'Kirsten Poulsen' × 'Vesuvius', the latter a single crimson Hybrid Tea from McGredy.

'Donald Prior' and **'Betty Prior'**

Priors of Colchester had a distinguished career, in which they won the Nurserymens' Championship of the National Rose Society, and bred two of the best Floribundas of the 1930s. 'Donald Prior' was crimson in brilliant degree, introduced in 1934, and bred from a seedling × 'D. T. Poulsen'. It was a leading variety for several years.

'Betty Prior' was single and pink, not at first sight a glamorous rose; but she had two great qualities, of insistence to bloom, and of hardiness. She is still widely grown in the United States, and in those parts of Europe where hardiness is essential. She was a seedling of 'Kirsten Poulsen', introduced in 1935.

'Baby Château'　*Medium　Crimson　Remontant*　P1　H3

The name refers to 'Château de Clos Vougeot', that darkest of red roses from Pernet-Ducher; 'Baby' refers to the flowers rather than the growth, and has been omitted as misleading by some. This introduction of 1936 was not of itself a great rose; indeed it was described by its breeder as a 'lame duck'. In spite of this, it proved to be the parent that transmitted to modern roses those fiery scarlet geranium colours, which perhaps have proved more arresting than restful. It is, therefore, one of the more important roses, even though its value in the garden was low. It was bred by Wilhelm Kordes, and was crimson, with no hint of the fires beneath.

There can be little doubt that the vivid vermilion scarlet was inherited from Polyantha roses, among which it first appeared in the sport 'Gloria Mundi'; but that and other similar sports did not transmit the colour to their progeny, probably because their sporting affected only their exterior cells, and not the interior ones where the sexual activity occurs. However the parentage of 'Baby Château' reveals that Polyantha enters into it, being 'Aroma' × ('Robin Hood' × 'Ami Quinard'). 'Aroma' and 'Ami Quinard' were red Hybrid Teas, the former from Cants and the latter, a very dark one, from Charles Mallerin. 'Robin Hood' was called a Hybrid Musk, although in reality it is a Polyantha, and was only excluded from that class by its size, because people thought Polyanthas should be dwarf. Its pollen parent was the crimson Polyantha, 'Miss Edith Cavell'. To complete the link with 'Baby Château's', namesake, Mallerin had used a rose bred from 'Château de Clos Vougeot' when he raised 'Ami Quinard'.

Such is the account given by Wilhelm Kordes in the *Rose Annual 1953,* but he apparently gave *Modern Roses* a different parentage, by substituting 'Eva' for 'Robin Hood'. Should that be correct, it merely places 'Robin Hood' one generation back, for it was a parent of 'Eva'. One boon which either 'Eva' or 'Robin Hood' might be thanked for, was that 'Baby Château' passed to her progeny an excellent standard of health.

'Rosenelfe'　*Medium − Pink Remontant*　P4　H2

The four syllables with which Herr Kordes would have pronounced this rose have a loving eloquence absent from the abrupt translation, 'Rose Elf'. It was introduced by Kordes in 1936, and in the United States by Henry A. Dreer in 1939; and it was the first Floribunda with flowers like small Hybrid Teas.

No doubt the war robbed 'Rosenelfe' of much of the fame she deserved. I thought her most beautiful in the summer of 1939, a clear and pleasant pink, the form of the flowers charming, the fragrance sweet, the placement of the blooms perfect. She was raised from 'Else Poulsen' × 'Sir Basil McFarland', the latter a pink Hybrid Tea from McGredy.

'Dainty Maid' *Medium + Pink Remontant* P3 H4 *
'Dainty Maid' is one of the most attractive single pink roses ever raised; the petals reflect the colour softly, and the yellow stamens illuminate it discreetly. The plants are vigorous, their dignity well served by their leaves. Not many nurseries stock it, more's the pity. It was raised by Edward Le Grice of North Walsham, Norfolk, and introduced in 1938. Its five petals are fairly large, deeper pink on the outside; one of its great advantages is resistance to rain damage. It was a seedling from 'D. T. Poulsen', a red Floribunda.

'Poulsen's Yellow' *Medium Yellow Remontant* P2 H1
This, the first true yellow Floribunda, came from Svend Poulsen in 1938, but as its colour faded, and the semi-double flowers were apt to be untidy, it had little chance of resurrection when rose growers resumed their operations after the war, and found a better alternative in 'Goldilocks'. There are two interesting facts about 'Poulsen's Yellow': the foliage was dark and glossy to an unusual degree; and it was bred from 'Mrs W. H. Cutbush' × 'Gottfried Keller'. The latter comes from 'Persian Yellow', and its sad story is related in the section Pimpinellifoliae.

'Pinocchio' *Medium Pink blend Remontant* P3 H2
Raised by Wilhelm Kordes, and introduced in 1940 as 'Rosenmärchen'. This rose became a useful parent, which might have been expected from its own origin, 'Eva' × 'Geheimrat Duisberg', namely a red shrub of mixed parentage crossed with a yellow Hybrid Tea. It was more double than usual for its period, and of somewhat unstable colour, usually light pink with deeper flushes, and some yellow within.

'Käthe Duvigneau' *Medium Crimson Remontant* P1 H2
The name and the time killed this excellent healthy rose in Britain, but it deserves mention as one of the early seedlings from 'Baby Château'. The pollen parent is given as *R. roxburghii,* although more likely it was a seedling derived from the species. It was raised by Mathias Tantau in Germany, introduced in 1942, and by the time my firm grew it after the war, it had to contend with 'Frensham'. Eventually we gave up the losing battle of trying to sell it.

'Floradora' *Medium + Vermilion red Remontant* P2 H2
There is an extraordinary neglect of this important rose in our rose literature. It was introduced in the United States in 1943 or 1944, and presumably in Germany some time previously, I have failed to discover when. It was raised by Mathias Tantau, and the parentage is variously given as 'Baby Château' × *R. roxburghii (Modern Roses);* and *R. multibracteata* × 'Baby Château' (Dr W. E. Lammerts). Neither is likely to be exact.

It was one of the first to exhibit the vermilion inheritance from 'Baby Château' in double flowers, but rather lighter and duller than the colour description indicates. The leaves were glossy and healthy, but not attractive in their abundance of cold light green. Not an elegant rose, it was unique at the time, both in appearance and descent. We know it was pollen parent to 'Queen Elizabeth', and we may strongly suspect that Tantau's breeding records might link it with 'Super Star'.

'Frensham' *Tall Crimson Remontant* P2 H1 **

Raised by Albert Norman, and introduced by my firm in 1946, 'Frensham' was so much better than all other red Floribundas in colour and vigour, that it was scarcely profitable for nurserymen to grow its rivals. From this grand entrance, it suddenly fell into trouble about 1955, by acting as a universal host to mildew. It is the prime example of an apparently fool-proof rose letting the pundits down. The most convincing explanation I have heard is that a particular form of mildew became prevalent after its introduction; perhaps, even, with its help. After twenty years in disgrace, 'Frensham', which had the hardihood to survive its invalid years in the hands of less particular gardeners, now appears to be rewarding them in its old form, without the mildew.

Mr Norman gave its origin as ('Miss Edith Cavell' × 'Edgar Andreu') × 'Crimson Glory'. He was not quite certain of the seed parent, having assumed that the cross occurred due to proximity, and from the appearance of the seedling. He was most probably right, being an observant and intelligent rosarian; and if so, we have in 'Frensham' a mixture of Polyantha, Wichuraiana, China and Hybrid Tea. From its unorthodoxy and sterility, it could indeed be such a hybrid.

'Goldilocks' *Short Yellow Remontant* P3 H2

'Goldilocks' was an important Floribunda in two ways, from being easily the best yellow up to its introduction in 1945, and from setting the style of the class firmly into double flowers of Hybrid Tea type, as 'Rosenelfe' had first shown to be possible. It also introduces us to an American breeder so successful with this type of rose he was nicknamed Papa Floribunda.

Eugene Boerner was born in 1893 in Cedarsburg, Wisconsin, and was always proud of the German stock he came from. He joined the Jackson & Perkins Company in 1920, and in 1930 became Director of Research in succession to Dr J. H. Nicolas. Nicolas had a great reputation for his knowledge of the rose, and for his scientific approach to breeding; his most lasting varieties were the yellow Hybrid Tea, 'Eclipse', and the yellow climber, 'King Midas', introduced in 1935 and 1942 respectively. The pink Hybrid Tea, 'The Doctor', was named after him, under his familiar title.

Jackson & Perkins (usually known as J & P) developed by means of an exhibit at the New York World's Fair in 1939; they had the acumen to rename 'Minna Kordes', a crimson Floribunda they had from Germany and to introduce it in New York as 'World's Fair'. The result was that in the 1950s they were claiming to be the world's largest rose growers with 17 million plants. Impressed by the virtues of quantity, Boerner applied it also to rose breeding. His fields of new roses on trial became too large to inspect on foot, so he suspended seats behind a tractor in order to oversee them. But it cannot be said that quantity yielded the rewards he hoped for; apart from the useful orange red 'Zorina', a Floribunda for cut flower growers introduced in 1963, Boerner's greatest successes were from 1945–1955. He died in 1966.

'Goldilocks' was a pleasant soft yellow colour, perfectly complemented by the grassy green of its leaves. It was raised from a seedling × 'Doubloons', the latter being a yellow climber from M. H. Horvath, of Mentor, Ohio, raised from interesting parents, a hybrid of *R. setigera* (the Prairie Rose) × a hybrid of *R. foetida bicolor* ('Austrian Copper'); it had been introduced in 1934. Thus 'Goldilocks' brought some new blood into Floribundas, and in due time passed it on to 'Allgold'.

'Lavender Pinocchio' *Short   Lavender pink   Remontant*   P4   H2
Raised by Eugene Boerner and introduced by J & P in 1948, 'Lavender Pinocchio' revived hopes of a blue rose. It has rather small semi-double flowers, light lavender pink, very pretty with their yellow stamens; it is much better grown under glass than outdoors in the British climate. It was derived from 'Pinocchio' × 'Grey Pearl'. The latter was an odd rose from McGredy, introduced by J & P in 1945, with a name which really needs no further description. It was rudely nicknamed The Mouse, from the greyness and the brown colour of its buds; its inability to grow also merited that title.

From 'Lavender Pinocchio' came most of the modern lilac pink roses. The parentage of Le Grice's 'Lilac Charm' has not been published, but I feel sure that 1961 introduction came from 'Lavender Pinocchio', which I saw in Le Grice's breeding house on a visit to him in the early 1950s. It may be said that we have improved the garden appearance of lilac pink roses, which are quite easy to raise. I myself have introduced 'Maud Cole', 'Lake Como', 'Atlantis', 'Lagoon', 'Seven Seas' and 'Harry Edland', and all of them related to 'Lilac Charm'. Le Grice raised 'Silver Charm' and 'News', the latter an interesting purple from 'Lilac Charm' × 'Tuscany Superb', a Gallica. It was introduced in 1968. Nearly every breeder has his crop of lilac varieties, but nobody can make them blue. That step demands chemical elements which do not exist in these lilac colours any more than in any other roses; until an accident of nature or intelligent research introduces those missing elements, we can go on crossing these lilac varieties until we are blue in the face, which is the nearest we shall get to producing anything blue from them.

'Fashion' *Medium −   Coral pink   Remontant*   P3   H2
What a lovely colour this rose brought to us in 1949! And what a harvest of rose rust bred upon its leaves! Regretfully my firm discarded it, as soon as we saw this beauty in peach and coral spreading devastation in the gardens of our customers. We spent the next few years subscribing to nearly every acknowledgement of order: 'Regret we do not grow Fashion'; and I fear our competitors profited thereby. It was raised by Eugene Boerner from 'Pinocchio' × 'Crimson Glory'.

'Masquerade' *Medium   Yellow to red   Remontant*   P3   H4   *
Few roses were so truly novel as this, with its strange habit of yellow buds, which admitted more and more red, until the old flowers were dark crimson, and the inflorescence spotted with dark dots among the gold. Had the rose world been familiar with *R. chinensis mutabilis,* the novelty were less; but that variety was rare. It is wonderful to suppose that the colour change of 'Masquerade' may have been latent in all the generations of hybrids from the China Rose until 1949.

'Masquerade' was bred by Eugene Boerner from 'Goldilocks' × 'Holiday', both those parents being raised by him too. 'Holiday' was a Floribunda, yellow and pink, with 'Pinocchio' as pollen parent; so 'Pinocchio' is well marked as a transmitter of unusual colours, on the evidence of 'Lavender Pinocchio', 'Fashion' and 'Masquerade'; with 'Circus' yet to come. The main objection to growing 'Masquerade' at present, is that no stocks are known to be free of the rose mosaic virus.

'Independence' *Medium* − *Deep vermilion* *Remontant* P2 H2
The colours and health promised by 'Baby Château' became reality when Wilhelm Kordes introduced his 'Kordes' Sondermeldung'; which means his special announcement, or news flash. Nobody knew how to describe the colour; orange scarlet was already trite, having been applied a good way across the spectrum. Words like cinnabar and red lead appeared in rose catalogues. The name was changed to 'Geranium', then 'Independence', and 'Reina Elisenda' was also used.

Apart from its colour when young, it was an ugly rose, horribly changing to magenta, with flowers too few for a Floribunda, too small for a Hybrid Tea, wagging on weak stems. But it brought pollen and seed which were tools to the benefit of the future. It was from 'Baby Château' × 'Crimson Glory'; not a straight cross, but a self-set seed from a plant of that parentage. Although it was introduced in America in 1951, and in Britain a year earlier, it had been on sale in Germany since 1943. 'Independence' was the first rose with a large flower to contain the pigment pelargonidum, responsible for geranium red colours.

'Rudolph Timm' *Medium* + *Pale pink* *Remontant* P4 H3 ******
An excellent rose for hardiness and health, but rarely grown because its flowers are very pale, semi-double, and not particularly exciting. It may yet prove important to the future, for I believe it has much to offer rose breeders, being another gift to them from Wilhelm Kordes. It was introduced in 1951, and raised from a significant strain ('Johannes Boettner' × 'Magnifica') × ('Baby Château' × 'Else Poulsen'). This being interpreted brings in a double dose of 'Baby Château' and 'Else Poulsen', with which we are already familiar, and mixes with them a Sweet Briar; for 'Magnifica' was a seedling of one of Lord Penzance's Sweet Briars, 'Lucy Ashton'. The importance of that new blood, and of 'Rudolph Timm' as a donor, have not, I think, been generally appreciated. My own tribute to 'Rudolph Timm' is to have raised 'Saga' and 'Margaret Merril' from it, and I have to own that the idea of using it was not mine, but Major-General Frank Naylor's.

'Queen Elizabeth' *Taller Pink Remontant* P2 H4 *********
Looking back through the years of my life as a rose grower, I think this is the best rose raised during that time. Its vigour ensures easy growth and good performance. It is not a rose for a particular region or climate, but appears to thrive everywhere. On a visit to Australia a few years ago, I was told that it is practically the only rose which is equally good all along that mighty coastline, wherever roses are grown, from Adelaide to Queensland; and also in Perth in the west.

It was raised by Dr W. E. Lammerts from 'Charlotte Armstrong' × 'Floradora', and introduced by Germain's Nursery of Los Angeles, in 1954. The remarkable vigour puts it out of place among the Floribundas, because it is twice as tall as many of them. The growth is upright and the flowers attractively pink, good for cutting or garden display. The colour is not a normal rose pink, but more like the lighter pinks seen in cyclamen or fuchsias.

No better hedge rose exists, but pruning can be a problem, for on it depends the height of the hedge and the covering of the base. The answer with 'Queen Elizabeth' is to have no fear of cutting some of the old wood down, to make it break into young growth and leaves towards the base of the plant. It usually responds to this treatment, and with some cut short, and some left tall, very handsome plants are the result.

Queen Elizabeth II was beginning her reign when this rose was named after her by the American raiser, and no kinder compliment in the world of roses could be made from one country to another. I believe that the suggestion came from Harry Wheatcroft when he saw the rose under trial.

'Spartan'   *Medium +   Coral pink   Remontant*   P3   H3   *

'Spartan' had a fine, rounded habit, and flowers above normal size for its time. It proved a valuable parent; and transmitted its quality of varying its colour from summer to autumn. It was more pink in summer, more orange in autumn. The habit of growth was also an advance, in covering the sides as well as the top with double flowers. It was bred from 'Geranium Red' × 'Fashion', raised by Eugene Boerner, and introduced by J & P in 1955.

'Allgold'   *Medium −   Yellow   Remontant*   P2   H1   *****

Introduced in 1956, 'Allgold' is one of the purest and deepest yellow roses ever raised, and has the added advantage of holding its colour without fading or changing perceptibly; quite a rare thing in roses. The plants are below average height, and their leaves are shiny, deep green, and resistant to disease. It is the best variety that Edward Le Grice ever raised, and one of the fastest Floribundas to repeat its flowers.

Some twenty years ago Le Grice told me of its origin, and how it justified the theory of making trial crosses. 'Goldilocks' was an obvious gift to rose breeders, and Le Grice sought for a mate to deepen its colour. He had been working with 'Mrs Beckwith', a yellow Hybrid Tea introduced by Pernet-Ducher in 1922, which had the failing of producing white flowers in its first flush, like many other yellow roses in those days, such as 'Julien Potin', and even 'Phyllis Gold'. He managed to raise 'Yellowcrest', which kept its colour but lost its leaves. Seeking a yellow with good leaves, he hit upon Cant's 'Mrs Beatty' (1926), in spite of its pale colour and frequently rounded centre; he crossed it with 'Yellowcrest', with the result of 'Ellinor Le Grice', which gave him the colour and foliage he wanted, although not quite the form of flower. It was rather globular, and the petals were frequently scalloped. That at least is Le Grice's version; the parents of 'Ellinor Le Grice' in the record books are 'Lilian' × 'Yellowcrest'. 'Lilian' was another yellow Hybrid Tea of Cants, and it is possible that Le Grice's memory was not too certain. Due to the war, the introduction of 'Ellinor Le Grice' was delayed until 1949, twelve years after the cross was made.

He made a trial of 'Goldilocks' × 'Ellinor Le Grice', and noted that the few seedlings were promising. Like a gold miner who sees the first glint, he explored more thoroughly, by raising eight thousand seedlings of the same cross, of which he introduced four: 'Golden Delight' and 'Honeyglow' in 1955; 'Allgold' and 'Copper Delight' in 1956. He himself quotes the dates a year later in each case, but his advertisements in the *Rose Annual* refute this. However, that is a trivial detail to put beside a brilliant exercise in rose breeding, in which careful observation and practical imagination led him to his target.

Edward Le Grice was born in 1902 and died in 1977. He was devoted to his profession, and known throughout the rose world not only as a rose breeder, but as a lecturer and the author of *Rose Growing Complete*. If the rose world had better men, more modest and gentle, I never came across them. He was a devout Christian, a lay preacher for his Baptist Church, set in the lovely countryside of his native Norfolk, and beside which he now lies. At the last meeting I attended in his company, I wrote down the following remark he made: 'People have to play for safety if they want to make a living; and that is quite the wrong way for a hybridist.'

'Circus'   *Medium* −   *Yellow & red   Remontant*   P3   H1
The neat flowers, small and shapely, had their yellow all flushed towards golden apricot, and marked with pink or red flushes, mostly on the outer petals. It came as a sensation in 1956, from Herbert Swim of Armstrong Nurseries; the parents were 'Fandango' × 'Pinocchio'. Although it was to prove a valuable parent, its career in cultivation was strange, for it divided into at least three separate types; one was vigorous and coarse growing, with too many buds in an ugly cluster, and pale flowers; the second was the true 'Circus'; and the third was much deeper in colour, not quite so strong as the true one, and with fewer petals.

Before these variations were appreciated, those who collect wood for propagation in nurseries had not unnaturally taken much from the most vigorous and least desirable of the three, as being the easiest supplier; and there followed a painful period of trying to get rid of it. But no matter how one selected the propagating material, that brute would come back. The attractive colour of the third type caused Harry Wheatcroft to introduce it in 1959 as 'Alison Wheatcroft'. A similar but more double sport, and I think a better one, was found in Livermore, California by F. B. Begonia and Paul De Vor, and introduced by Armstrong Nurseries in 1963 as 'Circus Parade'. For some reason these two sports are not so liable to revert as was the true 'Circus'.

'Iceberg'   *Medium* +   *White   Remontant*   P2   H1   ****
The way to grow 'Iceberg' is as a shrub or a standard, for although it can form an impressive bed, it will attract blackspot far more easily when crowded together. Moreover, repeated hard pruning appears to affect the colour of its leaves; if the plants are allowed to develop, the leaf colour is slightly grey green, a splendid foil for the white flowers. In contrast, on hard pruned plants, the mature foliage is hidden at the base, and the flowers are less favourably backed by leaves which tend to be yellow green. I can advocate another reason: it is a handsome, rounded shrub, ready to flower down its sides almost to the ground, an advantage that is lost in a bed.

It was said by Alexander Dickson in the *Rose Annual 1918,* that Hybrid Teas had given a new lease of life to standards. The practice of propagating roses at the top of a long stem, in order that they may be lifted up, is agreeable for close inspection and for the garden scene. But it lost much of its point in the days when most of the roses grown were tall Hybrid Perpetuals or delicate Teas. Even today, the choice of varieties grown thus is often thoughtless, and those with an elegant rounded habit should always be preferred to the stiff and upright.

Standard roses, known as Tree roses in America, and Rosiers tiges in France, may be propagated on the stems of a number of wild roses or hybrids, the main requirement being that the stem be long enough, stiff and straight, and compatible with the rose it is to receive. Standards should be staked against the wind, and pruned moderately by removing only the thinnest shoots, together with those that are damaged, frozen or obviously too old. The way to recognize those parts which are too old is by their ceasing to bear young growth, and even then it is best to shorten them instead of removing them entirely, to give them a year's grace in which to break into growth again. A standard is different from a bush, and cannot renew itself so many times in its life. If a plant is over-crowded with growths, some may be thinned out, but inexperienced pruners are warned that once a shoot is cut off, it cannot be replaced. Thinning out can all too easily leave the plant much slimmer than was intended.

Thomas Rivers of Sawbridgeworth in Hertfordshire is credited with having made Standard roses popular in Britain, much to the disgust of his associates, who referred to 'they rubbishy brambles'. Wild briar from *R. canina* was the stem favoured in Britain for over a century, it being abundant in the countryside, and a form of pocket money for needy countrymen. Dean Hole gave a humorous account, saying that when he saw his briar man among the worshippers at church, he knew it was time to order his stems, and the order once given, that apostate was absent from divine service for the next twelve months. There was not a reliable crop from these standards, and a gentleman is quoted in the *Rosarian's Year Book 1890,* as saying that unless the stems were carefully selected, the garden next year would be 'schwarming with absentees'. I remember sorting through the stems brought to our nursery; we paid according to the length, and returned the discards firmly. In the hopes of deceiving an inexperienced sorter, and of qualifying for the greatest length, some of our suppliers would cheerfully submit the long canes of blackberries. Improved prosperity, the diminished numbers of our agricultural population, the fact that gipsies deal more in scrap metal than their old natural resources, the clearance of briar clad land; all these factors have put standard roses on to cultivated stems these days. In Britain *R. rugosa* 'Hollandica' is most used; but types of *R. canina* such as 'Pfänder' or 'Polmeriana' are better.

In case you are wondering what happened to 'Iceberg', whose beauty as a standard provoked so long a digression, let us now credit it to Reimer Kordes, the son of the great Wilhelm. He introduced it in 1958 under the name 'Schneewittchen'. It was bred from 'Robin Hood' × 'Virgo', namely a shrubby Polyantha crossed Hybrid Tea. Do not be surprised to see quite a flush of pink in it occasionally.

'Meteor' *Shorter Vermilion scarlet Remontant* P2 H2 **
In 1951 Kordes introduced a significant seedling of 'Baby Château' called 'Gertrud Westphal'. It was single and scarlet, very short in growth, and revealed to many people for the first time the sweetness of Floribundas in flowering like a carpet on the ground.

'Meteor' was bred from 'Feurio' × 'Gertrud Westphal', and became the first popular short Floribunda, due to its well-shaped double flowers, and light vermilion scarlet colour. Its parentage betrays some strange facts, that of its grandparents, one was 'Baby Château' and all the other three were bred from 'Baby Château'; two of them came from the Hybrid Sweet Briar, 'Magnifica'. Reimer Kordes introduced 'Meteor' in 1958; in 1963 he followed with an excellent dwarf crimson, 'Marlena', from 'Gertrud Westphal' × 'Lilli Marlene'. Despite much work, progress in this potentially popular type has been slow; perhaps some breeders ought to have kept 'Gertrud Westphal' in their hybridizing houses. Obviously there will be a great many short Floribundas in the next few years, and the American nurserymen are beginning to call them Patio Roses, or Carpet Roses. A good name is badly needed; Dwarf Floribunda does not exactly pirouette upon the tongue.

'Honeymoon' *Medium Yellow Remontant* P4 H2 **
Introduced by Reimer Kordes in 1959 as 'Honigmond', and bred from 'Cläre Grammerstorf' × 'Spek's Yellow'. This is a much better rose in cold areas than in warm, because the yellow holds better, and the plants do not grow so tall. If encouraged by heat, it can become lanky. It is one of the big successes around the city of Aberdeen.

'Cläre Grammerstorf' deserves particular attention, as leading Sweet Briar blood into yellow roses. Kordes had been breeding with Sweet Briars, especially 'Magnifica', as a source of hardiness, because the market for his roses was in

Scandinavia as well as in Germany. He crossed a Sweet Briar hybrid with 'Peace', and introduced a rose called 'Kordes' Harmonie' from that cross in 1954. He then used 'Kordes' Harmonie' as seed parent to a Sweet Briar hybrid, whether the same one we do not know, and the result was 'Cläre Grammerstorf'. It is a coarse rose, with huge leathery leaves of a somewhat unpleasant light green, and bright yellow flowers. We may regard it as a stud rose for the future, for although its decorative value was such as to preclude people from buying it, in the hands of breeders it is transforming modern roses, particularly through its tough foliage, which resists disease, as well as in hardiness and vigour. The rather light leaves of 'Honeymoon' and 'Arthur Bell' are typical of the 'Cläre Grammerstorf' line, and Poulsen's 'Chinatown' has 'Cläre Grammerstorf' written all over it.

'Paddy McGredy' *Medium − Rose red Remontant* P2 H2 **

Some people call it deep pink; I have yet to learn where pink ends and red begins. Is pink not another way of saying light red? If so, surely deep pink equals red? It is convenient, I think, to use the agreeable words 'rose red' to bridge the gap.

'Paddy McGredy' came from Sam McGredy in 1962, its parents 'Spartan' × 'Tzigane'; the latter was a red and yellow Hybrid Tea descended from 'Peace', and assured of a short life in a cold climate by its thick, soft pith. Bad parents can have good children, which is fortunate for 'Paddy McGredy', who had the rust-laden 'Fashion' as a grandmother.

With 'Paddy McGredy' came the realization that Floribundas were able to produce flowers as large as Hybrid Teas, and the only difference between the two might well be whether the flowers were in large heads or not. To go a stage further, if Hybrid Tea flowers could be borne in abundance by Floribundas, what would be the use of the Hybrid Tea class at all? That stage has not been reached; but the National Rose Society was provoked into adopting in 1959 or 1960 the term Floribunda − H.T. type. The Americans had tried to use Grandiflora, which was justly disapproved, because Hybrid Teas had grander flowers still; but we must own that Floribunda − H.T. type dances upon the tongue less lightly.

Perhaps I should mention that on 26 February 1965, the title of the National Rose Society was changed to the Royal National Rose Society, by command of Her Majesty the Queen. I have tried to refer to it throughout this book by the name it was known to the rosarians of the relevant time.

'Pink Parfait' *Medium Pink Remontant* P3 H3 ****

This is a refined and elegant variety, with long petals for a Floribunda, in pink colours which are variable but always gentle; the base of the petals is cream, which sometimes trespasses higher into the flower. It was raised from 'First Love' × 'Pinocchio' by Herbert Swim, and introduced by Armstrong Nurseries in 1960.

'Arthur Bell' *Tall Yellow Remontant* P6 H3 ***

Most people feel slightly annoyed with 'Arthur Bell' when his yellow swiftly ebbs away; but the contrast of gold and primrose is not displeasing. A sweetly scented Floribunda, 'Arthur Bell' has an excellent record of health. He has been a channel for Kordes' Sweet Briar strain to pass through into Hybrid Teas as well as Floribundas. Raised by Sam McGredy from 'Cläre Grammerstorf' × 'Piccadilly', and introduced in 1965. If you wish to know who Arthur Bell may be, look at a bottle of Bell's Old Scotch Whisky.

'Escapade' *Medium* + *Rosy violet Remontant* P5 H1 ***
This is one of my own roses, bred from 'Pink Parfait' × 'Baby Faurax', and introduced in 1967. It has much of the Polyantha about it, derived from its little amethyst pollen parent; but it denies the normally dominant Polyantha influence, by bearing large flowers instead of small. They have about twelve petals, and open to show a white centre, with rosy violet around it. To see these wide open flowers basking in the sunshine is a pleasant experience.

'Escapade' is an unusual kind of rose, so much so that it evoked a comment in a Belgian rose magazine: 'Nous admirons l'esprit sportif de J. L. Harkness.' I didn't know whether it was a compliment to 'Escapade' or not. Strange to say, a year later Alec Cocker showed me a seedling of his, from 'Ma Perkins' × 'Baby Faurax'. It was 'Escapade's' twin.

'Escapade' can grow into a fairly big bush, and is a joy for cutting. If you cut it before the flowers are expanded, and let it open in water, the colour will develop perfectly, and will ensure your agreement that there is nothing else like 'Escapade' in the world of roses.

'Picasso' **'Matangi'** **'Old Master'** **'Priscilla Burton'** ****
I was told that it was the eye of 'Frühlingsmorgen' that suggested to Sam McGredy that developments might come from it. 'Frühlingsmorgen' is a hybrid from a Scotch Rose, a class in which broken colours were quite common; they were termed 'marbled', and if you look at some of the pink Scotch Roses, such as 'Andrewsii' or 'Falkland', it does not take much imagination to see how the colours could break and separate, to turn into 'Picasso' and its type, or as Sam McGredy likes to call them, his hand-painted roses.

At least, it doesn't take much imagination now that Sam has done it. It needed a good deal more beforehand, and he was the man who had it.

'Picasso' was perhaps a premature introduction, in the sense that its breeder was able to improve on it within a few years. The regular pattern of carmine and white upon the petals was something entirely new, and very beautiful when at its best. But it was not consistent at every flowering, and the variety suffered from dull foliage. However it was the first, and therefore a landmark in roses. It was introduced in 1971, and the parentage given is 'Marlena' × ['Evelyn Fison' × ('Orange Sweetheart' × 'Frühlingsmorgen')].

In 1974, 'Picasso' was succeeded by 'Old Master'. This is a vigorous grower, with large semi-double flowers; the carmine and white pattern upon them is dramatic. As in all 'Picasso's' successors to date, the foliage is dark and glossy. In this case the parents are given as {['Evelyn Fison' × ('Tantau's Triumph' × *R*. X *coryana*)] × ('Hamburger Phoenix' × 'Danse du Feu')} × ['Evelyn Fison' × ('Orange Sweetheart' × 'Frühlingsmorgen')]. Although it may not appear so, this formula is simpler than the genealogical sections of the Old Testament. Anyone who wishes to understand the sequence expressed within all those brackets may practise by numbering the names given above one to eight in the order they stand. Then this is what occurred:

7 & 8 gave a seedling, which pollinated 6, call the result A
2 & 3 gave a seedling, which pollinated 1, call the result B
4 & 5 gave a seedling, which pollinated B, call the result C
A pollinated C, the result was 'Old Master'.

In the same year (1974), McGredy introduced 'Matangi', the most Floribunda-like of the strain so far; in fact to my taste it had lost some of the exotic 'hand-painted' touch; but it is so highly spoken of around me, that I must recognize I am in a minority. The parentage: {('Little Darling' × 'Goldilocks') × ['Evelyn Fison' × (R. X *coryana* × 'Tantau's Triumph')]} × 'Picasso'. The pollen parent was 'Picasso' by itself; and I have a strong suspicion that the records have *R*. X *coryana* and 'Tantau's Triumph' in the wrong order.

It was obvious from his entries sent to the Trial Ground that Sam McGredy could play variations on his red and white patterned roses almost ad infinitum. At least two more of extraordinary beauty have been seen, of which his 1978 introduction is 'Priscilla Burton'. Whereas the beauty of the type hitherto showed in the fully expanded flower, 'Priscilla Burton' does not need to open, but is lovely before her central petals part from one another. This suggests that 'hand-painted' Hybrid Teas will be admirable; and meanwhile the industrious Sam McGredy is submitting to the trials Dwarf Floribundas and Miniatures in 'Picasso' style. The colours remain red and white, although the red varies from carmine towards crimson or scarlet. What a wonder it will be when the white is supplanted by yellow!

'Rob Roy' *Medium   Crimson   Remontant* P2 H3 *****
'Rob Roy's' rich and glorious crimson is the most splendid red to be found in roses, according to my eyes. The flowers are of Hybrid Tea shape, and although the petals are not too numerous, there are enough of them to make up a pretty flower, and to provide a first class buttonhole. It is an excellent garden rose of upright habit; and anyone who likes to grow roses under glass should make trial of this. There is little scent, unfortunately.

It was raised by Alec Cocker from 'Evelyn Fison' × 'Wendy Cussons', and introduced in 1971. Mr Cocker was highly delighted to receive a letter from France in connection with securing Plant Breeders' Rights there, asking for a letter of authority from Mr Roy for the use of his name!

'Southampton' *Medium +   Apricot orange   Remontant* P4 H3 ****
The colour range from 'Fashion' to orange is one of the most beautiful, but breeders were unable for many years to accompany that beauty with good health and hardiness. 'Fashion' itself, 'Woburn Abbey', 'Zambra' and 'Elizabeth of Glamis' were successive examples of this problem. It always seemed to me that the hope was to introduce 'Allgold' into orange colours; but 'Allgold' itself is not normally the best of parents, because it transmits to most of its seedlings small leaves and flowers. The breeder's principle then is to mate 'Allgold' with something strong, and use the ensuing seedling in the hope that 'Allgold's' desired qualities will turn up in its grandchild. No cross is thoroughly explored by observing its immediate results, because hereditary features more commonly skip a generation.

Accordingly I trusted 'Ann Elizabeth' to make good use of 'Allgold's' pollen; 'Ann Elizabeth' was a free growing pink Floribunda from Albert Norman, introduced in 1962. I selected a light yellow seedling, and from the cross ('Ann Elizabeth' × 'Allgold') × 'Yellow Cushion' came the kind of rose for which I was looking: flowers in the apricot to orange range, flushed scarlet, and leaves of remarkable health and fine appearance. Fortunately there was the added bonus of scent, which if not strong is certainly pleasant.

'Southampton' is a splendid garden rose. Its flowers open semi-double from a pretty Hybrid Tea bud; and I notice they stand both the sun and the rain, which should make every year a good year for 'Southampton'. It was named after that famous English city, after the Mayor had visited our nursery to approve the choice. I chose it for them, well knowing they had a reliable and healthy rose. It was introduced in 1972; and I shall be much surprised if it does not prove an important parent.

'Margaret Merril' *Medium White Remontant* P9 H2 ****
Much more beautiful than white, because a delicate blush is usually to be seen. The colour and form of flower are charming, but 'Margaret Merril's' great virtue is the chief absentee from the Floribunda class: scent. Some roses may have a sweeter scent, but not many I think. I do not know of any with a perfume so piquant and agreeable, so apt to concentrate one's attention upon the pure pleasure of inhalation.

I raised this rose from ('Rudolph Timm' × 'Dedication') × 'Pascali'. It therefore has the valuable Sweet Briar background of 'Rudolph Timm', and I am hopeful that it may be the means of bringing scent into pink, red and white Floribundas. The purpose of the cross was, I admit, quite different from the result. My seedling which acted as seed parent was a strange pink semi-double rose, which faded bright green; and I hoped 'Pascali' might encourage that oddity.

'Margaret Merril' was introduced in 1977, and enables me to end this account of Floribundas with a variety which has caught one of the best gifts of Wilhelm Kordes from the past, and tenders it, with something added, to the future.

HYBRID MUSKS

The Hybrid Musks should be dismantled as a class, and put where they belong, some in the Floribundas and some in the Polyanthas. The Rev. Joseph Pemberton was a great rosarian, with some fine achievements to his name including the origination of this class, but his enthusiasm led him astray when he invoked the Musk Rose as godmother to his new roses. It was more like a remote ancestor.

I have therefore transferred those with obvious affinity to *R. multiflora* to the Polyanthas, and kept under this heading those more like the Indicae, out of respect for custom. The reason a separate class was wanted, was to part bedding plants from flowering shrubs. This may be helpful horticulturally; although even that is questionable, because heights can be readily indicated, and not every gardener desires all his plants to be level. The Floribundas range from 'Meteor' to 'Queen Elizabeth', and the gardening public is quite able to deal with that situation.

We come up against a difficulty here, namely that all roses are shrubs, except the climbers and trailers. We may grow Hybrid Teas and Floribundas as shrubs, or we may grow Hybrid Musks in beds. The difference between a bush rose and a shrub rose is nil; the two words have exactly the same meaning, and when we use them to imply a difference, we are trying to say the shrub rose needs more elbow room. But so do the bedding roses, if we grow them as shrubs. A short study of practically any list of shrub roses will reveal many inconsistencies. Some are by breeders, well knowing that a shrub rose will not sell like a Floribunda, and introducing 'Chinatown' and 'Eye Paint' as Floribundas. And the specialist growers contribute, because their list of shrub roses is incomplete without, say, 'Viridiflora'. What the customer says after he planted three 'Viridiflora' shrubs to dominate his twelve bushes of 'Queen Elizabeth', I leave to your imagination.

The Rev. Joseph H. Pemberton was a curate at Romford in Essex from 1880–1903. Until 1914, he was diocesan inspector for St Albans, but resigned to spend his life growing roses. He lived in a round house at Havering-atte-Bower, and was an exhibitor at the 1877 National Rose Show in London. He said that he used to breed horses. His book, *Roses Their History, Development and Cultivation,* is a standard work. I have an edition dated 1908, in which the publishers advertise a gardening book by H. Rider Haggard. The impression one receives of Pemberton from reading him, and about him, is of an eager but practical enthusiast, sometimes too hasty in his reactions, insistent on achieving his object despite opposition, a slightly Gallic individual with English style. He served the rose and the National Rose Society with unusual flair and vigour. After he died, one of his gardeners took over his roses, and introduced some of them. His name was J. A. Bentall.

'Buff Beauty'   *Medium +   Light apricot   Remontant*   P4   H1   **
With its nodding flowers and biscuit colour, this rose often makes me think of Teas, although the form of the double flowers is somewhat confused. It has a sleepy, summery scent. The origin is strangely unclear, given the usual introduction date of 1939. It would appear that it may have been one of Pemberton's roses, which was held back because it had not the same look as his other Hybrid Musks; and so it appeared years after he had died in 1926. Somebody, somewhere must have more detailed information.

'Cornelia'   *Taller   Pink   Remontant*   P4   H2   ***
A large bush, which spreads fairly wide, and is well covered with dark leaves. The flowers are pink, with a touch of apricot to enliven them, especially in the autumn. This is an agreeable plant to grow, usually showing at least some colour through most of the season, and occasionally surprising one by its magnificence. The flowers are fragrant, double, trimly formed; perhaps smaller than one would expect in relation to the bush. Introduced in 1925 by Pemberton, without details of parentage. There is an attractive Hybrid Musk called 'Kathleen' raised by Pemberton from 'Daphne' × 'Perle des Jeannes', introduced in 1922; one can envisage 'Kathleen' by imagining a whitish 'Cornelia'. I suspect the word Jeannes is an error for either Jardins or Jaunes.

'Eva'   *Taller   Carmine   Remontant*   P2   H4
No elegant beauty, but it was valuable to rose breeders as a source of health and vigour. One of its seedlings was 'Pinocchio', from which came some of the most beautiful Floribundas; and by another line, it was an ancestor of 'Baby Château', and therefore of 'Queen Elizabeth' and the modern geranium scarlet roses. A tough looking plant, the leaves a fair way apart, the flowers held well above them in large uneven heads, semi-double, carmine with white centres. Raised by Wilhelm Kordes from 'Robin Hood' × 'J. C. Thornton', and introduced in 1933.

'Felicia'   *Medium +   Light pink   Remontant*   P4   H3   **
Nobody can appreciate 'Felicia' until they grow a mature and fairly large plant. Then the flowers, which looked pale and insignificant in the early years, show what a delightful display they can make. They have a lively touch of apricot pink within them, and are paler to the edges. Raised by Pemberton from 'Trier' × 'Ophelia' and introduced in 1928.

'Moonlight'   *Tall   Cream   Remontant*   P3   H2   **
A splendid rose, with dark shiny leaves and loose creamy flowers. It is almost a climber, and an asset to the shrub border. Raised by Pemberton from 'Trier' × 'Sulphurea', which is tall Polyantha crossed Tea. Introduced in 1913.

'Penelope' *Medium Light pink Remontant* P4 H5 **
This can be pruned and grown like a Floribunda, or allowed to grow into a large plant. In either case, there is a long interval between the amazing abundance of the first flower and the lesser second flush. One can help by removing the old flowers before they set seed in the summer. The flowers are light pink, opening from rounded red buds, and finishing near white. It is fragrant and charming, with honest green leaves. The second flowers may be allowed to set seed, because the hips are quite attractive. Raised by Pemberton from 'Ophelia', the pollen parent being in doubt. Introduced in 1924.

'Prosperity' *Tall Ivory Remontant* P3 H1 *
'Prosperity' can be charming; its buds are beautifully formed, and the flowers open into rather small rosettes. It is on the border line between this section and the Polyanthas, but its small dark leaves are not Polyantha type. It is a spreading shrub with occasional long shoots. Raised by Pemberton from 'Marie-Jeanne' × 'Perle des Jardins', that is Polyantha crossed Tea. Introduced in 1919.

'Vanity' *Climber Pink Remontant* P4 H3 **
I suppose 'Vanity' was not intended as a climber, but it is quite impossible to make a well clad shrub from it; as it is rather beautiful with its large single flowers, bright rose pink with yellow stamens, the most practical way to enjoy it is to treat it as a climber. Raised by Pemberton from 'Château de Clos Vougeot' seed; introduced in 1920.

'Wilhelm' *Tall Red Remontant* P1 H3
In my view a most uninteresting rose, but it does provide a red Hybrid Musk, without the scent associated with most of them; besides, so many people praise it, that I must be in the minority in my distaste for it. Raised by Wilhelm Kordes from 'Robin Hood' × 'J. C. Thornton', and a sister therefore of 'Eva'. It was introduced in 1934, and is known in the USA as 'Skyrocket'.

MINIATURES
The origin of the Miniatures is a complete mystery. I dutifully followed authority by mentioning *R. chinensis minima* earlier in this section, although no such wild variety has been reported from China or anywhere else. The story we rely on comes from a distinguished botanist, John Lindley, who wrote in 1820 that Robert Sweet had brought the Miniature rose home to England from Mauritius in 1810. That report may have been based on a statement by Robert Sweet in 1818, which merely says the rose came from Mauritius in 1810. The most perceptive gentleman of the period, in relation to this rose, was J. Sims, who described the Miniature rose in 1815 under the name *R. semperflorens minima.* He commented that the plants he saw were to the best of his belief raised from seed. We may well accept the hint he gave us, that the Miniature rose was originally a dwarf seedling from *R. chinensis semperflorens,* and presumably, therefore, raised in cultivation. The first one may have come from Mauritius; it appears that we have no evidence one way or another, apart from Robert Sweet saying so, whilst others said it came from China in 1800, or a few years later. This will not stop writers giving specific dates when it came from Mauritius, Madagascar or China. I can squash one assertion, that the Royal Horticultural Society's *Dictionary of Gardening* says it was in Britain in 1762. Their reference is not to a date, but to a plate number in *Curtis's Botanical Magazine.* Thus are fallacies born.

The first Miniature described was a single red, and the early lists of varieties are strong in reds. Miniatures were introduced to France from England by Louis Noisette, and in both countries became popular pot plants for sale in flower shops. In 1848, William Paul remarked of Miniatures that they were 'pretty objects cultivated in pots'. Their popularity waned later in the nineteenth century, when Teas and Polyanthas proved more marketable.

They collected a whole directory of names, Latin and vernacular. Miniature, Fairy and Pigmy roses were natural enough. The equivalents in Latin described dwarf Indian roses (as the Chinas were then thought to be) as *R. indica humilis* and *R. indica pumila*. Eventually the present name of *R. chinensis minima* was accepted in 1894, which is very nice, except that nobody can produce the plant to which the name belongs. One of the first names was 'Miss Lawrance's Rose', or *R. lawranceana*, in a generous variety of spellings. Mary Lawrance wrote one of the first books about roses, published in 1799. I do not know how she was associated with the Miniatures, but the name was also attached to one of the early popular red varieties, 'Gloire des Lawranceanas', in 1837.

A few cruel deceptions have been practised, perhaps not intentionally. One is to confuse Miniatures with *R. multiflora nana,* a completely different rose, by calling the latter the Fairy Rose, and recommending its seeds as producing Miniatures. One famous rose book actually provides this rose as the botanic name of Miniatures; and, worse still, I have seen it masquerading in one of the world's most important gardens as *R. chinensis minima.* Its seeds are very fertile, much more so than those of Miniatures, but I fear the results are not what the sowers expected.

Conflicting advice is given as to whether Miniatures should be grown from cuttings, or propagated on to a rootstock. They are indeed quite different in character according to the method chosen. The answer is, that if small plants are wanted, as is reasonable for growing in pots, or in specially selected areas, then they should be grown from cuttings. But if they are to go in the garden among other plants, miniatures from cuttings are insignificant, outgrown by even the shyest groundsel. They should be on a rootstock, which will multiply their size two or three times. They are perfectly attractive in either form. Beware however of buying plants on rootstocks which the nurseryman has deliberately dwarfed, by grafting on to the smallest rootstocks he can find. These are bad plants, and cuttings would be better.

While we are on the subject of cruel deceptions, do not be misled into trying to copy a formal rose garden in miniature, grass paths and all. These are pretty toys to see at a flower show, but quite impracticable for anyone whose devotion to the aim falls short of fanatical.

The main use of Miniatures has consistently been to grow them in pots, and bring them into the home for a few days while their flowers are most attractive. They are not house plants, and soon deteriorate unless they are put out again until their next flowering. The idea of pots can easily be extended to other containers, especially window boxes, tubs and troughs. In all such cases, one must remember that adequate soil is necessary. People who grow pot plants see to this by occasionally re-potting, and annually scratching out and replacing the top inch or two of soil. Just because window boxes and other containers are larger than pots does not mean that such attention can be skipped.

In the open garden, Miniatures may be used in rockeries, provided the soil is not a shallow basin; or near the front of mixed borders among other low plants, or to edge beds or borders. In the latter case, assuming the plants they edge around are higher, Miniatures should not be planted in their shadow, but on the sunny side. They can be a pleasant hobby, especially to the gardener who likes to root his own. Cuttings can be taken in early autumn, a short finger length from firm growth of the current year. They root quite easily, the yellows being the more difficult as a rule. Anyone who does this can have a never failing supply of little gifts to meet many occasions. Miniatures are just as hardy as ordinary roses; the main hazard to young ones is being lifted by frosty weather, and their owner failing to notice it, and to firm them back again when the ground is drier. Finally I should mention how charming they can be grown upon short standard stems.

We need a definition of what a Miniature rose is, because some of the introductions of recent years have been miniature in all but growth; one could not describe Jack's beanstalk as miniature, just because its flowers and leaves were tiny.

I suggest that a Miniature should have the appearance of a China rose in its leaves, not a Polyantha appearance. The leaves, flowers and growth should all be small. It is obvious from the amount of breeding at present practised that many new Miniatures will soon be arriving. These are the steps that led to them:

'Pompon de Paris'

I have only grown this rose in its climbing form; if I had any confidence that the Miniature could be obtained, I should have filled in its details above, and appended five stars; for a little pattern of the climber would be charming indeed. It used to be one of the most popular Miniatures of the flower markets. The flowers are a happy pink, bright against the dark green leaves, which are cut clean and small. I glimpsed the nearest sight of what the original may have been by pruning some climbers hard, and planting them in my greenhouse, so that the plants flowered like bushes next season, before the climbing shoots grew; very pretty. The origin is not clearly known, but it is thought that the rose was introduced about 1839.

'Rouletii' *Shortest   Pink   Remontant*   P1   H1

Some people say this is 'Pompon de Paris', but it does not look the same to me. It has an interesting history, and became the key to modern Miniatures. It appears that when the trade for Miniatures in pots died out, the Miniatures very nearly disappeared too, for they were of no great interest to gardeners in those days. They came to light again about 1918, in Switzerland, when a Swiss Army Medical Officer named Roulet saw plants of this variety in pots in a Swiss village. The villagers reckoned the rose had been in the village for a century. It was retrieved from the village of Onnens by Henri Correvon, a plantsman of Geneva, upon Roulet's report. Correvon introduced it in 1922, as *R. rouletii;* it is often spelt wrongly, with a double 't'. Of course it had no claim to naming as a species.

It is a very short plant, rather crimped if you ask me, with pink double flowers. There seems little doubt that it had been acquired in the days when flower shops sold Miniatures in pots, and that cuttings had been passed around among the people of at least two villages. The 'century' was no doubt an exaggeration, but on the other hand it is obviously considerably senior to its date of introduction. The fact that stands is this: but for Colonel Roulet and M. Correvon, there would be no Miniatures today.

'Peon' *Shortest   Red   Remontant*   P1   H1

The next stage in the resurrection of Miniatures took place in Holland, where John de Vink had a nursery in that fascinating Mecca of the nursery world, Boskoop; a small town which contains something like seven hundred nurseries, most of them only thirty-four metres wide, with a canal each side of them.

'Peon' was bred from 'Rouletii' × 'Gloria Mundi', and was a small plant with red flowers, the centre being white. Now it is one thing to raise a rose, and another thing to sell it; and we must not use the word sell to imply greedy commercialism, because selling is a two-way act. It makes available to the public an article they want, and of which they would have known nothing but for the salesman. In this case, the salesman who taught the world to grow Miniatures was Robert Pyle of the Conard-Pyle Co. in Pennsylvania. His first act was to change the name from 'Peon' to 'Tom Thumb', his second was to introduce it in the United States in 1936, and his third to follow it up with plenty more Miniatures, preferably with nursery rhyme names.

'Baby Gold Star'   *Shortest   Yellow   Remontant*   P2   H1
While John de Vink was mixing 'Rouletii' with Polyanthas, Pedro Dot had the audacity to marry it to Hybrid Teas. His home was San Feliu de Llobregat, near Barcelona, Spain. As a result of that address, around which there was a civil war, some of Dot's roses were not introduced until many years after they had been raised. He was breeding in the 1930s with a yellow Hybrid Tea called 'Eduardo Toda', which he had raised from 'Ophelia' × 'Julien Potin'; it was not introduced until 1947. By its parents, and by its effects upon 'Rouletii', I should think 'Eduardo Toda' could have been invaluable in breeding yellow Hybrid Teas. As seed parent to 'Rouletii' it produced 'Baby Gold Star', or 'Estrellita de Oro', as Pedro Dot named it.

'Baby Gold Star' was introduced in the United States in 1940. It is famous for bringing yellow into the class, but at a cost, for it is a plant with few shoots, and much blackspot. The flowers are brilliant yellow and very double.

'Pour Toi'   *Shortest   White   Remontant*   P2   H1   ***
One of the most perfect Miniatures ever raised, with a bushy plant insistently producing sweet little white flowers, touched with cream. It was raised by Pedro Dot from 'Eduardo Toda' × 'Pompon de Paris', and introduced by Meilland of France in 1946. The original name was 'Para Ti'. It also picked up the appellations of 'For You' and 'Wendy'.

'Perla de Alcanada'   *Shortest   Rose red   Remontant*   P1   H1   **
This is not quite what we expect of a Miniature, being a robust bush, although short. The flowers are flat, and there's no pretence of imitating a Hybrid Tea here. The rose red colour is uninteresting; and yet one cannot discount it, because it will grow, and exude health and greenery and rose-reddery. Raised by Pedro Dot from 'Perle des Rouges' × 'Rouletii', that is Polyantha × Miniature. It collected several names: 'Baby Crimson', 'Pearl of Canada', 'Titania' and 'Wheatcroft's Baby Crimson'. It was introduced by Meilland in 1944. It will be noticed that Meilland sponsored Miniatures in France, as Conard-Pyle had done in America. In due course the lead in England was taken by a little known nursery, Thomas Robinson of Carlton, Nottingham. Harry Wheatcroft also became interested, and introduced a few of Pedro Dot's varieties. But it was left to C. Gregory & Son of Chilwell, Nottingham to propagate and exhibit Miniatures seriously in the 1960s; Mr Gregory introduced Ralph Moore's varieties to Britain. Another famous nursery was renowned for making a pretty garden of Miniatures on a table at Chelsea Show, namely Murrells of Shrewsbury.

'Perla de Montserrat'   *Shortest   Pink   Remontant*   P2   H1   ***
A delightful little bush; its pink flowers are fairly light in colour, and well formed.

Raised by Pedro Dot from 'Cécile Brunner' × 'Rouletii', and introduced by Meilland in 1945. I envy Señor Dot that cross, for I can never get 'Cécile Brunner' to breed.

'Cinderella' *Shortest Pale pink Remontant* P2 H1 **

So pale as to be nearly white, this charming little plant came from De Vink by means of 'Cécile Brunner' × 'Peon'; so both pioneers of Miniatures succeeded with 'Cécile Brunner', the ideal parent for Miniatures. 'Cinderella' was introduced in 1952, and is very double.

Even more double was De Vink's 'Humpty Dumpty' introduced along with 'Cinderella' by Thomas Robinson in 1952. This is rose pink, has nearly a hundred small petals, and is so short that it looks all flower and no plant. Before we leave De Vink's varieties, we might mention a third charming pink, 'Sweet Fairy', introduced by Conard-Pyle in 1946, and raised from 'Peon' × unnamed seedling.

'Rosina' *Shortest Yellow Remontant* P2 H2 ****

Although this was raised in about 1935, it was obviously second choice in the raiser's judgement to the more double 'Baby Gold Star'. With that, and the sequence of wars, it was not introduced until 1951, by Meilland in France; and by Wheatcroft in England, using the name 'Josephine Wheatcroft'. It has also been sold as 'Yellow Sweetheart', the breeder's name being considered a little misleading for a yellow rose by speakers of English.

It is a splendid Miniature, with golden yellow flowers which open semi-double, but not before they have exhibited a pretty Hybrid Tea form in the buds and young blooms. The proportions of the bush are nearly perfect, the leaves attractive, and just the right colour to agree with the flowers. One of the sights I shall always remember is of 'Rosina' one winter day, her leaves rimmed with white frost, and the yellow flowers above innocently behaving as if it were full summer. The parents were 'Eduardo Toda' × 'Rouletii'.

'Baby Masquerade' *Shortest Yellow & pink Remontant* P1 H1 ***

Probably the easiest Miniature to grow, although one might think the flowers a trifle shaggy. It is not unlike 'Masquerade' in miniature, but the colour contrast is not so sharp, because the red is less in evidence; nor is the flower formation similar. In flower production and colourful effect, it is one of the most successful.

Mathias Tantau raised it from 'Peon' × 'Masquerade', and it was introduced in 1956. It has also been known as 'Baby Carnaval', not in England as one might guess from the spelling; and the raiser's German version of its name is 'Baby Maskerade'.

'Easter Morning' *Shortest White Remontant* P2 H1 ***

This variety introduces us to the most enthusiastic, prolific and wise of modern breeders of Miniatures, Ralph S. Moore of Sequoia Nursery, Visalia, California. The difference between Ralph Moore and other breeders, is that Miniatures have been his speciality, his favourites among roses through the whole of his career. He has introduced more than a hundred varieties. Like Edward Le Grice in England, he is a devoted follower of Christ, whom he serves in his Presbyterian church.

Ralph Moore followed De Vink and Pedro Dot by using 'Rouletii' when he started to breed roses in the 1930s. But his researches went beyond anything that had been done in Europe. He soon discarded the idea that both parents had to be as short as possible, because he found that only one parent needed to be short. This gave him the freedom of the genus, and one of his successful parents for breeding Miniatures was in fact a Climber, 'Golden Glow'.

A significant factor in Ralph Moore's career was a Climbing Miniature which he discovered in his seedlings about 1940; he named it 'Zee'. It was pink, with very small leaves and flowers, and its trailing growth was of moderate length. Its parentage is of absorbing interest, being 'Carolyn Dean' × 'Peon'. We know about the pollen parent, having discussed it in this section; so let us look at 'Carolyn Dean'. She came from 'Etoile Luisante' (a coppery pink Polyantha) × 'Sierra Snowstorm'. The latter was one of Moore's own varieties, raised from 'Gloire des Rosomanes' × 'Dorothy Perkins'; we know 'Dorothy Perkins' well, as a rambling pink Wichuraiana hybrid; but 'Gloire des Rosomanes' is of great interest, a Bourbon rose, an important ancestor of Hybrid Perpetuals, the plain 'Ragged Robin' then used as an understock in California. What an inheritance that humble 'Zee' had received: Polyantha, Bourbon, Wichuraiana, Miniature. It laid the foundation of Moore's future success.

'Easter Morning' is a smart little white rose, the flowers like miniature Hybrid Teas, the growth neat and tidy, the leaves firm and shiny. It was raised from 'Golden Glow' × 'Zee', and introduced in 1960.

'Little Flirt'   Shortest   Red & yellow   Remontant   P2   H1   **

This is on the border line between Miniature and Dwarf Floribunda, although most people consider it a Miniature from its short growth. The leaves and flowers are a little larger than Miniatures ought to have. It is colourful, orange red with a lighter centre, the reverse yellow; but the colour fades off in the old flowers. An easy grower; and although the Royal National Rose Society warns that it may get blackspot, I must say it has been a healthy rose in my experience. Raised by Ralph Moore from (*R. wichuraiana* × 'Floradora') × ('Golden Glow' × 'Zee'). A fascinating parentage; if you care to look up 'Floradora' in the Floribunda section, you will see what it has added to Moore's strain.

'New Penny'   Shortest   Pink   Remontant   P2   H2   ****

A shining little rose; the foliage glitters and the pink flowers gleam against it. I am puzzled by the usual description of orange red, because although the buds are salmon, it is quite a light pink in general effect. Either it behaves differently whether in America or Britain, or else we have the wrong variety. We have a useful one, not only as a handsome plant, but for its fertile pollen. Raised by Ralph Moore from (*R. wichuraiana* × 'Floradora') × unnamed seedling. Introduced in 1962.

'Starina'   and   'Darling Flame'   P2   H2   ****

These two excellent Miniatures point out that European breeders are not content to leave the field to Ralph Moore. They both came from Meilland. 'Starina' is vermilion scarlet, a plant with many flowers of exquisite shape. It was raised from ('Dany Robin' × 'Fire King')× 'Perla de Montserrat', and introduced in 1965. If it has a failing, and one hesitates to express ingratitude at so good a rose, it is to be seen when the flowers are fading at the end of their career.

'Darling Flame' was introduced in 1971, under the denomination 'Minuetto'. It is a striking rose, with a colour on the vermilion side of orange; the parents were ('Rimosa' × 'Rosina') × 'Zambra'.

'Fairy Moss'   'Kara'   'Paintbrush'   'Dresden Doll'

These four are the early products of Ralph Moore's imaginative effort to breed Miniature Moss roses. At no time has the Moss rose been an easy subject for breeding, for the prototypes were sterile sports. However sterility is not always so complete as it appears and Pedro Dot raised 'Golden Moss', introduced by the Conard-Pyle Co. in 1932; it came from 'Frau Karl Druschki × ('Souvenir de Claudius Pernet' × 'Blanche Moreau'), that is Hybrid Perpetual, Hybrid Tea and Moss. I fear the name was a considerable exaggeration.

Ralph Moore made a cross 'Mark Sullivan' × 'Golden Moss'. Now 'Mark Sullivan' was an unhealthy Hybrid Tea from Charles Mallerin, who called it 'Président Chaussé'. Moore's cross was successful to the extent of producing a mossy Hybrid Tea; nothing great, but encouraging. So he went along for another generation by the cross: unnamed yellow Hybrid Tea × ('Mark Sullivan' × 'Golden Moss'). From the progeny, he selected a pure yellow seedling, and tried a third generation by putting its pollen on to 'Rumba'. This gave him the plant which after all that work was merely the tool he had been trying to forge for future use. It was a tool shaped like a mossy yellow Floribunda, and he called it 'Goldmoss'.

Breeders need more than one iron in the fire, and he had also been using a purple Moss, 'William Lobb'. A cross 'Pinocchio' × 'William Lobb' had given a promising seedling; and when that seedling received the pollen of 'New Penny', it produced the first mossy Miniature in 'Fairy Moss'. This was introduced in 1969, and was rose red.

By combining his two strains of Moss hybrids, and using 'Fairy Moss' also, he has opened the door to all sorts of modern Moss roses. It is a wonderful example of the rose breeder's art, but like all new developments, the prototypes are not necessarily absolutely right. 'Kara' is a single pink, 'Paintbrush' is buff yellow going white, and 'Dresden Doll' double pink. The moss is certainly there, but not with the Victorian charm we expected. Sad to say, the plants I have seen of these mossy Miniatures have been susceptible to blackspot. But these are teething troubles; and even if they were not overcome, what an example Ralph Moore has set!

CLIMBING HYBRID TEAS

It seems totally illogical to go to the trouble of dividing bush roses into Hybrid Teas and Floribundas, and then to neglect to do the same with Climbers. In my forty-three years of working in nurseries, I am well aware that a prospective purchaser of a climbing rose is nine times out of ten thinking about Hybrid Tea flowers around his windows. He is perfectly right to do so, because large flowers are particularly appropriate for the normal distance from which climbers are seen; if he wants Climbing Hybrid Teas, then he should be given such a class to choose from, and not a mixture of all sizes and types of flowers under the indigestible title 'Repeat Flowering Climbers'.

Climbing Hybrid Teas are normally plants of stiff growth, capable of flowering from the same system of branches for many years, and not too prompt in growing new basal shoots. For those reasons, it is essential to avoid losing shoots, a mischief easily done by leaving them untied. It is not sufficient to let shoots wave freely until the annual pruning; rather they should be tied in when they are noticed in the summer. Until that is done, they should annoy the conscientious gardener like a door banging in the wind.

Their eventual size is usually underestimated, to the regret of those who planted them too near one another. Four good strides from plant to plant ought to be considered the minimum distance. When they have been firmly planted, they should not be tied to a support until the soil is perfectly settled. Indeed it is best to wait until they grow, and then tie the new shoots into a fan shape, securing as far as possible the more horizontal positions first. As a guide to the distance between the trained shoots upon their support, elbow to finger tips will serve. Thereafter pruning will consist mainly of shortening the side shoots which the trained shoots bear. Do not leave the pruning late, because climbers are often the first roses to grow in the spring; it is a task for late autumn or even winter. Usually it takes three years for a climber to look as if it is really in business. From that time onwards, it is normally capable of bearing hundreds of flowers each year. I should add that Climbing Hybrid Teas do not flower as long as Hybrid Tea bushes; many are decidedly stingy in the autumn, and for them I have used the term 'Summer +', which means that the autumn flowers may be somewhat far apart on the plants. Many of these however, are most beautiful when they are most valuable, the first 'real' roses of the summer, in flower some weeks earlier than bush roses, especially when given a wall on which the sun shines.

Most of the ensuing varieties are sports from bushes of the same name, and it is not uncommon for these sports to occur in more than one place. Some have been all growth and little flower, and unfortunately the customers discover it before the nurserymen, who sell them before they bloom. 'Lady Sylvia, Climbing' and 'Peace, Climbing' are two to keep clear of. The readiness of Hybrid Teas to climb is clear indication that they are descended from one or more climbers; it helps to confirm the opinions of those who think the original of *R. chinensis* was a climber, and that Teas are children of the far growing *R. gigantea*. A nurseryman once told me that he could make any Hybrid Tea give him a climbing sport, by repeatedly taking propagating wood from the base of the stems; I don't know how successful he was, but privately I thought he had an excellent chance of raising the kind that don't flower.

'Allen Chandler' *Climber Crimson Remontant* P3 H3 ***
I am sorry to start off the Climbing Hybrid Teas with one which is semi-double, but I would make exceptions all the way for this excellent rose. Sad to say, it is becoming rare. It has large flowers of brilliant crimson, a fine sight. Amenable to staying within a desired space, it does not usually go very high. Raised by Mr Chandler from seed of 'Hugh Dickson' and introduced by George Prince of Oxford in 1923, when the National Rose Society described it 'one of the greatest acquisitions of recent years.'

'Aloha' *Climber Pink Remontant* P3 H2 ***
Do not use to cover a large space, because it may take years to grow to any height. On the other hand, it has advantages as a short climber, and may be grown as a shrub. The flowers are stuffed full of pink petals, the outside being darker than the inside. Maybe it is small for a Hybrid Tea, but in shape and fullness gives a good imitation. Raised by Eugene Boerner from 'Mercedes Gallart' × 'New Dawn', and introduced in 1949.

'Christine, Climbing' *Climber Yellow Summer +* P2 H2 *
Many bright yellow Climbers have come and gone since this sport was introduced in 1936. I know of none to equal its golden display about midsummer. The best plants I know are on walls of houses; it is apt to go about half way up a two storey house.

'Compassion' *Climber Apricot pink Remontant* P7 H3 ****
The sweet scent and pleasing colour of 'Compassion' have made a favourable impression on the rose world since my company introduced this rose in 1973; but it has another valuable feature of making basal growths with more freedom than common in the class. The colour varies from light to salmon pink; the deeper the pink, the more apricot. It has abundant foliage, dark and glossy, and is a fairly vigorous grower. I raised it from 'White Cockade' × 'Prima Ballerina'.

'Crimson Glory, Climbing'   *Climber   Dark red   Summer* +   P8   H1   *
No longer a favourite in Britain, but still popular in many other countries. Why don't we like it? The foliage a trifle dull? The old flowers too purple? Some mildew? Admittedly the dark red flowers are worth paying for, and lovely to smell. Discovered by Miller in 1941; introduced in the United States by Jackson & Perkins in 1946.

'Easlea's Golden Rambler'   *Climber   Yellow   Summer*   P3   H2   *
The name is misleading; think of it as Easlea's Golden Climber instead. It has large yellow flowers, with red marks on the outer petals. A vigorous grower, slightly more lax than most climbers because of its longer side shoots, it is best planted where its extremities are not too far out of reach, on a fence or pergola. Walter Easlea originally worked for William Paul & Son of Waltham Cross, until he made his own nursery at Leigh-on-Sea in Essex. Hybridizing was his chief interest, and he raised a Hybrid Tea called 'Lamia', which was an unusual colour, like smoked salmon with a bit more red in it. Readers of *Rose Annuals* of the period cannot fail to gather the impression that Easlea enjoyed the affection and respect of his contemporaries. No parentage is given for his 'Rambler', and it was introduced in 1932.

'Elegance'   *Climber   Primrose   Summer*   P2   H3   **
Grows fast and far, with a wicked armoury of thorns. If you have some thicket or corner over which you and nature are arguing, with nature getting the better of it, then I suggest you put 'Elegance' there, and give nature a Pyrrhic victory.
   The flowers are a surprise, perfect in their Hybrid Tea form though slightly smaller, lovely creamy yellow. I never tire of looking at them, and I cannot remember seeing one after the summer flush. This healthy and hardy rose came from Dr and Mrs Walter D. Brownell, of Little Compton, Rhode Island, from 'Glenn Dale' × ('Mary Wallace' × 'Miss Lolita Armour'), a mixture of *R. wichuraiana* and Hybrid Tea. It was introduced in 1937. The Brownells set out to breed bush roses which would endure harsh winters, and introduced them as Sub-Zero roses; and although they made quite a reputation thereby, in retrospect their more valuable work may prove to have been with climbers and ramblers. 'Elegance' could yet be valuable for breeding yellow Hybrid Teas.

'Ena Harkness, Climbing'   *Climber   Crimson   Summer* +   P5   H2   ***
The best way to grow this famous red rose is to plant it as a climber by a wall or fence. The foliage looks darker, and the flowers larger than in the bush form; I don't know why that should be. Moreover the sting is drawn from the chief failing of the variety, that she hangs her head, for as a climber she hangs it just sufficiently to afford a perfect view. The sport occurred in two nurseries, Gurteen & Ritson of Horley, Surrey, and R. Murrell of Bedmond Hill, Hertfordshire. It was introduced in 1954.

'Etoile de Hollande, Climbing'   *Climber   Crimson   Remontant* −   P7   H3   ***
Dark red and fragrant, one of the best Climbing Hybrid Teas to decorate the wall of a house in early summer. Opinions differ upon its subsequent performance. I do not expect to see many blooms after the first generous flush, but Norman Young in *The Complete Rosarian* claims that his plant was in flower for 161 days from mid May to the end of October; and Graham Thomas declares it 'recurrent'. It is well worth growing, and will normally go two storeys high upon a house, after a slow start. The sport was introduced by M. Leenders of Tegelen, Holland in 1931. Since writing this

I have seen a plant covered in bloom at midwinter, and have therefore changed Summer + in favour of Remontant minus.

'Golden Dawn, Climbing' *Climber Yellow Summer +*   P3   H2   **
This Climber was introduced from three sources: Armstrong of California in 1935, George Knight & Sons of Homebush, New South Wales in 1937, and E. B. Le Grice of North Walsham, Norfolk in 1947. In Britain we grow Le Grice's sport, and a very good one it is. The shoots are usually thick, closely clad with 'Golden Dawn's' attractive foliage, a little crinkle in it, a suggestion of colour to the leaf edge; the flowers are large, double, light yellow with a flush of red on the outside. Split centres are common, but easily forgiven, as they are not usually noticed until the flower is well open. A good one for wall and fence; although vigorous it is not usually a tall plant.

'Guinée' *Climber Dark red Summer +*   P4   H2   *
Charles Mallerin was quite a genius at capturing colours beyond the normal range, and this climber is the best of all roses to plant for those people who want their red ones so dark as to approach black. How the result is valued depends on the eyesight. I can look at a flower of 'Guinée' in my hand, and think it marvellous; but on the plant from a distance, the flowers are only dull dots to me. Other people, I gather, obtain a completely different visual impression. 'Guinée' grows quite easily, although the leaves are dull; it will climb most of the way up a two storey house. Whether you plant it or not depends how much you want the darkest red rose. Raised by Charles Mallerin from 'Souvenir de Claudius Denoyel' × 'Ami Quinard', and introduced in 1938 by Meilland in France and the Conard-Pyle Company in USA.

'Mme Abel Chatenay, Climber' *Climber Bicolour pink Remontant* P3 H3 **
Fortunate are those with an old plant of this in their gardens, for I fear that nurseries have given up propagating it, due to loss of vigour. It is one of the most free and continuous blooming Climbers of the type, and the only way I can see you getting it, is to beg some cuttings and root them under mist. We described the famous Chatenay in the Hybrid Teas, and it is superb as a climber. When Walter Easlea introduced it in 1917, he said 'the flowers are often of superior quality to the original dwarf form' and that is perfectly true. The sport was apparently discovered by Courtney Page, Secretary of the National Rose Society at that time.

'Mme Caroline Testout, Climber' *Climber Pink Remontant*   P3 H4   *
One of the earlier Climbing Hybrid Teas, and one of the more vigorous. It has gone straight up to the roof of countless houses, surrounding bedroom windows and gutters with bright pink flowers, sometimes inconsiderately, having regard to the colour of the masonry. The lower part of the plant is commonly an uncompromising array of thorny stems, not a leaf to be seen. But it is a rose to flower freely and long, so that sweeping pink petals from the terrace can be a regular task. It came from Chauvry of Bordeaux in 1901.

'Mme Edouard Herriot, Climbing' *Climber Coral orange Summer +* P3 H3   *
Spectacular when it behaves itself, that is by avoiding blackspot, which cannot be depended on. Although capable of a fair height, it is more often quite a short climber in England, easily recognized by its striking coral orange colour. If you see that

interesting colour, and find the plant has many large, flat thorns, it will almost certainly be Herriot. Introduced by Ketten Bros of Luxembourg in 1921.

'Mme Grégoire Staechelin' *Climber Pink Early summer* P7 H6 ****
If you don't mind a rose which has finished blooming before most have started, you may find a home for this gorgeous thing. Having one short time in flower, it makes a rare spectacle of it. Large double pink roses, delightfully creased as a dainty skirt might be, cover most of the plant and issue a sweet fragrance. It is hardy, despite being raised in sunny Spain, and we grow it on walls with chilly aspects very well. It can be kept within one storey height if desired, or allowed to grow higher. Don't remove the old flowers, because they turn into large hips, and no more will follow in any case. Raised by Pedro Dot from 'Frau Karl Druschki' × 'Château de Clos Vougeot' and introduced in 1927. The Conard-Pyle Company brought it out in the United States in 1929 as 'Spanish Beauty'.

'Mrs Pierre S. du Pont, Climbing' *Climber Yellow Summer* + P2 H2 *
The only place I have seen this fine yellow rose is in Paris, where it is so good that one assumes it should do well in all places of similar climate; and I wonder why it has not aroused more interest in England. In France they grow it successfully on pillars and pergolas, as well as on walls. The sport came from V. S. Hillock, Arlington, Texas in 1933. I should think there was probably also a French one.

'Mrs Sam McGredy, Climbing' *Climber Salmon to red Summer* + P2 H4 ***
The only sensible way to grow this darling of the 1930s is as a climber, in which form it is more robust than the bush ever was. The purple colour of the young leaves and the coppery colour of the young flowers are both entrancing, and at different times. There is some risk of blackspot. A leafy plant which seems to promise to leap out of bounds, but normally keeps to first storey height. Sports were found in Holland by G. A. H. Buisman & Son of Heerde; in France by the Widow Guillaud & Fils of Isère; and in the United States by the Western Rose Company of Van Nuys, California. The Dutch sport introduced in 1937, is the one grown in Britain.

'Paul's Lemon Pillar' *Climber Cream Early summer* P3 H4 *
Enormous pale lemon flowers, of high centred form, justify the continued planting of this rose. It flowers early, and then stops. I tried to grow it on one of our more inhospitable walls, in the hope that it would flower late enough for the Summer Show; but all it did was to refuse to flower until its head was over the wall. It does not like cold places. I could never see that it was a good rose for a pillar, it needs to be trained like a fan on a wall or fence. It is vigorous, and has the class of bloom one cannot forget. Raised by Paul & Son of Cheshunt from 'Frau Karl Druschki' × 'Maréchal Niel', and introduced in 1915.

'Shot Silk, Climbing' *Climber Orange pink Summer* + P5 H3 *
This charming rose has just the colour and foliage to make a sparkling climber; if it was more generous after its first flush of bloom, it would be everybody's choice. I have often been surprised at the affection this niggard inspires in its owners. The sport first appeared in Australia, and was introduced by George Knight & Sons in 1931.

CLIMBING FLORIBUNDAS

I take the members of this class to be those plants which are either sports from

Floribundas, or seedlings with flowers and foliage which could pass in a Floribunda. This class has taken some knocks, because some of the original Climbing Floribundas belied all expectations by scarcely deigning to flower at all. 'Else Poulsen, Climbing' was a prime example. It is a shame to damn them all for the transgressions of a few; and some of the modern types are exemplary in their flower production. We can expect great developments in this class. Their cultivation is similar to that for Climbing Hybrid Teas.

'Allgold, Climbing'   *Climber   Yellow   Summer* +   P2   H1   *
A handsome plant, needing its foliage alone to establish that. The bright yellow flowers are unfortunately not plentiful, but very effective. Introduced by Gandy's Roses, North Kilworth, Rugby, in 1961.

'Altissimo'   *Climber   Crimson   Remontant*   P2   H3   ***
This is the nearest we can find to a red 'Mermaid'. The large blooms are brilliant red, virtually single, and beautiful indeed. One could wish they appeared in greater abundance. Raised by Delbard-Chabert of Paris, and introduced in 1966.

'Circus, Climbing'   *Climber   Yellow & red   Summer* +   P3   H1   *
The rich colour of 'Circus' is most effective as a climber; and it will grow on cold walls. Found by Bernice L. House of Tyler, Texas, and introduced in 1961 by Armstrong Nurseries.

'Danse du Feu'   *Climber   Scarlet   Remontant*   P1   H3   ***
The double flowers grow close together, almost too close, and are produced as generously in autumn as in summer. The colour is on the orange side of scarlet, very effective but not vivid. It has to be balanced against the health and remarkable freedom of this variety that it finishes life somewhat atrociously purple. A moderate grower, with abundant foliage. Raised by Charles Mallerin from 'Paul's Scarlet Climber' × seedling of *R. multiflora,* and introduced in France in 1953. J & P brought it out in the United States in 1956 as 'Spectacular'.

'Golden Showers'   *Climber   Yellow   Remontant*   P3   H3   ***
A bushy kind of climber, but one which is in flower for a long time. The flowers are bright yellow, and open loosely; they can be attractive when wide open, with the dark stamens to be seen inside. A plant that is all gloss and smartness, from its bright leaves and yellow blooms. It does not usually grow very large. Raised by Dr W. E. Lammerts from 'Charlotte Armstrong' × 'Captain Thomas', and introduced by Germain's of Los Angeles in 1956. The Royal National Rose Society warns that it may need protection against blackspot, but in my experience it is not unduly prone to that disease.

'Handel'   *Climber   Pink & white   Remontant*   P6   H2   ***
A flower of fair size and good formation, most of it creamy white, flushed with pink and rose red, especially at the petal edges. From that recipe, it makes an exquisite bloom. I have greatly admired 'Handel', which nearly always has at least a few pretty flowers on it from summer to late autumn. Occasionally one sees a plant suffering from blackspot on its handsome leaves, and but for that it would be one of my five star roses. Raised by Sam McGredy from 'Columbine' × 'Heidelberg', and introduced in 1965.

'Iceberg, Climbing' *Climber   White   Remontant* P2 H1 **
The best of the Climbing Floribunda sports, in my opinion. I have been impressed by the cover given by the foliage, a good backcloth for the white flowers. Introduced by Cants in 1968.

'Masquerade, Climbing' *Climber   Yellow to red   Summer* + P3 H4 **
Whether to admire the spots of many colours which form a bunch of 'Masquerade', may be left to individual taste. Here is the climber to make the most of that strange colour change, and it is perfectly good and effective. Nobody is likely to walk past a plant in flower, without a second look, and maybe a third. It was discovered by C. J. Dillon of Northumberland, and introduced in 1958.

Some people train 'Joseph's Coat' as a climber, to obtain a similar effect over a longer period; but 'Joseph's Coat' is really a bush, and will not always climb far enough.

'Morning Jewel' *Climber   Pink   Summer* + P2 H3 ***
Worth growing for the sparkle of it in the summer. The foliage glistens, the warm pink of the semi-double flowers bursts out cheerfully. It is not quite so co-ordinated after its first flush, but produces flowers sporadically. One looks forward to it each year. A trouble free plant in my experience, and one of the best to fill the area it grows upon without leaving blank spaces. Do not expect it to cover a large space. Raised by Alec Cocker from 'New Dawn' × 'Red Dandy', and introduced in 1969.

'Pink Perpetue' *Climber   Pink   Remontant* P2 H3 ****
This flowers freely over a long period. The petals are bright pink inside with a deeper colour outside. I confess to finding the colour cold, but for those who like it, no better climber exists. The flowers are sufficiently double and lasting to cut for the house, and the plant is vigorous without being tall. Raised by C. Gregory & Son from 'Danse du Feu' × 'New Dawn', and introduced in 1965.

CLIMBING MINIATURES
It is pure mirage for us in Britain to visualize Climbing Miniatures growing no more than head high on slim posts, and flowering remontantly.

Yet this tantalizing vision may be near reality; and I have a horrible feeling that we have not made adequate trial of a class so potentially lovely. The Climbing Miniatures on sale in America and Australia are mostly from Ralph Moore, in nearly every case from the pollen of 'Zee', which we discussed under 'Easter Morning' in the Miniatures. Of these I have grown 'Jackie, Climbing' (which is not a sport, despite its name), 'Papoose' and 'Little Showoff'. The latter two flowered in summer only, and although 'Jackie, Climbing' made a better hand of blooming again, its colour and appearance were not endearing.

The other Climbing Miniatures are mainly sports from the little bushes, and we know that if a climbing sport appears, it brings no guarantee of height or flower freedom. Miniatures have a delicate balance of charm; let quite a small thing be wrong, and the variety is spoiled. I think this applies with greater force to their climbing forms, and while I wish I was more familiar with the new American varieties, I do not believe I should find my ideal among them. But it may be there tomorrow.

I visited Australia's specialist in Miniatures, the enthusiastic Roy Rumsey of Dural near Sydney. He had a climbing sport from a Miniature called 'Over the Rainbow'; and he attached the word 'Climbing' in front of it with the greatest pleasure.

'Nozomi'   *Trailer   White   Summer*   P1   H1   **

This comes from Japan, and the name means hope. The little green leaves might remind one of *Cotoneaster horizontalis*. The flowers are palest pearl, single, small and only seen in summer. It is doubtful how far Climbing Miniatures intend to grow, until they have been observed for some years. This one appears quite content with head height or less. It is being recommended as a ground cover rose, for which purpose one allows it to trail over the ground. My personal opinion is that this is an inelegant and untidy way to grow roses, and the problems of weed control that arise are far in excess of the trouble saved by any weeds that may be smothered. Raised by F. T. Onodera of Urawa, Japan, and introduced in 1968. The parents were 'Fairy Princess' × 'Sweet Fairy', of which the former is one of Ralph Moore's Climbing Miniatures, raised from 'Eblouissant' × 'Zee'.

'Perla Rosa, Climbing'   *Climber   Pink   Summer*   P2   H1   *

In habit this is almost ideal; we grew it on a stout bamboo cane, as a short pillar, and the plants held their flowers out delightfully. The brash pink colour and the short flowering season were against it. Introduced by Pedro Dot in 1947; the original 'Perla Rosa' was one of Dot's varieties too, bred from 'Perle des Rouges' × 'Rouletii', that is Polyantha and Miniature.

'Pink Cameo'   *Climber   Pink   Summer*   P2   H1   *

Not unlike the foregoing; the pink flowers are deeper in colour. Raised by Ralph Moore from ('Soeur Thérèse' × 'Wilhelm')× 'Zee'. Introduced 1954.

'Pompon de Paris, Climbing'   *Climber   Pink   Summer*   P2   H1   ***

The ideal way to grow this is to let it ramble along a low wall, such as might border a terrace. It is a beautiful plant in leaf and flower; but it forgot about being a Miniature when it decided to climb, because it will go up to a second storey window. This is one to treasure. The records do not reveal its origin.

SPECIES continued

R. gigantea   *Climber   White   Early summer*   P3   H2

The Giant Rose of north Burma and south-west China; so called from its great growth. As Graham Thomas pointed out at a conference in 1968, it was as well no larger ones were subsequently discovered, for if so the name became nonsense. The flowers are creamy white and single, fairly large for a wild rose, but by no means gigantic. Outdoors in Britain, one can scarcely hope for more than the odd flower from it. I once had a plant with shoots up to ten paces long, and having kept it a few years for very few flowers, hoped to see it in full bloom; but frost ended its life, always a likely fate of this rose in Britain. C. C. Hurst took it to be the pollen parent of three of his 'Stud Chinas', his main grounds being a comparison of characteristics. Nobody has disproved him as far as I know; and in that case *R. gigantea* is an important parent of modern roses. Some rosarians believe it to be the source of the Tea scent. It has been known as *R. odorata gigantea,* which is calling it a variety of the non-existent wild Tea rose, a strange procedure. A pink variety exists, *R. gigantea erubescens.*

GIGANTEA HYBRIDS

Because most western rose breeders have been concerned with breeding hardy roses, it follows that the tender *R. gigantea* has been of little interest to them. That should not stop research by breeders in warm climates. If Hurst is right, the Chinese used *R. gigantea* centuries ago, and we have hardy Hybrid Teas and Floribundas as a result. The following examples show that beautiful roses may be discovered from *R. gigantea;* if they are initially confined to the warmer parts of the earth, they may eventually be crossed with hardier roses, so that hybrids preserving their chief beauties can be grown everywhere.

'Belle Portugaise' *Climber Pink Midsummer* P3 H2
Given a warm wall and some shelter, this can be grown outdoors in England, as was successfuly shown for some years at the Royal Horticultural Society's gardens in Wisley. But the operation will normally be at risk in cold climates; it is a rose for places like California and the Canary Islands, or even the south of France. It was raised by Henri Cayeux, of the Lisbon Botanical Garden, and introduced in 1903 or shortly after. Both the dates and parentages vary in different authorities, but there is agreement that one of the parents was *R. gigantea.*

This climber is light pink, with the outside of the petals deeper; the flowers are double, and open loosely, that is to say the large petals are well apart. It has a silky look of summer about it. The English version 'Belle of Portugal' is sometimes used, although no great linguistic difficulty would seem to be solved thereby.

'Cooper's Burmese Rose' *Climber White Midsummer* P3 H2
This rose is also known as *R. cooperi,* although there is no evidence that it is a species; and those who appreciate that fact refer to it as 'Cooperi'. Why not use the more informative name that heads this paragraph? Burma is Burma, but Cooper may live anywhere.

An expedition in Burma collected seed, which was sent to Cornwall from Rangoon by Cooper, and distributed to interested people in England. I find no record to tell who raised this particular seedling, but a plant of it was reported well established at the National Rose Society's Trial Ground in Haywards Heath in 1937; and another, less happy, in the Royal Botanic Garden, Edinburgh. It can grow in Scotland, according to a report in the *Rose Annual 1976* of a vigorous plant at Crathes Castle near Banchory, well to the north east of that country. Crathes Castle is of some interest to British rosarians as having employed the young Millar Gault, future superintendent of Regent's Park in London where he created Queen Mary's Rose Garden. So beautiful and popular was it under his care, that even James Bond spent a few reflective moments in it!

'Cooper's Burmese Rose' has white flowers and highly polished leaves, leading to the theory that it may be a hybrid between *R. gigantea* and *R. laevigata.*

'La Follette' *Climber Pink Midsummer* P3 H2
The assumption must be that this was raised from 'Belle Portugaise', but there is no certainty. It came from Cannes, where it was raised by Mr Busby, gardener to Lord Brougham; the date given by Jäger is 'about 1910'.

If Hurst required convincing evidence that Teas came from *R. gigantea,* 'Belle Portugaise' and 'La Follette' provide it. They have the silky, long petals and attractive pointed form we associated with Teas. 'La Follette' is far too tender to attempt in any but the most temperate parts of Britain; but in Southill Park in Bedfordshire, there is a magnificent specimen in a greenhouse, covering a large wall and most of the roof. When my brother saw it several years ago, he estimated it was bearing over 1500 lovely rich pink blooms.

'Lorraine Lee' *Medium   Pink   Remontant*   P2   H1

Alister Clark of Bulla in Victoria, Australia, was an energetic and imaginative breeder of roses, and fond of using an enormous plant of *R. gigantea* which grew in his garden. He admitted that his records did not always go to the extent of revealing his pollen parents; but even without that sophistication, it was through his name that many people in the world learned to respect Australian rosarians.

'Lorraine Lee' is a pretty little rose from Clark's *R. gigantea* line; although it looks like a China, both in leaf and flower. We grew it successfully in our nursery in Hitchin for some years, and admired the bushy growth, great freedom of flowers, abundant little leaves so glossy, and the warm pink colour touched with apricot. The buds are well formed, and the flowers open small and semi-double. The parents are stated to be 'Jessie Clark' × 'Capitaine Millet'; the former was a seedling from *R. gigantea,* and the latter a seedling from 'Général Schablikine', which accounts for the China look. 'Lorraine Lee' was introduced in 1924 by Hackett & Company of Adelaide. At Hitchin we also grew 'Lorraine Lee, Climbing', which grew so far as to elicit the gibe that one needed binoculars to study the few flowers it bore. I understand it does better in Australia.

'Sénateur Amic' *Climber   Red   Early summer*   P4   H2

This can be grown in sheltered warm parts of Britain. It is bright carmine red, and opens to a flower that is virtually single. The buds are attractively long and pointed. Raised in France by Paul Nabonnand of Golfe Juan, and introduced in 1924. The parents were *R. gigantea* × 'General McArthur'.

'Susan Louise'

Many areas of the United States are suitable for Gigantea Hybrids; we may hope that somebody in that country will try to use *R. gigantea* to breed huge rose bushes: something the size of a lilac bush, covered with flowers like 'Peace'. The example was set by Charles E. Adams of San José, California, who obtained 'Susan Louise' from the seed of 'Belle Portugaise'. Introduced by the Stocking Rose Nursery in 1929, she is semi-double, pink, scarcely known in Britain. Of course she is nothing like my vision of the lilac bush; I wonder if she might lead to it?

12. Synstylae and Hybrids

The name of this section means styles together. One has only to see a flower to judge how apt the title is, for the styles protrude from the middle of the flower, fused together in a slender column as if they were one. In all other respects the recognition factors are the same as for the Indicae, namely pinnate leaves, smooth hips, stipules joined to the leaf stalk, and styles protruding; in the Indicae, the styles are separate, and they do not protrude so obviously.

The base of the styles is later incorporated in the fruit; so that hips of the Synstylae usually end with a slight protrusion, like a short beak. The styles are not numerous in this section, therefore the seeds are few and the hips small.

Botanists suggest there are twenty-four species; but it is my belief that most are merely forms of one another. Nearly all of them are trailing plants capable of growing a long way, because their natural habitat forced them through shrubs or trees in search of the sun. This immediately suggests how they may be used horticulturally; and those who wish to breed ground-cover roses surely need look no further for source material.

Nearly all the Synstylae come from China; one might ask whether there is some clue to the evolution of the rose, in that each sub-genus or section appears to have a particular region, as if there was originally one prototype of each, from which its descendants varied and travelled. Nature is rarely as simple as that, and there are sufficient exceptions to confound the theorist, of which the Synstylae offer three, in the form of a species each from India, Europe and America.

I renew the reminder that the recognition factors apply to the species, but not necessarily to the hybrids.

SPECIES

R. anemoneflora *Trailer White Summer* P4 H2
The anemone-flowered rose is not a true species; but it will not do for every writer to change the accepted order of things, and therefore I meekly follow authority until such time as the difficult task of assessing the Synstylae is achieved. They cross fertilize one another readily, and even if seed were newly imported, there is no guarantee that it would not have been made a hybrid in the wild.

This is a tender rose, with small double flowers resembling *Anemone nemorosa*. They are pink in the bud and open white. It has also been known as *R. triphylla*, from having some of its leaves composed of three leaflets; and *R. sempervirens anemoniflora*. Indeed there is quite a resemblance to *R. sempervirens* in the flowers. It was discovered by Robert Fortune in a garden in Shanghai, and sent to England in 1844.

R. arvensis   *Trailer   White   Summer*   P6   H5
The Field Rose; after the Dog Rose, perhaps the most common British wild rose; and
it comes after it in flowering too, about ten days later. Also common in western and
central Europe, it is easily recognized by its long trailing growth over the ground or
low bushes, by its thin stems with some purple colour in the young bark, and by its
clear white flowers. It has had several names: *R. repens* and *R. serpens* refer to its
creeping habit; *R. silvestris* because it may be found in woods, to which the Synstylae
are adapted; and *R. candida* for its whiteness. It has also been called the White Dog
Rose, by a misapprehension of relationships, and of course the Field Rose, which is a
translation of *R. arvensis,* and serves to prove that a variety of habitats suits it, from
woods to fields.

Two more claims to fame have been made for it, that it was the white rose of York,
on the grounds that Yorkshire was full of it, whereas the rival claimant, *R.* × *alba*
would have been less common; and that it is the rose Shakespeare knew as the
musk-rose. A case can be made for the second claim, because the lovely lines from *A
Midsummer Night's Dream,* 'I know a bank whereon the wild thyme blows', refer to a
place in the countryside embellished with wild flowers. *R. arvensis* is the only wild
rose in Britain that can be taken for a Musk, and it is indeed the most closely related.
Shakespeare's musk-rose 'quite over-canopied' the pretty scene; which only *R.
arvensis* could do, being the solitary wild climbing rose in Britain; it is true that the
real Musk Rose had arrived, probably by about 1540, and was to be the only climbing
rose available to gardeners for a long period; but I cannot see Shakespeare mixing a
cultivated plant with the natural flora of the English countryside, 'Where oxlips and
the nodding violet grows.' He knew it too well. And if anyone seeks to remind me
that the play was set near Athens, I shall ask if Bottom is a common name in Greece.

ARVENSIS HYBRIDS
Sometime early in the nineteenth century, a series of hybrids of *R. arvensis* was
introduced to British rosarians as Ayrshire Roses. They had many advantages in
those days, when there were scarcely any climbing roses to be had: they were hardy,
they grew fast, they could cover banks or rough places, and they did not object to
some shade, a rare thing for roses. 'Wilderness Rose' was the epithet used by Thomas
Rivers.

They would be called ramblers if they were still grown today; I have tried to avoid
the word rambler, having had to explain its difference from a climber at regular
intervals in the course of my profession. I think trailer is better. A climber climbs up;
a trailer trails along; but a rambler can ramble anywhere.

'Dundee Rambler'   *Trailer   White   Summer*
The Ayrshires appear to have started in Scotland, with some mystery, for the Earl of
Loudon is said to have obtained the seeds originally responsible from an expedition
that went to Canada in 1767. But *R. arvensis* is not native to Canada; the botanist
who collected a common British plant would not have advanced his standing; and the
seedlings raised were clearly related to *R. arvensis,* and eventually sold as Ayrshire
Roses. The report came from Joseph Sabine, Secretary of the Royal Horticultural
Society, in 1822; and I think that with a time lag of fifty-five years from the
expedition, we are entitled to doubt it. Moreover, I suspect that there was quite a
long period between 1767 and the introduction of Ayrshires, which so far as I know
are not mentioned in eighteenth-century catalogues. Perhaps there were two lots of
seed, and a wrong identification at some stage.

'Dundee Rambler' did not come from Loudon Castle in Ayrshire, but from Mr Martin of Rose Angle, Dundee, who raised 'several of our prettiest varieties', according to Thomas Rivers. This one was double and white. The date of introduction is unknown. Mr Martin's strangely named abode tempted him to dub some of his Ayrshires after it: 'Angle' and 'Angle Blush' are puzzling rose names without that knowledge.

'Splendens'   *Trailer   Blush   Summer*
Of interest because it was one of the varieties which was also called 'Myrrh-scented'; a 'peculiar scent', says Rivers. The buds were red, the flowers light pink and double. Origin unknown.

'Ayrshire Queen'   *Trailer   Purple red   Summer*
In the absence of any plants, we cannot be sure how much this rose departed from the appearance of its clan. Thomas Rivers raised it from 'Blush Ayrshire' × 'Tuscany'; the latter is a French Rose, and we may guess at the colour it gave from considering Edward Le Grice's 'News', which was fathered by 'Tuscany Superb'. 'Ayrshire Queen' was introduced in 1835, as the only dark Ayrshire known; we may note that its English raiser was canny enough to put the Scotch name on it. But only thirteen years later, it had failed to get into William Paul's comprehensive list of roses in *The Rose Garden*.

Thomas Rivers gave a warning against duds concerning an Ayrshire named 'Lovely Rambler', or 'Crimson Ayrshire': 'its petals too flaccid, to be much esteemed; it is mentioned here to prevent its two imposing names from misleading the amateur.'

'Crimson Ayrshire'? Wasn't that dark?

'Bennett's Seedling'   *Trailer   White   Summer*
This double white was raised by Mr Bennett, gardener to Lord Manners at Thoresby in Nottinghamshire; and was also known as 'Thoresbyana'. It was a double form of *R. arvensis,* white, with a good reputation for freedom of flower. Introduced in 1840.

'Ruga'
A rose one would like to know more about; it was said to be a hybrid between *R. arvensis* and a China, and to have been raised in Italy early in the nineteenth century. William Paul adds a significant sentence to his approving notice of it: 'A good seed-bearer.' It was light pink, fading to white, 'very sweet'. It is listed in *Modern Roses* as *R. × ruga*.

SPECIES & VARIETIES continued

R. filipes   R. helenae   R. longicuspis   P6   H5   **

These three are easily confused, so if we look at them side by side we may understand them better. All three are vigorous trailers; *R. filipes* and *R. longicuspis* are capable of growing shoots as long as three tall men in a summer; *R. helenae* is not quite so ambitious. Their natural way of growing is to form a tangled mound, from which the long shoots explore the surrounding jungle. Sooner or later a young shoot will grow fast upwards through the mound, and its hooked thorns will catch in branches above. Then it is away into a tree, with the object of growing through the tree and flowering in the sun. The result is a remarkable floral display, and to achieve it the shoots will grow yards and yards. This habit teaches us that if we wish to train these roses through trees, we should copy nature by letting them form a mound first, instead of tying them to the tree trunk as soon as we plant them. Usually such sites are difficult; a rose suddenly transplanted to the foot of an elm, after a year of luxury in a nursery, finds problems in securing its food and moisture; it may need a few years, and plenty of water, before it is ready to ascend. Then one can help guide it into the tree. Don't plant it next to the tree trunk, but rather under some low branches.

All three have small creamy white flowers with prominent yellow stamens. The clusters of flowers borne by *R. filipes* and *R. longicuspis* can be enormous. Presumably the plants are not always certain of reaching the light, and to insure against failure, they are able to bear over a hundred flowers in one great cluster. *R. helenae* also bears many blooms, but in more compact heads. They flower in summer only; *R. helenae* is likely to be the first of them to bloom.

One cannot climb up to smell the flowers, so it is fortunate that their delicious fragrance is expelled into the air. This may be a device to attract the rose's normal insect visitors to an unaccustomed destination, the top of a tree. It is a pity if these roses flower in cold or windy weather, for one of their sweetest gifts is then lost and blown away. Graham Thomas made the point in the *Rose Annual 1965* that the scent of the Synstylae comes not from the petals, but from the stamens. That observation leads to several questions about so interesting a change in the rose's normal chemistry. Is it a survival from some evolutionary period before flowers had petals? Is it forced upon the plant by the speed of its growth, a short cut as it were? Is it done because much of the foliage is in the shadow of the host plant, slow to inhale and activate the necessary elements? Do the petals themselves usurp some of the normal functions of the leaves? Is it done because the stamens can eject the volatile oils more easily than a petal, the stimuli for ejection being less up in the air than near the ground? Can we steal this virtue from the Synstylae, and make more roses breathe fragrance out of stamens as well as petals? To what extent are the stamens in other roses fragrant? I don't know the answers to any of these, I am only asking the question. (One of the Royal National Rose Society's Presidents, John Clarke of Wilmslow, was very fond of introducing controversial matters with those innocent and diplomatic words, 'I am only asking the question'.)

The young shoots grow so fast, that for quite a length at their ends the stems and the leaves show colours which may be immature, but are pleasant to see; sometimes they are almost red. And the final beauty of their year is hundreds of tiny hips, of which *R. helenae* is the most handsome bearer.

It is doubtful whether true stock of *R. filipes* exists in Britain, unless it is the vigorous rose called 'Kiftsgate', after the Gloucestershire garden in which it was found to be notable. The name of the species is from the word filipendula, which means hanging by a thread, and is an allusion to the thin flower stalks. *R. helenae* was named after the wife of E. H. Wilson, a famous plant seeker, and 'longicuspis' means having a long pointed end; I confess I am not certain which part of the plant it refers to, but the hips are so small that the term long is only true in relation to their size.

R. moschata and R. brunonii

R. moschata is the Musk Rose, familiar to everybody by name, but who has seen it? It was reported to have been brought to England from Italy by Thomas Cromwell, which puts the date before 1540, in which year he lost his head. For three hundred years, it was generally described as growing three or four metres high, flowering late in the summer, or even early autumn. For much of that time, it was the only climbing rose grown in gardens; and there were reckoned to be plenty more in its native places, in Spain, North Africa and Madeira.

By the early twentieth century, *R. moschata* was being described entirely differently, as growing much bigger and flowering early rather than late. The original had obviously been supplanted and was virtually lost to cultivation. It then appeared that there was no use going to Spain, North Africa or Madeira to look for it, because it was as rare there as in England. We must therefore suppose that far from being a native of that region, it came, like most of the Synstylae, from much further east. There is a French account from the late eighteenth century of a plant cultivated in Ispahan, known as the Chinese Rose Tree. Seeds were sent to Paris, and proved to be the common (as it was in those days) Musk Rose. If the people of Ispahan named it Chinese, it is strange that the plant explorers did not note its presence in China or about the Himalayas. One should read three fascinating articles upon the subject, by Norman Young in the *Rose Annuals* of 1960 and 1962, and by Graham Thomas in 1965; 'The Mystery of the Musk Rose' in *Climbing Roses Old and New* by Graham Thomas describes his efforts to discover it again, and summarizes the affair in masterly fashion. Seed was eventually discovered in Spain, and plants from it are growing in the Royal Horticultural Society's garden at Wisley.

According to Thomas Rivers in the 1840 edition of *The Rose Amateur's Guide,* 'The White Musk Rose is one of the oldest inhabitants of our gardens, and probably more widely spread over the face of the earth than any other rose.' In that case, how extraordinarily thorough has been its eclipse! We find ourselves left without any wild rose we can identify as *R. moschata.* The conclusion must be that it never was wild, but rather a form of one of the Synstylae, or a hybrid between two of them which came true from seed, apart from its variations between single and double. Whether it originated in China, or in some country to the west of China, we have no idea. Nor do we know when it completed its journey to the Mediterranean area.

The supplanter of the Musk Rose appears to be *R. brunonii.* This is a vigorous plant, notable for its leaves, which are so coppery red when young, and apt to point downwards. It is a plant which bears so much foliage, you think it might choke itself. It bears creamy white flowers in great abundance about midsummer. I grew it at Hitchin quite successfully in the open, despite its reputation of being tender.

Another complication for the future is growing up in regard to *R. brunonii.* Its name is given in *Modern Roses* as *R. moschata nepalensis* or the Himalayan Musk Rose. We have in the Royal National Rose Society's gardens a wonderful plant labelled 'Paul's Himalayan Musk', which is nothing like *R. brunonii,* having duller and smaller foliage, as if it had met *R. multiflora* in its career; it is blessed with the greatest sweep of blossom one can imagine, a multitude of tiny flowers, pale, with a touch of lilac pink in them.

MOSCHATA HYBRID
Many roses are said to have *R. moschata* as a parent, although we cannot check those statements now. Most of them fall more naturally under other headings, for example the Noisettes among the Indicae; but there is one beautiful rose to be mentioned here:

R. × **dupontii**   *Tall   Blush white   Midsummer*   P5   H2   ******
'Dupontii' grows as a spreading shrub, and makes good use of its breadth to cram in as many flowers as it can, whether on high shoots, low shoots, in the middle of the bush or at its limits. The time this abundance is especially seen is during the three

years between the plant's establishment and full maturity; which prompts the suggestion of thinning out old wood frequently and thoroughly. It is better to look down upon a plant full of bloom than to look up at a lot of greenery.

The flowers are single, creamy white with a faint blush, fragrant and symmetric; the word that conveys their nature is bridal. The leaves are soft grey green. It is thought to be a cross between *R. gallica* and *R. moschata;* it is known to have been in existence in 1817, and is named after André Dupont, who was the founder of the rose collection at the Luxembourg Gardens in Paris, and director until succeeded by Eugène Hardy.

SPECIES & VARIETIES continued

R. multiflora   *Taller   White   Summer*   P4   H2
One of the least attractive of wild roses, but one of the most generous and amazing parents. Its leaves are dull, its white flowers small, and it is in such a hurry to drop its petals, that you will be lucky to see the bushes in bloom at all if the wind is blowing. The small hips are as dull as the leaves, but the birds can see them and make haste to eat them. In spite of all these disabilities, it has had a great influence on modern roses; also upon the rose industry, which in America in particular uses *R. multiflora* as a rootstock. Unfortunately it is also the best indicator of virus, in the sense that if a virus is present in the rose being grafted, it is liable to exhibit itself in plants grown on *R. multiflora,* whereas it may remain latent and unseen if a different rootstock is used. There are pink varieties, *R. multiflora cathayensis,* with a larger flower, and *R. multiflora carnea,* which is double.

R. multiflora is a hardy shrub from East Asia. It was for some years known as *R. polyantha,* a name it gave to its first offspring after it arrived in Europe.

R. multiflora nana   *Shorter   White   Summer* +   P4   H2
A dwarf form of *R. multiflora,* and with much more charm. The petals are wider, and remain on the plants longer. Presumably it is a hybrid, because it has all the signs of a remontant rose; if grown from spring sown seed, the young plants will flower in three months, and seed has been sold as the 'Fairy Rose' for that purpose. The seedlings show variation, from single to semi-double, from white to pink, from good to bad. Although it is said to flower all through the season, my experience is that after a splendid show in summer, it is apt to be spasmodic for the rest of the season, and sometimes to remain dull green and flowerless. The short plants spread fairly wide. I have no information regarding its origin.

R. multiflora platyphylla   *Climber   Pink   Summer*   P2   H1
Famous for its romantic name, the Seven Sisters Rose. It is an intrusive plant, with thick canes and large leaves, wrinkled and coarse; it grows with vigour, gets mildew, and bears huge trusses of small flowers. Their colour is inconsistent, from light to deep pink, with a suggestion of lilac. It looks a greedy rose to me, and grows fast until late in the season, so that its unripened wood may fall victim to the frost. It was a cultivated rose in China, and came to London in 1815. The varietal name refers to its broad leaves.

R. multiflora watsoniana
This is an oddity, known also as the 'Bamboo Rose'. It has strangely deformed leaflets, long and narrow, sometimes patched with white. No beauty, but it does

indicate what strange tricks *R. multiflora* can play. Whether it came from a Japanese garden, or from one in Albany, New York, is the choice offered by the reports of its origin.

MULTIFLORA HYBRIDS
Descendants from *R. multiflora* normally have three points of identification: clusters of many small flowers; dull, rough looking leaves, usually light green; and stipules which are not only deeply toothed, but prominent as that small feature goes. The main characteristic is the small flowers, and in favour of it we accept leaves and stipules showing affinity to some other parent.

POLYANTHAS
'Pâquerette'
Credit for the first Polyantha, and thus for a significant contribution to modern roses, belongs to Guillot Fils of Lyon-Monplaisir, France. 'Pâquerette' set the pattern for the new class, of being short and flowering in clusters. I have read a statement that *R. multiflora* is the only rose with a tendency to breed dwarf varieties. This is untrue. Not only have we the evidence of the Miniatures to show that *R. chinensis* does the same, but from my own breeding experience I know that *R. californica* follows suit. In all probability, there are others, too.

Seeds of *R. multiflora* were apparently sent to France from Japan about 1860; there is more than one account of when and to whom, and of course there may have been more than one consignment. It is assumed that *R. multiflora* was pollinated by a China, and thus produced 'Pâquerette', a dwarf, white and remontant rose. The name is frequently printed as 'Ma Pâquerette', occasionally as 'La Pâquerette'. It was introduced in 1875.

'Mignonette'
In 1879, the second Polyantha came from the widow Rambaud of Lyon; it was white, 'Anna-Maria de Montravel'; in 1880, Guillot introduced 'Mignonette', the first to show some pink with the white in its double flowers. It is presumably of similar parentage to 'Pâquerette'.

'Gloire des Polyantha'
Although there were only a few Polyanthas by 1887, Guillot brought this variety out as the glory of them in that year. It was a seedling from 'Mignonette', and a considerable advance in colour, being bright pink. Sudden colour changes were to be a particular feature of the class, as we shall see.

'Marie Pavié'   *Shorter Pale pink Remontant*   P4 H1   *
This blushing rose had some interesting characteristics; it had scarcely any thorns, a good scent, and pretty double flowers. It was raised by M. Allégatiere of Lyon, and introduced in 1888. A climbing sport appeared from it in 1904. The name in several authorities is 'Marie Pavic'.

'Perle des Rouges'
White in 1875, pink in 1887, and now the reds were appearing. This was cherry red, raised by M. Dubreuil of Lyon, and introduced in 1896. There had been one called 'Red Pet' in 1888, but it was more of a China than a Polyantha.

'Katharina Zeimet' *Shorter   White   Remontant*   P4   H1   *
A little plant of great refinement; the double white flowers are carried daintily apart,
and shown against leaves darker than in most of the class. It was introduced in 1901,
and survived in most collections of Polyanthas until the class succumbed to the
success of Floribundas. The stems are thin, the flowers fragrant. Peter Lambert of
Trier raised it from 'Etoile de Mai' × 'Marie Pavié', both of them Polyantha. It was
popular in the United States, under the name 'White Baby Rambler'.

The Polyantha class collected a number of names as it proceeded, of which Baby
Ramblers was one. They were Fairies, Pets, Daisies, Dwarfs and Pompons. The two
most commonly in use were Polyantha Pompon and Dwarf Polyantha.

In the year he introduced 'Katharina Zeimet', Peter Lambert brought out another
white Polyantha called 'Schneewittchen', which name was later used for the famous
'Iceberg'.

'Mme Norbert Levavasseur' *Shorter   Crimson   Remontant*   P2   H1
The name proved too much for the Americans, who promptly called it 'Red Baby
Rambler', and ensured its popularity. This rose is an important one in the
development of the Polyantha, for it was the parent of 'Orléans Rose'. It was deep
red, although the colour went wickedly blue. Levavasseur et Fils raised it from
'Crimson Rambler' × 'Gloire des Polyantha'; 'Crimson Rambler' was a genuine
climber, not a baby one. Introduced in 1903.

'Orléans Rose' *Shorter   Rose red   Remontant*   P2   H1
In 'Orléans Rose', the pattern of Polyantha roses was set for the future, mainly
because it provided many of them itself, by sports and its seed. It was also to be
responsible for the eclipse of the class, because Svend Poulsen grew from its seed
'Else' and 'Kirsten Poulsen'.

Geranium red is the colour of 'Orléans Rose' according to several authorities; a
quite amazing statement to those of us who have seen 'Independence', and
remember growing 'Orléans Rose' year after year. It was much nearer pink; and to
call it rose red is generous enough to it. Raised by Levavasseur et Fils from seed of
'Mme Norbert Levavasseur', and introduced in 1909.

'Ellen Poulsen' *Short   Pink   Remontant*   P3   H2
I remember this rose with affection, for it was one of the most free and continuous in
flower, and had an air of refinement about its foliage. The colour was deep, between
pink and rose red. It was raised by Dines Poulsen from 'Mme Norbert Levavasseur'
× 'Dorothy Perkins', and had some of the deeper, burnished colour of *R.
wichuraiana's* leaves. Introduced in 1911.

'Echo' *Short   Pink to white   Remontant*   P3   H1
Quite different from the other Polyanthas. It was a dwarf, remontant sport from the
climber 'Tausendschön', and much the same colour, rose pink with a white centre,
and a tendency to lose the pink. The flowers were different from the rest of the class,
for instead of the neat blooms of 'Marie Pavié' or the pompons which were
developing through 'Orléans Rose', 'Echo' had fairly wide blooms with the outer
petals curving up to make a bowl-shaped flower. It was introduced by Peter Lambert
in 1914. Then came an extraordinary series of sports, from one to the next: 'Greta
Kluis', red, in 1916; 'Anneke Koster', red, in 1927; 'Dick Koster', pink, in 1929,
culminating in the attractive 'Margo Koster', orange salmon, in 1931.

'Miss Edith Cavell' *Shorter Bright crimson Remontant* P2 H1

This rose began the career of a famous breeder, Gerrit de Ruiter of Hazerswoude, Holland. He was cutting budwood of 'Orléans Rose' in August 1914, when he found a shoot bearing red flowers. After propagation and trial, he found it to be good, and it was introduced by Jan Spek in 1917. If the date of discovery is correct, which it should be, for De Ruiter himself stated it, and August 1914 is the kind of date one remembers, then a remarkably short time passed in working up stock for introduction. The Dutch have nothing to learn about propagation; they will turn one rose bush into thousands in twelve months, by grafting every eye under heat, starting in early winter. The grafts are joined in three weeks, and have shoots in six or seven, which provide more eyes for the next batch of grafts. De Ruiter said he had four plants of 'Miss Edith Cavell' in 1915, and allowing 20 possible grafts per plant, that would give the propagator 80 young plants by the winter. Say he struck ten from each, and he has 800; and he would be capable of multiplying by ten again, to have 8000 by the summer. If he wished, he could then propagate out of doors to have 80,000 plants on sale for autumn of 1917. These figures leave out of consideration the stock of old plants which remain from each stage. Such haste is by no means the rule, but there was an incentive applying to sports, that somebody else might find a similar one.

'Miss Edith Cavell' was a great improvement on any red in the class; dark yet brilliant, its little flowers were so close in the large trusses as to make a crimson carpet. The name gave some trouble, because another 'Edith Cavell' was introduced in England in 1918 by Chaplin Brothers, a cream Hybrid Tea. De Ruiter's variety was prefixed for a time by Nurse, and finally settled for Miss.

De Ruiter specialized in Polyanthas, and in finding sports among them, but it was some years before he began to breed roses. He soon made a name at that, and one of his sons, Gysbert, has continued since his father's death. Breeders cannot foresee what others will get from their roses; 'Miss Edith Cavell' led to 'Robin Hood', and thus to 'Iceberg'.

'Coral Cluster' *Shorter Coral pink Remontant* P2 H1

This rose is the first to suggest that the Polyanthas had a surprising colour change in store. It was a sport of 'Orléans Rose', introduced by R. Murrell in 1920, and promptly recognized in the *Rose Annual 1921* as 'quite a new shade amongst the polyanthas'. The colour is pale, and the coral touch most pleasing.

'Baby Faurax' *Shortest Amethyst Remontant* P4 H1 *

R. multiflora astonishes us again with flowers of dark amethyst in 'Baby Faurax'. They are small, very double, and fragrant. The plant does not distinguish itself by growing very much, being stumpy and rather ugly, which is a shame because the flowers are pretty. I recommend anyone to try it, because this is the nearest thing to a blue rose, and an interesting curiosity. The best way to grow it is in a pot in the greenhouse; let it stand outside after flowering. It is certainly not a Miniature, despite the descriptions to be found in some catalogues. It was raised by Leonard Lille of Lyon, and introduced in 1924. Speculation about its parentage has not found an answer, apart from a suggestion it may be a dwarf version of one of the Multiflora Climbers.

'Superb' *Shorter Crimson Remontant* P2 H1

Dark crimson, with neat, small flowers; this was discovered by De Ruiter and introduced in 1927. He said it was one of the 'Orléans Rose' group, without indicating which variety it sported from. Frequently listed as 'Superba', a name already shared by four other varieties. The value of 'Superb' is shown by the ensuing sports from it.

'Golden Salmon'   *Shorter   Orange   Remontant*   P2   H1
The promise of 'Coral Cluster' was abundantly fulfilled by 'Golden Salmon'. Here, and for the first time, rose colours moved into that part of the spectrum we call orange. How and why the Multiflora Hybrids broke into completely new colours by a series of sports is a mystery. It would be an interesting enquiry, to seek a relationship between the act of sporting and the formation of the colour compounds.

De Ruiter discovered this sport in plants of 'Superb', and he named it 'Goldlachs'. It was introduced in 1926. He followed it in 1929 with one of its own sports, said to hold its colour better, for 'Golden Salmon' unfortunately ended its career in disgrace from magenta. 'Golden Salmon Supérieur' (or Improved in Britain) was thenceforth generally grown instead,

'Robin Hood'   *Medium + Red   Remontant*   P2   H2
We now come to a Polyantha different from the 'Orléans Rose' type. It is usually called a Hybrid Musk, and grows into a spreading bush, with narrow, dark, smooth leaves. The flowers are red, with white at the centre, small, opening with a semi-double appearance, and multitudinous. It was raised by the Rev. J. H. Pemberton from a seedling × 'Miss Edith Cavell', and turned out to be a valuable parent in the hands of Wilhelm Kordes. Introduced in 1927.

'Gloria Mundi'   *Shorter   Orange vermilion   Remontant*   P2   H1
From 'Superb' came this sport, introduced in 1929. It was a wonder of the rose world, the first of the orange vermilion colours, which were later to become so common in the Floribundas and Hybrid Teas. The Dutch salesmen wore a single little flower in their buttonholes, and filled their order books on the strength of it. De Ruiter discovered it, and similar colours followed in the next few years. 'Paul Crampel' came from Kersbergen in 1930, the name borrowed from a vivid and popular pelargonium much used for bedding; and 'Gloire du Midi', a sport from 'Gloria Mundi', from De Ruiter in 1932.

'Gloria Mundi' marks the climax of the Polyanthas, because in the 1930s their shortcomings became obvious with Floribundas beside them; they faded out of the rose catalogues soon after 1945. The neat little flowers were seen to be small beside 'Else Poulsen' and 'Donald Prior'. Their tendency to succumb to mildew contrasted with the health of 'Kirsten Poulsen' and 'Dainty Maid'. Their leaves were outdone by the handsome influence of the Indicae upon Floribunda foliage. And worst of all, they were not stable. The series of sports had one great drawback, that they were even happier to revert than they had been to sport. Thus a carefully planned bedding scheme was spoiled, because half the flower, or a stem, or complete bushes reverted to one of their originals, or part way back. That the nursery trade could have done more to keep the stocks pure is probable, but only as a delaying measure. Henceforward the Polyantha class, with all its beauty, was to be represented by roses of different character, such as 'Ballerina', which follows.

The wonderful colours of 'Golden Salmon' and 'Gloria Mundi' were no help to breeders at all. These sports were of the kind where only the exterior tissue changed; the interior tissue, including the sexual system, behaved as if the sports had not occurred. A possible exception to this is 'Miss Edith Cavell', one of the ancestors of 'Baby Château', through which the pelargonium colours eventually came to modern roses.

'Ballerina' *Medium + Light pink Remontant* P1 H2 ***

A splendid, dense plant, often with a squared-off look, and nearly always in good health and vigour. The flowers are small and single, light pink with a white eye; when a basal shoot arises, it bears a huge head of them, like a mop. This rose went unnoticed by most British nurserymen, until Fryers of Knutsford had the perception to advance it. A group of plants can form a handsome clump.

No doubt this was one of Pemberton's seedlings, for it was introduced by his successor, J. A. Bentall, in 1937. We have no information as to its parents, but in the same year a very similar variety appeared in Germany, raised by Peter Lambert, and named 'Mozart'. It's parents were 'Robin Hood' × 'Rote Pharisäer', and it varies from 'Ballerina' in having a deeper pink around its white eye; its foliage is slightly more inclined towards the multiflora type. Slightly taller than both 'Ballerina' and 'Mozart', and also charming, is 'Belinda', which came from Bentall in 1936, and looks like a sister of 'Ballerina'.

In 1977 my firm introduced the first good red rose after 'Ballerina's' style. It is 'Marjorie Fair', bred from 'Ballerina' × 'Baby Faurax'. The flowers are a cheerful carmine red with a white eye.

'Bashful' 'Doc' 'Dopey' 'Grumpy' 'Happy' 'Sleepy' 'Sneezy'

Separated from Snow White and from one another, the names of some of the seven dwarfs do not exactly dignify a rose variety. They were raised by De Ruiter, and introduced by C. Gregory & Son as Compacta Roses in 1954–5; while the firm of Willicher Baumschulen presented them in Germany under the following names: Giesebrecht, Degenhard, Eberwein, Burkhard (what a splendid version of 'Grumpy'!), Alberich, Balduin and Bertram respectively.

Their character was to grow short, with as many small flowers upon them as could be crammed in their limited space. 'Grumpy' in particular disobeyed with an occasional long shoot. Had they not come out en bloc as a family, I think nobody would have taken notice of them, for they are inelegant, their colours are dull reds or pinks, and the flowers stay until they wither. The best I can say of them is that they exhibited an interesting if unlovely aspect of Multiflora Hybrids, one which might be further investigated. Of the four parentages supplied, three were between 'Robin Hood' and Polyantha seedlings. 'Dopey' and 'Happy' are red; 'Bashful' is single, red with a white eye; the others are brash pinks.

'Yesterday' *Medium Pink Remontant* P6 H1 ***

Elegance can dignify Polyanthas, as this variety demonstrates, with its small, burnished leaves, and airy sprays of little flowers. The flowers are pink, and they admit in a pleasing way a suggestion of lavender as they age. 'Yesterday' is an unusual rose, apt to send up occasionally long shoots; it is particularly effective as a little hedge or as a standard. The flowering period is long, and the fragrance very sweet.

The parents I used to raise it were ('Phyllis Bide' × 'Shepherd's Delight') × 'Ballerina'; my firm introduced it in 1974. I find pleasure in seeing the narrow petals open out flat around a little tuft of yellow stamens. Perhaps 'Yesterday' will lead the Polyanthas to their tomorrow.

CLIMBING POLYANTHAS

Bred from *R. multiflora* × 'Rêve d'Or', it indicates the reluctance with which multifloras accept yellow, and that when they do, they lose it as fast as they can, and multiflors accept yellow, and that when they do, they lose it as fast as they can, and fade to white. I learned this anew when trying to raise a yellow 'Ballerina'. 'Aglaia' starts pale yellow; I include it because it is believed to be a parent of 'Trier', and is therefore of importance in the development of the rose. It was raised by a grower named Schmitt of Lyon, and introduced by Peter Lambert in Germany in 1896.

'Blush Rambler'   *Climber   Light pink   Summer*   P5   H1
One of the most charming of the older climbers; its cupped flowers were well described as blush, and they had a pleasant scent too. Raised by B. R. Cant from 'Crimson Rambler' × 'The Garland', and introduced in 1903. The flowers are a little larger than one might expect; the growth is clean and pleasant, with all the multiflora coarseness removed.

'Crimson Rambler'   *Climber   Red   Summer*   P2   H1
Famous for a simple reason: it was the first red climbing rose to be introduced. To Chinese gardeners it was 'Shi Tz-mei', or 'Ten Sisters'. To the Japanese, 'Soukara-Ibara'; and when Robert Smith saw it in Japanese gardens, and sent it home to Edinburgh, his friends in Scotland called it the 'Engineer's Rose', for that was Mr Smith's calling.

A nurseryman from Slough, Charles Turner, purchased it, and introduced it in 1893 as 'Turner's Crimson Rambler'. *The Rosarian's Year Book 1894* remarked: 'It has been so universally admired, and is so thoroughly distinct, that we understand there has been an enormous sale for it, and it has been distributed everywhere in our Islands, on the Continent, and in America.' Queen Victoria was reported to have gone to Slough to see it. The American introduction was in 1895, by Ellwanger and Barry of Rochester, New York.

'Crimson Rambler' had the coarseness and mildew which multifloras of a particularly vigorous nature are liable to. It was easily surpassed when red Wichuraiana Hybrids arrived; but the familiar name kept it in the catalogues for some years, and breeders made good use of it. The question we have no answer to, is how did the Chinese or the Japanese cajole it from *R. multiflora?*

'Goldfinch'   *Climber   Yellow to white   Summer*   P6   H2   *
I like this rose, its smooth stems, pleasant leaves, and pretty little yellow flowers; yes, even when they have turned white. Although it has not been grown for sale very much in the past thirty years or more, one frequently sees surviving plants. It is a refined Multiflora Hybrid, and a healthy one; the plants do not normally climb high, which is all the better for enjoying their scent. Raised by Paul & Son from seed of 'Hélène', and introduced in 1907. Peter Lambert had introduced 'Hélène' in 1897, its parentage a mixture of Hybrid Tea, 'Aglaia' and 'Crimson Rambler'. One questions whether the pollen of 'Crimson Rambler' had achieved fertilization.

'Paul's Scarlet Climber'   *Climber   Scarlet   Summer*   P2   H1   *
Sometimes I suspect there may have been a hint of the pelargonium colour in this climber, but the suspicion is apt to fade as the vivid scarlet turns to dull red. Despite that failing, it was one of the most popular climbers from 1916, when William Paul & Son introduced it, until 'Danse du Feu' provided a similar colour in autumn as well as

summer. It does not normally grow into a large plant, and when it does, the growth seems to be at the expense of flowers. Being hardy and long lived, 'Paul's Scarlet' will produce its semi-double flowers for many years from the tens of thousands of plants about the world. In the United States, a form called 'Blaze' was raised by Joseph Kallay of Painesville, Ohio, and introduced by J & P in 1932. It was supposed to be remontant, but we in Britain could not see any difference from the original.

'Phyllis Bide' *Climber Yellow & pink Remontant* P2 H1 **
Pale yellow, pale pink, in a fluffy little flower; it is one of the most truly remontant climbers, old or new; and the colour is deeper in the autumn. Ideal to grow on a pillar, or as a weeping standard, it can also be kept as a shrub. The leaves are small and firm, the plant as a whole is pleasant and friendly, one becomes fond of it. Raised by S. Bide & Sons of Farnham, Surrey, who are nurserymen; it was introduced in 1923. The parentage given is 'Perle d'Or' × 'Gloire de Dijon', but I do not believe it. My guess at the pollen parent is 'William Allen Richardson'. I know from breeding with 'Phyllis Bide' that its progeny take strongly after multifloras.

'Rose Marie Viaud' *Climber Purple Summer* P1 H1
A strange dark purple, which reflects little light, and summons one nearer to see what manner of thing is this. The flowers are small, very double, the leaves large, and the shoots are smooth, with few thorns. Raised by Igoult from a seed of 'Veilchenblau', and introduced by Viaud-Bruant in 1924. It is sure to have mildew on its flower stalks.

'Tausendschön' *Climber Pink & white Summer* P3 H1
The pink climber with a large white eye, which sported to the dwarf 'Echo', and thence to the various Koster roses, to the great benefit of those who grew roses in pots for the flower market. It was raised by J. C. Schmidt from 'Daniel Lacombe' × 'Weisser Herumstreicher'; which is a mixture of *R. multiflora*, 'Général Jacqueminot' and 'Pâquerette'. Introduced in 1906.

'The Garland' *Climber Blush Summer* P6 H5 *
Remembered with affection for its sprays of little flowers, soft pink touched cream, held aloft and slightly aloof, but sending a message of fragrance to all who came near. It looked quite regal, as if it could stretch out and turn the far distance into bloom if it so wished. It is credited to Mr Wells, who lived at Redleaf, Tunbridge Wells, Kent; it was introduced in 1835. The parentage is given as *R. moschata* × *R. multiflora,* but if so the pollen parent was probably *R. multiflora carnea,* which was known to be in Europe in 1804. We do not know when *R. multiflora* itself arrived, all we know is that it was in France in the 1860s. Thomas Rivers thought 'The Garland' was from the seed of the Noisette Rose, by which he would mean 'Blush Noisette'; that is an attractive theory.

'Veilchenblau' *Climber Light lilac Summer* P4 H1 *
The 'Violet Blue' seedling of 'Crimson Rambler', with light but handsome foliage, and clusters of flowers of an interesting, unusual colour. Those who are repelled by the so-called blue roses might well start their conversion here. 'Veilchenblau' has a soft, respectable colour, light but not highly reflective. Grow it where it has some shadow in the afternoon, and you will see it at its best. Raised by J. C. Schmidt, and introduced in 1909.

SPECIES continued

R. sempervirens   *Trailer   White   Summer*   P2   H3
Which, being translated, is the Evergreen Rose, for this species retains its foliage
through most of a mild winter. It is a trailer with white flowers, native to southern
Europe and North Africa; and therefore a fellow fugitive with *R. arvensis* from the
normal eastern haunts of the Synstylae. Has also been called *R. alba, R. balearica* and
R. atrovirens.

SEMPERVIRENS HYBRIDS
French rosarians experimented with *R. sempervirens;* and it has been suggested that
the Arvensis Hybrids perhaps owe something to it. However the two species are
sufficiently similar to require no intervention from *R. sempervirens* to account for the
Arvensis Hybrids, especially as most of them came from Scotland, where *R.
sempervirens* would perhaps not feel at home. The thought of evergreen roses may
appear tempting, until one remembers that the leaves have to fall eventually, even if
they wait for the spring growth. Nurserymen defoliate their plants before despatch,
some by turning sheep into their fields, others with chemicals, or by machines to
knock the leaves off. Amateurs find it easier to prune leafless plants; and often
enough they are sufficiently relieved when leaf fall releases them from the task of
spraying. It therefore seems that the chemical companies have most to gain from such
an advance, and maybe they will subsidize rose breeders to get it? We should take
note that here is another gift among wild roses waiting to be accepted.

'Adélaïde d'Orléans'   *Climber   Blush   Midsummer*   P2   H2
The Sempervirens Hybrids most worthy of mention were due to the work of M.
Jacques, who was gardener to the Duc d'Orléans at the Château de Neuilly. He
introduced this climber in 1826. The leaves are persistent, the shoots tenuous and
long. The blush colour is very pale, except for pink flushes upon the outside of the
semi-double flowers. The Duke in whose domain the rose was raised became King
Louis Philippe. Adélaïde was one of his daughters.

'Félicité et Perpétue'   *Climber   White   Summer*   P3   H1   ***
Raised by M. Jacques and introduced in 1827, this white climber is one of the easiest
to grow, a truly beautiful plant. The rosette style of the flowers is charming, and all
the better for the little touches of red upon them. The flowers are small, set off
perfectly against a dark and discreet background of leaves. Although *R. sempervirens*
is tender, 'Félicité et Perpétue' is so hardy as to be a useful rose in unfavourable
conditions. It may be grown on walls, or practically any support suitable to bear a
fairly vigorous climber. In a sheltered place, it holds its leaves through most of a mild
winter. The advice generally given is to prune as little as need be.

The name is that of two saints, Christian women who were thrown to wild beasts in
Carthage in AD 203. The Church always unites their names, usually as Félicité-
Perpétue; or at least with hyphens each side of the 'et'; but in this small instance the
rose world is at variance with the Church. Many gardeners, not well versed in the
Saints, have planted this rose under the impression it is perpetual flowering. It is
recorded as a sport of *R. sempervirens,* but I believe it must be a hybrid.

'Little White Pet'   *Short   White   Remontant*   P3   H1   ****
Here is 'Félicité et Perpétue' reduced by a sport to a short bush, with the same sweet

flowers on it not just for summer, but all the season long. A beautiful rose to own, far better than many white Polyanthas and Floribundas falsely claimed to be superior. It is usually listed as a Polyantha, sometimes as a China, and often as 'White Pet'. Raised by Peter Henderson & Co. of New York, and introduced in 1879.

SPECIES continued

R. setigera *Tallest Pink Late summer* P4 H4
The only member of the Synstylae native to America, *R. setigera* is a shrub or Climber as you like to grow it, with long arching growths, capable of layering themselves like blackberries when their tips come to the ground. It has little affinity to the Synstylae; the flowers are larger, bright pink instead of the normal white. It varies from most roses in its partial segregation into male and female forms, the best seed bearers having poor pollen, whereas the pollen of the worst seed bearers is highly fertile. Most wild roses have finished flowering when this one starts; therefore natural hybridity is unlikely; does a need for other pollen cause the sexual segregation?
    R. setigera is a common wild rose in the east of the United States, and in the Middle West. It is called the Prairie Rose. Its name means bristly.

SETIGERA HYBRIDS
Several breeders have experimented with *R. setigera*, with Americans taking the lead, for they would naturally hope that a native rose would breed varieties at home in their country.

'American Pillar' *Climber Carmine & white Summer* P1 H2
A grower of almost objectionable zeal, after the fashion of *R. multiflora platyphylla;* it varies from most multifloras in its highly glossed leaves. The flowers are single, rosy carmine with a large white eye, and are borne in spectacular profusion. It is a rose that gives easy results, and though welcome in the days when choice was limited, it is clearly less beautiful than most of its successors. This tough, long lived plant responded to being cut down by growing with unabated vigour, and all this in spite of regular mildew. Raised in 1902 by Dr Walter van Fleet from (*R. wichuraiana* × *R. setigera*) × a red Hybrid Perpetual. The introduction by Conard & Jones is dated 1908.

'Doubloons' *Climber Yellow Summer +*
Potentially the most interesting Setigera Hybrid, having been bred from two hybrids, one from *R. setigera* and the other from *R. foetida bicolor*. It was raised by M. H. Horvath of Mentor, Ohio, and introduced by J & P in 1934. How much its popularity was due to the golden yellow climber in the catalogue's picture, we in Britain cannot judge, for few were grown over here, and when they were, the description 'rich gold' turned into 'buff yellow'.
    Horvath introduced several Setigera Hybrids, into which he guided the blood of *R. wichuraiana* and Hybrid Teas; I fancy he would be disappointed that his work did not lead to more conspicuous success, but at least 'Doubloons' played its part in fathering 'Goldilocks'. Horvath was fond of pirate names for his Setigera Hybrids, among which are 'Captain Kidd', 'Jean Lafitte' and 'Long John Silver', all introduced in 1934. But whatever was 'President Coolidge' doing among them?

SPECIES continued

R. sinowilsonii *Climber   White   Summer*   P2   H3
It is worth a journey to see the huge leaves of this rose, dark and polished. Only in a warm climate or sheltered place would one plant it, because of tenderness; and only then if there is room for it to climb a great way. The flowers are white, of secondary interest. A plant is growing in the Royal National Rose Society's garden at St Albans. The name acknowledges a famous plant explorer: E. H. Wilson's Chinese rose.

SINOWILSONII HYBRID

'Wedding Day' *Climber   White to pink   Summer*   P5   H1   ******
This beautiful variety could pass as a hybrid of any of the Musk type of the Synstylae, and I see little to affiliate it particularly to *R. sinowilsonii;* however the accomplished gardener who raised it, Sir Frederick Stern of Sussex, informs us that it was a seedling of that species. He was one of the few gardeners in England who kept stock of *Hulthemia persica.*

'Wedding Day' is not over hardy, a trait we took advantage of in Hitchin, by growing it in an exposed place, which had the result of keeping it as a fairly short and most attractive pillar rose. Given ideal conditions, it is reported to grow fairly large. The leaves are small, nothing like those of its seed parent. The single flowers are in close clusters, in which abundance aids charm: white, single, with yellow stamens, and a sweet scent. Unlike most of the Synstylae, the petals do not drop easily, which means that 'Wedding Day' can preserve her charm through winds which denude *R. soulieana* and most of the others. The price to be paid is that when they have all faded pink, the flowers look jaded, although the first stages of the change, when pink and white are still together, are pleasant. It was introduced in 1950.

SPECIES continued

R. soulieana *Tallest   White   Summer*   P4   H5
The leaves of *R. soulieana* are grey green; the flowers are white with enough stamens to turn the effect into ivory. It is a strong, arching shrub, and bears attractive orange hips.

R. wichuraiana *Trailer   White   Late summer*   P5   H4
With this we may include *R. luciae,* for the two are so similar that there is argument as to whether one is a variety of the other, or whether they are the same. In either case, *R. luciae* ought to be the specific name, having five years priority; but custom is robbing it of that honour. The accepted name is of a German botanist (not Japanese as sometimes reported) Dr Wichura, who visited China in about 1860.

R. wichuraiana is a beautiful wild rose, with a habit of trailing far along the ground, rarely ascending other plants. Its leaves are small, polished, clean cut, and they shine as brilliantly as any. The single white flowers stand out like stars against that foliage.

In the United States, it is called the Memorial Rose, from a practice of planting it to cover graves, conceived long before rose breeders began to talk of ground cover roses.

WICHURAIANA HYBRIDS

The species has contributed generously to our gardens, by providing the roses usually described as ramblers; and it is ready to transmit its polished leaves to bushes too.

The ramblers are in fact an assortment of climbers and trailers, with some beautiful uses. They are the best plants to grow as weeping standards, which means budding them on a tall stem of some suitable understock, and allowing them to cascade. In order to help them do so, it used to be the practice to tie weights to the end of the stems.

The simplest way to grow these roses is by tying to a post, the beautiful result being termed a pillar rose. They are also beautiful if they can grow over the top of a wall or other object, and hang down. Arches and pergolas are suitable for them, and as a general rule they can be planted on any support which invites their flowers to hang down to the view. They are even lovely on houses, especially grown over a porch, provided the owner does not let them go up to the roof, for he will have some complicated problems in pruning and training in that event; to allow a Wichuraiana Hybrid to grow into a large plant on a house wall is usually asking for mildew.

Earlier in this century, Wichuraiana Hybrids were grown in large pots for the decoration of ballrooms, receptions and similar functions. B. R. Cant & Sons of Colchester continued this custom up to about 1965 by exhibiting such pot plants as a background to their display at Chelsea Show. They did well to maintain the plants, and have them timed for the Show year after year. Regular visitors began to recognize those plants as old friends. At one Chelsea Show I remarked upon this to Billy Douglas, then of McGredy's, and he said, 'If Cants gave those plants a slap on the pot, and said Chelsea Show, they would get here all on their own.'

It is not difficult to grow most of the varieties from cuttings. The wood to use for rose cuttings, assuming they are to be rooted in the open ground, not under mist, is hard wood of the present season. Wait until late summer or early autumn, so that the wood is ripe, and take cuttings about 20 cm long. The wood at the base of the shoots is usually best, being ripest. It is as well to remove the bottom two eyes in this particular case, before planting the cuttings out so that about a third of their length is left exposed. See that they are firm in the ground; they will probably need to be firmed again after frosts, when the soil has dried. Do not lift them until the next autumn.

Pruning is not difficult, apart from getting in a tangle, which may be avoided by doing it bit by bit through the season. Tie new shoots in as they appear; trim the side shoots back after they have flowered; at the same time, if the plant has many shoots, cut out the old in favour of the young, so that the young may ripen before winter. But don't cut all the old shoots out as a matter of course; keep them until you see adequate replacements in the form of the young. Complete any pruning, of which there should not be much left, well before spring, because growth normally starts earlier than one expects.

'Pink Roamer'   *Climber   Pink   Early summer*

The credit for the first hybrids of *R. wichuraiana* belongs to Michael Horvath, then of Newport, Rhode Island; later of Mentor, Ohio. The Arnold Arboretum having received *R. wichuraiana* from Louis Späth of Berlin, distributed it, and the nursery where Horvath worked was one of the recipients. Horvath's first crosses were made in 1893, resulting in four varieties being introduced by W. A. Manda of South Orange, New Jersey. 'Pink Roamer' was the first, in 1897. The parents of all four were *R. wichuraiana* × 'Cramoisi Supérieur'. The fate of all prototypes is to disappear as a result of the success they engender, and 'Pink Roamer' was no exception. It was a single pink with white at the centre, and the colour did not hold well in England. One of the four was a blush pink variety called 'South Orange Perfection', a bewildering name until we know where Mr Manda lived.

'May Queen'   *Climber   Pink   Early summer*   P3   H2   *
A charming rose, of restrained growth for the class; the small pink flowers open fully
double to show the old fashioned quartered form in a neat way. This is perhaps the
result of marrying *R. wichuraiana* to the Bourbon pollen of 'Champion of the World'.
Raised by W. A. Manda, and introduced in 1898; in that year another 'May Queen'
came from Conard & Jones, who later changed their name to the Conard-Pyle Co.
Two 'May Queens' have caused some confusion, but the difference in the
contemporary descriptions appears to be that Conard & Jones' version was not so
double, had a white centre, and was more prostrate.

'Gardenia'   *Climber   Cream   Early summer*
This variety stole a march by its name, for the gardenia was a South African flower,
considered the acme of elegance for the decoration of the wealthy. For a short time
the buds of this rose are yellow, and led people into expectations that they had a
yellow rambler. 'One of the best yellows', says the *Rose Annual 1909;* but the effect
is not far from white, like 'Albéric Barbier'. Raised by W. A. Manda from *R.
wichuraiana* × 'Perle des Jardins', a Tea.

'Jersey Beauty'   *Climber   Cream   Early summer*   P4   H2   **
A rare variety now, but too beautiful to lose. A pillar of 'Jersey Beauty' is a column of
glistening leaves, adorned with small but lovely single flowers, creamy white, given
yellow by the stamens. No florist could better its perfect arrangement. The sweet
fragrance, and the persistence of the leaves into winter are two more good points.
Against it must be set the modern gardener's distaste for roses which are single and
only flower briefly in summer. Raised by W. A. Manda from the same parents as
'Gardenia', and introduced the same year.

'Albéric Barbier'   *Climber   Cream   Summer +*   P3   H1   ***
The French breeders were by now interested in *R. wichuraiana,* and began to
produce good varieties from it. Barbier & Co of Orléans were the most successful. It
is strange that nearly all the early Wichuraiana Hybrids flowered early in the
summer, for their wild parent blooms later. 'Albéric Barbier' was introduced in
1900, raised from *R. wichuraiana* × 'Shirley Hibberd', a Tea; it was the best up to
that date for giving some flowers in the autumn. The buds are small, well formed,
opening to semi-double flowers. It is vigorous, with persistent foliage, and one of the
best roses to try in an inhospitable site. Our standards change; we should say it is
cream with rather small flowers. An old description reads 'large double yellow
blooms, fading to creamy white'.

'Dorothy Perkins'   *Climber   Pink   Late summer*   P2   H1
'Orléans Rose' set a standard of form and growth to which Polyanthas were expected
to conform, and 'Dorothy Perkins' did the same for a class to be known as
Wichuraiana Ramblers. I first learned how lovely roses are from a plant of Dorothy
in the backyard at home, when I was about seven. But I would not wish it back,
because after the masses of small pink flowers comes the mildew.
    It must be one of the most famous roses of the twentieth century, and we note that
suddenly the flowering time has been put back, for 'Dorothy' blooms nearly a month
later than its predecessors. It was raised by Mr Miller, an employee of Jackson &
Perkins, who introduced it in 1901. The parents were *R. wichuraiana* × 'Mme
Gabriel Luizet', a Hybrid Perpetual.

In the matter of sports 'Dorothy Perkins' also imitated 'Orléans Rose'. Within eight years there appeared pink, white and red ones. 'Lady Godiva' came from Paul & Son in 1907, its gentle pink colour misleading catalogue writers into such gaffes as 'flesh coloured sport'. In 1908 came 'Christian Curle' from Cocker, and 'Dorothy Dennison' from Dickson, both pink but quite different. B. R. Cant introduced 'White Dorothy' in 1908; and the 'Red Dorothy Perkins', otherwise known as 'Excelsa', came from Walsh in 1909.

'Minnehaha' *Climber Pink Late summer* P2 H1

This could pass as a sport of 'Dorothy Perkins', but the raiser informs us it came from *R. wichuraiana* × 'Paul Neyron', a Hybrid Perpetual. It is paler than 'Dorothy', with slightly larger blooms. The raiser, M. H. Walsh of Woods Hole, Massachussets, brought out several famous varieties of this class, including 'Excelsa', 'Hiawatha' and 'Lady Gay'. 'Minnehaha' was introduced in 1905.

'François Juranville' *Climber Pink Midsummer* P4 H1 ***

I think this is the most beautiful of the Wichuraiana Hybrids; the gentle pink flowers are backed by gleaming dark leaves, in perfect harmony. It was raised by Barbier from *R. wichuraiana* × 'Mme Laurette Messimy', a Hybrid China; introduced in 1906. The colour has a touch of salmon in it. Barbier had a few varieties of similar character, of which 'Léontine Gervais' was much esteemed. It was introduced in 1903, having been raised from *R. wichuraiana* × 'Souvenir de Catherine Guillot', a Tea. Although from a catalogue one could have chosen 'Léontine Gervais', through mention of its coppery shades, the less mixed pink of 'François Juranville' makes a better sight.

'Dr W. van Fleet' *Climber Blush white Summer* P5 H3 *

A vigorous grower, less pliable than most of the class, and distinguished by the flower form, its petals being a little longer, so that the young flowers look like small Hybrid Teas before they open semi-double. It is fragrant and healthy, with handsome leaves, large for this class. Dr Walter van Fleet came from Glenn Dale, Maryland, and raised some famous roses, including 'American Pillar'. This rose, bearing his name, is his best in my opinion; it was introduced in 1910, and raised from (*R. wichuraiana* × 'Safrano') × 'Souvenir du Président Carnot', that is a Tea and a Hybrid Tea added to the species.

'Iceberg'

In 1908 (or 1909 in some versions, 1910 in still others), Paul & Son of Cheshunt introduced some Wichuraiana Hybrids which were not climbers, but bushes. This illustrated the potential charm which the species could offer bush roses, although the varieties did not last long. 'Iceberg', the name of which is now attached to a popular white Floribunda, was raised from 'Jersey Beauty' × 'Nellie Johnston', a Tea; and it was not a climber according to contemporary descriptions, although it appears as one in some records. 'Amber' was a short grower, the colour probably less than the optimism of the name; it was a seedling of 'Jersey Beauty'. My firm grew 'Valerie' for many years, a pleasant yellow rose introduced by Chaplin Brothers in 1932. It was stated to be a Wichuraiana Hybrid, and looked like one in all but its yellow, although I never saw a note of its parentage.

'Sander's White' *Trailer White Late summer* P6 H1 ***

Nobody grows this as a trailer, so far as I know, because its flowers hang down; it is tied to a post or a fence, or grown as a weeping standard, and it is a beauty, with double little white flowers against its shining dark leaves. It looks heavy with flowers, and smells sweet.

Although the breeder is usually recorded as Sanders & Sons of St Albans, I believe it was really Sander, an orchid specialist from Belgium with an English branch nursery at St Albans. In the *Rose Annual 1916,* George M. Taylor reports that a box of flowers arrived in Sander's Belgian office for their consideration, and a British visitor who happened to be present persuaded them to introduce the white rambler, in which, as orchid growers, they were not greatly interested. If that is true, the raiser's name has gone unknown and with it the parentage. That Sander raised it is unlikely. It was introduced in 1912.

'Dr Huey' *Climber Red Summer* P2 H2

The commercial value of this rose far exceeded its beauty, because it became a popular rootstock among American nurserymen, under the name 'Shafter'. Being a hybrid, it had to be propagated by cuttings, and eventually rose mosaic virus invaded it; which is one reason why the majority of European nurserymen prefer rootstocks grown from seed, through which virus is not so easily transmitted. 'Dr Huey' is dark red, rather a dull colour, and has bright green foliage. It was raised by Capt. George C. Thomas of Beverly Hills, California, from 'Ethel' × 'Gruss an Teplitz', in 1914; but its introduction was delayed until 1920. 'Ethel' was a seedling of 'Dorothy Perkins'; 'Gruss an Teplitz' is a most interesting red rose, a mixture of Bourbon, Tea and China.

'Emily Gray' *Climber Yellow Summer* P3 H2 *

The best yellow by far. It is not golden, but rather chamois yellow, and is still a familiar sight in British gardens. The growth is vigorous; the leaves are easily recognizable, red in their youth, maturing to rich glossy green. From a pretty bud, the flowers open semi-double. This rose does best for gardeners who neglect their pruning, provided they do not lose shoots to the wind, because it does not like being cut about. Its vigorous appearance derives from the density of the leaves and the thickness of its shoots; it does not replace lost growth as readily as one would expect.

A medical man from Horsham in Sussex raised it, Dr A. H. Williams, whose practice had been in Harrow. He was President of the National Rose Society in 1933–4. We may remark that it was a great success for an amateur to raise the yellow which had eluded the professionals. 'Emily Gray' came from 'Jersey Beauty' × 'Comtesse du Cayla', and was introduced in 1918 by B. R. Cant & Sons.

'Max Graf' *Trailer Pink Summer* P2 H1

In 1919, this highly significant rose was introduced by James H. Bowditch of Pomfret Center, Connecticut; thirty-five years later, Wilhelm Kordes was to show why it was important.

Its origin is obscure; according to Kordes, it was found in a garden in the United States. From its appearance, being a trailer with leaves suggesting *R. rugosa,* it was assumed to be a hybrid between that species and *R. wichuraiana;* we may consider it to be the first ground cover rose. And it was soon found to be exceptionally hardy. It could just as reasonably be placed in the Rugosa Hybrids as in the Wichuraiana Hybrids, but its offspring suggest that this is the place for it. It is vigorous, bears single pink flowers larger than those of *R. wichuraiana.* If the parentage has been correctly assumed, it is a hybrid between two species whose resistance to blackspot is high, and therefore of potential value to breeders. The future developments appear a few pages on, under Kordesii Hybrids.

'Albertine' *Climber   Pink   Early summer*   P4   H4   *
With so much vigour as sometimes to outgrow its welcome, 'Albertine' was introduced in 1921, and became a firm favourite. For this its wonderful display when in full flower was responsible. The buds are a lovely salmon red, and the open flowers light pink; the flowers are large for a Wichuraiana Hybrid. Introduced in 1921, and raised by Barbier from *R. wichuraiana* × 'Mrs Arthur Robert Waddell', a Hybrid Tea. The only caution to be observed in recommending it now is: beware of mildew.

'New Dawn' *Tall   Blush white   Summer +*   P5   H3   ***
'Dr W. van Fleet' produced a sport, which is shorter and more remontant than itself, but in all other respects the same. As regards the growth, it is possible to treat 'New Dawn' as a climber, but by nature it is a beautiful shrub, and looks much better grown thus. It needs space, for it spreads wide if little pruned, and makes a glorious mound of fragrant, pale, shapely flowers. Or if it is much pruned, it grows like a Floribunda three or four times normal stature, and will provide many long flowering stems, beautiful for arrangements of mixed flowers; it can also be grown as a handsome hedge.

The claims of remontancy are true in comparison with 'Dr W. van Fleet', but fall short of what we expect a remontant rose to be. It does flower in the autumn, but not nearly so freely as in the summer. It was discovered by Somerset Rose Nurseries, New Brunswick, New Jersey, and introduced in 1930 by Henry A. Dreer of Philadelphia. The optimistic title of Everblooming Dr W. van Fleet has been tacked on to it.

A distinction that no other rose can share with 'New Dawn' is that of being the first variety in which the discoverer's rights were protected in law. The United States led the world in this respect, after being one of the last countries to accept authors' copyrights. Their Plant Patents Act came into effect in 1930, with 'New Dawn' holding Plant Patent No. 1.

'The Fairy' *Medium   Pink   Late summer +*   P3   H1   ****
A pretty bush, wherein 'Lady Godiva' proved well able to sport, and to change her character more than is usual; for 'The Fairy' I am sure is a deeper colour in flower and leaf than 'Lady Godiva'; and the growth is entirely different, from vigorous climber to bush. It is difficult to give a height for 'The Fairy', which often remains short, but sometimes rises hip high. As to the remontancy with which it is usually credited, it flowers late in summer in such profusion, and for so long a time, that there is scarcely the opportunity for a repeat performance. It is delightful, the little rose pink flowers in their lovely sprays all fresh against the small dark leaves. When other roses are jaded by the centre of summer, this follows them with a smile on its face. Introduced by J. A. Bentall in 1932; and in America by the Conard-Pyle Company nine years later.

'Crimson Shower' *Trailer   Red   Late summer*   P2   H1   ***
One of the last roses to come into bloom; and one of the last Wichuraiana Hybrids to be raised, as breeders turned their attention to more remontant climbers. It has the typical small double flowers of the class, in a deep glowing crimson, the best red colour of them all. No better red rose exists to grow on a pillar.

Raised by Albert Norman and introduced by my firm in 1951. The parentage is always quoted as a seedling of 'Excelsa', but I have an idea there was more to it than that.

'Temple Bells'   *Trailer   White   Summer*   P3   H1
A trailer which is being recommended for ground cover. It has myriads of small polished leaves, and abundant prostrate growth. The flowers are small, white. An interesting variation, raised by Dennison Morey of Santa Rosa, California. It was introduced in 1973.

SPECIES continued

R. kordesii   *Medium* +   *Rose red   Summer* +   P2   H3
'Max Graf' was not at first sight valuable to breeders, because of infertile pollen and few hips. Wilhelm Kordes tried to breed from it despite these disabilities, and he reported that over many years he collected only three or four hips from a large plant. In 1941 he raised two seedlings, one of which resembled *R. rugosa,* and died of frost in its first winter. The other was *R. kordesii;* leaving aside its bright foliage and flowers, it had two rich gifts to offer Herr Kordes: it set seed freely, and was very hardy. But there was hidden in its cells a third gift, still greater: it proved compatible with modern roses, having increased its chromosomes from the fourteen of its parents to the twenty-eight of Hybrid Teas and Floribundas. The key was now given to admit into modern roses the combined qualities of two of the healthiest wild roses, namely 'Max Graf's' parents, assumed, but with some certainty, to be *R. rugosa* and *R. wichuraiana. R. kordesii* breeds true from seed, and has therefore been accepted as a species, although I should have thought it more consistent of the authorities to denote it a hybrid species.

KORDESII HYBRIDS
Such was the fertility of *R. kordesii,* that its raiser sent to the National Rose Society's trial ground over forty hybrids in 1951. Most of them were climbers; some were vigorous shrubs. Their vigour, abundant foliage and freedom of flower ensured that those entries from Wilhelm Kordes were never to be forgotten by the trial ground judges of that period. If there could be a criticism, it would ask for greater elegance. Perhaps for this reason a continuity of varieties has not flowed into British gardens since the introductions of the 1950s, although many are grown in Germany. British breeders have preferred to seek climbers from Hybrid Tea and Floribunda sources; nevertheless the gifts of *R. kordesii* are certain to flow into modern roses, as is proved by the example of 'Silver Jubilee' in the Hybrid Teas.

Although these roses are almost universally said to be remontant, it is my experience that the second blooming is much less spectacular than the first.

'Dortmund'   *Climber   Red; white eye   Remontant* –   P1   H2   *
The picture of well-being; abundant glossy foliage backs large single flowers, red with a white eye. For all its vigour, it does not usually reach a great height, and is therefore an excellent pillar rose. Raised by Wilhelm Kordes from pollen of *R. kordesii* used upon an unnamed seedling. Introduced 1955.

'Hamburger Phoenix'   *Climber   Red   Remontant* –   P1   H2   *
Dark red, semi-double flowers. Wilhelm Kordes said that his firm sold forty thousand plants of 'Hamburger Phoenix' in 1957. It has the usual Kordesii

appearance of bursting with vigour, and looks so broad and full of leaf that one expects it to climb further than it does. It is generally agreed that modern gardens require such climbers; and not the type that travel yards and yards. Dark red, semi-double flowers. Raised by Wilhelm Kordes from *R. kordesii* × seedling, and introduced in 1954.

'Leverkusen' *Climber Yellow Remontant* P3 H1 **
The introduction of yellow into Kordesii Hybrids would appear difficult, as neither *R. rugosa* nor *R. wichuraiana* accept that colour easily. Wilhelm Kordes solved the problem by the cross *R. kordesii* × 'Golden Glow'. The latter is a significant rose, used also by Ralph Moore in breeding miniatures. It is a yellow climber bred by Dr and Mrs Brownell from 'Glenn Dale' × ('Mary Wallace' × unnamed Hybrid Tea); thus Kordes used a yellow variety which already had *R. wichuraiana* from two sources, well diluted with Hybrid Tea. 'Leverkusen' has double flowers of clear light yellow; it is more truly remontant than 'Dortmund' and 'Hamburger Phoenix' in the sense that the autumn bloom is comparable with the summer. Introduced in 1954.

'Parkdirektor Riggers' *Climber Crimson Remontant* − P2 H2 *
A pillar of this rose in full flower is a wonderful sight, for the crimson is bright and deep. Abundant dark green foliage. It is a fine looking plant, unless it gets mildew on its young growths, which sometimes occurs. Raised by Reimer Kordes from *R. kordesii* × 'Our Princess', the latter being the likely reason for the mildew. Introduced in 1957.

'Ritter von Barmstede' *Climber Pink Remontant* P3 H1 **
One of the more truly remontant climbers, this has double pink flowers, and makes an attractive pillar. The parents were *R. kordesii* × a Polyantha; and some of the Polyantha influence can be seen in its flowers and leaves. However the flowers are not particularly small, a point to note when buying this variety, for two completely different roses have been sold as 'Ritter von Barmstede' in Britain. That with the deeper colour and larger flowers is I believe the true one, and certainly the more attractive. Raised by Wilhelm Kordes, and introduced in 1959.

OTHER SYNSTYLAE SPECIES
Like most British rosarians. I am not familiar with these; further, I am not confident that they are all true species, and not convinced that true stock can be located without a journey to those parts of the world, principally China, where they are wild. However they are supposed to be as follows: *R. cerasocarpa*, something like *R. moschata*, with red hips, the name meaning cherry fruited. *R. crocantha*, similar to *R. helenae*, the name suggests that its thorns are coloured saffron. *R. fargesii*, similar to *R. moschata*, but beware, there is also a variety *R. moyesii fargesii* in the Cinnamomeae. *R. gentiliana* and *R. henryi* are in complete confusion, as to whether they are the same or different, existent or not; and a hybrid called *R. polyantha grandiflora*, of unknown parentage, has been distributed under their names. *R. glomerata* and *R. rubus* take after *R. helenae*, their names mean respectively the rose with round flower heads and the blackberry rose. *R. leschenaultii* is between *R. brunonii* and *R. moschata* in appearance. *R. maximowicziana* tends towards *R. multiflora*. *R. mulliganii* is like *R. helenae*. *R. phoenicia* has a different place of origin, Turkey and the region about; it was C. C. Hurst's opinion that this was a parent of the Damask Roses. It is allied to *R. moschata*, and I wonder if some of the Musk Roses of the old days owed anything to *R. phoenicia?*

13. Gallicanae and Hybrids

It is perhaps pompous to allot a section of the Eurosa to one species; if so, we plead that species' importance; the French Rose, *R. gallica,* is the archetypal rose of the west. It was by no means confined to France, but grew across central and southern Europe into Asia. Therefore it was native to nearly all the sources of Western civilization of which we have knowledge; and from the care it received long ago, it became the progenitor of most of the garden roses grown by western man from Nebuchadnezzar to Napoleon.

The factors of recognition here take a further step. We reached the Synstylae by the points: leaves pinnate; hips smooth; stipules joined; styles protruding. In the Gallicanae and henceforth, the styles protrude only a little. When looking into the flower, one sees the stigmas, but very little of the styles that support them. In order to recognize the succeeding sections, in all of which the styles are of this unprotruding nature, we consider how the flowers are borne. In the Gallicanae and the Pimpinellifoliae, the flowers are on the whole borne singly. Thereafter they are borne in large heads. The difference between Gallicanae and Pimpinellifoliae is in the leaflets, usually not more than five in this section, and usually not under seven in the Pimpinellifoliae. I am not too happy that the Gallicanae conform sufficiently to the rule of bearing their flowers singly, for in cultivation one can easily find *R. gallica versicolor* with large heads of bloom. However, the botanists seem quite clear upon this point, and as I have never seen *R. gallica* growing wild, I accept their authority. The hybrids do not necessarily take their character entirely from *R. gallica.*

SPECIES & VARIETIES

R. gallica *Medium – Pink Summer* P4 H2
The student of *R. gallica* must discipline himself to observe some sort of order. He is dealing with a rose which is both variable and historic, two factors which pose problems of identity insoluble by any means other than swallowing a series of assumptions. Let us begin by seeing what it looks like.

It is a shrubby rose, not very tall, spreading easily by suckers. The leaves are soft to the touch, light green, and not at all glossy. The stems are closely covered with pliant bristles, but by few thorns. The flowers are large as wild roses go, and fragrant; they are carried in a particularly pleasing manner, opening wide and smiling up at one, well above the foliage, on top of the plant. The colour is pink, with sufficient natural variations for deeper pink and light red specimens to occur, but it does not change in the other direction so as to become white. The hips are small, not decorative.

On considering its history, we may assume it has had some significance in the lives of people for many thousands of years. But only since the sixteenth century have we been able to identify it. We may assume on a balance of probability that Medes and

Persians, Minoans and Myceneans, Greeks and Romans, Egyptians and Carthaginians were growing and using it; on the other hand it is just possible that some of those civilizations were not entirely incapable of raising hybrids doomed to perish with them. The history of the rose is a blank page until the past three or four hundred years; the old references omit the things that matter: how roses evolved, what they meant to ordinary people, and in particular their identity. One might as well write a history of the daisy or the dandelion for all the reality that is to be got from the early days.

The facts that matter are that *R. gallica* was ready and willing to cross itself with other roses, and that it had some economic uses, of which the most important was medicinal, the most profitable cosmetic, the most sensible decorative and the most artful culinary.

It has had several other Latin names, of which the best known is *R. rubra*. There is a dwarf form, *R. gallica pumila*.

R. gallica officinalis *Medium* – *Red Midsummer* P4 H1
This varies from the species in that its flowers are red and semi-double. Before Linnaeus established an orderly system of naming plants in the eighteenth century, this was called the Red Rose. It is also known as the Apothecary's Rose, a reference to its uses in medicine, and as the Provins Rose, because that French town specialized in making conserves and medicine from it, innocently laying traps for unwary rosarians of the future by inviting confusion with the Provence, or Cabbage Rose.

The English added to the general confusion by calling it the Red Damask. It is certainly no Damask, but it is a bright cerise red. Those who have plants of 'Rosa Mundi' (*R. gallica versicolor*) may expect to see it revert to red flowers occasionally, and these are normally *R. gallica officinalis*. The red colours of old European roses derive almost exclusively from this variety; which explains their purple cast. The darker crimson, and those removed from the purple side of the spectrum, derive from the colour of *R. chinensis semperflorens*. I might add here that the China Roses brought many gifts, especially remontancy and good foliage; but they had little fragrance, a quality in which the old roses of the west were strong.

R. gallica versicolor *Medium* – *Red striped blush Midsummer* P4 H1 **
The striped flowers make a brave, eccentric show, one of the sights of the rose world. They are red with blush white stripes, or in some blooms where the colours are fairly equal in area, they could be expressed the other way round with equal accuracy; but as it sported from *R. gallica officinalis,* the red is the original colour. This is generally known by the lovely name 'Rosa Mundi'. It is similar to *R. gallica officinalis* in all respects save its colour. In 1659, the statement was made in *The Garden Book of Sir Thomas Hanmer* that 'Rosa Mundi' was 'first found in Norfolk a few years since upon a branch of the common red rose'. When this is borne in mind, and it is noted that the first list of roses grown in Britain was by John Gerard in 1596, without mention of such a striped rose, we can assume Sir Thomas Hanmer's account worthy of belief. A striped rose had been described in 1581 by M. de l'Obel, and recorded by Clusius in 1583; but its absence from that time until 1659 needs some explanation, if it was as good as 'Rosa Mundi'. The story has grown that 'Rosa Mundi' is of ancient origin. It has been connected with the Fair Rosamund, who was mistress of Henry II, and died about 1177. Crusaders have been credited with bringing it home from the near East: these are legends.

GALLICA HYBRIDS

Before looking at the outstanding Gallicas, it is seemly to pause and express the thanks which all rosarians must owe to Graham Stuart Thomas for his work in identifying, and bringing back into cultivation many of those roses known as Old-Fashioned, or Old Garden Roses. ('But we've got a *new* garden,' said an outraged customer).

Thousands of roses had been raised in Europe before *R. chinensis* came to change them, to act in a dual capacity as mate and executioner. In the 1930s, they were for the greater part gone for ever. Those that remained were likely to be found in old gardens, and nameless. A few true rosarians had done their best to preserve them, notably Edward Bunyard of Maidstone, Kent. Graham Thomas was working with a wholesale nurseryman, Thomas Hilling of Chobham, Surrey, and it is to the eternal credit of the latter that he encouraged and supported an activity so unlikely to attract a wholesale nurseryman. Hilling acquired a collection of shrub roses, and Graham Thomas pursued his studies with patience and intelligence; having found a rose, he often had to search for its identity, his best aid being illustrations and descriptions in old publications. It stands to his integrity that few of his identifications can be faulted; we may appreciate his difficulties by saying that in 1848 William Paul described 471 Gallicas in *The Rose Garden*. Eventually Thomas Hilling printed a price list of several hundred roses of which most contemporary rosarians had never heard; fortunately the enterprise (which was jam to the horticultural journalists) caught the public fancy. From a nurseryman's point of view, Hilling must have had a difficult operation. Graham Thomas eventually became manager of Sunningdale Nurseries, where he continued to build up his collection; and he issued '*The Manual of Shrub Roses*', a concise and helpful guide to the genus. In effect it was a descriptive catalogue, price three shillings, to augment the nursery's price list. Mr Thomas eventually accepted a post as Garden Adviser to the National Trust, an organization with the purpose of acquiring and maintaining such areas and properties as are important parts of the nation's heritage, and which would have been lost without that intervention. The National Trust has a collection of old garden roses at Mottisfont, Romsey, Hants; and the Royal National Rose Society likewise at Chiswell Green Lane, St Albans.

I do not propose in this section to describe a long list of varieties, for this has been done with better knowledge by Graham Thomas in '*The Old Shrub Roses*', and if I am to be honest, he has more affection for them than I have. My purpose is to show how the old roses of Europe were changed by successive assaults from *R. chinensis* into the Hybrid Perpetuals, forerunners of the Hybrid Teas.

R. × francofurtana   *Tall − Pink Midsummer*   P5   H4   *
Also known as *R. turbinata*, which means shaped like a top, a reference to its hips. It derived its official name from having been grown in Frankfurt, Germany, but its origin is unknown. It is assumed to be a hybrid between *R. gallica* and *R. cinnamomea*, and was first described by C. Clusius in 1583. It is a pleasant plant, especially where its pendulous stems can contrast with upright surroundings. The pink flowers are double, about as large as those of 'Rosa Mundi'; the colour gets lighter towards the rim of the flower. The petals are folded, and when they open out they reveal many stamens. I like its fragrance.

R. × richardii
The Holy Rose, or *R. sancta;* also St John's Rose. It is thought to be a hybrid between *R. gallica* and *R. phoenicia*. This short, erect bush bears pink flowers, and is

interesting on account of having been discovered in Ethiopia. C. C. Hurst assumed it was taken there from the Near East long ago. It is also connected with the Rose of the Tombs. After a garland of roses had been extracted from an Egyptian tomb in the 1880s, it was examined by the Belgian botanist, Professor F. Crépin. He expressed his emotion upon seeing a simple tribute thought to be about 1500 years old, and gave the opinion it was one of the Gallicanae, probably this one. It is not cultivated in Britain to my knowledge.

'Scharlachglut' *Tallest Bright red Midsummer* P3 H7 *

Plenty of room is needed for 'Scarlet Fire', as it is commonly called in Britain, because it surrounds itself with long arching shoots. It may be used as a climber by those who like a fight. The raiser said it provided good cover for birds. The flowers are brilliant scarlet red, large and single; and the hips grow into big, red, decorative fruits. A fair question would be whether the flowers are sufficient rent for the area taken up. 'Scarlet Fire' does not look like a Gallica, its leaves could pass as those of modern roses. It is an interesting cross, 'Poinsettia' × 'Alika'. The former is a Hybrid Tea, something like a lighter 'Ena Harkness'; 'Alika' is known as *R. gallica grandiflora,* and was brought from Russia in 1906. According to the descriptions, it was a red Gallica with no trace of purple in it. Were I beginning to breed roses, I should be interested in crossing 'Scarlet Fire' with red Hybrid Teas, seeking double remontant progeny, and breeding with them. It was raised by Wilhelm Kordes, and introduced in 1952.

GALLICAS

The Gallica Roses, or French Roses, normally have soft, light coloured leaves; with their summer flower their glory vanishes, for their foliage is dull, and likely to be host to mildew. As they have no further flowers, perhaps mildew can be forgiven; they seem to grow the following year without ill effect. So far as we can tell, they are the oldest type of cultivated roses known to the west. Naturally the varieties have changed over the centuries; we cannot point to one, and say that the Romans grew it. Most of the existing sorts were raised in France, in the nineteenth century or perhaps the eighteenth. Thomas Rivers had a suggestion to lengthen the flowering period: 'two plants of each variety should be planted; one plant to be pruned in October and the other in May'. The catch about pruning roses which are not remontant, is that the new wood of one year will not flower until the following year. Therefore do not cut it all away. Long new growths should be shortened half way or a little more; side shoots should be shortened by cutting off their thin ends.

'Belle de Crécy' *Medium + Mauve Midsummer* P7 H1 *

Begins pink, looks more slate-coloured when open, and ends mauve; a typical example of the palette of this class; it is one of those to show a green eye in the centre of its double flower. Introduced by M. Roeser, Crécy-en-Brie, France.

'Camaieux' *Medium − Striped Midsummer* P3 H3 *

'Sometimes pretty,' says William Paul, 'but a small, bad grower.' Hesitant in amending the master's words, I should say rather that it is sometimes fantastic, and that the growth is not so bad as to damn it. The colour is rosy purple with blush white splashes and stripes, quite a crazy mixture. It bows out with the rosy purple greyed over. Appears as 'Camaien' or 'Camaieu' in the old books. Credited to J. P. Vibert of

Angers, France; most authorities leave the raiser blank, and give 1830 as its date of introduction. Somewhat similar, and perhaps more easily grown is 'Tricolore de Flandre', raised by Louis van Houtte of Gand, Belgium, and introduced in 1846.

'Cardinal de Richelieu' *Medium + Purple Midsummer* P4 H1 **
The stems and leaves have a smoother, shinier look than other Gallicas, and the flowers are in a class of their own for rich royal purple. They are stuffed full of petals, folded when young, bending over backwards as the flower opens. The raiser is thought to be M. Laffay of Bellevue, France, and the date of introduction 1840. But there is some doubt as to whether it was really a Dutch rose called 'Rose Van Sian'. Many Gallicas were raised in Holland in the eighteenth and early nineteenth centuries, but few Dutch varieties survived competition with the French.

'Charles de Mills' *Medium Crimson Midsummer* P4 H1 *
I have had little joy from this variety, which the experts describe as tall, and proceed to extol its young flowers. 'Charles de Mills' does not grow tall when I plant it, and I do not admire its short buds, which look as if someone had sliced off the top of them. It improves on opening, and the colour is rich dark red, leaning upon purple support, with the latter predominating by the time the flowers are old. Origin unknown, but that may not mean it is particularly old, because I do not find it in Rivers (1840) or Paul (1848), either under this name or the alternative, 'Bizarre Triomphant'.

'Gloire de France' *Medium Pink Midsummer* P4 H1 **
Amid the stripes and strange colours of the Gallicas, one needs a gentler colour; and so far as they may be said to possess one, 'Gloire de France' may serve. It is pink, with an increasing suffusion of lilac as the flower develops. Its origin is unknown; it was in cultivation in 1819.

'Président de Sèze' *Medium + Mauve Midsummer* P4 H1 *
Double flowers, which open quartered, but not neatly. The colour is purple red to the centre, lilac pink to the perimeter, daring or daunting according to the beholder's eye. Credited to Mme Hébert; I have found no details about her, nor of the introduction date.

'Surpasse Tout' *Medium Red Midsummer* P3 H1 *
'Beats the lot', thought its raiser confidently. In a way, it does, because I do not know a better red Gallica, apart from *R. gallica officinalis*. This is more double, with a symmetrical flower. The colour is cherry red, not quite free from purple, fading to rose red. It was in cultivation in 1832, but its origin is unknown.

'Tuscany' *Tall Maroon Midsummer* P3 H2 **
By the description of the Velvet Rose in Gerard's *Herball* of 1597, it was either 'Tuscany' or its twin. Velvet Roses were well represented in nurserymen's catalogues in Britain in the eighteenth century, there being several varieties. The name fits this particular rose well, describing its dark maroon red colour aptly. 'Tuscany' grows more upright than most Gallicas, stiff where they are lax. This is an advantage in showing off the particular kind of flower it bears, especially when the stamens can be seen, dusty yellow against the velvet red. There is a good form of it, 'Tuscany Superb', rather more double, and it is probable that these two Tuscanies are the 'Velvet Semi-double' and 'Velvet Double' of the eighteenth century catalogues.

One could speculate from the name and the known dates that it could be one of the oldest garden roses in existence.

DAMASKS

For all their fame, Damasks are strangely elusive. There is no such rose as *R. damascena*, with or without an X, in spite of its imposing appearance in books about roses. It represents the first hybrid assumed to have inaugurated the class. In C. C. Hurst's opinion it was between *R. gallica* and *R. phoenicia*, the latter a member of the Synstylae. That origin is undated, unplaced and unknown; it is surmise. Upon the name and the antiquity of the class, other high rise blocks of supposition have ascended: connecting the rose with Syria because Damascus is there, with the Crusaders because they went to Syria, and with the Greeks and Romans, merely because they had roses. Surmise may of course be right, but it is not fact.

Damasks are reported in Italy in the sixteenth century, and the Damask Rose was said by Richard Hakluyt in 1582 to have been brought to England by Dr Linaker, physician to Henry VII and Henry VIII. The presumption is that it came from Italy, which Dr Linaker is known to have visited, before 1524, in which year he died. In 1596, John Gerard recorded the Common and the Lesser Damask Roses. A confusion speedily grew up through a red Gallica being taken for the Common Damask, thereby imprinting on the public mind the misconception that Damasks were dark in colour.

For so famous a class, there were few varieties. One cannot identify all the roses in eighteenth-century catalogues, but it appears that half a dozen Damasks were about their limit. The early nineteenth century saw a big increase however; the very thorough William Paul listed 201 in 1848; Graham Thomas retrieved 20 for his *Manual of Shrub Roses,* a comprehensive twentieth-century collection; most modern rose catalogues have none. William Paul's list is divided into 87 Damasks, 7 Four Seasons, 23 Roses de Trianon and 84 Damask Perpetuals. In fact there is one more. Mr Paul considerably numbered each variety in his book, but when he came to 'Queen of Perpetuals', he described it by one word. It was 'Worthless' and dismissed from his count. A few of his Damasks, however, would be in other classes in a modern assessment.

When we ask what a Damask is like, and how do we recognize it, the answers are vague. This is no clearly defined class of uniform members and it does not stand out obviously from Gallicas and Centifolias. Damasks are usually more robust; their growth tends to be lax, waving away from the centre to form an open bush; their leaves are, if anything, even lighter green.

R. × damascena trigintipetala   *Taller   Pink   Midsummer*   P3   H3
This is the staple of the famous 'attar of rose' industry in Bulgaria. It is pink, and one would only plant it in the garden out of interest, not expecting much from it in the way of garden decoration. But we should remember that out of the thousands of years the rose has been cultivated, only since the late nineteenth century has it been used primarily as a garden plant. Its oldest use on record is to supply perfume.

It is a strange thing that perfume, which one would have thought an inessential frippery, has been regularly made and used even by poor people; and although in its more exotic forms it is a luxury of the rich, that has not stopped the poor from freely using such fragrances as they could obtain. Perfume, by ancient belief, had the power to disinfect; and who can deny that a housewife of old was indeed caring for the health of her family if she swilled out a fouled room with a bucket of mint water?

Even today, disinfectants and polishes boast of smelling of pine trees. Perfume was also believed to prevent infections, and in the days of plagues, all unaware that their real enemies were more usually fleas, people used to carry herbs in their hands, and plug them into their ears and noses, so that noxious exhalations from the infected might not enter through the apertures of their bodies. In London's Old Bailey, it was until quite recently the custom to scatter herbs on the floor surrounding the judge, and to put flowers on his desk, to keep the jail-fever away from him; and of this practice tokens still remain. The ideas of purification by perfume extended to anointing the dead, worshipping the gods and cleansing contaminated things, as Saladin was reputed to have done with five hundred camel loads of rose-water, brought from Damascus to clean a Mosque in Jerusalem after he took it back from the Infidels (or Crusaders, depending on which side one was) in 1187. While the great and articulate were doing these things with perfume, ordinary people used it to attract their lovers, or because they liked the smell of it, or to disguise their own aroma, to some extent as we use soap today.

In ancient times, rose-scented oil was made by soaking rose petals in a substance which would absorb their perfume; and one lay ready to hand in Mediterranean civilizations, namely the oil from olives, although other oils could be used, and other fragrances imparted to them. When rose oil became a popular commodity, it would be necessary to ensure a supply of fragrant rose petals for making it, and therein most probably lies the origin of rose growing as a profession pursued in the course of commerce.

The next development took advantage of the volatility of rose scent, by the process of distillation; this involves boiling petals in water, and guiding the steam through a cooled pipe, thereby turning it back into water by condensation. The result of this process is rose-water, because some of the perfume accompanies the water through the process of condensation. It is thought that this particular discovery was made in India or Persia; and the oriental origins of rose perfumery are clearly shown by the famous name 'Attar of Roses'.

Attar is a Persian word, and attar-gul means essence of roses. Some confusion has come of the alternative word Otto, but if it is remembered that Otto, far from being a German gentleman, is more like a Turkish one, and that the Ottoman Empire once extended Turkey's rule, then otto of roses may be understood as a natural corruption of attar.

The production of attar of roses was a sophisticated step ahead of making rose-water, and it arose from the realization that only a small part of the perfume was passing through the distillation, because most of it was not soluble in water. It was however soluble in other dissolvers, especially in alcohol and oils. The object therefore was to remove the droplets of perfume from the petals, capture them in a dissolver, distil them out of it, and because of their volatility, hold them in some kind of fixative. The product would thus be rose perfume, or attar of roses, pure in relation to the efficiency of the process. It is scarcely necessary to point out that perfume droplets are but a microscopic proportion of a petal's contents, and therefore a large heap of petals yields a small amount of attar, which is thus extremely expensive, and sold as a concentrated ingredient for use in blending with other perfumes.

Credit for this ingenious invention belongs to some unknown person, but there is a story from India about the origin of attar, to be enjoyed rather than believed. It centres upon Princess Nur Mahal (Light of the Palace), who was due to be rowed along a canal with her husband, the Emperor Jahangir Khan. Whether from an exuberant joy in celebration, or because the canal stank (a possibility which the tellers of this tale are too kind to mention, but which could show Nur Mahal to be a lady of admirable resolution and resource), she had rose petals thrown upon the face of the water. She observed an oily film upon the canal, and from it learned how to capture rose perfume. Those were the days of the Mogul Emperors, who left many enduring testimonies to the artistic and technical skill of India, not least the Taj Mahal, which was built in memory of Nur Mahal's niece, Mumtaz Mahal.

The famous country for attar of roses is Bulgaria, where the roses are grown in a district due east of Sofia, halfway between it and the Black Sea. Kazanluk (spelt Kazanlik in most western records) is the best known town, but there are others in the Valley of Roses, an area about sixty miles long from Klisura to Stara Zagora. It is presumed that the Bulgars learned the art from the Turks, when the Ottoman Empire ruled their country. The roses grown for attar are Damask Roses (*R.* × *damascena trigintipetala*), and some others of similar type. It would be of great interest to know that rose's origin, whether the Turks brought it, and how long it has been grown for attar; because a rose with such a commercial use could well be a survivor from ages past; but history hides the answer from us. Around the plantings of Damask Roses are hedges of *R.* × *alba semi-plena*.

Bulgaria receives special mention for the size of the industry there; but that country was not an exclusive producer. From India to the Mediterranean and along North Africa from Egypt to Morocco, attar was made to satisfy the needs of various localities; and from North Africa, long under French influence, the skill naturally went to South France, where the Provence Rose (*R.* × *centifolia*) was for some years the favourite variety for perfumiers.

R. damascena versicolor   Tall   Blush & white   Midsummer   P4   H1

The York and Lancaster Rose; and a poor uninteresting thing it is, with pale flowers. A close look is needed to see that some flowers are light pink, some blush to white, and some a mixture of the two colours. *R. gallica versicolor* has in the past been mistaken for York and Lancaster. I take the story of York and Lancaster plucking their white and red roses from the same bush as symbolic of tearing England apart. The 'Wars of the Roses' is a deceitful euphemism for the actions of those murderous Dukes.

'Celsiana'   Tall   Pink   Midsummer   P4   H1   *

A Damask with light leaves, sharp little thorns and thin flower stems. The nodding pink blooms are short at the centre, but open their blunt ended petals into a fragrant semi-double flower. It promptly turns towards a white colour. The origin is uncertain; varieties named 'Cels' and 'Double Cels' used to be grown, perhaps this is the second under a latinized name. It has been stated that M. F. Cels imported it to France from Holland.

'Madame Hardy'   Taller   White   Midsummer   P5   H1   ***

One of the most wonderful roses, provided its lax, ungainly growth may be forgiven; a further pardon is required in case the weather sweeps away its intricate flowers. I do so pardon it, because it has a bloom different from any rose, and the memory of it is good. Imagine a flower to cover the palm of your hand, yet flat as an open daisy, with white petals overlapping one another, showing their tips in many perfect circles from near the centre to the outside. The impression is of hundreds of them. A green eye of carpels rests in the middle, like an emerald in the snow. A bloom like that is remembered all your life. And to be honest, you will not find one every year. It was raised in the Luxembourg Gardens in Paris, named after the director's wife (we have already met M. Eugène Hardy in these pages) and introduced in 1832.

'Quatre Saisons' *Tall   Pink   Summer* +   P5   H1   *

The Four Seasons Rose was a bit of Gallic hyperbole, akin to Perpetual and to the naughty modern epithet, Ever-blooming. But the name at least indicates how impressed were the people of old by a rose which flowered in the autumn, however shy it was. No other rose in the west would flower in autumn, except under abnormal circumstances. Because this was the only type capable of remontant bloom, it is assumed that it must be the one to which allusions were made in the classics of old. And we should certainly be hard pressed to suggest any other, although it is likely that the existing varieties have changed. It is generally known as the 'Autumn Damask', or *R.* × *damascena semperflorens;* which is, I suppose, a Latin precedent for naughty modern epithets. The question to ask is where did its timid tendency to be remontant come from? Nobody has found a convincing answer yet.

'Quatre Saisons' is light pink, a hard colour where a gentle one might be expected. The flowers are by no means symmetrical, for the petals are folded in all directions, but the scent is good. It is not a handsome plant, nor are most Damasks; the long shoots bend out leaving the plant sparse and open.

'Quatre Saisons Blanc Mousseux' *Tall   White   Summer* +   P4   H1   *

Question: do we put this with the Moss roses, or leave it here? I follow my own precedent of having accorded the Miniatures their own mossy varieties. This is similar to 'Quatre Saisons' except for being white, and for having well-defined moss upon the seedpods and sepals. One can see the small prickles becoming closer on the flower stalk, as if preparing for the change into moss. Also known as 'Perpetual White Moss' and 'Rosier de Thionville'. It is a sport from 'Quatre Saisons'.

Other Damasks

If these added to our knowledge significantly, I would have chosen them; but in each class I have looked for those which were important, because they tell the story of the rose as I wish to relate it. In some classes, of which this is one, those steps have worn smooth in time and become indistinguishable; especially as no parentage records exist to show how they developed from one to another. It would have been pleasant to dwell on 'La Ville de Bruxelles', pink, from Vibert 1849; 'Leda', the Painted Damask (shades of 'Picasso'!), white with a touch of red on the rim; 'Marie Louise', a big pink rose from the Empress Josephine's garden, unkindly named after Napoleon's next wife; and 'Hebe's Lip' a late arrival in 1912 from William Paul, looking as if a Damask had met the Sweet Briar 'Janet's Pride', its creamy flower tipped red.

CENTIFOLIAS

These old roses have mostly been known by three common names: Cabbage roses, Provence roses and Cent-feuilles. Each one is a source of misguidance, as we shall see. The official name is *R.* × *centifolia.*

The earliest English name, from John Gerard in 1597, is the Holland or Province rose. The origin of Centifolias is not clearly proved, but the evidence suggests that they were raised in Holland, and grown to good effect in Provence in the south of France. Hence they acquired the name Provence (or Province in John Gerard's spelling) much to the annoyance of some Dutch rosarians, who protested that they should be Holland roses. Unfortunately there was already a red Gallica familiarly known as the Provins rose, from being grown in that town, miles north of Provence; the two were inevitably muddled.

In England, the familiar alternative was Cabbage roses, which probably advanced in popular use during the Napoleonic wars, when any name was preferable to a French one. Few people look upon the cabbage as a thing of ethereal beauty, and the idea grew that the name implied roses the size of cabbages. Those who thought so were of course disappointed. The name was given because the petals folded over the centre of the flower, and delayed revealing it, as all good round cabbages do.

The French name Cent-Feuilles, and the Latin name Centifolia, imply that the flowers contain a hundred petals; or to put not too mathematical a meaning to it, a great many petals. This is an exaggerated claim for many Centifolias. Unfortunately it provided an exact parallel with the hundred-petalled rose reported from Ancient Greece and Rome by Theophrastus and Pliny. Theophrastus was wary of hearsay evidence. He introduced that multipetalled rose with the honourable caution, 'for there are some, they say, which are even called hundred-petalled.' In Pliny's 'Natural History', written over three hundred years later, the observations of Theophrastus shine through, just as today those of Graham Thomas can clearly be seen in the descriptions of old garden roses written by his successors. Pliny was not so careful about hearsay, and committed himself to the Latin word, centifolia; and in the eighteenth century, Linnaeus applied it as a specific name for these roses. By the nineteenth century, the connection between the two had become fixed in many minds, and the history of the Centifolias was confidently traced to the Garden of Midas, out of Herodotus, about BC 550, through Italy and up to the present day. Such an account appeared in the *Rosarian's Year-Book 1896*, written by the Rev. G. E. Jeans, a vicar in the Isle of Wight. It was reprinted in the *Rose Annuals* of 1921 and 1945, a gospel thrice accepted, but quite unreliable.

The truth of their origin was sought by C. C. Hurst, who concluded that they were complex hybrids evolved in Holland in the sixteenth century, and not perfected until the eighteenth. (But when is any class perfected?) The species he took to be in their pedigree were *R. gallica, R. phoenicia, R. canina* and *R. moschata*. The quickest route to join them, he says, would be by a marriage of 'Quatre Saisons' (the Autumn Damask, which he calls *R. bifera*) and *R. × alba*. He may have been correct; 'Quatre Saisons' is a most convincing answer, because it sported to a Moss, which the Centifolias proceeded to do in turn. Hurst's studies compel respect by his knowledge and his examination of plant cells. Without benefit of the latter, I cannot subdue the thought that the growth of Centifolias suggests a marriage between 'Quatre Saisons' and Gallicas.

To round off the affair, let us remember that the Dutchmen in the sixteenth century could just conceivably have been in the tracks of Greeks before Christ.

'Bullata' *Tall Pink Midsummer* P5 H1 *
A bullate leaf is one in which the surface is above the veins, as in a primrose, and for that noticeable character this double pink rose is named. The French called it 'Rosier à Feuilles de Laitue', which is the Lettuce-leafed rose. Official name: *R. × centifolia bullata*. Presumably it was a sport from an original Centifolia; and we may note that this is a class of few seeds and many sports. Nobody knows how old 'Bullata' is, apart from knowledge of its existence early in the nineteenth century. It opens, fragrantly, in the form typical of Centifolias. A ladybird on the edge of an outer petal would be like a mountaineer looking into the quiet crater of a pink volcano.

'Chapeau de Napoleon' *Medium   Pink   Midsummer* P4 H1 **

The official name of this fascinator is *R.* × *centifolia cristata;* and although it is not a Moss, it is known also as 'Crested Moss'. The old name, 'Crested Provence', was more accurate in its day. No other rose copies its strange practice of imitating little fronds upon its sepals; before the buds open, some of these growths join in an outline for which Napoleon's hat is an apt picture. The flowers are pink, double. This rose was first recorded by J. Prévost, after some unknown botanist had sent it to him from Switzerland. It was introduced by Vibert in 1827.

'Petite de Hollande' *Medium* + *Pink   Midsummer* P3 H1 **

This may be one of the old Centifolias, for at least its Dutch past is acknowledged, and I have found no news of its origin. It has other names: 'Petite Junon de Hollande', 'Pompon des Dames' and 'Normandica'. It is a charming Centifolia, forming a spreading bush. It makes good use of its spread by covering itself with small double pink flowers. A neat and pleasing rose, which I have had in my garden for many years with great satisfaction. The flowers are flatter and less fragrant than most Centifolias, half way towards rosettes. This flower formation is carried a stage further by the shorter 'De Meaux', which has pompon flowers, and would be an absolute beauty if it could keep off its addiction to blackspot. 'De Meaux', which is pink, also has other names, *R.* × *centifolia pomponia,* 'Pompon Rose' and 'Rose de Meaux'. It is credited to Robert Sweet in 1789, but this is more likely to be an identification than a raising, for it was on sale in England in 1770.

'Spong' *Short   Pink   Early summer* P3 H1 **

This and 'De Meaux' belonged to a class which William Paul called The Miniature Provence, or Pompon Rose. I have never understood why Graham Thomas says it grows four feet high, because mine do not reach my knees. When its little pink flowers come into bloom, no bush is so spruce and attractive. This prettiness is of short duration, for the petals hang on into ugly old age, and for the rest of the season the Centifolia foliage is less than inspiring. It is said to have been introduced by a gardener whose strange name it bears, 1805 and 1820 being two dates in the books; Hurst identifies it with a rose mentioned in 1789 under a name to which silent amazement seems the only response, 'The Great Dwarf Rose'.

'Tour de Malakoff' *Tall   Mauve pink   Midsummer* P4 H1

If you like to grow an arching shrub of wayward disposition and revolting colour, this is the one for you. At least it is different from anything else. Surely this is a Centifolia of Gallica descent, inheriting the crazy Gallica colours; it starts up magenta, changes down to mauve pink, and finally meets its doom all greyed over in a proper spirit of ashes to ashes. I have written off Malakoff from my future itineraries; it must be an extraordinary place on this evidence. The rose came from Soupert & Notting of the Grand Duchy of Luxembourg in 1856.

MOSS ROSES

These should really be included with the Centifolias; but long tradition, stretched by sentiment, puts them in a class by themselves. We have seen that Damasks and Miniatures can also be mossy; but the Moss roses really belong to Centifolias, from which they began as sports. Their official name is *R.* × *centifolia muscosa.*

Their charming character derives from little glandular growths, like modified bristles, growing closely all over the seed pod and sepals. Why these growths should so concentrate in one area is a mystery. It is perhaps a chance shuffling of the rose's resources. The formation of flower, colour, scent and reproductive organs is a complicated piece of vegetative engineering, to be carried out to a precise schedule; an intruder need cause no great surprise where all the forces are mobilized.

Their origin is unclear. The first mention of them according to Hurst is in an index of plants by Hermann Boerhaave of Holland in 1720. Subsequently it was claimed that they had existed around Carcassonne in the south of France since 1696. But that date is arbitrary, being based on a statement by F. du Castel in 1746 that they had been known in Carcassonne for half a century; which might mean anything from twenty years. Those dates indicate the time; the place we cannot decide on; Holland and the South of France are equally likely, as being the places with most Centifolias, and we do not know that Boerhaave proved the plant to be of Dutch origin.

The Moss is a disappointing rose to grow, lanky and mildewy; most of them are best trained along a fence made out of posts and wires (not a solid fence, because that abets mildew). The long growths should be tied down, and their thin ends removed. The following year they should flower; and the best pruning of them is to cut the flowers; let the trained shoots live until they are too old to be useful, or until they are superfluous in relation to the new growths. As items of garden decoration, or as free standing shrubs, they are usually poor. Paul records eighty-four varieties, and more were introduced as a result of keen eyed rosarians scanning the seed pods and calyces for the slightest sign of moss; with the result that some of those sent out looked as mossy as a man in slight need of a shave.

'Blanche Moreau' Tall White Midsummer P3 H1 *

A good white Moss rose, with dark leaves for its class, a help to the colour. The mossy growth is also dark, which renders it less dainty and conspicuous than one might wish. Lanky growth. The name does not mean white moss, but refers to the raisers, Moreau-Robert, of Angers, France. They raised it from 'Comtesse du Murinais' × 'Quatre Saisons Blanc', and introduced it in 1880.

'Common Moss' Tall Pink Midsummer P4 H1 *

Taken to be the original, as *R.* × *centifolia muscosa;* 'Old Pink Moss' has been a familiar name for it in England, and it has also been known as 'Communis' and 'Pink Moss'. It is the best Moss to grow if the object is to enjoy the moss, other than which there is no point in growing Moss roses. In this case it is fresh and green, an attractive embellishment to the pink buds. And of course it is in the bud stage that Moss roses should be seen, not when the open petals hide its raison d'être.

In 1788 a white sport was introduced by Henry Shailer in England as 'Shailer's White Moss'; it was followed about twenty-five years later by another English sport from a Mr Salter of Clifton, Bristol; he named it 'White Bath'; under that name or 'White Moss' it became more popular than Shailer's variety; whether any perceptible difference existed between the two sports seems doubtful.

'Laneii' and 'William Lobb' *

Both these roses are a splendid purple; I have been told from time to time that my 'Laneii' is 'William Lobb', but I believe them to be different; they both came from M. Laffay in France; he sent 'Laneii' to Lane's Nursery in Berkhamsted, who introduced it according to *Modern Roses* in 1854; while 'William Lobb' came out in France in 1855, with the additional name 'Duchesse d'Istrie'.

On the face of it, a perfect means of the same variety growing under two names.

But there is one strange fact. According to William Paul in 1848, flowers of 'Laneii' were exhibited at Chiswick in 1847, which is a long time before the date of introduction of either rose. Upon turning to Jäger's *Rosenlexikon* I find the date of 'Laneii' is 1846. This makes better sense; and as Jäger agrees with 1855 for 'William Lobb', we suddenly see the likelihood of two different varieties, for it is not to be thought that Laffay would introduce his own rose eleven years later than a foreigner.

I obtained 'William Lobb' for comparison, and find these major differences: 'Laneii' is a stubby bush which spreads wide; 'William Lobb' is taller, makes a bigger and more lax plant. 'Laneii' holds a deep colour in its later stages; 'William Lobb' becomes paler.

Both are bold purple roses, good to look at. As far as moss goes, they are poorly endowed; perhaps that is why 'Laneii' reverted to that name after a period as 'Lane's Moss'.

PORTLANDS

The Gallicas, Damasks and Centifolias were the old garden roses of Europe. To them may be added a fourth class, the Albas, which are akin to the Caninae, and therefore appear in that section. The early nineteenth century is a kind of watershed: the years behind were scented by Gallicas, Damasks, Centifolias and Albas, beyond memory; the years ahead were to see those roses shaken from their thrones in double quick time. The Portlands were the first hint of what the China rose was about to do.

'Duchess of Portland' *Medium   Red   Summer* +   P2   H3
The proper name of this rose is 'Paestana', under which it is said to have arrived in England from Italy near the end of the eighteenth century. From England it went to France, where André Dupont, gardener to the Empress Josephine, named it 'Duchess of Portland'. As it gave that name to a new class, I retain it. It was also known as the 'Scarlet Four Seasons', expressing a suspected relationship with the 'Autumn Damask'. The name 'Paestana' alluded to the reputation of that area in ancient times. It was a Greek colony on the Gulf of Salerno, called Poseidonia until the Romans took it and named it Paestum. The roses of that place had long been famous, and their best publicist was the poet Virgil, who died in 19 BC. His epithet, 'biferique rosaria Paesti', means 'the twice-bearing rose gardens of Paestum', and fixed in people's minds the idea that Paestum was particularly favoured by having twice as many roses as anywhere else. This may have occurred from the bushes repeating their flowers, but more probably from some of them being forced into early bloom by the use of hot water. There is some doubt as to how near to a greenhouse the Romans approached, but it seems clear that they used earthenware pipes to circulate hot water, and an obvious corollary would be some kind of shelter to save heat, and exclude wind and frost. The satirist Seneca, who in general appears to have been a somewhat unpleasant busybody, and eventually was obliged to accept an invitation from Nero to commit suicide, protested against the practice of forcing plants into bloom, as part of the Roman madness of turning nature upside down. Truly there is nothing new without its objectors.

Somebody, upon finding a red rose which was to some degree remontant, remembered his Virgil and bestowed the appropriate name of 'Paestana' upon so valuable a discovery. We do not know who he was. We assume the rose came from a chance cross between a red China and 'Quatre Saisons', the 'Autumn Damask'. There is a plant named 'Paestana' in the Royal National Rose Society's garden at St Albans, believed to be the correct variety. It is more like a Gallica than a Damask, the flowers taking after *R. gallica officinalis*. Whether the one parent was Gallica or Damask, there can be little doubt that the other was a China. As the first evidence that the roses of east and west were marrying, this variety has its place in the rose's history.

'Comte de Chambord' *Tall Pink Remontant* – P4 H1

The Portlands were not a clearly defined class, but spent much of their career as Damask Perpetuals, in the opinion of those who grew them. This variety is clear pink, not unlike the colour of 'Mme Caroline Testout', the flowers about two-thirds the diameter of a garden Hybrid Tea. The young flowers are well formed; their outside petals stretch around a regular, globular centre; then, very swiftly it seems, the centre opens into several rows of little petals, all folded, and pointing outward. The end product is blowsy. Growth rather lax. Introduced in 1860.

'Jacques Cartier' *Tall Pink Remontant* – P3 H2 *

A pretty pink rose; when fully open it reminds me of an over double carnation, because although it opens with a rounded centre like 'Comte de Chambord', the petals finally point up instead of out. Pleasing in colour, well filled as a shrub, but disappointing in scent. It was introduced by Moreau-Robert in 1868; but shortly afterwards, everyone was growing Hybrid Perpetuals, and the Portlands were forgotten.

BOURBONS

The China rose had apparently mated with western roses first in Italy, giving birth to the Portlands. Its second significant marriage had been with the Musk rose in the United States: the Noisettes came from it. The third important liaison came to light in the remote island of Réunion in the Indian Ocean, giving rise to the Bourbons, so named because the island was then called the Île de Bourbon.

These three classes, with help from the Chinas and Teas, were leading to Hybrid Perpetuals, and thence to the Hybrid Teas we know so well today. Their spontaneous creation occurred in three different continents within a time of about twenty years, so far as we can tell. These bare facts may stimulate thoughts about the nature of the world we live in; but my task is to attend to the roses, not to dream. I content myself by asking whether the plant material would have been transported and used with such despatch today?

Whether Réunion was truly the point of origin is not completely certain. The story wavers in detail from one authority to the next, and the best check point we have is Thomas Rivers, who quoted one of the 'many fables . . . told by the French respecting the origin of this rose', and having done so, proceeds: 'This is pretty enough, but entirely devoid of truth. Monsieur Bréon, a French botanist, and now a seedsman in Paris, gives the following account, for the truth of which he vouches: – "At the Isle of Bourbon, the inhabitants generally enclose their land with hedges made of two rows of roses, one row of the Common China Rose, the other of the Red Four Seasons. Monsieur Perichon, a proprietor at Saint Benoist, in the isle, in planting one of these hedges, found amongst his young plants one very different from the others in its shoots and foliage. This induced him to plant it in his garden. It flowered the following year; and as he anticipated, proved to be of quite a new race, and differing much from the above two roses, *which, at the time, were the only sorts known on the island."* Monsieur Bréon arrived at Bourbon in 1817, as botanical traveller for the Government of France, and curator of the Botanical and Naturalization Garden there.'

We leave Thomas Rivers there, as his dates from that point perhaps lack the guidance of Monsieur Bréon, whose statement is indeed a modest one, with no claim for the discovery which is generally credited to him. He obviously took an interest in Monsieur Périchon's rose, and sent seeds of it to Monsieur Jacques, the gardener of the Duc d'Orléans at the Château de Neuilly near Paris. We already met M. Jacques in connection with *R. sempervirens*. He received the seeds in October 1819, and four or five came up in 1820. M. Jacques distributed stock to some French rosarians about 1823, and it was known for a time as 'Bourbon Jacques'.

All this leads us back to the question of how it arose. It was subsequently claimed that the rose of Réunion existed also in Mauritius, and had been sent to the Luxembourg Gardens in Paris from that island in 1821. And again, that it existed in the Calcutta Botanic Garden under the name 'Rose Edouard'. Whether a similar cross occurred in more than one of these places; or whether the rose was transported from one to another in the ordinary course of sea voyages, we have no means of knowing. The sea routes offered that possibility; Mauritius and Réunion were ports of call between India and the Cape of Good Hope. What is certain is that 'Rose Edouard' has been known in India for many years; the Indians call it the 'Temple Rose', and they have used it as an understock. The important point is that the Bourbons appear to have come by seed from a plant which was a hybrid between China and Damask, so far as the history and appearance of the class informs us.

Bourbons were chiefly enjoyed for their large petals, wide and silky in comparison with the folded petals of the older roses. This gave the flowers a fine circular appearance, and made the colours appear brighter. They were splendid in the autumn, a reason to treasure a rose in those days; but after a few years rosarians in the cooler countries were noting that the Bourbons were not so fine in the summer. The truth was that they needed heat in the growing season; that of high summer was adequate to make glorious blooms in the autumn, but the shoots which grew in the cool springs of the north were incapable of forming perfect blooms in midsummer. Thomas Rivers had noted that the main task in pruning them was to remove their frost-killed wood. From these slightly tender causes they lost their popularity, and were trodden down by their own hungry progeny, the Hybrid Perpetuals. Their heyday was the period about 1830–70; and many of the survivors of the class are those in which hardier but less graceful roses changed the delicacy of the Bourbon flower. The official name of the Bourbon rose is *R. × borboniana*.

'Gloire des Rosomanes' *Tallest Red Remontant* P4 H4

The date of introduction was 1825, which allows little time for J. P. Vibert to raise it from those supplies that may have come his way from M. Jacques. As it was accepted as a Hybrid of the Bourbons by 1832, it ill becomes me to question its origin at this late date. All of the original seedlings from Jacques are said to have died out; but I wonder if, just possibly, this could have been one of them? It is a tall, ranging plant, with abundant growth. Thomas Rivers concluded that as it outgrew any partners, the best place for it was tied to a pillar, as a climber. 'As a pillar rose', he says, 'it will form a splendid object'. The flowers are red, semi-double.

Under the name 'Ragged Robin', it has been used as a rootstock on which to propagate roses. It has also been used as a rose hedge, and is still advertised for this purpose in Britain; most rosarians would suppose there are better hedge roses, but this is an effective one, provided the growth suits the site. It can be produced cheaply, and is a great improvement on hedge roses which used to be advertised in the British press, to the scandal of the rose trade; for they were the discards from fields of Dog Roses grown as understocks, those too small and crooked for their purpose. They could be bought for a few shillings a thousand from the Dutch growers, who otherwise burnt them; and many an innocent citizen who sent off his money for a rose hedge was astounded when it came in an envelope through his letter box, and landed on the doormat with a dry bounce. After many representations, the editors learned to refuse those advertisements.

'Bourbon Queen' *Tall Pink Remontant* – P3 H2 *
The rose we know under this name is a cheerful bright pink bush, which proved so hardy that it is a common survivor from plantations otherwise long forgotten. The flowers are double, the outer petals slightly deeper in colour than the inner, which tend to crinkle. The leaves are dark green, unobtrusive. It seems that a number of names were used, 'Bourbon Queen', 'Queen of Bourbons', 'Reine des Îles Bourbon', and 'Souvenir de la Princesse de Lamballe', being some; and we cannot be sure they all applied to the same rose; in the old days, some nurseries were unscrupulous in giving an old variety a new name, a charge which brought this reproof from William Paul: 'I am sorry that my experience does not allow me to meet this assertion with a direct negative. *Old Roses have been sent to this establishment under new names, and charged at high prices.* This, however, might occur by mistake, and seldom happens with *the respectable growers*.' As a grower myself for over forty years, how well I know those detestable mistakes. 'Ena Harkness', out of familiarity, becomes EH to the whole staff. Then comes a rose 'Ernest H. Morse', soon known as E. H. Morse. 'Tom, fetch some E. H. Morse from Bill.' Tom is new; he has only heard of one of these roses. So, 'Bill, they want more E.H.' As soon as one gap is plugged, some genius opens another. An inattentive moment, and a couple of hundred 'Red Dandy' labels enter the pigeon hole of 'Red Devil'. It shouldn't happen, but it does. Deliberate misrepresentation is rare these days, I hope. Every trade has its unscrupulous operators, and from what I have seen in the rose trade, ours are unscrupulous on some inverted principle, to put themselves one up in their game. They see life as a contest between sharp wits, their swindles as triumphs rather than frauds. It never occurs to them that they could live just as well without their sharpness; they have the true irresponsibility that sees no consequences of an action.

To return to 'Bourbon Queen', if we have the right variety, it came from Mauget of Orléans in 1834 or 1835.

'Souvenir de la Malmaison' *Medium Blush white Remontant* P6 H2 ***
This is the best, the most beautiful advertisement for the Bourbons. 'Queen of Beauty and Fragrance' they called it, most truthfully. The wide, pale flowers shine against leaf and soil like water lilies upon a dark pond. The bushes are short for the class, the scent is sweet, and the flowers are double. A more vigorous form exists, with the word 'Climbing' attached to it, but it is neither so remontant nor so charming. A sport with so few petals as to be virtually single came from a famous rose garden in Dublin, was named 'Souvenir de St Anne's', and was introduced by T. Hilling & Co. of Chobham, Surrey in 1950. It could well be taken as the emblem of purity.

'Souvenir de la Malmaison' was raised by Jean Béluze of Lyon from 'Mme Desprez', another Bourbon. The pollen parent is said to have been a Tea. It was introduced in 1843.

'Boule de Neige' *Tall White Remontant* – P8 H1 *
When the double flowers open without damage from the weather, their symmetric form is beautiful to see; but all too often the sequence from tight round bud to petal crammed bloom is spoiled. If it is allowed to proceed, it ends like a snowball, as the outer petals stretch backwards towards the flower stalk. Raised by François Lacharme of Lyon, and introduced in 1867.

'Zéphirine Drouhin' *Climber Pink Remontant* P5 H1 ***
Famous as the 'Thornless Rose', although it is not completely without prickles. It may be grown as a climber, although preferably not on a wall, as mildew is likely there; better on a fence, and best of all as a pillar; it may also be grown as a shrub, or even as a hedge. In the latter case, it may be pruned to keep the required height, with the longer growths being tied down into the hedge.

At first sight it is one's least favourite pink, in the area between pink and red, often denoted in the catalogues by that word of warning: 'cerise'. But let them open, and the small flowers express the warmth of summer, not this summer but some old remembered days of warmth, when roses innocently quartered their centres without disgrace, and were expected to breathe a gentle fragrance into the air. I know nothing of the raiser except his name, Bizot; he introduced this rose in 1868, and it has been generally cultivated and enjoyed for over a century. In 1919, Alexander Dickson introduced a lovely pale pink sport, 'Kathleen Harrop', in all respects save colour the same.

'Mme Pierre Oger' *Tall Pink & white Remontant* P7 H2 ***
On her day, one of the most beautiful rose blooms in the world, with a combination of colour and form which cannot be mistaken, for no other rose is similar. Imagine a small saucer, for the size and outline. Break the rim into the rounded curves of petals, delicate pink melting into white. Let the centre contain shorter petals and stamens, not crowded, but decently existing without knowing where to go. Such a saucer, if in porcelain, would be locked safely within its showcase as a great treasure.

This beauty has her failings; she needs the sun to respond to; she has not the best of figures, being on the lanky side; and her health is delicate for she catches blackspot.

She arose as a sport from 'Reine Victoria', which is similar except for her plainer pink colour. 'Reine Victoria' came from J. Schwartz of Lyon in 1872; 'Mme Pierre Oger' from M. A. Oger of Caen in Northern France, for whom Eugène Verdier of Paris introduced it in 1878.

'Mme Isaac Pereire' *Taller Pink Remontant* P6 H1
This has shaggy double flowers in which strident pink fights a losing battle against the inroads of magenta; from it arose a sport, 'Mme Ernst Calvat', which is more resolute in maintaining its pink identity.

These two are generally applauded and extolled as examples of the beauty of old garden roses. I cannot see why. Like Johnny the soldier, I am at a loss to understand why the rest of the platoon persists in marching out of step. For if 'Mme Pierre Oger' is Cinderella, these two are the Ugly Sisters fortissimo.

Their long branches are clad with dull foliage, nasty little thorns and mildew. Their flowers, revolting in colour, frequently ameliorate that sin by failing to open at all. Few shrubs can rival their ungainly habit, to avoid which the experts propose they should be grown as climbers; and for a wall facing a neighbour one wishes to annoy, they are ideal subjects.

I now recall one distinguished voice to summon to my aid, that of my old employer, Willie Slinger, a Yorkshireman who became proprietor of the Donard Nursery Company, just where the Mountains of Mourne run down to the sea in County Down. I spent three blissful years there in my youth, ostensibly learning how to be a nurseryman. Some years later, I listened to the two Willies, Slinger and Harkness, talking at Chelsea Show about the interest in old garden roses revived by Graham Thomas. Willie Slinger approved the idea, but expressed wonder at the choice of varieties. The stars of his youth had been passed over, he claimed, and the rejects put in their place. 'Calvat always was rubbish', are the four words I recollect verbatim.

Willie Slinger had been apprentice at the Harkness Nursery in Leeming Bar, Yorkshire in the 1890s. I repaid the compliment likewise at his nursery in the 1930s. He was a brilliant nurseryman and exhibitor; the stars of his youth had been those most ephemeral of all roses, the exhibition varieties. I still have a letter of his, written to Willie (Bill) Harkness in 1937 after a show at Leeds, where they were in competition. The local paper had awarded not only the Rose Trophy, but also that for Sweet Peas to Harkness, in a fit of journalistic generosity. So Willie Slinger writes to his rival: 'Congrats on whacking me for that Cup. I see according to the papers you also won the Sweet Pea Cup, which was probably news to you but did not surprise me in the least. Let me know if you are entering for the F.A. Cup, the Boat Race or the St Leger, and I will get my money on you.' When I told him of the death of Bill Harkness, he wept. I last heard from him after his eightieth birthday, when he wrote to say that the future was bright; as a baby he had been quite unable to walk, whereas on entering his ninth decade, he could not only walk, but even run, a short way. Therefore his prospects at eighty were better than when newly born.

Back to the Bourbons! 'Mme Isaac Pereire' was raised by M. Garçon of Rouen, and introduced by M. Margottin in 1881. 'Mme Ernst Calvat' (also known as 'Pink Bourbon') came from the widow of J. Schwartz in 1888. To give the devils their dues, they are both fragrant.

HYBRID PERPETUALS

The name of this class is not so artificially devised as appears at first sight. If there are Hybrid Perpetuals, then there must have been a previous class called Perpetuals for them to be hybrids of. Such was the case. 'Perpetuals' were a miscellany of all those roses which flowered in the autumn, but which could not readily be assigned to such recognizable classes as Chinas, Teas, Bourbons or Noisettes. The Perpetuals contained derivatives from the Portlands, the Autumn Damask and many others; even from Scotch roses, for 'Stanwell Perpetual' was reckoned amongst them. Their change to Hybrid Perpetuals flowed mainly from crosses with the Bourbons. The French name for the new class was much more accurate, being the equivalent of Hybrid Remontants; to describe a plant that flowers more than once in the season, remontant is a more honest term than perpetual.

Hybrid Perpetuals therefore began as a medley; the Portlands and Bourbons were their principle progenitors, with Teas and others entering later. As the class progressed, it found its identity as a race of strong, upright plants, bearing large flowers, and blessed with a fortunate if deceptive name. Many flowered well in the autumn; but some spent the late summer growing long shoots with no flower buds on them, and their autumn flowers were scanty. Thousands of different varieties were raised, most in France, with the result of ousting the old garden roses, and of giving the rose a completely new social status of its own.

Hybrid Perpetuals were showman's flowers, large, full of petals, long lasting;

although to us the centres of many would look crimped and rounded. Nevertheless, they brought the rose into flower shows in full force, in such size and beauty as to fan the exhibitor's ardour into a fanatical flame, and to tempt others to imitate him. In England, the outcome of this was the first Grand National Rose Show in London in 1858, organized by some names by now familiar to us, such as Canon Hole, Thomas Rivers, George and William Paul. So far as we know, this was the first show on a national scale devoted exclusively to roses. Rose societies began to form themselves, primarily for the purpose of organizing rose shows; in December 1876, the National Rose Society was constituted, with Dean Hole as its President, and it soon announced that its first Great National Rose Show would be held on 4 July, 1877. The Rev. Joseph Pemberton was there, and wrote his memories of it in the *Rose Annual 1918,* describing a scene of chaos to which he generously contributed by trying to insert his own roses after having been too late in submitting his application to enter. There was no room on the staging for all the entries, many of which had to be lined up on the floor, six deep.

I heard old stories of exhibiting, as retailed to me by our rose grower, Ernest Barker, when I worked with him in the rose field in my youth; and also from Willie Slinger. The flower heads were shown on stalks a few inches long, each in its own tube of water; except that one expert thought they liked whisky in it, a practice he abandoned upon finding his exhibit dismantled and the whisky drunk from the tubes! These tubes were set in rectangular boxes of regulation size, surfaces covered with moss, and the object was to show the flowers with nothing to distract from their perfection. Classes were for a number of different varieties, one of each, 12, 24, and up to 72 for the nurserymen's championship; and other classes admitted duplicates, threes, and sixes of the same variety.

Some Hybrid Perpetuals would hold their shape for several days, and if their colour held, they were good for more than one show. Ernest Barker was once despatched by Robert Harkness to a show with the order to be sure to bring back a certain flower, and hand it over to Robert at Hitchin Station that night, for he would take it to the next show. When Mr Barker's show was closing, and he was thirsty, he fell to a tempter who offered him a shilling and ninepence for that bloom, reflecting that the boss might not need it, and that the sum represented fourteen pints of beer. His return to Hitchin Station was unostentatious, but to no avail, for his employer was waiting. 'Where's that flower?' With all the sad sincerity he could summon, and he had a lot of it, Mr Barker replied, 'It blew'.

A scandal developed in Staffordshire, when the flowers of one exhibitor did not blow, whereas all around his box, the roses of his rivals opened dismally in the heat of the day. Intrigued by these iron blooms, some rosarian made a close inspection of them, and found the cultural secret. The petals had been discreetly made to support one another by the use of gum! The cheat was challenged, and his prize taken away from him. He retorted that nowhere in the regulations was there a prohibition of the use of gum; and on appeal, the National Rose Society upheld him with reluctance, for in the letter of the law he was right. His prize was restored, but his future entries refused.

A favourite dodge was to leave one's best flowers concealed until the last moment. Competitors were good judges, and usually knew which entries ought to win. If they had entered several classes, there was no sense in winning one by a mile, and losing others by an inch. Better weaken this exhibit a little, since it is clearly in front, and strengthen another. Once that had been done, and no time remained for another change, the person who had been waiting for that moment would reach under the bench for the two or three flowers which changed his weakness into strength.

The Hybrid Perpetuals were vigorous plants. They made it easy to grow roses. Their normal habit was to flower in summer off wood of previous years, and then to grow long thick shoots, head high in some varieties; those were the bases for the future. Those long shoots were likely to have no flowers, the autumn bloom coming from the same sources as that of summer. This habit of growth required plenty of food and moisture; and from it grew the beliefs that roses were gross feeders and needed a heavy soil, that is one retentive of moisture.

The exhibitors of the nineteenth century made roses popular, established Rose Societies, learned the fine arts of cultivation, and therefore did much for the good of the rose. On the debit side, they encouraged varieties of no use for garden decoration; for among the vigorous Hybrid Perpetuals were the weak and the ugly, loudly recommended on the strength of a few inches of them at the shows. An article by T. W. Girdlestone in the *Rosarian's Year-Book 1890* said of the roses of his time 'the general effect produced by them in the garden is almost always incredibly poor'.

'Rose du Roi'

This was an important rose, bridging the gap between old and new. It was also highly valued as a red beauty. We may take it for a Portland, an Autumn Damask, a Perpetual or a Hybrid Perpetual, with good authority to quote for each. I think Portland may be correct, but it fits well here as being the chief progenitor of the Hybrid Perpetuals. It was known in Britain as 'Crimson Perpetual'.

It was raised as a seedling in 1812, in the gardens of the Palace of Saint Cloud at Sèvres; early nineteenth century accounts say that the seed parent was declared to be 'Paestana' or a similar Portland. There appears to be no evidence, but every horticultural sense points to 'Paestana'. Rivers and Paul both allude to some embarrassment over the name, which appears to have arisen because St Cloud was a royal palace, and the gardens came under the administration of Comte Lelieur. He named the new seedling after himself, 'Rose Lelieur'; but an official of the royal household overturned that decision, to name it 'Rose du Roi', much to the mortification of the Comte, from whom the affair elicited a resignation. After all the fuss, the gardener who had raised it, by name Souchet, introduced it in 1815. Says Rivers: 'Every gentleman's garden ought to have a large bed of Crimson Perpetual Roses, to furnish bouquets during August, September, and October; their fragrance is so delightful, their colour so rich, and their form so perfect.' But his bidding has been ignored by modern gentlemen; this rose is extremely difficult to find, and I have never seen it.

'Princesse Hélène'

According to William Paul, this was the first *striking* variety in the class. It was introduced in 1837, and it is fitting to remember it, because its breeder was M. Laffay of Bellevue, France. By general agreement the credit for the early development of Hybrid Perpetuals is given to him. I have never seen this rose, and doubt whether it is now to be found. It was rosy-purple.

'La Reine'   *Medium + Pink Remontant –*

A large pink rose, with which M. Laffay convinced many people that Hybrid Perpetuals were the roses of the age. It was introduced in 1841–3, the dates varying in different authorities. Also known as 'Rose de la Reine', which was the original name; and 'Reine des Français'.

'Baronne Prévost' *Tall   Pink   Remontant*   P5   H1
This variety is still in existence. It is pale pink; the quartered centre shows that the
early Hybrid Perpetuals had much of the old garden roses about them. From Desprez
of Yèbles, France in 1842.

'Géant des Batailles' *Medium +   Crimson   Remontant*
The first important red variety. 'Rose du Roi' may have been expected to launch the
Hybrid Perpetuals into a sea of red; but of the 106 varieties listed by William Paul in
1848, it is clear that deep reds were absent. Where the word crimson appears, it is
qualified by the addition of purple, or preceded by such adjectives as rosy or cherry;
nearly all the 106 followed their presumed Damask ancestor by being pink. Another
influx of red China was needed to make crimson Hybrid Perpetuals, and it is believed
to have been injected into this variety, possibly through 'Gloire des Rosomanes'.
'Géant des Batailles' was to prove an important rose in the future of the class. It was
raised by M. Nérard, and introduced by Guillot Père in 1846.

Only two varieties in Paul's list appear to have been deep red. 'Mélanie Cornu',
from M. Cornu in 1841, was 'crimson tinged with purple'. 'Cymédor', from Guillot
Père in 1846, was 'dark red, peculiar colour'.

'Général Jacqueminot' *Tall   Red   Remontant*   P6   H2
Affectionately known as 'General Jack' in English speaking countries, this variety
had a long spell in favour from its introduction in 1852 (or 1853.) About its
parentage, the same supposition is made as for 'Géant des Batailles'. But one could
quite reasonably go further, and suppose the 'Géant' to have been the other parent.
Its arrival fortified the sound base established by the 'Géant', from which to breed
red Hybrid Perpetuals and Hybrid Teas in the future. 'General Jack' was one of the
better looking plants in the class, not so coarse as most in leaf and stem; nor in bloom,
for the flowers were slim for a Hybrid Perpetual; they attracted the florists, who grew
'General Jack' for market for many years. It was fragrant, and stands as a significant
parent of modern roses.

'Général Jacqueminot' was raised by an amateur, M. A. Roussel of Montpelier. It
is a sad little tale. M. Roussel raised seedling roses as a hobby, but found no good
ones up to the day he died. His gardener, M. Rousselet, found 'General Jack' in the
last lot, after his employer's death.

Plenty of other names descended on the rose; but what is not generally known is
that six years previously, M. Laffay had introduced a Hybrid China under the same
name, 'Général Jacqueminot'.

'Victor Verdier' *Tall   Red   Remontant*
One of the most important Hybrid Perpetuals for introducing Teas into the class.
'Jules Margottin' × 'Safrano' were the parents quoted by its raiser, François
Lacharme; it was therefore a Hybrid Tea by parentage; and although the Hybrid
Perpetual character dominated it, something else showed through. It was noted as
being distinct in its smooth wood, lovely foliage and resistance to mildew. On the
debit side was rust, so devastating that Foster-Melliar owned to 'the early shoots
being often quite bare of leaves by the end of August'. Introduced in 1859.

'Charles Lefebvre' *Tall   Crimson   Remontant*
This is what the exhibitors wanted, dark red and large. Introduced in 1861, it was a
popular variety until the end of the Hybrid Perpetual's reign towards the turn of the

17 *Dr W. van Fleet, a Wichuraiana Hybrid, from the chapter Synstylae. This shows how it may clothe a fence*

18 *R. kordesii, from the chapter Synstylae. Although here encouraged to trail, it is naturally more upright*

19 R. gallica versicolor, or Rosa Mundi, from the section Gallicanae. Believed to have originated about 1650

20 Madame Hardy, a Damask, from the section Gallicanae. A rose of 1832, capable of impeccable beauty

21 Chapeau de Napoleon, or Crested Moss, from the section Gallicanae. Note the bud, with its strange fronds

22 Common Moss, from the section Gallicanae. The mossy buds have intrigued generations of rose lovers

23 Zéphirine Drouhin, the famous 'Thornless Rose', a Bourbon from the chapter Gallicanae

24 Roger Lambelin, a Hybrid Perpetual from the chapter Gallicanae. Famous for its white edged petals

25 Golden Chersonese, an Ecae Hybrid from the section Pimpinellifoliae. A large and glorious plant

26 R. foetida bicolor, or Austrian Copper, from the section Pimpinellifoliae, 'a blaze like one of Turner's sunsets'

27 *Marguerite Hilling, placed in this book in the section Pimpinellifoliae, as a Spinosissima Hybrid*

28 *Celestial, an Alba, from the section Caninae. Note the handsome plant growth, typical of Albas*

29 Complicata, placed in this book as a Macrantha, in the chapter Caninae. Here it has invaded its neighbour

30 R. foliolosa, from the section Carolinae; a wild rose from Arkansas, of lovely growth

31 R. moyesii, from the section Cinnamomeae. One of a group noted for the beauty of the hips

32 Scabrosa, a Rugosa, from the section Cinnamomeae. It flowers for months, and has handsome hips

century. It was notable for smooth wood, many of the class being fiercely thorned; and with gratitude, it was taken as fairly free from mildew; for which it compensated by getting rust. The raiser was François Lacharme of Lyon, and the parentage he reported was 'Général Jacqueminot' × 'Victor Verdier'. It was also known as 'Marguerite Brassac' and 'Paul Jamain'.

'Beauty of Waltham' *Taller Pink Remontant* P4 H2
Both the Pauls were by now raising English Hybrid Perpetuals. Paul & Son of Cheshunt were to have their major success in 1868 with a red seedling from 'Général Jacqueminot' named 'Duke of Edinburgh'. William Paul & Son of Waltham Cross introduced 'Beauty of Waltham' in 1862, a fine, healthy, long-lived pink rose, with rather flat flowers thick with petals. Until recently there were several plants of it in the village of Hinxworth in Hertfordshire, giving an excellent account of themselves.

'Marie Baumann' and 'Horace Vernet'
'The growth as a cutback cannot be called more than fair, and the foliage is not large. The wood is weak and pliable . . . the stem is not stiff enough . . . the flowers generally fall over with their faces to the ground . . . decidedly liable to mildew.'

In those words Foster-Melliar draws his pen picture of 'Marie Baumann'; he then proceeds: 'It is especially noted as one of the most reliable of Roses . . .'

And so it was, but only to put in an exhibition box.

As to 'Horace Vernet', the *Rosarian's Year Book 1890* explains that it 'only succeeds as a maiden'. In other words, there was no sense in buying a plant of it, because its maiden year had then elapsed. It was necessary to propagate it oneself every year, and throw it away after its first season.

These two instances reveal the dangers to the rose of too much emphasis on exhibition points. 'Marie' and 'Horace' were famous for many years, and no doubt gardeners bought them. Worse, their success on show led to a demand for similar varieties, to the great weakening of the Hybrid Perpetuals. They were not, of course, the only two. 'Duchesse de Morny' was reckoned to be best as a maiden. The famous 'Alfred K. Williams' was difficult to keep alive, even to transplant successfully. 'Gustave Piganeau' grew very short in its first year, and progressively shrunk thereafter. Fortunately for rosarians of the present day, such varieties have a very poor chance of emerging with any credit from the Trial Grounds about the world.

'Marie Baumann' was carmine, raised by A. N. Baumann of Bolwyller, France, from seed of 'Alfred Colomb', introduced 1863, and also known as 'Mme Alphonse Lavallée'. 'Horace Vernet' was red, raised by Jean-Baptiste Guillot from seed of 'Général Jacqueminot', and introduced 1866. 'Duchesse de Morny' was pink, from Eugène Verdier in 1863. 'Alfred K. Williams' (which was usually called 'A. K. Williams') came from J. Schwartz in 1877. It was carmine, and is said to be a sport of 'Général Jacqueminot', which makes its behaviour difficult to understand, and prompts one to disbelieve that statement. 'Gustave Piganeau' was carmine, from Pernet-Ducher in 1889, said to be a cross 'Charlotte Corday' × 'Baronne Adolphe de Rothschild', both of which were Hybrid Perpetuals, the latter usually known in America and England as 'Baroness Rothschild'.

'Mme Gabriel Luizet' *Taller Light pink Remontant* – P4 H1
This was much better stock than the miserable clutch we have just regarded, being something of a garden rose with the vigour expected of its class. It had the reputation

of holding its leaves later than most of its fellows, which indicates resistance to rust; but it was not so free from mildew. The pleasant light colour, sweet fragrance and pointed shape were exquisite, but the autumn flowering was sparse. Raised by Jean Liabaud of Lyon, and introduced in 1877.

'Ulrich Brunner' *Taller   Rose red   Remontant* P5 H2
A famous Hybrid Perpetual, due to its health and long life; but it is not interesting. The light red colour is dull for a rose, and the inner petals are slow to stretch out from the rounded centre. Perhaps it was better eighty years ago, when it was internationally popular, especially in the United States. The correct name is 'Ulrich Brunner Fils'; from Antoine Levet of Lyon, who introduced it in 1881. The parentage is in doubt, whether a seedling of 'Anna de Diesbach' or of 'Paul Neyron'. The former was also known as 'Gloire de Paris', a pink Hybrid Perpetual from François Lacharme in 1858. 'Paul Neyron' is a famous name; it had the reputation of being the biggest rose in the world, but needed plenty of sun, otherwise it was coarse. Therefore it was popular in France and the United States; reports of its splendour came to me until a few years ago from rosarians in Egypt and Sudan, for apparently many plants went to Egypt in its heyday. In Britain, the petals usually look crimped, but given decent weather they open out like a pink paeony robbed of its silkiness. It came from Antoine Levet in 1869.

'Her Majesty' *Medium   Pink   Remontant* −
Raised by Henry Bennett, the English cattle-breeder, who had recently amazed rosarians with his Pedigree Hybrid Teas. If the rose world wanted enormous flowers, Bennett was ready to oblige, and he took several boxes of 'Her Majesty' to compete for the first Gold Medal offered by the National Rose Society in 1883. So huge were his blooms, that the Gold Medal was 'granted by acclamation', says Foster-Melliar. But: 'one of the objections to it was that when staged it would dwarf all the other roses'. One imagines that a cattle-breeder when he turns his hand to roses would not be short of dung for them.

Bennett delayed introducing it for a year, due to selling most of his stock to an American grower; and from its triumphant introduction in 1885, when plants at half a guinea were eagerly sought, there followed one of the swiftest downfalls on record. By 1890 we may read that Alexander Hill Gray saw it in France, 'overwhelmed with the original sin of mildew'. The Rev. Joseph Pemberton summed up 'Her Majesty' in these ungallant terms: 'Few and scentless were its flowers, and perched upon the top of a stiff, mildewed, spotted stem it savoured of stubbornness and self-conceit.'

The parents were declared by the man who kept his pedigrees so carefully to be 'Mabel Morrison' × 'Canary': a white Hybrid Perpetual and a cream Tea, both with few petals. Contemporary rosarians found it difficult to believe.

'Mrs John Laing' *Medium + Pink Remontant* P7 H2 ******
The shortcomings of 'Her Majesty' were fully atoned by Henry Bennett when he introduced in 1887 this most lovely of pink roses. The flowers are shapely and wide, of confident beauty and sweet scent. The colour is serene, cool; for the pink has a hint of lavender in it. Of all the Hybrid Perpetuals, I take this as the best. It is a seedling of 'François Michelon'.

'Roger Lambelin' *Tall   Red & white   Remontant* P6 H1 *****
The dark red petals are marked with a narrow white outline; and as the flower is

something like a carnation in form, the effect is interesting; perhaps more so in the vase than on the bush. This strange tracery of the petal edges appears in several Hybrid Perpetuals, all of them sports, and suggests a resource that breeders might turn to. 'Baron Girod de l'Ain' is another variety to show it, being a sport from 'Eugène Fürst' and introduced by Reverchon in 1897. The parent from which 'Roger Lambelin' sported is generally stated to be 'Fisher & Holmes', but the growth and flower form are so different that it must be doubted. Graham Thomas is much nearer the mark, I think, with 'Prince Camille de Rohan'. That rose was famous because it was the darkest of reds, so dark as to be dull. It was raised by Eugène Verdier, introduced in 1861, and was also known as 'La Rosière'. It was thought to have deteriorated to some extent in size of flower by the 1890s, and had the reputation of getting rust; that warning must also be given in respect of 'Roger Lambelin', which came from the widow Schwartz in 1890.

'Frau Karl Druschki' *Taller White Remontant* P1 H3 *
Here we see the Hybrid Perpetuals in a state of metamorphosis, as they yield their favoured place to their successors, the Hybrid Teas. By its parents and blooms, 'Frau Karl Druschki' could pass as a Hybrid Tea; but the buds, the leaves and the growth are those of a Hybrid Perpetual. The snowy purity of its open flowers made it famous. The red flush on the outer petals is hidden as soon as the blooms expand, showing the high pointed centres and great size we have learned to anticipate with pleasure. On the debit side, there is no scent, some mildew, and a papery texture to the petals, which the rain may easily spoil. The best way to grow this rose is to treat it as a lightly pruned shrub. It may need some support as its longer branches reach out, and will repay such encouragement with a veritable tree of snowballs.

Peter Lambert, of Trier in Germany, first showed this white seedling at the Stuttgart Exhibition in 1899. Those who were present were enchanted, and it aptly earned the name 'Schneekönigin', which is 'Snow Queen'. At a show in Trier in 1900, a competition was held to choose a rose worthy to be named 'Otto von Bismarck', the prizes being the honour and three thousand marks to go with it. Peter Lambert entered his white rose, but lost, and had the satisfaction of hearing the lamentations of the jury when later in the day they visited his nursery and saw their discard growing. I do not know for what reason the winner's introduction was delayed until 1908; it was a pink Hybrid Tea, bred by Hermann Kiese of Viselbach-Erfurt; it had a short run.

Peter Lambert was more successful in Berlin, where his rose was selected to bear the name of 'Frau Karl Druschki', wife of the President of the Society concerned in that exhibition. A pity he did not leave it as 'Snow Queen', or 'Reine des Neiges' or 'Schneekönigin', happy versions in three languages. I regret to say that the British reverted to 'Snow Queen' in the 1914-18 war; and the Americans, for whom no rose could compete with 'American Beauty', simply called it 'White American Beauty'. The parents were 'Merveille de Lyon' × 'Mme Caroline Testout', namely Hybrid Perpetual × Hybrid Tea.

'Hugh Dickson' *Tallest Crimson Remontant* P5 H3
Like an indignant protest from one of the last of the condemned race, 'Hugh Dickson' waves red flags at the end of uncommonly long arms. It was introduced in 1905, and bears the name of the raiser. As much a climber as a shrub, it is poor value for so popular a rose, because the colour relates to the plant like a flag to its pole. The clear crimson is bright and pleasant, the flowers wide but not full; if it is planted

amongst other shrubs, its flowers will appear unexpectedly amongst them, and its ungainly stature will not be noticed.

I believe a confusion arose in the public mind between the two Dicksons, 'George' and 'Hugh'; it was expected that Hugh had the huge, double, dark, richly scented red flowers; whereas it is light crimson, and not strongly fragrant. The parents were 'Lord Bacon' × 'Gruss an Teplitz', the former being a little known Hybrid Perpetual.

In the *Rose Annual 1917*, George Burch wrote an article 'The Decline of the Hybrid Perpetual Rose'. It was due, he said, not merely to the advance of Hybrid Teas, but also because the quality of bloom was no longer that which the old exhibitors grew so well. The knell was rung in the *Rose Annual 1925* by the Rev. J. H. Pemberton. His article was entitled 'The Passing of the Hybrid Perpetual'.

14. Pimpinellifoliae and Hybrids

This section of the Eurosa includes some of the most beautiful wild roses in the world. Their peculiar grace and clear colours establish them as ornaments of the garden, wild as they are. All are Asian, one of them spreading across Europe to the shores of the Atlantic.

The factors of recognition are those which led us to the Gallicanae: pinnate leaves; smooth hips; stipules joined to their leaf stalks; styles not protruding from their tube; flowers that are frequently solitary. The difference from the Gallicanae is in the number of leaflets composing the leaf. Whereas they normally have five, the Pimpinellifoliae do not usually have less than seven. We might also note that most of the species in this section are marked by black or dark red hips.

The name describes roses with leaves like a *Pimpinella* which is the Latin name for a kind of Burnet. Imagine a slender leaf stalk, with three or four tiny leaves neatly arranged each side of it, and one at the terminus, the whole like a dainty fern, little more than finger size. Except for *R. foetida,* leaves composed of nine leaflets are common; *R. sericea* may have seventeen.

Four of the species are early flowering yellow roses of great beauty. Their habit is to flower upon wood grown in the previous year. Having equipped themselves with slender branches in readiness, they clothe them with single yellow flowers like big buttercups, each on a tiny flower stalk, so that the flowers fit close to the branches like great jewels worn on a finger. When a branch is so adorned, it tends to arch down under its delicate load, showing its beauty all the better. Do not prune off the ends of such shoots, but leave them full length, for they are more graceful in that way. Pruning consists in removing old sections of the plant during the winter; the plants may be left unpruned for about four years, until it becomes obvious that they need to be thinned out to encourage more new wood.

These four species may in fact be only two; *R. ecae* and *R. primula* are a similar pair; as also are *R. hugonis* and *R. xanthina.* An interesting paper, 'Relationship between Species in the Genus Rosa, section Pimpinellifoliae' was written by Dr Andrew Roberts and published in the *Botanical Journal of the Linnaean Society* in June 1977.

SPECIES & VARIETIES

R. ecae *Taller   Yellow   Late spring*   P4   H2   *

In every Army there seems to be an observant plantsman, and very often his activities are the only lasting benefit obtained from military operations. Dr J. E. T. Aitchison was a botanist, and also served in the British Army in the second Afghan War as a Medical Officer; he probably did not meet Dr Watson, that beguiling chronicler of Sherlock Holmes, who claimed to be a veteran of the same campaign. But he did encounter a wild rose clad with clear yellow single flowers; it grows fairly straight, its branches usually trying to point up, less ready to arch down than those of its three yellow sisters. It is the least amenable of them in cultivation in Britain, but was still worth the effort until its hybrid 'Golden Chersonese' appeared. The name means that it is E.C.A's rose, those initials referring to Mrs Aitchison. It grows wild from the east of the Caspian Sea into Afghanistan.

ECAE HYBRID
'Golden Chersonese'   *Taller   Yellow   Late spring*   P6   H2   *****
This glorious plant is a hybrid from *R. ecae* × 'Canary Bird', combining the gold and the upward reaching nature of *R. ecae* with the greater flower size and grace of 'Canary Bird'. Its time in flower is early, brief, fragrant and spectacular. Thereafter the bushes are handsome in leaf and dark stems. Raised by E. F. Allen of Copdock, Suffolk, and introduced by Hillier & Sons in 1969. Mr Allen was subsequently President of the Royal National Rose Society in its centenary year, and is now the Society's Hon. Scientific Adviser. His rose is one of the most beautiful plants ever introduced to gardeners.

SPECIES AND VARIETIES continued

R. farreri persetosa   *Taller   Pink   Midsummer*   P4   H3   ***
I have never seen *R. farreri* itself, this seedling being the only form in cultivation in Britain, so far as I am aware. It is a remarkable plant, growing more than head high, with thick stems, as if it were a giant. But the giant puts on the clothes of a baby, tiny leaves and flowers so small that a finger print could hide one. To maintain his ferocity he seeks to cover himself with bristles, but only achieves another charm thereby, so closely and attractively are they set. The bright pink of the flowers, with yellow stamens alight, is charming indeed. Plant it where it will stand out against its background; it doesn't mind a little shade, but needs to be fairly close to the view, its parts being so small. It was called the Threepenny Bit Rose in Britain, but that name has been rendered void by two currency changes since that small silver coin was lost from the pockets of Britons, and found in their Christmas puddings. Dr Roberts concluded that there were grounds for removing *R. farreri* from the Pimpinellifoliae, and transferring it to the Cinnamomeae.

R. foetida   *Tall* −   *Yellow   Midsummer*   P4   H1
The 'Austrian Briar' or 'Austrian Yellow', the ultimate source so far as we can ascertain of the yellow in modern roses; for which reason we should be ashamed to call it by a stinking name, but in gratitude ought to restore the euphonious pre-Linnean name, *R. lutea*. Our forefathers did much better: they took it for the Yellow Sweet Briar.

'Austrian Yellow' is an upright shrub, rarely a big plant, with bright green leaves a little larger than most of this section. The flowers are bold, unfading yellow, single, and prominent. The wood is the colour of dark chocolate. It rarely sets seed, and thereby propounds this mystery: how wild can a wild rose be without seed?

The first English reference to the Yellow Rose, the only one then known, was by John Gerard in his *Herball*, 1597. He had the right idea, namely that it was not wild at all, but 'by Art so coloured, and altered from his first estate, by grafting a wilde Rose upon a Broome-stalke'. Whilst that method of cultivation is not generally practised in modern rose nurseries, it aptly sums up the mystery and the marvel of the case. One can only guess where it originated, Iran to Turkey maybe; I know of no convincing theory as to how it came into being. It appears to have been widely cultivated in Iran, Iraq and Turkey, and its petals used for making jam. Without human intervention, it would most probably be extinct. The connection with Austria is due to a report that it was brought to Holland by Clusius from Vienna probably in the 1560s. Botanists used Latinized versions of their names; Clusius was Charles de l'Ecluse; Linnaeus was Carl von Linné.

R. foetida bicolor *Tall* – *Red & yellow* *Midsummer* P4 H1 **

Well known as 'Austrian Copper'; and in France as 'Rose Capucine', which means the Nasturtium Rose, and prepares one to expect its vivid colour. When it is in full bloom, it qualifies on the distant view as a burning bush. There is an echoing memory of its glory in an article by the Rev. H. Temple Frere in the *Rosarian's Year Book, 1890:* 'One of the grandest, though but ephemeral, sights I have lately seen was the Copper Austrian Briar, in the garden of a village shoemaker, as big as a small haystack, and a blaze like one of Turner's sunsets.'

It is a sport from 'Austrian Yellow', to which it occasionally reverts; I have a plant with a plain yellow branch on it. The petals are nasturtium red on the inner side, yellow on the outer side, that colour being the distinction between 'Austrian Copper' and 'Austrian Yellow'. In other respects they are virtually the same, including the mystery surrounding their origin. A sport which was yellow with red streaks on the petals used to be sold as 'Jaune Bicolor', and although I believe it to be lost, it is very likely to occur again.

R. × hemisphaerica *Tall* *Yellow* *Summer* P1 H1

This rose first came to the notice of Europeans in an unusual way, about the year 1600. At an exhibition in Vienna, apparently devoted to arts and crafts, there was to be seen a contribution from Constantinople. Accounts vary as to whether it was a paper model of a Turkish garden, or whether it was Turkish wallpaper; but in either event it featured double yellow roses, as unknown to Europeans in those days as double sky-blue ones are today. The botanist Clusius instituted enquiries, which had the happy result of obtaining from the Turks their double yellow rose. It proved difficult to propagate, and most of the seventeenth century passed before it was safely established in England; but in France and Italy the growers were more successful; and in those countries it was widely grown for its flowers to be sold.

It therefore follows that *R. × hemisphaerica* was the only double yellow rose known to Europeans for about two hundred years. English growers went to great lengths to cultivate it, but with difficulty, because the British climate was not to its liking. Old accounts offer many theories how to propagate and how to grow it. One method of propagation suggested was to bud 'Austrian Yellow' on to a rootstock, and then bud *R. × hemisphaerica* on the growing shoot of 'Austrian Yellow'. It was with a sigh of relief that British rosarians welcomed 'Persian Yellow' when it arrived, for they could then cease their struggles with *R. × hemisphaerica*.

It has had many names in its career, of which the most common was *R. sulphurea*, or the Sulphur Rose. It was for a while thought to be a Centifolia, and was called the 'Yellow Provence'; another Latin name, *R. glaucophylla,* indicated the sea green colour of the leaves. Of its history before 1600 we have no information at all, only its mute evidence as to the skill and good taste of some ancient Ottoman or Persian rosarians. The French had a dwarf form of it, called 'Pompon Jaune', a sport, the only kind of variation one could hope for, as *R. × hemisphaerica* was sterile.

R. foetida persiana *Tall Yellow Midsummer* P4 H1
Upon the introduction of this rose from Iran in 1837, *R.* × *hemisphaerica* was quickly abandoned in Britain. Who would not favour a deeper yellow rose, which actually consented to grow, to be propagated and to flower with an accommodating generosity found wanting in its predecessor? 'Persian Yellow' had the brilliance of *R. foetida,* and no double yellow rose could rival it until the Noisettes in the 1860s; for brightness it stood alone, until Joseph Pernet-Ducher made it father to the Pernetianas.

I am much obliged to Mr Nigel Raban, President of the Royal National Rose Society 1977–8, for making me free of his efforts to substantiate the accounts of 'Persian Yellow's' introduction to Europe. He provides a sweet example of how little details go astray when history is written. From a dozen sources, all highly respectable, we can compile the following dossier of alternatives:

'Persian Yellow' was brought *(introduced, sent, sent in the diplomatic bag)* from Persia in 1838 *(1835, 1837)* by Sir Henry Willock *(Wilcock, Willcock, Willcocks, Willocks),* K.L.S. *(F.L.S.),* Envoy Extraordinary and Minister Plenipotentiary *(then British Minister; while Her Majesty's Minister to the Court of Persia)* at Teheran.

Mr Raban was intrigued to discover that Sir Henry actually left Persia in early 1827, eleven years before he was supposed to have brought the rose. He enquired from the Foreign and Commonwealth Office, and from the Royal Horticultural Society, in order to establish the following facts:

Captain Henry Willock was chargé d'affaires in Teheran from 6 October, 1815 until 2 September, 1826, when his functions ceased. He was knighted in London on 30 June, 1827. 'Persian Yellow' was received from him by the Horticultural Society's garden in May 1836.

I leave future writers to build their own presumptions from there; and I wonder, if Mr Raban should investigate other rosy stories, how much will have to be crossed out of the rose books?

FOETIDA HYBRIDS
There have been many important hybrids of *R. foetida;* but most of them are to be found under the heading of the other partner to the marriage: the yellow Scotch Roses under *R. spinosissima,* the Pernetianas under Hybrid Teas. Both of these were in the past considered Hybrid Austrian Briars. The hybrids here recorded are by no means the sum of *R. foetida's* importance. To assess its generosity, one has only to look at the yellow roses in modern gardens, and remember that Joseph Pernet-Ducher made them possible with his 'Soleil d'Or' out of 'Persian Yellow' in 1900.

'Gottfried Keller'
While the golden sun was rising for Joseph Pernet-Ducher in France, somebody in Germany was trying to do exactly the same thing, but with less success. Herr Doktor Franz Müller of Weingarten had also been using 'Persian Yellow', and he too introduced a hybrid from it. The trouble with 'Gottfried Keller' is that it is not a Hybrid Tea at all, and therefore it was passed by, all the world being dazzled by 'Soleil d'Or'. However this variety is of interest, because it proves that the idea of using 'Persian Yellow' was not exclusive to Pernet-Ducher; and it was later to be used by Poulsen of Denmark as a parent of 'Poulsen's Yellow'.

'Gottfried Keller' was bred as follows: [('Mme Bérard' × *R. foetida persiana*) × ('Pierre Notting' × 'Mme Bérard')] × *R. foetida persiana*. This means that a seedling of the first pair was pollinated by a seedling of the second pair; the resultant seedling was pollinated by *R. foetida persiana*. When breeders use a succession of anonymous seedlings, their parentages are worse than algebra to follow. Dr Müller's reasoning was intelligent. 'Mme Bérard' was a Climbing Tea with some yellow in it, thereby offering vigour and colour. 'Pierre Notting' was a Hybrid Perpetual, a less obvious choice, being red, but we cannot criticize it as we don't know what the seedling from it was like.

I have never seen 'Gottfried Keller', and can only pass on the description from August Jägers *Rosenlexikon* that it was light apricot yellow, deeper yellow on the back, with seven to ten petals, and of average growth. Both this work and *Modern Roses* put the introduction date as 1894, but other authorities say 1902. I do not know which is correct; the latter date seems to have started with an article by George M. Taylor in the *Rose Annual 1925*. I would think 1894 is to be believed, and the subconscious reason for rejecting it is disbelief that anyone was so much in advance of Pernet-Ducher in this field of research.

The best known rose of Dr Müller's is 'Conrad Ferdinand Meyer'. I think he was a trifle unlucky.

'Lawrence Johnston' *Climber Yellow Midsummer* P6 H3 *
A spectacular bright yellow climber, which will turn a wall into a sheet of gold before most roses are out in the summer. The flowers are semi-double, the leaves bright green. Raised by Joseph Pernet-Ducher from 'Mme Eugène Verdier' × *R. foetida persiana,* the former being a pink Hybrid Perpetual. Pernet-Ducher saved two seedlings from the cross, but preferred 'La Rêve', which he introduced in 1923. The only plant of 'Lawrence Johnston' was purchased unnamed by Major Johnston, who grew it in his famous garden at Hidcote in Gloucestershire under the name 'Hidcote Yellow'. Eventually Graham Thomas obtained permission to exhibit it in 1948, and introduced it as 'Lawrence Johnston' through his firm, Sunningdale Nurseries of Windlesham, Surrey.

'Réveil Dijonnais' *Taller Red & yellow Remontant* P3 H2
The vivid colour of 'Austrian Copper' shines in the shaggy, semi-double flowers of this rose. The plant is aggressively leafy, so shiny and light green as to detract from the flowers; it is highly susceptible to blackspot. Raised by Messrs Buatois of Dijon from 'Eugène Fürst' × 'Constance'; that is, a red Hybrid Perpetual with one of Pernet-Ducher's seedlings from 'Rayon d'Or'. It was introduced in 1931.

SPECIES continued

R. hugonis *Taller Primrose Late spring* P4 H2 *
This popular wild rose is similar to *R. xanthina,* but not, I think, quite so beautiful; of the lovely yellows with flower studded branches, it was the first to be generally known in the west, thanks in part to American nurserymen extolling it as the 'Golden Rose of China', with a generously coloured photograph. Primrose is a fair description of the colour; and unless the plant is regularly thinned out, the flowers will be found small; the petals tend to curl inwards, chilling their beauty thereby.

The stock of this rose in the west came from seed raised in Kew Gardens; knowing the hybridity of wild roses, we cannot be certain that our *R. hugonis* corresponds with a wild plant in China. It was discovered by the Rev. Hugh Scallan, who was known as Father Hugh, and lent his name to the rose. James Veitch & Sons introduced it in 1908. They were famous nurserymen, of an address nowadays most unlikely: King's Road, Chelsea.

HUGONIS HYBRID
R. × cantabrigiensis   *Taller   Cream   Late spring*   P4   H3   ******
A large fragrant shrub, easy to grow, with an abundance of single cream flowers
borne in the elegant way of *R. hugonis,* only with blooms more handsome, if paler,
being larger, and opening wide and firm. It was raised at the Botanic Garden of
Cambridge, England, from *R. hugonis × R. sericea hookeri.* Raised in 1931, its date
of introduction is a matter of imperceptible circulation. My firm was growing it when
I joined in 1937. The correct name, vide *Modern Roses,* is *R. × pteragonis
cantabrigiensis.* Perhaps I should also mention here 'Earldomensis', named after the
home of Mr Courtney Page, who was Secretary of the National Rose Society from
1915 to 1947. It was raised in his garden from *R. hugonis × R. sericea pteracantha,*
and introduced in 1934. It is one of the most beautiful, the flowers frail, perfect and
pale; but it is not easy to grow; we recently lost our lovely plant in the Royal National
Rose Society's gardens, and it is not clear whether we can find a replacement.
Graham Thomas is an advocate of 'Headleyensis', raised from *R. hugonis* at Headley
in Surrey about 1920; I regret I do not know it well, and must attend to my education
on that point.

SPECIES & VARIETIES continued

R. primula   *Tall   Primrose   Late spring*   P6   H2   ******
The 'Incense Rose' has affinity with *R. ecae,* but is much lighter in colour, and forms a
shorter and wider bush. The 'incense' arises from its aromatic leaves, and is
perceptible in humid weather. *R. primula* was discovered about 1890, and
introduced in 1910. For some years it was thoroughly muddled with *R. ecae,* and
grown under that name in the United States.

R. sericea   *Taller   White   Early summer*
R. sericea breaks the wild rose's normal fashion of having five petals, by forming
many of its small flowers, but not all of them, out of four petals. The five-fold nature
of sepals and petals is one of the distinguishing marks by which the genus *ROSA* is
identified from other genera, and at first sight the anomaly of having four petals
would appear to exclude a plant from the genus. On close inspection, however, it will
be seen that one of the four petals is normally larger than the others, and has a cleft at
the centre of its outer rim, which if continued could have split the petal, and
established the normal five. Perhaps we may pause and wonder whether the rose's
five petals may have been responsible for its fascination for human beings.
   There must be a whole unwritten history of the significance of the rose in forms of
religion, the symbols of which were often the sun, numbers, and geometric shapes.
Circles, hexagrams and pentagrams illustrated the cycle of seasons and of time, the
powers and balance of the known world, with mankind protectively enclosed. Three,
five, seven and many other numbers were chosen for their coincidence with natural
phenomena, odd numbers being favoured as communicating security from the equal
balance possible around a central symbol or person, who might be protected, fought,
revered or sacrificed. The sun's position in the sky was of particular importance to
those who dwelt in the latitudes where it was most noticeable that the equinoxes of
spring and autumn brought nights and days of equal length, and the solstices of
summer and winter marked the daylight at its longest and shortest periods
respectively. Of these significant changes in the year, from which so much of the
rhythm of natural life appeared to take its time, the summer solstice was an especial

religious festival, and it happened that in the northern hemisphere the rose was in flower at that time, revealing the five-sided shape of a pentagon, its petal points suggesting extensibility to the magic symbol of a pentagram, a small organism the emblem of the balance of the whole cosmos; the significant number of five petals had its parallels at the end of every person's hands, in their senses, and in many other symbols and likenesses chosen by human imagination. But the essential fact for us is not the details of the religious procedures, but rather the fact that the rose was in bloom at a very significant time to lend itself to their decoration, and to offer some symbolic expression of their philosophy. The written evidence about such usage is minimal, which is not surprising, for rites were often the secrets of the tribe, the learning of the priests was by memory, jealously guarded by the priesthood, who secured the exclusiveness of their position in part by inviolate secrecy, to constitute one of the earliest and most effective trade unions in history.

Apparent to all mankind was the paradox that the beautiful and fragile blossom of the rose grew upon a bush which was ready to draw blood by its armoury of thorns. The ancients might have equated this with deceit, but seeing the truth more clearly, they read it as a fact of life, that pleasure and pain may not be far apart; if one was careless in love, scratches were a likely reward; that human beings were complex, with resources and passions which could not be read upon a pretty face. But it worked the other way too, for the face of a rose multiplied its delight when one approached it, and sensed its fragrance.

There is a degree of beauty which startles a person from everyday life, and suggests a plane of experience where he cannot long remain; it can pierce people to the point of tears, letting them share for a second the blaze of 'some heart once pregnant with celestial fire'. The world is well filled with things to impart this inspiration, as if to be certain mankind cannot miss it, and it is an important part of their story that roses invoke this response in many people. The curtains of daily life soon shut out the brightness, but the fact remains that we experience those moments of exaltation, and therefore we are stimulated by what the genes of a rose have performed. The natural suggestion prompted by this phenomenon is that an evolutionary exaltation of human life is one possible outcome of our genetic factors; the natural result of those moments when roses have been the agents of inspiration is the world-wide wish to grow them.

The rose is a transient flower, soon changing from youth to age, and thereby invoking a powerful parable of the course of human life. That a rose should be made so beautiful, and fade so soon, reminds man born of woman of his own mortality, for 'he cometh up, and is cut down, like a flower'.

R. sericea pteracantha *Taller White Early summer* P2 H2 ******
We had better return to business; *R. sericea* is a native of the region to the north and east of the Indian sub-continent, that is of the Himalayas, Manipur, Burma and into China. The species is not often seen in cultivation, because this extraordinary variety is so much more interesting on account of the huge thorns described in the name, which means the silky rose with winged thorns. The silkiness is on the underside of the leaves, and may not be obvious, but there is no mistaking the thorns. They are joined to the stem by a long base, and jut from it like a triangle with a hook on the top; they look as thin as a membrane, and when young are red and almost translucent, so that a shoot of the variety at that time, with its huge red thorns and ferny leaves, is a thing of beauty. The flowers are as small and white as those of *R. sericea,* and are of little moment. In order to maintain a supply of new growth, it is necessary to prune

out the old wood frequently; there is little beauty once the thorns have become old and lost their redness.

The name has been changed from *R. sericea* to *R. omeiensis* and back to *R. sericea* again. A very fine variety of *R. sericea* is 'Heather Muir', believed to be a seedling of the species raised by Edward Bunyard of Maidstone, Kent, and introduced by Graham Thomas through his Sunningdale Nursery in 1957; which was many years after Mr Bunyard raised it, for he sold the seedling, and Mr Thomas brought it to the general knowledge from the garden of the purchaser. 'Heather Muir' does not have the thorns of *R. sericea pteracantha,* but it possesses an attribute otherwise absent from the species, that of fine large flowers. It is a spectacular shrub in late spring to early summer when in bloom, and a tall and handsome plant whilst in leaf.

R. spinosissima   *Short   White   Late spring*   P5   H5
The wild Scotch Rose is easy to recognize, from its obvious signals of short growth, clear white flowers, black fruit and plentiful prickles.

Most wild roses grow into large shrubs, but the Scotch Rose forms a low thicket, knee high, and sometimes much shorter. This difference is environmental, as I discovered on the island of Herm, close to Guernsey. Herm is an exposed, grassy hillock, and when walking across it I noticed black hips brushing my bootlaces among the grass. Some friends from Guernsey instructed me that it was the Herm Rose, and that according to local belief, it could be grown nowhere except on Herm.

I took that for an old wives' tale, and I took some seeds, and of course had no difficulty in raising plants from them. They promptly showed themselves true Scotch Roses, by growing three times as high as on Herm, so to the extent that the dwarf nature of the plants was caused by their home on Herm, I suppose the old wives had some justification.

The white flowers are very clear, because the petals are clean cut, and stretch open to a symmetric outline. This appearance is the more effective for the flowers being borne individually on short stems, rather than sharing one stem to a cluster. As a result, they are framed against green, not against each other. A closer examination will show that the female organs keep low in the centre of the flower, the stigmas scarcely sticking out at all, and thus contributing to the spruce and tidy appearance of the flower. The scent is fresh and agreeable, although not particularly strong.

The dark seedshells are a regular trademark of the Scotch Roses, and the impression that they are black is fair enough for identification purposes, even if a closer inspection may show that many are dark chestnut brown. The sepals of the flower remain in an erect position on the fruit for some time, and the black surface is smooth and polished, with occasionally a few hairs growing on it. Scotch Roses ripen their seeds well before summer is over.

The prickles and bristles are straight, sharp and abundant, especially on the flowering branches, and on the suckers which grow from the roots. The suckers are apt to have hooked thorns as well as straight ones, and in short, a thicket of Scotch Roses is no comfortable place to traverse.

The leaves are small, and are elegantly divided in a fern-like pattern into leaflets each about half an inch (1.25 cm) long. The number of leaflets varies, five, seven, nine or eleven, of which seven is the most usual; those with eleven are most likely to be found on the suckers. The leaves lose their clear green colour as the summer passes, and take on much dull purple, especially towards the edges. They are closely set, without much space of stem between one leaf and the next. The stems are brown.

This tough little wild rose appears to have been known in England not originally as the Scotch Rose, but either as the Pimpernel or Burnet Rose. I have failed to discover when the Scotch name took precedence, as it certainly has, for rarely do I recollect anyone in real life talking about these roses as Burnets, much less Pimpernels. Certainly they have been generally known as Scotch Roses since before 1800. Linnaeus named the wild Scotch Rose *R. spinosissima,* which means the thorniest rose, a good and pointed description.

The Scotch Rose grows wild in a great rectangle, of which the western corners are Iceland and northern Spain, and the eastern deep into central Asia. It has become naturalized in North America. It inhabits harsher climates than most roses, and can be considered one of the hardiest. Its favourite homes are in poor soils such as most roses abhor, not only inland but also in the wind by the sea, which it approaches by sand dunes, or looks down on from the cliffs.

To live in such conditions, the Scotch Rose has its own survival techniques, the most obvious of which are the suckers that grow from its roots, and by which it forms close thickets. It has extremely fertile pollen, over 90 per cent of the grains being viable, according to tests reported by Gordon Rowley of Reading University. It flowers early, and in consequence can laugh at short summers or bad weather, because its seed is quickly ripe. The short growth is a necessary protection from wind damage. It conquers starvation by the simple process of not eating much, but allows its leaves to reduce activity, discolour, and fall well before the autumn. Thus the growth in late summer is much restricted, and tender shoots are not left to the winter's mercy, which is a strained quality in most of its natural habitats.

Such are the general observations we may make on the appearance, names and habitat of the Scotch rose as we see it today. It was described as follows in *A Niewe Herball or Historie of Plants,* which was a translation in 1578 by Henry Lyte of a work by a Flemish herbalist named Dodonaeus: 'Amongst the kindes of wilde Roses, there is founde a sorte whose shutes, twigges and branches are covered all over with thicke small thornie prickles. The flowers be small single and white, & of a very good savour. The whole plant is bare and low, and the least of al both of the garden and wilde kind of Roses.'

And although the Scotch Rose is not particularly common in south-east England, we have a delightful quotation from John Gerard's *The Herball or Generall Historie of Plants,* 1597, to say that it 'groweth in a pasture as you go from a village hard by London called Knightsbridge unto Fulham, a village thereby . . .' Perhaps just where Chelsea play football nowadays?

Among the wild populations of Scotch Roses, people have discovered many variations; and naturally, the variations to cause most interest were those of colour. Gordon Rowley states that he received cuttings from Scotch Roses growing at the head of Loch Coruisk in Skye, sent to him by Dr M. B. E. Godward of London University, and containing from the one area colours varying from yellow to deep pink. It may be optimistic to express those colours so definitely, for colour is comparative, and where there is no yellow, then cream becomes yellow, and where there is no pink, blush becomes pink. However it is undeniable that the Scotch Rose does depart from its clear white to cream, and occasionally with marks of pink or red.

Moreover, when these wild roses are grown from seed, they occasionally produce flowers with more than five petals. Thus, given a stock which departs from the white colour, and departs from the five petals, the possibility of developing colours and double flowers clearly exists. It was exploited in Scotland, under the following circumstances, which were related by Robert Brown to Joseph Sabine, Secretary of the Royal Horticultural Society, and recounted in the *Transactions of the Royal Horticultural Society, 1822*.

Robert Brown was a partner in the nursery of Dickson & Brown of Perth, and in 1793, he and his brother dug up some wild Scotch Roses from the Hill of Kintoul, near Perth, and brought them to their nursery.

One of these plants bore flowers slightly tinged with red, and a plant was raised from it, whether by seed or a cutting we are not told. The offspring 'exhibited a monstrosity, appearing as if one or two flowers came from one bud, which was a little tinged with red'. Seed was taken from it, and gave rise to plants with semi-double flowers, from which seed was taken in turn, so that by 1802 and 1803 Dickson & Brown had eight good double varieties of which to dispose.

Mr Sabine cautiously listed the eight varieties, 'as nearly as I have been able to ascertain'. They were one white, one yellow, two 'lady's blush', one light red, one red, one 'dark marbled' and one bicoloured. This instantly reveals the wide colour range capable of starting straight from the wild; and not only in single toned colours, as in white and red, but also in the readiness of the Scotch Rose to produce mixed colours. The bicolour, of course, has different colours on its inner and outer petal surfaces; the 'marbled' was to be a particular speciality of Scotch Roses, and it means a colour which is veined, mottled or dappled with one or more other colours. In nearly all Scotch Roses, whatever the colour, the base of the petal will be found to be white or greenish yellow.

The stock disseminated from Perth started the Scotch Roses on a hectic skate to popularity, although they were not allowed to enjoy it for very long. A Glasgow nurseryman, Robert Austin (of the firm Austin & McAslan) obtained the varieties from Perth in about 1807, and by 1822 was offering over a hundred different sorts, and eventually published a catalogue of 208 Scotch Roses. In 1832, G. Don listed 25 doubles, 149 singles and 14 botanical varieties.

The Scotch Roses came to London in 1805, the year of Trafalgar, when William Malcolm of Kensington purchased six of them from Dickson & Brown; Lee & Kennedy of Hammersmith, and Lee of Bedfont were also early purchasers, and the latter proceeded to raise seedlings himself.

In the early days, the varieties were named descriptively; for example, Mr Sabine in 1822 starts off with:

DOUBLE WHITE SCOTCH ROSES

The Small Double White	Large Double White
Large Semi-Double White	Whitley's Double White

and proceeds in similar style through Double Yellow, Double Blush, Double Red, Double Marbled, Double Two-Coloured and Double Dark Coloured Scotch Roses, covering twenty-six varieties. But there was already a two-fold difficulty in identification, as people in different places raised their own varieties, gave them names, and thought their own strain the best.

The Large Semi-Double White for example, seemed to Mr Sabine the model of the Redouté painting of 'Rosier Pimpernelle blanc à fleurs double'. The Double Blush evoked some faint lyric stirrings, causing the plain colour names to become 'The Princess of Blush' and 'Double Lady's Blush'; and a notable form of the latter was listed as 'Anderson's Double Lady's Blush', which sounds as if Mr Anderson had his hands full.

Mr Sabine had observed with satisfaction that here was a class of roses almost exclusively the produce of his own country. But was it? There also existed the 'Dutch

Double Blush', known in Holland as *R. spinosissima flore pleno,* and on a Redouté plate as 'Rosier Pimpernelle rouge à fleurs double'.

British growers offered Scotch Roses years before Robert Brown raised his; this is proved by John H. Harvey in his interesting books *Early Gardening Catalogues* and *Early Nurserymen;* also in the *Rose Annual 1976*. 'Marbled Double' was on sale in 1750, 'Scotch Painted Lady' in 1760 and 'Burnet-leaved Double' in 1775. Thomas Rivers said that 'Painted Lady' was a French hybrid; and his list of Scotch Roses contains many French varieties. 'Painted Lady' was a favourite name, the rose being white with red stripes, the title to be echoed two centuries later by Sam McGredy exploring the same race to create his 'hand-painted' roses.

Thus there was considerable confusion, and in 1840, Thomas Rivers noted of his fellow nurserymen: 'In some of their catalogues, two or three hundred names are given, but in many cases these names are attached to flowers without distinctive qualities.'

Before the vogue slithered into the past, a fascinating variety was introduced in 1838, under the name 'Stanwell Perpetual'. 'The Stanwell Perpetual, I believe was raised from seed in Mr Lee's nursery at Stanwell,' says Thomas Rivers; and there has been some confusion about Mr Lee, whose gardens, according to Joseph Sabine, were in Bedfont, beyond Hounslow. Stanwell is next door to Bedfont, and not in Essex, as some authorities suppose.

'Stanwell Perpetual,' is 'one of the prettiest and sweetest of autumnal roses,' according to Thomas Rivers. It is generally accepted to be a cross between *R.* × *damascena semperflorens* and *R. spinosissima*. Its double blush pink flowers, sweetly scented, are still a delight, and with the greyish green foliage can provide beautiful little arrangements for the house.

At last the Scotch Rose had yielded a good autumn flowering variety, at the cost of losing its stubby growth, but with the gain of losing its suckers too. But perpetual was the reverse of the Scotch Rose's nature. Of all the roses in their day the Scotch were the soonest over, at their close before the others opened. As the nineteenth century reached its halfway mark, people were taught by the China rose to expect longer periods of flower, and so the hundreds of little Scotch jewels disappeared from the catalogues, leaving as the most common survivors 'Scotch Yellow', an invaluable colour in those days, and 'Stanwell Perpetual'.

Owing to their tenacity in survival, they did not vanish entirely from gardens. Some were preserved; others spread themselves, seeded, and quite possibly changed in some ways, thus becoming candidates for rediscovery in the twentieth century. The problem of identification is close to insolubility; there were so many, of such little variation, with different growers having their own strains, or taking someone else's, interchanging English colour names, Latin names and fancy titles, that it is only with tongue in cheek that we can match the survivors of today with the sweet names of yesterday. It is clear that in a short time any competent breeder could re-create a whole range of them again, and only their brief flowering period suggests that such an exercise would be unprofitable.

Briefly though they bloom, their short burst of colour is glorious, and worth travelling many miles to see. A visit to a rose garden must be for their sake alone, because apart from some wild roses, no others will be in flower. They are not plants for frost pockets, because they flower before the time of spring frost is over, and a cold spring can spoil the show.

The Scotch Roses acquired their deep yellow colour from *R. foetida,* the Austrian Briar; some of the forms were therefore gaunt in growth, and are to be avoided in favour of the typical low Scotch habit. Most of the nurseries who sell the 'Double Yellow Scotch' will provide such a plant, the best selection being 'Williams' Double Yellow', which is a good dwarf habit, and is heavily scented. Instead of the normal reproductive organs, the centre of its flower has a bunch of little green growths, and consequently there are no hips.

Those who have not seen purple Scotch Roses are due for a pleasant surprise, for in full flower they are a sight of rich and royal splendour. One of the best is 'Mrs Colville', which has single flowers, purple with white at the petal base surrounding yellow stamens. This is one of the few Scotch Roses with red fruit instead of black, because it is a hybrid with another species, thought to be *R. pendulina*. Another excellent variety is 'William III', very short growing, with about fifteen petals; it changes from crimson-purple to a Victoria plum colour, turns paler, and ends the season with black hips.

I advise every true rose lover to have in his garden three Scotch Roses: a yellow, a purple and 'Stanwell Perpetual'.

In their heyday, Scotch Roses were grown as Standards, which at least prevented them from suckering. Says Thomas Rivers: 'the yellow, and one or two of the more robust varieties made good heads, but in general they form a round and lumpish tree, in ill accordance with good taste.' We would, I am sure, agree with him, and conclude that the best way to grow them is in a clump of three or more plants of each variety.

R. spinosissima altaica *Tall   White   Early summer*   P5   H6   *
Western and Central Asia. The name represents one of its homes, the Altai Mountains, which straddle the border between Russia and Mongolia, and give rise to the perfectly correct inference that this is an extremely hardy rose. It blooms early, usually before mid-summer, with glistening creamy white flowers, which are purely single of five petals, set along thin branches, in comparison with which they look large. The scent is fresh and pleasant. The shining maroon black hips are a compelling sight in late summer and autumn. The leaves are sub-divided into narrow, attractively cut leaflets, usually in nines although the number varies. It is not so thorny as most Scotch Roses, indeed the upper part of the branches is often quite smooth, the slender prickles and bristles appearing more at the base of the stems. This rose will sucker freely, especially if grown from cuttings, and can form a dense hedge. It is an attractive shrub, for which purpose budded plants should be used. On account of its hardiness, for which it got much credit through growing in Siberia, Wilhelm Kordes used it in the hope of breeding frost-proof roses for northern Europe; and similar endeavours took place in Canada and the United States. Thus it is an ancestor of the attractive shrub 'Golden Wings' from America, and of 'Frühlingsmorgen' from Germany. Through 'Frühlingsmorgen', it has some ancestral credit for 'Picasso' and all the 'hand-painted' line therefrom. It was recorded in 1818, and has borne other names, *R. baltica, R. grandiflora,* and *R. sibirica;* it was for a time considered a separate species as *R. altaica.*

R. spinosissima dunwichensis *Short   White   Late spring*   P5   H5
This interesting variation was found in Suffolk. It is similar to *R. spinosissima* in all respects, except for a more prostrate habit.

R. spinosissima hispida *Tall   Ivory   Early summer*   P5   H9   **
A strong and upstanding shrub, more upright and open in habit than other Scotch Roses, and with larger leaves, flowers and seed pods. It has another identity clue in

the colour of the flowers, which contain more yellow than those of *R. spinosissima altaica,* the variety with which it is most likely to be confused; nor is it quite so prone to sucker. Beautiful as the flowers are, they are fleeting, and gone before mid-summer, and the true glory of this variety is autumnal, when its large black hips present a sight that one is tempted to term dramatic. The name refers to the thin prickles and bristly hairs, which are closely set on most of the shoots. The leaflets normally number nine, but as with nearly all roses, are apt to vary in number. This variety came from Siberia, and was already on record in 1781. Wilhelm Kordes used it to breed for hardiness, and the best known variety it fathered is the extremely vigorous shrub, 'Frühlingsgold'. It has had the dignity of being recorded as a species in its own right as *R. hispida,* and also as *R. lutescens,* but is now generally accepted to be a variety of *R. spinosissima.*

R. spinosissima myriacantha   *Short   White   Late spring*
More of botanic than garden interest, this rose of countless thorns is a variety of *R. spinosissima,* recorded already by 1820. The flowers are white, often smaller than those of the species, sometimes showing a slight pink blush. The leaves are more glandular, and the prickles more numerous.

R. spinosissima nana   *Short   White   Late spring*
Not necessarily a dwarf form, as one would have expected from its name; the wild Scotch Rose is quite short, and its height is governed by environment. I am not aware of any strain having been discovered which is genetically dwarf. I include this one to make that point, and to mention that its main difference from *R. spinosissima* is in having flowers which are semi-double instead of single.

SPINOSISSIMA HYBRIDS
'Andrewsii'   *Shorter   Pink & cream   Late spring*   P4   H2   *
It is rare for Scotch Roses to flower other than early in the season; imagine my surprise, therefore, on visiting the Royal National Rose Society's gardens in the autumn (on 13th October to be precise) to find 'Andrewsii' in full bloom. It is semi-double, fresh pink with cream at the stamens' base, and some veining in the petals.

'Bicolor'   *Short   Pink & white   Late spring*   P3   H2
It is possible, though not certain, that this is one of the earliest Scotch Roses, for a list in 1822 refers the 'Large Double Two-Coloured Scotch Rose' to *R. spinosissima bicolor; Modern Roses 7* refers the varieties 'Grahamstown' and 'Staffa' here, so the message seems to be, when in doubt call it bicolor; there has been much doubt in identifying Scotch Roses. This is typical of them, forming a short thicket by its suckers, and flowering early. The flowers are semi-double, with a bare two rows of petals. This rose is pink, with a touch of lilac in it, going pale towards the petal edges, and the underside of the petals is practically white, with a touch of pink.

'Double White'   *Medium   White   Late spring*   P5   H1   *
The flowers are fully double, and open half way to hold their petals poised in that position. This charming and expectant posture is usually given a rude reward by the weather, so that more often than not, 'Double White' finishes up in a bruised condition; but not before we have explored closely to discover what the expectancy is about, and found to our pleasure a delicious lily-of-the-valley scent. Normally a little

taller than the typical Scotch Roses, but otherwise similar in its small leaves, with
abundant thorns and suckering thicket growth. A double white was among the first of
the Scotch Roses to be raised and introduced in 1802 or 1803, but it is impossible to
say which of the old varieties is now being offered under this name. Possibly 'William
the Fourth', which Thomas Rivers described as 'the largest white pure Scotch Rose
known'.

'Falkland' *Medium   Pink   Late spring*   P5   H4
A charming and typical Scotch Rose, with a more greyish cast to its leaves than most,
a feature which accords agreeably with the pleasing soft pink of its semi-double
flowers. It has a pleasant scent, and dark seed pods, along with the other attributes we
expect in Scotch Roses: close growth, suckers, many prickles, small leaves and an
early flowering time.

'Frühlingsgold' *Taller   Cream   Early summer*   P6   H2   *
Completely different from the typical Scotch Roses, because it is a hybrid invoking a
Hybrid Tea, in the cross 'Joanna Hill' × *R. spinosissima hispida,* made by Wilhelm
Kordes, and introduced in 1937. It turned out to be a big shrub, with few thorns,
bearing large semi-double flowers of creamy yellow, sweetly fragrant. A fine
specimen plant; I know of a splendid hedge of it, the top beyond the reach of
upstretched arms.

'Frühlingsmorgen' *Tall   Pink   Early summer*   P5   H2   *
Raised by Wilhelm Kordes from ('E. G. Hill' × 'Cathrine Kordes') × *R. spinosissima
altaica.* This is apt to be an ill-furnished shrub, with leaves which do not look the
picture of happiness. The flowers are glorious, five petals to cover one's palm, cherry
pink with much yellow to the centre, and long dark stamens against the yellow. It has
a powerful aroma, like sweet hay. Introduced in 1942.

'Golden Wings' *Tall   Cream yellow   Remontant*   P3   H2   ****
This valuable shrub has wide single flowers which attract the eye like a magnet, so
that the bush is a joy to look at even when it has few blooms on it. Its attraction lies, I
think, in the deep colour of its stamens and stigmas at the heart of its creamy spread.
It is half way, or perhaps three-quarters, towards being modern rather than Scotch.
Raised by Roy Shepherd of Medina, Ohio, from 'Soeur Thérèse' × (*R. spinosissima
altaica* × 'Ormiston Roy'). 'Ormiston Roy' is an interesting hybrid from S.
Doorenbos of The Hague, from *R. spinosissima* × *R. xanthina.* Roy Shepherd is the
same whose distinguished *History of the Rose* has frequently been referred to in these
pages. This rose of his was introduced in 1956.

'Harisonii' *Tall   Yellow   Early summer*   P5   H1
'Harison's Yellow' is an interesting rose which hovers between *R. spinosissima* and
R. foetida in classification. While Europe was welcoming 'Persian Yellow', Americans had their own double yellow rose in advance, maybe rather a gaunt plant, the
flower certainly not of outstanding form. But it was there before 'Persian Yellow' was
familiar, and rapidly passed across the United States. It was introduced in New York
about 1830, under circumstances not exactly clear; it appears to have been found in
the garden of a New York lawyer named George Harison, and to have been obtained
by one nurseryman and passed to others. Speculations as to its parentage cannot

outgrow that status; 'Persian Yellow' is ruled out, by not existing in the west, except possibly in Sir Henry Willock's garden in England. The most reasonable explanation to my mind is that it came from a double yellow Scotch Rose, which already had *R. foetida* breeding in it.

'Lutea' *Medium* + *Yellow Late spring* P4 H3

The Yellow Rose in the old days was the Austrian Briar, *R. foetida,* and for some centuries, the only yellow roses in cultivation in Europe were *R. foetida* and *R. hemisphaerica.* Scotch Roses however, even in the wild, occasionally produce flowers with a touch of yellow in them, and amongst the first batch to be put on sale by Robert Brown was 'the small yellow'. Twenty years later, four double yellows were listed, respectively entitled the Small, the Pale, the Large and the Globe. But in 1840, another eighteen years on, the best that so excellent a commentator as Thomas Rivers can say is: 'Lady Baillie, Marchioness of Lansdowne, and Mrs Hay, are all pretty, pale sulphur-coloured roses; from the seed of these it is very probable that some good yellow varieties may, at some future time be raised. . . . Sulphurea and one or two other straw-coloured varieties may be planted with the double yellow Austrian Briar, and most likely some pretty sulphur-coloured roses will be the result of this combination.' When we ask why there were no better yellow Scotch Roses, it turns out that they were considered to be Austrian Briars, and not Scotch at all. This alone is a tribute to their brilliance of colour. There is no doubt that Rivers' advice about Austrian Briars had already been followed when he wrote it, and that the brilliant yellow of the Scotch Roses was a prime reason for growing them through most of the nineteenth century. 'Lutea', sometimes known as 'Lutea maxima' is a single variety, with more brilliant foliage than most Scotch Roses have. The best double yellow variety is described under the name 'Williams' Double Yellow'.

'Marguerite Hilling' *Taller Pink Midsummer* + P4 H1 ****

Some eyebrows may be raised on the foreheads of learned rosarians who find 'Marguerite Hilling' and 'Nevada' in the Scotch Roses, for it is the custom to align them with *R. moyesii,* because the raiser of 'Nevada' claimed that to be the parent. Whether he was right or wrong does not alter the fact that apart from being roses, they have no visible relationship to *R. moyesii* whatsoever. But when one looks at them, their black seed pods, the marbled colour of 'Marguerite Hilling', it does not seem irresponsible to call them Scotch in all but their smooth wood. 'Marguerite Hilling' is a beautiful shrub, with wide single blooms, the warm pink of it imperfectly covering the white underneath. In size of flower, in freedom, in colour, in its extra blooms after the summer flush, it is most desirable and enjoyable. The foliage could be better, it is soft, light and dull. But what is that to set against such floral exuberance? A sport from 'Nevada', introduced by Thomas Hilling in 1959.

'Mary Queen of Scots' *Medium* − *Lilac Late spring* P4 H1

Raisers of Scotch Roses were fond of using names which were either royal or Scottish, and this combination of both was unlikely to escape their notice. Dr Archie Dick notes in the *Rose Annual, 1973* that this is supposed to have been brought from France by Mary Queen of Scots, and rediscovered in Ireland in 1921. He carefully refrains from expressing any trust in that legend. Considering that Mary was dead two centuries before Scotch Roses became of popular interest, and three hundred and fifty years before the rediscovery, it would appear difficult to construct a logical train of events connecting her with the rose. It is a typical Scotch Rose, of lilac pink colour, with the underside of the petals greyish pink, and a marvellously compact, rounded grower.

'Mrs Colville' *Medium – Purple Late spring* P3 H5 **

A glorious variety, which covers itself with rich purple flowers, and presents a spectacle which commends attention. The early flowering time and the close thicket of growth are typically present in the character of Scotch Roses, but the seed pods are not, for they are more red than black; and the stems are not quite so bristly. The flowers are single with a touch of white at the petal base near the stamens. This rose obviously is not of pure Scotch blood, and the generally accepted conjecture is that one parent was *R. pendulina*.

'Nevada' *Taller White Midsummer +* P4 H1 ****

The rose from which 'Marguerite Hilling' sported, and whose excuses for appearing here are made under 'Marguerite's' description. A fine large shrub, many of its branches are so crowded with wide white flowers that leaves and stems are entirely hidden. The flowers are single; some appear later in the season, but never in summer's glorious profusion. Raised by Pedro Dot in Spain from 'La Giralda' × *R. moyesii*. 'La Giralda' was a Hybrid Tea, bred from 'Frau Karl Druschki', signs of whose pale foliage may be imagined in 'Nevada'. As to *R. moyesii*, the probability is that the breeder's record was in error. I raised some hybrids from 'Nevada', amongst them one with a stem which could have passed for *R. moyesii,* but the plant was weak, and died before any useful conclusion was drawn. I should not be surprised if the pollen parent of 'Nevada' was *R. spinosissima hispida.* It was introduced in 1927.

'Stanwell Perpetual' *Medium Blush Remontant* P6 H1 ***

A beautiful rose, which expresses to us, whether accurately or not, much of what we consider to be the essence of the old-fashioned roses. The flowers are a delicate blush colour, turning paler in hot weather, and they have many petals, rather short, folded and arranged in the most complicated way, to give an impression of artless simplicity. It flowers well both in summer and autumn, and I think better in the autumn, when the colour is unfaded and the flowers larger. A few autumn flowers in a vase are quite delightful, and are helped by the small, neat leaves, which are greyish green. The scent is sweet, and comes out better indoors, for on the bush I do not find it particularly strong. It is a strange sort of grower, not particularly tidy, because it likes to send out long shoots which bend outwards from the plant. The shoots are closely covered with small prickles. The origin is conjectured to be *R. × damascena semperflorens × R. spinosissima,* and it was raised by Mr Lee, and introduced in 1838. Mr Lee lived close to where London Airport now sprawls.

'William III' *Shorter Purple Late spring* P3 H3 ***

A beautiful plant, free-flowering and low growing, with a rich and very noticeable purple colour, which to the uninitiated is almost unbelievable upon a rose. The flowers have about fifteen petals, and the colour lightens with age. The underside of the petals is pale. A typical thicket-forming Scotch Rose, compact as a hedgehog, scented, with small grey green leaves, the usual abundant thorns, early flowers and black fruit. It must surely be the case that anyone fortunate enough to own this will consider it one of the dearest treasures of his garden.

'Williams' Double Yellow' *Short   Yellow   Late spring*   P6   H1   ***

The best yellow Scotch Rose was generally considered to be one raised by John Williams of Pitmaston, Worcester, and introduced in or around 1828. Mr Williams was famous for his apples and pears. It was known in its early days as 'Williams' Double Yellow Sweet Briar', presumably on account of its rich scent, and is most probably, though not certainly, the variety sold under an assortment of names such as 'Scotch Yellow', 'Double Yellow', 'Old Yellow Scotch' and 'Lutea plena'. If that was not enough, the Scots also called it 'Prince Charlie's Rose', more out of sentiment I suppose than for any logical reason. It is a splendid bright yellow colour; its rather shaggy flowers have green carpels in the centre instead of the female organs, and hence it has no fruit. The consistency with which this variety produces its flowers year after year is admirable, and so is the stability of their colour, for unlike most yellow roses, they show little sign of going pale. However they have another disadvantage, of not shedding themselves, and remain on the plant until they have turned brown with age. The foliage is darker and more shiny than in most Scotch Roses, the growth bushy and compact. It is generally believed to have been raised from *R. foetida*, and Thomas Rivers says so definitely. The other parent must presumably have been a double Scotch Rose.

SPECIES & VARIETY continued

R. xanthina *Tall   Yellow   Late spring*   P2   H1

Here is a case of the double variety being granted the specific name. It has shaggy double flowers, with many narrow petals, and quite loses the beautiful grace of those lovely single species of the Pimpinellifoliae, *R. ecae, R. hugonis, R. primula* and of its own single types. I first met this rose in Ireland in 1935, where we grew it at the Donard Nursery as 'American Species'; nothing could be less appropriate, for it is Chinese. Later it bore the name of the proprietor of the nursery, as *R. slingeri*. It is closely allied to *R. hugonis*. Why there was so much indecision about its name I cannot understand, for the records state that it has been known since 1906.

'Canary Bird' *Tall   Yellow   Late spring*   P4   H1   *****

A joy each spring, when its dainty flowers turn the branches into yellow gauntlets arched down for perfect viewing. The colour is clear yellow, fresh and spring-like, not brazen in the slightest. A pleasant perfume surrounds the bush, and the ferny leaves are a pleasure all through the summer. The flowers are small, yet large in proportion to the leaves and stems behind them. This may not enjoy the more exposed and chilly areas, but the cost of a bush is slight compared with the pleasure that will ensue should the experiment be successful.

The species ought to be *R. xanthina spontanea,* but we are not sure whether it is now in cultivation. 'Canary Bird' was long thought to be that species, but appears to be a seedling probably raised in a Botanic Garden, and quietly passed around. Some of the stocks in Britain came from a fine form in the Botanic Garden at Edinburgh.

Other Species

The other species of the Pimpinellifoliae, of less interest to gardeners, and indeed little known at the present time, are *R. elasmacantha,* a pale yellow shrub from the Caucasus; *R. graciliflora,* pale pink, from China, *R. koreana,* from Korea as one would expect, a pale blush species, like an intermediary between *R. farreri* and *R. spinosissima;* and *R. turkestanica,* also announcing its address, cream white, and probably a variation of *R. spinosissima.*

15. Caninae and Hybrids

The last three sections of the Eurosa are the Caninae, the Carolinae and the Cinnamomeae; and although we might suppose that we have examined most of the world's wild roses, the truth is that these three sections contain about thirty, seven and fifty-six species respectively; that is, approximately two-thirds of the whole. Many of them are similar to one another, and perhaps not worthy of specific rank; many are plants without that special appeal that tempts gardeners to plant them; we shall therefore limit our inspection to the more beautiful and interesting of them.

The recognition factors are the same that led us to the Gallicanae and Pimpinellifoliae, that is pinnate leaves, smooth hips, stipules well joined to their leaf stalks and styles not protruding; from that point, the Gallicanae and Pimpinellifoliae were hived off by generally bearing their flowers singly; these three final sections bear their flowers together in heads, although it would not be hard to point to exceptions to the rule. The Caninae are distinguished from the other two by having thorns generally curved, and placed well apart, even though there may be many of them.

The name means Dog roses, derived from *R. canina,* which gave its name to the section. It is usually claimed that this name arises from the use of that rose as a cure for hydrophobia; whether any syrup or extract could be an effective cure seems doubtful; I should have thought the name arose from the shape of the thorns being likened to that of the teeth of a dog.

The Dog Roses are the typical wild roses of Europe, which is their chief home, although many spread well into Asia, and some into North Africa. Of the thirty species, only three are not European, two being Asian and one, of which there is some doubt, having been found in Mexico.

They hide within themselves a function unique amongst plants. Wherever a sexual union is the cause of birth, it is normal for male and female parents to make an equal contribution of their generative atoms to the embryo. In the Dog Roses, the contribution is unequal. The female imparts twenty-eight chromosomes and the male only seven. This extraordinary procedure has set a barrier against breeders, and explains why they have used the Caninae with little success. Those who wish to know how the unequal numbers of chromosomes are delivered in the embryo should read 'Why the Caninae Roses are Different' by Ann P. Wylie of the University of Otago, Dunedin, New Zealand. It is printed in the *New Zealand Rose Annual 1976.*

SPECIES

R. canina *Taller Blush white Midsummer* P5 H7
A hardy wild rose, so familiar to Europeans that they would not plant it in their gardens for all its prettiness. Its flowers are lustrous and fragrant, just off white by a

blush of pink. The hips are bright red, and make a good show in the autumn. Familiarly known as the Dog Rose, and as the Briar. It has been used as a rootstock on which to bud or graft roses, a process accurately described by William Shakespeare, although the commercial application appears to date from the nineteenth century. Such rootstocks were grown by the tens of millions, chiefly in Holland, Germany and Denmark, from seed collected all over Europe, as far as Hungary, Yugoslavia and Romania. Needless to say the seed beds exhibited a rare assortment of forms and types; for those who gathered them went after rose hips without wasting time on a botanical analysis of the plants which bore them. It was a common remark on rose nurseries that no two of their plants of *R. canina* looked the same; and that was considered a disadvantage for raising upon them an even crop of roses. Therefore the growers of rootstocks began to make selections of the best types, and after ascertaining that they would come reasonably true from seed, due to the peculiar sexual operations of the species, they established their own plantations as a source of seed. These selections are known as Edelcaninas. The best, I believe, is 'Pfänder', from J. Pfänder of Beuren, Wurttemberg, Germany, made before 1930. It is hardy and vigorous, and although it contracts mildew, that does not necessarily affect the rose it bears. It can also be grown as a standard stem, which is done by planting one year seedlings of reasonable development, allowing them to grow naturally for two years, apart from some thinning out, and then digging them up and cutting away all the shoots except the one most suitable, which is then planted ready to receive the benefit of being budded.

'Inermis' is much favoured in Germany for being hardy and not too thorny. It has dark wood, for *R. canina*. It came from a grower named Gamon of Lyon in about 1905. 'Pollmeriana' is the most handsome, with shiny leaves, suggesting that it may be a hybrid between *R. canina* and some other species. Unfortunately it gets blackspot, which causes the leaves to fall and the sap to dry up: unless sap flows freely, one cannot bud roses. Herr Pollmer came from Groszenheim in Germany, and introduced his strain before 1928. There are a dozen or so other selections, but the writing is on the wall for the lot of them, because they all share *R. canina's* ability to make suckers. I am ashamed to say that the rose trade bore this with equanimity when labour was cheap, and most of their customers employed gardeners. When the rose became everyman's plant, and the horticultural industry began to pay better wages, even now by no means high in the industrial scale, there was soon a cry for roses without suckers; and *R. canina* and its strains are rapidly being abandoned in consequence.

The hips of *R. canina* are a source of Vitamin C; Rose Hip Syrup was an important supplement in the diet of children in Britain in the last war, when citrus fruit disappeared from the shops. While I should not quarrel with the wartime name, I might point out that a hip is the fruit of a rose and of no other plant; just as the grape is the fruit of the vine. One might as well say Vine Grapes as Rose Hips. Hip is an old English word, sometimes spelt hep, which misleads pronunciation, but avoids misunderstanding with the bones in our sides. The word is in danger of becoming obsolete, and I suppose an alternative would be welcome. My suggestion is 'seedshell', because the red fleshy part is derived from the pericarp, which means 'the shell around'. Having mentioned grapes, I should add that the flesh of hips makes excellent wine; I heard of a German Vintner who thought the British stupid to import wine, for in his opinion hips were as good as grapes. A British wine maker told me that garden roses provide hips as good if not better than wild roses for the purpose. I have not put these assertions to the test, but intend to!

CANINA HYBRIDS

'Abbotswood' *Taller Blush Midsummer* P5 H7
This gives evidence that the Dog Rose can become double, or at least semi-double;
and that is the way to visualize this variety, as a Dog Rose with more petals. It was
found in a hedge surrounding a garden called Abbotswood in Gloucestershire.
Introduced by T. Hilling & Co in 1954; but semi-double Dog Roses have been
known in the past.

'Andersonii' *Taller Pink Midsummer* P5 H7
A deep coloured hybrid of the Dog Rose, and with larger flowers. Miss Willmott
stated in *The Genus Rosa* 1910–14, that it was to be found in many old gardens. It
was re-introduced by Hillier & Sons, a deservedly famous nursery at Winchester,
England, in about 1935.

R. × **hibernica** *Medium* + *Pink Midsummer* P5 H4
The Irish name refers to its discovery near Belfast about 1800. It is considered to be a
hybrid between *R. canina* and *R. spinosissima,* and its appearance bears it out. A
compact shrub, like a pink Dog Rose, with some cream in it, giving a hint of the
marbled manner of the Scotch roses. It has dull grey green leaves, and a sweet scent.

'Kiese' *Tall Light red Midsummer* P3 H7 *
Of interest, being from 'Général Jacqueminot' × *R. canina;* and of beauty
particularly for its fine red hips. The leaves are bright and glossy, the flowers
cheerfully cherry red, with a few petals more than a single. It was bred by Herman
Kiese & Co of Viselbach-Erfurt in Germany; but the intention was to create a
rootstock. It has had less credit than it deserves as a healthy shrub with handsome
hips. Introduced in 1910.

ALBAS

Along with the Gallicas and Damasks, the Albas constitute the truly old garden
roses; the Centifolias made the fourth group. Their origin is unknown. C. C. Hurst
concluded that they were derived from *R. canina* as a mother, and a Damask as the
male. Modern authorities believe the species of the Caninae may have been *R.
corymbifera.* From their appearance we may well associate them with the familiar
Dog Rose.
   Their hallmarks are pale colours and noble bushy plants, with tough foliage,
slightly blue green. They are immune to mildew and blackspot in my experience, but
not to rust. They are strong, hardy, enduring, fragrant, delightful. They have a host of
names, as partisans sneaked credit from their beauty: 'Bonnie Prince Charlie's
Rose', 'The Jacobite Rose', 'The White Rose of York'. Officially they are *R.* × *Alba.*

'Celestial' *Tall Light pink Summer* P5 H1 ***
The pretty buds open light rose pink, a delicate colour; the expanded flowers have
about five circuits of petals, those to the centre being narrow, and allowing a view of
the stamens, not always to be seen in so full a flower. It therefore has a flower of great
charm, with a pleasant scent, and proceeds to exhibit it to perfection on large bushes
with sea green leaves. This is a delightful rose to own. Its origin is unknown and some
of the old names credited to it may have belonged elsewhere. Often referred to as
'Céleste'.

'Félicité Parmentier' *Medium* + *Blush* *Summer* P3 H1 **
The flower form of the Albas is often intricate, always charming. Of both qualities we have evidence here. The buds are round, and soon show a gap at the top as they open; they are then white, with a pale blush. As soon as the centre petals show their colour through the gap, they are seen to be pink, and the flower opens, pink in and white out; it has many petals, folded; and the centre is quartered; the flower looks short, as if the top had been sliced off. The middle petals expand, and as they do so they stretch out a white topside, and conceal the pink of their reverse, so that the centre looks parti-coloured. They end apologetically and delicately blushing in the most charming of flowers. The plants are not so tall and strong as most Albas, nor is the fragrance so sweet. The stems are obliged to bend under the weight of bloom they carry. Origin unknown; like 'Celestial' it was already being grown in the nineteenth century.

'Königin von Danemarck' *Tall* *Pink* *Summer* P8 H1 *
Not quite typical of the Albas; it obviously has some different relation. It is the deepest colour amongst them, retains their charming flower form, but loses their nobility of plant growth. The double flowers expand with the petals still curved towards the centre; only late in their career do they relax and stretch out straight. The flowers are large for the class, the growth on the pendular side, the fragrance glorious.

'Maiden's Blush' *Taller* *Blush white* *Summer* P5 H1 **
A fine, upstanding plant, with firm sea green leaves and a sweet scent. On close inspection the flowers have not the subtle charm of 'Celestial'; they fade paler, and keep the centre petals folded over the stamens. There are forms known as Great and Small Maiden's Blush. This was already a favourite in the early nineteenth century, and one hesitates to guess how much older it may be. The records start at Kew Gardens in 1797, but we know that 'Maiden's Blush' in various forms was on sale in England in the period 1750–70, and there seems little doubt that the White Rose of John Gerard in 1597 was an Alba. The French had several names, with an extra word tacked on to denote a particularly choice colour; and when the emotive name 'Maiden's Blush' was invented in England, and the even more intimate 'Cuisse de Nymphe' in France, taking the blush from her cheeks to her thighs, it is safe to assume that various roses were promptly accorded those names. 'Incarnata', 'La Sèduisante', 'La Virginal', 'Cuisse de Nymphe Émue' and *R. alba regalis* are just a sample of the directory.

'Maxima' *Taller* *White* *Summer* P3 H1 *
A large and handsome shrub with double white flowers. This is like 'Maiden's Blush' without any pink in it, and is taken to be the 'Jacobite Rose'. Its origin cannot be traced, but not for want of names, of which the most likely to be met are 'Great Double White', *R.* × *alba maxima* and *R.* × *alba plena*. It is, I think pointless to search for the origin of these roses, because it is lost in the mists, well, not of antiquity, but of the eighteenth and early nineteenth centuries.

'Mme Legras de St. Germain' *Taller* *White* *Summer* P6 H1 ***
A beauty in snowy white, the double flowers are large for the class. They open to show the centre perfectly round, whereupon the outer petals stretch out, and the inner unwrap themselves from the central ball to stand, each one folded, closely around the centre of the flower. It puts me in mind of a powder puff. The plant is

vigorous and handsome, the fragrance like that of 'Celestial', perhaps stronger. Origin uncertain, it may quite probably have been raised in France in about 1840.

'Pompon Blanc Parfait'   *Tall   White   Summer*   P2   H1   *
This grows as an open bush, the branches well apart, which is in contradiction to the closely clad habit of its classmates. I should not be surprised if it has some extra Centifolia or Damask blood. Whether one wishes to grow it, excusing its inferior habit, depends upon the fascinating flowers. They are white with a slight blush, and change from round buds into pompons, made of many small petals. The outer three rows extend flat, the inner petals are folded, and just reveal the stigmas. These flowers are carried on top of short side shoots for nearly the whole length the branches are exposed to the sun. A disappointment is the slight scent; a bonus comes in the form of a few flowers in the autumn. Introduced in 1876, by Eugène Verdier. Also known as 'Pompon Parfait', which is asking for confusion, as there was a Hybrid China of that name.

'Semi-plena'   *Taller   White   Summer*   P4   H5   *
The largest plant in the class, with pretty buds, which open to loose, semi-double flowers. I should say it has the least interesting flowers of the Albas. As a tribute to this superb class, let us say that any owner of 'Semi-plena' would be fond of his plant. It is a noble grower, handsome in leaf; and it is the only Alba to be relied on for a brave show of red hips. The Scots take it for 'Bonnie Prince Charlie's Rose'; it is assumed to be *R.* × *alba suaveolens,* planted along with the Damasks in the Valley of the Roses in Bulgaria. It may provide some Attar; but the scent is not markedly pervasive, and it should be, for that is what suaveolens implies.

MACRANTHAS
Nobody, I think is very clear where *R.* × *macrantha* belongs. Its birth certificate must be sadly disfigured from the number of parents that have been proposed; I do not intend to list them all, but *R. gallica, R. canina* and *R.* × *alba* are amongst the candidates. Upon asking ourselves which class it most resembles, no clear answer appears. I have therefore placed it as a class of its own among the *Caninae,* and if this is not exactly correct, it is at least convenient. In associating 'Complicata' with the Macranthas, I am guided by its appearance.

R. × **macrantha**   *Trailer   Blush   Midsummer*   P4   H5   *
Found in France in 1823, this rose was bound to attract notice by the pleasant width of its single flowers. They are pale in colour, regularly formed, and fragrant, with the stamens making them a smaller imitation of 'Mermaid'. The stigmas sit up like a little toadstool. Although it trails, it does so as a shrub rather than a rambler, and needs appropriate placing. It mounds itself up to head high, and then goes outwards. Attractive red hips follow in autumn.

'Complicata'   *Taller   Pink   Midsummer*   P3   H2   *
Single pink flowers of great beauty adorn this ungainly plant. Rarely satisfied with its own place, it sends long branches to pry into its neighbours. The beauty of the blooms is the reason for growing it; they continually earn reprieves for its awkward habit. Its origin is unknown, but it is often referred to as 'Gallica complicata'.

'Lady Curzon'   *Taller   Pink   Midsummer*   P4   H2
From Charles Turner of 'Crimson Rambler' fame; and I am sure that if anyone had

told him that 'Lady Curzon' would survive 'Crimson Rambler', he would have had a good laugh at such folly. 'Lady Curzon' was introduced in 1901; it is considered a hybrid between *R.* × *macrantha* and *R. rugosa rubra.* The beauty of it is the large single flowers, pink with attractive veining, cream stamens within. The plants send out long shoots, and are apt to stray out of bounds.

SPECIES continued

R. coriifolia and R. corymbifera

These are of interest to us only because the Laxa understock is the variety *R. coriifolia froebelii;* or so the experts say. The Dutch stock growers don't believe them. They say it is a selection from *R. corymbifera,* which is like a Dog Rose with downy leaves; and the Dutch call the understock *R. corymbifera* 'Laxa'. I would as soon interfere as intrude upon two experts in the boxing ring. Suffice it to say that this rose has a dual economic importance in Great Britain. It has proved the rootstock to eliminate suckers, or all but a few of them; and it has been the means of British growers growing their own rootstocks instead of importing them from Holland, Denmark or Germany. For years the Continentals produced them so cheaply that the British found it more profitable to buy than to grow; and when the price became less attractive, the British had little experience of the art. Dr G. A. D. Jackson of the University College of North Wales, in Bangor, was interested in the germination of rose seeds, and received money in support of his research from the rose trade and the Royal National Rose Society. He engaged a research assistant, Dr J. B. Blundell; their studies of rose seeds resulted in a technique for breaking the dormancy of the seeds, and in Dr Blundell turning from research to put his skill into the commercial application of his ideas. This he now does in association with Gordon Sutton of Wisbech, Cambridgeshire; in 1977 the first large sowing resulted in the sale of over ten million stocks, many to the Continent; and, I should say, having seen them, superbly grown and of the highest quality.

A rose seed is like a small brazil nut, with a woody shell and a skin to protect the embryo. Such a seed is called an achene, a word which means closed up (literally, 'I don't gape'). And rose seeds are closed up, because nature has no intention of allowing them to germinate in a hurry. Those native to the colder regions must wait over winter for kind spring weather; but how many springs are kind? They are treacherous more often than not, the promise of early sun falsely kept by frost.

Therefore a rose seed is restrained from its willingness to grow by substances within the flesh of the hip, the woody seed coat, and the interior skin. The name given to the inhibitor is dormin; it loses its restrictive power slowly, so that rose seeds are freed from it over a long period, and therefore do not all spring to life at one signal from the sun, to die together in one frost.

Not all rose seeds behave like this. Some germinate freely. They are the denizens of the more temperate zones, a remarkable instance of natural provision in the genus.

To return to 'Laxa', the great criticism of it used to be its susceptibility to rust. Fortunately it is not the same rust that lives on popular garden roses, nor is it transferred to them. But any disease is bad, and a nurseryman is a fool indeed if he does not take the proper measures to keep his fields of 'Laxa' free from rust.

R. eglanteria *Taller Light pink Midsummer* P10 H7

The Sweet Briar, the Eglantine; Pemberton was fond of reminding us that the children in Essex called it Sweet Maria, to rhyme presumably with Briar. The botanical name for many years was less romantic: *R. rubiginosa,* which means rust coloured, and refers to its glandular hairs. The name *R. rubiginosa* came through a rare mistake by Linnaeus, who transferred the original name *R. eglanteria* to 'Austrian Yellow'; and after many years, we have got back the old name, as is right and proper having regard to its place in the poetry of the English language. Maybe 'Austrian Yellow' will be treated with similar kindness in the future.

The Sweet Briar's charm is the scent from its leaves, diffused when the glands are bruised, especially after a shower of rain. Miss Willmott informs us in *The Genus Rosa* that this perfume is not easily captured from the leaves: 'the water distilled from them yields a perfume far from agreeable unless mixed with some other ingredient.' It is certain that one Sweet Briar in a small garden, even from an inconspicuous position, can spread its pleasant aroma over the little property in a most agreeable way.

The plant is similar to the Dog Rose; it is more prickly, the leaves are not quite so large, the flowers are usually more pink. When I used to go 'briaring', that is getting standard stems from *R. canina* in the countryside, I learned the easiest way to distinguish *R. canina* from *R. eglanteria* in the middle of winter. The Sweet Briar is the one with the hips left on it, for the birds prefer the taste of the Dog Rose.

R. eglanteria has been used as a rootstock in Europe, and is probably the first species to have been taken for that purpose. I cannot say I liked it very much, from what I saw of the Sweet Briars which turned up among our stocks of *R. canina,* due to promiscuous seed gathering in Europe. It is prickly, and fond of making a tap root, which at least had the advantage of going down deep, and thus earned the species a reputation of being a useful stock in soil where roses had been grown for a long time.

EGLANTERIA HYBRIDS

We cannot doubt that improved forms of the Sweet Briar were grown in Europe as soon as the indigenous populations took any interest in roses at all. The Sweet Briar was one of Gerard's sixteen cultivated kinds of roses in 1597. English catalogues in the 1700s offered several varieties, including doubles, and a yellow. William Paul in 1848 has a list of fifteen Sweet Briars, including a pink one called 'Monstrous' and another pink with mossy buds, called 'Mossy'. Some of those old varieties may not be true Sweet Briars, but they provide a decent background to the work of Lord Penzance, and remind us that there were Sweet Briars before his famous introductions in the 1890s. It should be noted that many of the hybrids disappoint in the one great distinguishing glory of the species, its scented leaves.

'Janet's Pride' *Taller Pink & white Midsummer* P5 H2 *
Very different from the wild rose; its flowers are semi-double, pink with white running through them from the centre, whilst the leaves are dull, rough in texture, a solid background more attractive than they sound. They are not very fragrant. 'Janet's Pride' was noticed growing by a lane in Cheshire, and was introduced by Paul & Son in 1892. It has been suggested that it was the same as 'Clementine', an older variety, under which name it is known in the United States; but William Paul listed 'Clementine' in 1848 with the terse description 'rosy blush, distinct'; which does not sound appropriate to 'Janet's Pride'.

Penzance Hybrids
Lord Penzance (of Godalming in Surrey, not of Cornwall) was nearing his eightieth year when his sixteen hybrids of the Sweet Briar were introduced in 1894 and 1895

by Keynes, Williams & Company of Salisbury, as 'Quite a new Feature in Roses'. Lord Penzance contributed a paper, 'Experiments in Rose Hybridization', in the *Rosarian's Year Book 1892;* it reveals his serious interest in the subject; he conveys the news that Henry Bennett had been trying to breed with 'Persian Yellow', and had sown 'hundreds of hips' from its crosses without result. We are obliged to conclude that Bennett's use of that rose was at least contemporary with Pernet-Ducher's.

Lord Penzance noted that the energies of the rose world were devoted mainly to Hybrid Perpetuals, and that the assessment of roses related to their performance as exhibition blooms. His criticism was that 'our existing system tends to shut out all but a very few forms'. As for the favourite Hybrid Perpetuals, 'I should be sorry to insure the lives of most of them for five years, short of a very handsome premium'. His Sweet Briars certainly live very much longer. And his lesson is to the point. The whole is gravely hurt if attention is paid exclusively to one part.

People who plant Hybrid Sweet Briars should remember the word Briar, and give plenty of space. The variety which can be kept fairly compact is 'Lady Penzance'. The others are apt to send long shoots where they may be unwelcome, across paths and over fences. The only point in growing them is for the leaf-scent, and I have therefore abandoned all of Lord Penzance's in which that quality is imperceptible; but there is one named 'Minna', pink, introduced in 1895, and said to have very aromatic foliage. I'm sorry to say I have never come across it. Should one Sweet Briar be chosen, I take 'Lady Penzance' as the best. It can easily be trimmed to stay within bounds; the flowers are small and fleeting, but the leaf-scent is sufficient to haunt the garden, like an agreeable ghost on a damp summer evening. It was introduced in 1894, having been raised from *R. eglanteria* × *R. foetida bicolor*. The official name, given for some reason quite obscure to me, is *R.* × *penzanceana*. The single flowers are the colour of prawns with a touch of yellow, and the hips small and dark.

'Catherine Seyton' has quite a large single pink flower, and 'Rose Bradwardine' a smaller one. 'Meg Merrilies' is red, with fine hips. 'Lord Penzance', claimed to be from *R. eglanteria* × *R.* × *harisonii*, is like a paler 'Lady Penzance'. After them we have 'Lucy Ashton', white with a pink rim, of interest as being the parent of 'Magnifica'. All these were introduced in 1894.

'Magnifica' *Taller Rose red Summer*
A self set seed from 'Lucy Ashton' gave rise to 'Magnifica', otherwise known as *R. eglanteria duplex*. It was introduced in 1916 by a nurseryman named H. A. Hesse, of Ems in Germany; his one other variety of note was a white trailing Wichuraiana Hybrid, 'Fräulein Octavia Hesse', raised in 1910, and which my firm grew with much pleasure until a few years ago. 'Magnifica' was more significant, because German breeders used it, notably Wilhelm Kordes. From that breeding line came 'Rudolph Timm', and therefore 'Margaret Merril' in the Floribundas; and 'Gertrud Westphal' and therefore 'Marlena' of the short growing Floribundas. We should also recall that from an unidentified Sweet Briar came 'Harmonie', thence 'Cläre Grammerstorf', which introduced Sweet Briars into yellow Hybrid Teas and Floribundas. The motive, as so often in Kordes' breeding, was hardiness.

'Fritz Nobis' *Taller Pink Midsummer* P5 H5 ****
This lovely plant is no Sweet Briar in appearance, nor are its leaves scented; but it has as its parents 'Joanna Hill' × 'Magnifica', and I place it here for its father's sake. When in full bloom, it is one of the most handsome shrubs in the world; the double pink flowers with their crinkled petals stand on the bush as if it were a flower shop.

Their size accords well with the large plant; it is the nearest we have to Hybrid Teas on a large shrub, but more by the width of flower than by depth. The leaves are dark and healthy, the hips round and red. Raised by Wilhelm Kordes, and introduced in 1940.

SPECIES continued

R. pomifera   *Taller   Pink   Summer*   P4   H7   **

The Apple-bearing Rose; or just the Apple Rose. It was known for many years as *R. villosa,* and is a fine, handsome plant, spreading wide, the leaves downy, but bright and clean cut for the Caninae. The flowers are clear and lovely, the rose pink of them full of kindness and good cheer, the petals slightly creased like new clothes not quite shaken out. This rose will make a glorious hedge where it may have sufficient space. The name is given for the hips, which do not resemble apples at all, but are more like big, hairy, red gooseberries. There is a semi-double form named 'Duplex', or 'Wolley-Dod's Rose'.

R. *pomifera* is native to northern Europe (but not Britain) and western Asia; it is a hardy species, since Scandinavia is one of its homes. *R. tomentosa* is probably a hybrid from it, but not so handsome; and *R. sherardii* may be another. The most similar common British species is *R. mollis,* a short growing plant, whose plump, round, red hips may be seen on dykes in Scotland; it is by no means confined to Britain, but grows across Europe and into Asia.

R. rubrifolia   *Taller   Pink   Summer*   P2   H7   ***

The famous rose with red leaves; or to be more exact they have a dull bloom on them, like a purple grape. The leaves and stems when young often come close to purple. It is an unmistakable rose in the garden, mainly at peril from the scissors of the lady of the house, for it embellishes many a flower arrangement. The growth is not always full of vigour, and I think the reason may often be that it does not like to be in wet ground. The flowers are of brief account, light pink and small, in a bunch which quickly becomes sepals and stamens, as the petals blow away faster than apple blossom.

Great clusters of small hips decorate the bushes in the autumn, round and cheerfully red, until the birds eat them. One might think it easy to grow plenty more plants from the seeds, but it is one of the most obstinate roses to germinate, and the chances are that in the first spring less than one out of a hundred seeds will grow. The seed needs to be stratified for over a year, by mixing the hips with sand and peat, and turning the mixture over every two or three months. Then, if the mice and birds have been denied access, a spring sowing should be successful.

R. *rubrifolia* does not mind some shade. It is a native of central Europe, roughly from the Pyrenees to Austria, mainly in hill country. Of its other Latin names, the best known is *R. ferruginea,* which inaptly likens the rose to rust on iron. There is a hybrid from the Central Experimental Farm in Ottawa, Canada, claimed to be *R. rubrifolia* × *R. rugosa,* and named 'Carmenetta'. It has some of *R. rugosa's* small thorns, which look quite effective on the purple stems; but the smooth wood and natural grace of *R. rubrifolia* are more to my liking.

R. glutinosa and R. serafinii

R. *glutinosa* is like a prickly little Sweet Briar; but its leaf-scent smells more of a pine tree. Its name and scent come from the sticky glands on its leaves. It is from southern

Europe into Asia, roughly Spain to Iran. *R. serafinii* is also short and thorny, the flowers pink, the growth dense, the hips red and showy. First found in Italy, it also grows in the south of France, Sardinia and Corsica.

Other Species
The remainder of the Caninae are some twenty species which we had better leave for the botanists to consider; they are unfamiliar to gardeners for want of attractive horticultural features; in some cases they are no doubt forms of one another, or so close as to defy ready recognition. The one from America is *R. montezumae,* said to be like a Sweet Briar, and to have been discovered in Mexico in 1825. The probability is that it got there by the aid of some creature from the Old World, with wings or arms.

16. Carolinae and Hybrid

We may call this the American section, for its seven charming species all originate from the United States or Canada. To European eyes, they interpret the natural scene of North America as it is imagined, by the red and yellow colours in their leaves before they fall. Other roses show such colours, but that pretty grace is particularly noticeable in these.

The factors of recognition are the same as led us to the Caninae, with the variation in the final step that whereas the thorns of the Caninae are usually curved, here the thorns are straight; this holds good for both the Carolinae and the next (and final) section, the Cinnamomeae. The difference between the two is that when the Carolinae have set seed, their sepals soon fall from the hip; but the Cinnamomeae retain their sepals.

SPECIES & VARIETIES

R. carolina *Medium + Pink Summer* P3 H4
The names of the species of the Carolinae have been chopped and changed, so that if one refers to *R. carolina* in Willmott's *The Genus Rosa,* one arrives at another species altogether. In that work it appears as *R. humilis;* other names in past use were *R. pennsylvanica, R. parviflora, R. virginiana humilis* and *R. pratensis.* Its vernacular name is the Pasture Rose.

It is a shrub of medium height, sometimes tall, with small pink flowers of no great floral beauty, but with interesting sepals, long and thin. The leaves are more notable, smartly folded at first appearance, and opening to show themselves finely toothed; they are light green, and although not at all glossy, their appearance is bright. Round red hips in autumn. *R. carolina* is native to the eastern parts of North America, from Southern Canada to Florida. There is a white variety, *R. carolina alba;* and a pink one with its petals divided into three segments, *R. carolina triloba.* The species *R. subserrulata* comes from Missouri to Texas, and is very similar to *R. carolina.*

R. carolina plena *Short Pink Summer* P3 H1 *
A charming variety, in which the attractive leaves of the species look even better by being closer together on a short plant. The flowers are double, pink fading white, pleasant in form and colour change. This is presumably the 'Double Dwarf Pennsylvanian', which was on sale in England in 1770, painted by Redouté as *R. parviflora flore multiplici,* and thereafter lost from general notice until Mrs Doris Lynes of Taberg, New York, discovered it again after the Second World War.

R. foliolosa *Medium Pink Late Summer* P4 H4 *
A strange and interesting species, marked by its narrow leaflets. It has few thorns, and flowers later than most wild roses, not all at once but with afterthoughts as it

were; there were still two flowers when I looked at it last autumn, on 13th October. The flowers are quite deep in colour, the buds surrounded by the wispy ends of the five sepals. The hips, like the flowers, are usually scattered rather than en masse; they are rose red, small and round. The autumn foliage assumes delightful red and yellow colours, effective even though the leaves are small. The name means the rose covered with leaflets. This species is not common in the wild, its centre being Arkansas.

R. nitida   *Short   Pink   Summer*   P4   H6   **
Its name means lustrous, which it truly is, from the moment the tiny leaves trust their polished dark green to the spring, until they yield to the fall in a blaze of scarlet. The little flowers of summer are bright lilac pink, and the little hips of autumn are red and round. The growth is short, the plant as compact and neat as one could wish. It will sucker freely on its own roots, therefore if it is to be grown into a neat border, budded plants should be used; not that wild roses look happy in regimented lines; a little clump of plants as part of a rose border is perhaps the prettiest way of growing *R. nitida*, which always looks to me smart as new paint. It keeps short, is very hardy, its thorns are thin and numerous, the young wood is tinged with red, and the leaflets are narrow. Unlike most roses, its native places are poorly drained, bordering marshes, in the region chiefly from Massachusetts to Newfoundland.

R. palustris   *Tall   Pink   Late summer*
Although this species is not one to attract gardeners, it may possibly add another grain to the store of the rose's capabilities, because it naturally grows in the places roses hate: swamps. It is called the Swamp Rose, and the Latin name has the same meaning, of living in boggy ground. The flowers are deeply coloured. We have a fine hybrid in the Royal National Rose Society's gardens under the label *R. palustris* × *R. rugosa*. It is more than head high, of handsome upright habit, and gives a splendid display of oval hips, bright red. *R. palustris* comes from the south-east of Canada and the north-eastern United States.

R. rudiuscula   *Medium   Pink   Summer*
I do not know this species, which is from Oklahoma and Wisconsin. But we have a superb hybrid of it in the Royal National Rose Society's gardens, marked *R. rudiuscula* × 'Subglauca'. That hybrid is a tall plant with pink flowers, but its glory is its hips, masses of them, deep red, fat and round.

R. virginiana   *Tall − Pink   Late summer*   P4   H8   ****
One of the most handsome wild roses in the world; everything about it is right. The leaves are bright and clean, and furnish the plant to the ground. The growth is neither lanky nor lax, but designed to make a mound of its chosen area with simple grace. The flowers are bright pink, borne near the leaves; they are fairly large for a wild rose, and advertise themselves cheerfully for quite a long period. The red hips are sufficient reason for growing the rose, and, if all that were not enough, the leaves glow with red and yellow before they fall. As a specimen bush or as a hedge, *R. virginiana* is pure delight. Usually it keeps within bounds vertically and laterally; in Britain we expect a plant to remain less than head high, and to be content with about four square metres of ground, provided budded plants are used. On its own roots it will make a splendid thicket by its suckers.

In all probability, this was the first American rose to be taken to Europe and cultivated there. It was on sale in England in 1760, not only itself but also 'Virginia

Red'; a reference by John Parkinson in 1640 fits it. Its habitat is mainly in the area from New York into Canada.

VIRGINIANA HYBRID
We might hope for a flourishing race from *R. virginiana,* but it has not yet arrived.

'Rose d'Amour' *Tall – Pink Late summer* P3 H2 *
This pink rose is semi-double, otherwise it is like *R. virginiana,* but not so similar as to pass as a variety; it is therefore presumed to be a hybrid, and an attractive one too. Nobody, I think, can be quite sure of disentangling the names involved here. 'Rose d'Amour' is a name going back at least to 1759, and another old name for it is 'St. Mark's Rose'. A similar rose, with narrower leaves and stipules, appeared under the name 'D'Orsay Rose', presumably in the nineteenth century, although nobody seems to know when. As being a double or at least a semi-double version of *R. virginiana,* 'Rose d'Amour' was for a long time sold as *R. virginiana plena,* until the authorities substituted the name *R. × rapa.* Graham Thomas confesses that for some years, until he noticed they were different and segregated them, he had 'D'Orsay Rose' and 'Rose d'Amour' mixed under the name *R. virginiana plena.* I have an even graver confession: my own firm, alert to the new name, but indifferent to the hybrid symbol, was selling *R. rapa* until I pointed out that what we had was actually *R. virginiana.* Jean Gaujard of France put the cap on it all by introducing in 1936 a Hybrid Tea called 'Rose d'Amour'. If we stir in the old botanical names of *R. lucida* and *R. lucida plena,* we have all the clues and little clarity. Rapa alludes to a small turnip, and describes the shape of the hips.

17. Cinnamomeae and Hybrids

The riches of only a few sections have been plundered to dress our modern roses: especially the Indicae, Synstylae and Gallicanae. It is obvious that the genus has much in store to encourage the seekers of the future; and surely the Cinnamomeae is their treasure house, a great assembly of some fifty-six species as near as one can determine at present, well knowing that some will be proved in time to be hybrids.

They take their name from the Cinnamon Rose, which has little in common with that healthful spice unless one has an imaginative nose. Gerard in 1597 said the leaves smelt of cinnamon, and Parkinson in 1620 said it was the flowers. Most of their successors have sniffed in vain; my guess is that some old pharmacist brewed a substitute for cinnamon from its leaves.

This is a varied section, for which we take the general steps that led us to the Carolinae, and then claim that the sepals remain persistently on the hips of the Cinnamomeae. The variations are from wonderful beauty to scrubby vegetation; for easy reference I have kept them more or less in alphabetical order, the less interesting sharing a paragraph, the beauties set on their own. We do not know whether some apparently negligible species might stand in the future with the importance of *R. multiflora* or *R. gallica;* the least may prove to be foremost.

SPECIES & VARIETIES

R. acicularis   R. albertii   R. amblyotis   R. arkansana   R. banksiopsis   R. bella
R. acicularis means the rose with thorns like needles, no way to ingratiate itself. It should be the world's hardiest rose, for it grows in the northern temperate regions as near as it may to the North Pole, in Canada, Alaska, Mongolia, Russia and Scandinavia, for which reason it bears two names, the Arctic Rose and the Circumpolar Rose. It also spreads south to the United States, Japan and China. Of medium height, it has pink flowers, which one could match from a cheap bag of confetti. *R. albertii* is similar to *R. willmottiae;* it comes from central Asia.

R. amblyotis is rose red, known as the Kamchatka Rose, because it is native to that part of East Russia north of Japan by a thousand miles across the sea of Okhotsk. *R. arkansana* has bold lilac pink flowers, round, dull red hips, and like several other species from North America, its leaves show yellow autumnal colours; that is, if the rose I know truly is this species, for it has been a victim of mixed up names, and ours is considerably bigger than the botanists say it should be. *R. banksiopsis* and *R. bella* are both from China, with hips of the type of *R. moyesii.*

R. beggeriana   *Tall   White   Late summer*   P3   H3
A pale kind of rose, with light foliage and white flowers. I regret to say that the darkest thing one can depend on is blackspot, which likes this species. The hips are small, and lose their sepals sooner than a member of the Cinnamomeae ought; the

species flowers intermittently over a long period, so that the hips from the first flowers are ripe before the last blooms are over. A native of Western China.

R. blanda   *Taller   Pink   Summer*   P4   H4
A fine upright plant, with fairly large flowers for a wild rose, its lilac pink lightened by pale stigmas. The leaves are dull, like shadows in the background. This should prove hardy, for it is the Hudson's Bay Rose, and the Labrador Rose,thus revealing its homeland, which also includes much of the northern United States, and across to Vancouver. It is almost as variable in its forms as the Dog Rose. The stipules are worth a look, as being probably the largest in the genus; and we may note also that it has few thorns. Canadian plant breeders have used it, without any sensational success, and on the recommendation of E. F. Allen, Scientific Adviser to the Royal National Rose Society, British breeders are now experimenting with it.

R. californica   *Tall   Lilac pink   Summer +*   P4   H3   *
I shall have to speak up for this rose, for all my mentors decry it; even the almost infallible Graham Thomas, who dismisses it offhand as of no particular garden merit. Perhaps my stock of it is different, for it is known to be a variable rose in its native habitat, centred upon the state suggested by its name. Let me tell you what it is really like.

It grows into a shrub around head high, and will sucker everywhere on its own roots, and even to some extent when it is a budded plant. The leaves are fairly small, tending to be round for a rose, and are I admit somewhat nondescript. The stems are smooth in between the prickles, and somehow look unlike a rose, almost as if they belonged to some wiry perennial.

The flowers are the thing, carried in great heads; they are neat and small, would barely cover the face of a wristwatch, that is mine, not Madame's. Their colour is lilac pink, light, with the lavender or lilac accentuated more definitely than in any wild rose, and yellow stamens to decorate it. A flurry of pollen and scent escapes from their five little petals.

The heads have so many flowers from the different stages of buds, that colour is present for a long time; and it is rare for a year to go by without a lesser, but acceptable contribution arriving in the autumn, by which time the round red hips are present, but not prominent.

I can scarcely believe my eyes when I see it dismissed as pink and uninteresting, and the double variety, *R. californica plena,* extolled in its stead; no shearer in Australia ever took the wool off a sheep as thoroughly as the double Californica trimmed the individuality from the single; and the colour, too; it really is pink and uninteresting.

R. caudata   *Tallest   Red   Midsummer*   P4   H9   *
Probably a close relation of *R. macrophylla,* this comes from western China, and is a fine big plant with wonderful bright red hips. The flowers are red, and quickly over. The hips are like those of *R. moyesii,* of a lovely slim shape. Bunches of them hang down, each hip on a slender stalk, formed like a long red flask, on the neck of which the remains of the sepals hang like five old claws. The name means it has tails, a reference to the sepals.

R. cinnamomea   R. corymbulosa
The Canell or Cinnamon Rose of John Gerard had double flowers, and to him the species with its single flowers was a lesser form. It is not an interesting garden plant in

either state; the single one is the true *R. cinnamomea,* its flowers deep lilac pink, the hips round, deep red; not large. It is widely distributed across Asia and Europe, and like *R. blanda* has wide stipules. The double one has many names, of which *R. cinnamomea plena* is the official one; it is also 'Rose de Mai', 'Rose de Pâques', 'Rose du Saint-Sacrament', 'Stevens Rose' and *R. majalis.*

I have never studied *R. corymbulosa,* which was introduced from China by E. H. Wilson in 1907 or 1908, and is said to be allied to the next species, *R. davidii.*

R. davidii *Taller Pink Summer* P4 H8
One of the type of *R. macrophylla,* and therefore notable for its hips, bright red and large, the old sepals playing their trick of elongation. The flowers are pink. The stems grow stout and strong up to about head high, and then reach out from the plant in a great arch. *R. davidii* comes from the area where China joins the east of Tibet.

R. davidii elongata *Taller Pink Summer* P4 H7
This variety differs from the species in having larger leaflets and hips; but this is not necessarily an advantage, as the impression it gives when in flower and fruit is that neither are over abundant.

R. davurica R. elegantula R. elymaitica
R. davurica is of little interest, probably a variety of *R. cinnamomea,* from north-east China. *R. elegantula* must be regarded with suspicion, for the various descriptions attached to it are inconsistent, unless it is a chameleon. *R. elymaitica* is a thorny bush from Iran, with the reputation of not being hardy, and is practically unknown in cultivation; I have never seen one.

R. fedtschenkoana *Tall White Late summer* + P4 H4
A pale and ghostly species, its flowers white, and the green of its leaves turning grey; the ashen aspect is all the clearer for the contrast of the young shoots, which are briefly purple. This unusual rose may fit into some planting scheme which asks for different colours of foliage; it can scarcely be described handsome on its own. It is not always happy in cultivation; I have seen it looking like a sick albino, persuading its owner to dig it up for fear of some unknown plague. The name it bears is that of a Russian botanist, Olga Fedtschenko, who discovered it in Turkestan about 1875.

R. forrestiana R. giraldii R. gratissima R. gymnocarpa R. hemsleyana
R. holodonta R. laxa R. macounii
I suspect that *R. forrestiana* has been mixed up since its fairly late introduction from China about 1920; otherwise how can it be similar to *R. farreri, R. moyesii* and *R. multibracteata,* as various authorities declare? *R. giraldii,* by the plants at the Royal National Rose Society's gardens, is an interesting species, letting its shoots spread down to the ground like a bush pretending to be a weeping willow. It indicates better than measurements and words can convey the rich assortment of rose bush shapes; roses may be shrubs pointing up, aside or down; in domes, pyramids, columns, Roman candles; either tall or short; the leaves a solid block to the view, or a tracery through which one can see. Apart from its unusual habit and foliage, *R. giraldii* is not greatly distinguished in flower or hips, for both are small and scattered, pink and red respectively.

R. gratissima is one unknown to me, although it is said to be like *R. californica. R. gymnocarpa* is a spruce bush, small in every way; growth, pink flowers and red hips.

The name means that the hips are naked, that is without any hairs at all. You may imagine it between a Scotch Rose and *R. farreri* to get a rough (and rather too thorny) idea of it. It was first discovered in British Columbia, and grows wild from there down to California and Idaho, perhaps taller than we see it in cultivation in Britain. A preference for growing in partial shade no doubt elongates it in the wild.

R. hemsleyana is probably a form of *R. macrophylla;* and *R. holodonta* a variety of *R. moyesii,* under which it is described. *R. laxa* is a white species from Central Asia, nothing to do with the rootstock of that name, but notable as a hardy rose of the type of *R. cinnamomea. R. macounii* is probably a form of *R. woodsii,* from Canada and the northern United States; it is pale pink and very hardy.

R. macrophylla *Tallest Pink Midsummer* P5 H10 ***
For some strange reason, *R. moyesii* is familiar to most rosarians, but *R. macrophylla* is not. These two are equally beautiful in their hips, for which they are primarily grown. *R. moyesii* has perhaps the more remarkable flower, and *R. macrophylla* the more graceful growth.

The name means the rose with large leaves, hardly a helpful title as the leaves are not much bigger than normal. The stems, the flowers and the hips are more interesting. The stems for their smoothness and purpled colour when young; the flowers for the way they stand out, deep pink with the centre neatly surrounded by a circlet of yellow stamens; the hips for their elegant shape, like little scarlet bottles among the dark stems. The old sepals, instead of reaching down, open like the points of a star, and show at the end of the hips a little circle where once the stigmas grew. A wild and wonderful shrub which needs plenty of room to grow. One of the earliest species of its type to be brought to the west, it came from the Himalayan region early in the nineteenth century.

R. macrophylla rubricaulis *Tallest Pink Midsummer* P5 H10 ***
The stems are still darker, otherwise it is similar to the species. It has the reputation of being less hardy, but looks well enough in England. Hillier & Son of Winchester introduced it, having grown it from seed sent from the Himalayas.

MACROPHYLLA HYBRIDS
'Auguste Roussel' *Taller Pink Midsummer* P5 H2
Raised by Barbier of Orléans from *R. macrophylla* × 'Papa Gontier', the latter being a pink Tea. That fascinating cross surely suggests it is high time more breeders thought of *R. macrophylla,* although in this instance 'Auguste Roussel' seems to have been an immediate end of the line. It is a large pink bush, usually described as a climber, because of the arching shoots it inherits from *R. macrophylla.* The flowers acquired some size and petals out of the Tea, but nothing in the way of hips from *R. macrophylla.* Introduced in 1913.

'Doncasterii' *Tall Rose red Midsummer* P4 H10 ***
Not as tall as *R. macrophylla,* which means that instead of looking up at the hips, one looks down on many of them. It spreads out, all the better to display its striking, scarlet load of fruit. The branches are dark, some with fine, close prickles, others smooth. The hips and flowers are both handsome, the flowers rose red.

Whether it is from a seed of *R. macrophylla,* or is a hybrid between that species and *R. moyesii* is open to speculation. It was introduced in about 1930 by E. Doncaster of J. Burrell & Co., a nursery in Cambridge. I remember Mr Doncaster as a gentle old man from whom I had my first lessons in hybridizing. I knew too little of roses then to ask him about the origin of 'Doncasterii', but I am glad his name is remembered.

SPECIES & VARIETIES continued
R. manca   R. marrettii   R. melina   R. mohavensis
I have never noticed *R. manca,* for apparently nobody has loved it enough to make it known in cultivation. It is said to be a short growing pink rose from the southern part of the Rocky Mountains. *R. marrettii* from Sakhalin is a hardy species with dark stems and pink flowers. *R. melina* has light pink flowers and round hips of deep red colour. It comes from Colorado and Utah, where it is known as the Blackstem Rose, and grows about a metre high according to the books. In cultivation in England it is larger. *R. mohavensis* comes from southern California, and may be a form of *R. woodsii.* Its flowers are pink.

R. moyesii   *Tallest   Crimson   Midsummer*   P3   H10   **
Greatly admired for its flowers and hips although not so much for its growth, which is thorny and soars up like a rocket, to waste its sweetness on the birds of the air. This may be dealt with either by planting it on a level lower than the viewpoint, or else growing one of its less lanky forms. It is a mountain plant, from the south-west part of China that runs towards Tibet. The name is a compliment to the Rev. J. Moyes of the China Inland Mission, whose assistance and hospitality were appreciated by E. H. Wilson, the plant seeker who found it late in the nineteenth century.

The flowers are beautifully regular in their parts. The five petals, of a strangely dark but lustrous crimson, scrupulously share their allotted space. Within them, the stamens stand in a neat and dense ring, their purpled stalks and yellow dust a perfect eye to the red petals. I should not describe the hips as if they were exclusive to *R. moyesii,* because it is not fair to the related species, especially *R. caudata, R. davidii, R. macrophylla* and *R. sweginzowii.* The fruit of all these roses is such a harvest festival as to send us into the winter singing. The first impression is colour, a brilliant scarlet; then fruitfulness, from the great number of hips; and size, for they look bigger than they are, being elongated by the clenched sepals at the ends; the lasting impression is shape, like little red flagons, the seeds in the slim body, the neck leading to the old sepals; and the whole crop hanging upside down like gorgeous lanterns. Why no jeweller has copied them I cannot understand. They are nature's perfect pendants.

R. moyesii fargesii   *Taller   Rose red   Midsummer*
Similar to *R. moyesii,* the flowers lighter, the growth slightly less, the leaves smaller, the hips perhaps larger. It is probable that stocks of this variety are mixed. It is quite different from *R. fargesii,* which is a member of the Synstylae, similar to *R. moschata.*

R. moyesii rosea   *Tallest   Pink   Midsummer*   P3   H10   **
Also known as *R. holodonta.* While a pink flowered *R. moyesii* induces some sense of wishing for the red, there is no disappointment whatever in the hips; they are very fine. This pink form is said to be more common than the red in the wild state in China, and may well be the true species.

MOYESII HYBRIDS AND SELECTIONS
'Fred Streeter'   *Taller   Pink   Midsummer*   P2   H10   ***
Those who listened to Fred Streeter's radio talks are not likely to forget the flavour of that old countryman, sweet as a nut, his knowledge and love of plants flooding

away any inhibitions he may have had about talking to the British public; he did it as if in the potting shed with an old friend. There was also a Hybrid Tea bearing his name raised by Kordes and introduced by Wheatcroft in 1955. I managed to find and grow it for him after it had been generally dropped, in response to an appeal when he was in his nineties.

This other 'Fred Streeter' is presumably a seedling of *R. moyesii rosea,* although that is not certain for it may have been from *R. moyesii;* it was raised in Petworth in Sussex where he was head gardener; and was for a time known as 'Petworth'. The flowers are bright cherry pink, the hips very fine, and the growth is more compact than in most types of *R. moyesii.* It was introduced in 1951 by George Jackman & Son of Woking in Surrey, at that time a general nursery with a particularly good reputation for Clematis.

'Geranium' *Taller Red Midsummer*   P2   H10   *****
If we wish *R. moyesii* to be red, and of manageable shrubby growth, we have the best form of it here. We may have a quiet smile at the name, for the variety came from the Royal Horticultural Society's famous gardens in Wisley, Surrey; and although no such rule existed at the time, they ought to have known better than to give a rose the name of another plant. Some purists seek to veil that solecism by calling it 'Geranium Red', but merely fall into the arms of Eugene Boerner, who introduced a Floribunda of that name in 1947.

This excellent form is no doubt a seedling of *R. moyesii,* and was introduced in 1938. The hips are glorious, abundant and plump, painted in sealing wax scarlet.

R. × highdownensis *Tallest Light red Midsummer* P2 H10 ****
Probably a seedling of *R. moyesii,* just as 'Geranium'; but the pundits have dignified it as a hybrid species. The flowers are effective, the contrast of stamens and lighter red as pleasing as that within the darker *R. moyesii.* The hips are truly magnificent, being larger, darker red and more bristly than in most forms of *R. moyesii.* A fine plant, handsome in leaf, needing a little more space than 'Fred Streeter' and 'Geranium'. It was raised in Highdown, the garden of Sir Frederick Stern of Goring-by-Sea, Sussex, and was introduced in 1928.

R. × pruhoniciana *Tallest Crimson Midsummer* P2 H10 ***
A noble plant, given the space it needs. It has much of the typical *R. moyesii* habit, of going high; but it arches over to redeem itself, making a pretty tracery of leaves and stems through which the view is not hidden. This open habit is common to all the derivatives from *R. moyesii,* and best disguised in 'Geranium' and 'Sealing Wax'.

The flowers are darker than those of *R. moyesii,* and are something to be remembered. The hips are good, but not always as numerous as one might wish. This is thought to be a hybrid of *R. moyesii,* the other parent being somewhat speculative, with *R. multibracteata* the current favourite.

'Sealing Wax' *Taller Pink Midsummer* P2 H10 **
The name describes the hips; and fine though they are, I think one does better to plant 'Geranium'. The two were raised at Wisley and introduced by the Royal Horticultural Society in 1938.

R. × wintoniensis *Tallest Pink Midsummer* P2 H8
If the parentage is correct, this hybrid might yet prove to be important. It is given as

R. moyesii × *R. setipoda.* Most of its character is *R. moyesii,* plus the Sweet Briar scent of *R. setipoda's* leaves; or shall we say a hint of it, for I do not notice it without some hopeful nasal research. Introduced by Hilliers in 1935, and named for their home town, Winchester.

SPECIES continued

R. multibracteata *Tall Pink Summer* P3 H3 *
The rose of many bracts; which may be seen as pale modified leaves beneath the flowers. This is a dainty rose, with countless little round leaflets on the thin stems. The flowers are of matching size, small stars of pink with yellow stamens. A charming shrub, head high or more, well rounded; placed near plants with broad leaves, it stands to advantage from the contrast. The hips are small, and not particularly noticeable. It comes from Western China.

 R. multibracteata is fairly late in flowering, and is quoted as having been introduced into Herr Tantau's breeding line, from which some ten generations later came 'Super Star'. It is therefore blamed for the tendency of some modern roses to be late in flowering. This may not be quite fair. The late flowering is in part associated with the amount of growth that some of those roses have to make first; and as far as I know, we do not have inside information from Tantau's breeding records to show the progression from *R. multibracteata* to his late hybrids.

 One of these hybrids is 'Cerise Bouquet', said to be raised by Wilhelm Kordes from *R. multibracteata* × 'Crimson Glory', and introduced in 1958. It is a tall arching bush, with semi-double flowers of the nature one might expect of its name; and it certainly has the bracts. I questioned Herr Kordes about this rose, and was told it was not his at all, but one of Herr Tantau's. Herr Tantau was apparently not at all pleased to learn it had been introduced; I was politely asked not to grow it.

R. muriculata R. murielae R. nanothamnus R. nutkana
R. muriculata is probably a form of *R. nutkana.* The flowers are lilac pink, and it comes from British Columbia and south to California. *R. murielae* is Chinese, and has grey green leaves, white flowers. It is a more dependable species in cultivation than *R. fedtschenkoana,* should one require a wild rose with greyish leaves. *R. nanothamnus* is a pretty species, like a short growing *R. webbiana.* Dr Andrew Roberts has investigated its system of reproduction, with the surprising conclusion that it behaves so much after the style of the Caninae that it should be classed with them. It comes from China and central Asia. *R. nutkana* is American, from the western seaboard, and inland to Wyoming. It was used for a while as a stock for standard roses, or tree roses to use the American term. It is pink, and has a good show of hips.

R. pendulina *Medium* + *Red Early summer* P3 H7
One of the more handsome European wild roses, from the south and centre of the continent. It is known as the Alpine Rose from its habitats, and is particularly unusual on account of having few thorns. The flowers are light purple red; the stems are also purple when young, and arch over. The hips are handsome, not in the class of *R. moyesii,* but good. It is one of the species which looks as if it should be useful to breeders, without actually proving so. By tradition, it is a parent of the Boursaults, although this cannot be taken for certain; and of the Scotch rose, 'Mrs Colville'.

PENDULINA HYBRIDS
BOURSAULTS

The Boursaults arose in France early in the nineteenth century; they are yet another evidence of the China Rose's power to mate with western roses, although we cannot be perfectly certain which western rose was the partner in this case. The general opinion is *R. pendulina*, arrived at because the surviving Boursaults are so thornless as to suggest a parent of the same character, and therefore point to *R. pendulina*. In truth, there is no proof that the China Rose was involved, other than by comparing appearances; but the foliage was sufficient to convince most rosarians.

Unlike the fruitful partnerships which occured about the same time or later, and yielded Portlands, Noisettes and Bourbons from three different continents, the Boursaults were sterile; as first generation hybrids between a remontant and a non-remontant rose, they were none of them remontant; and their sterility prevented any trial for remontancy in subsequent generations.

They have an official name, *R.* × *l'heritierana;* a hybrid species title which in theory covers the similar seedlings expected from a cross of two pure species; but which, as we have realized long ago, means nothing if one of the species is not pure, for then the seedlings are all different, and no plant exists to claim the name. And in a great many cases among roses, one of the parents is not a pure species, the China Rose being a prominent example. The name *R.* × *l'heritierana* was derived from the name of a French botanist, Charles L'Héritier. The class name was after Henri Boursault, also a French botanist; for some time the term *R. boursaultii* was used.

'Mme. de Sancy de Parabère'   *Climber   Pink   Midsummer*   P3   H1
I take this as the best survivor of the Boursaults. It is a pleasant Climber, with loosely formed double flowers of a gentle rose pink. The wood is smooth. Its origin has usually stood to the credit of A. Bonnet & Fils of Nantes, with the introduction as 1874. But in the *Rose Annual 1973,* E. F. Allen points out that a French record in 1885 states that the rose had been in cultivation forty years already. (See the *Journal des Roses* of August 1885.) It will generally be discovered in the records without the first 'de' in its name. August Jäger adds a snippet of information, namely that it had the synonym 'Virginian Lass'.

'Morlettii'   *Taller   Pink   Early summer*   P2   H1
Known for many years as 'Inermis Morlettii', which means Morlet's Thornless. The stems suggest that *R. pendulina* is one parent; for although they are brown rather than purple, they have the same smooth look about them. Some authorities equate this rose with the previous one, but in the specimens I have seen, this is more of a shrub, its pink flowers are smaller, and its wood is a deeper colour. August Jäger suggests one parent may have been a Noisette. Credited to Morlet of Avon, France in 1883.

SPECIES & VARIETIES continued

R. persetosa   R. pinetorum   R. pisocarpa   R. prattii   R. pyrifera
R. persetosa has been considered a variety or hybrid of *R. macrophylla.* It came from western China in about 1895, and has pink flowers. *R. pinetorum* is perhaps a hybrid of *R. nutkana;* I have not met it, but learn that its flowers are pink. *R. pisocarpa* is amusing, for its name means that its hips are like peas, and so they roughly are for size, although not in colour. The little bunches of hips are notably varied in colour,

from greenish yellow to red. It is a pleasant bush, growing upwards first, and then reaching out and down to the ground. It comes from the Pacific coastal region of North America, from Alaska to California. *R. prattii* is Chinese, I do not know it as I should, the descriptions read like a cross between *R. multibracteata* and *R. macrophylla. R. pyrifera* is the rose with fruit like pears. The flowers are white, which is a disappointment to me, as the one I know is lilac pink, and presumably an error. The hybrid rose with remarkable fruit to fit this description is 'Herbstfeuer' from Kordes in 1961, a red shrub of no great floral beauty, but enormous hips. It surely has no affinity with *R. pyrifera,* but for want of knowledge of its parents it is difficult to assign it to its right place. *R. pyrifera* comes from the Rocky Mountains.

R. rugosa *Tall Lilac pink Remontant* −
The original species is officially named *R. rugosa typica* or *R. rugosa rugosa.* Its identity, however, is only approximate, because successive sowings of seeds have thrown up varied progeny; such seedlings are of use if some kind of naturalized planting is desired, especially in coastal areas, as *R. rugosa* is normally willing to grow near the sea. For gardens, however, the selected forms or hybrids are much better, especially as budded plants, whereby their natural desire to sucker is controlled.

R. rugosa typica and most of its forms are marked by valuable attributes in leaf, flower and fruit. The leaves are large and wrinkled (the Latin for a wrinkle is *ruga*), making the plants into a solid block; they are more resistant to the usual fungus diseases than any other rose. The flowers are large for a wild rose, and in most cases continue to arrive spasmodically over a period of several months. The hips are like small tomatoes, and ripen quickly.

Such valuable tendencies ought to establish Rugosas in popular favour, but they somehow miss being loved as they deserve; how can one say why? Does the solidity of the plant fail to express the ethereal nature of the rose? Does consistency in performance detract from the rose's charm of transience? Are roses so much treasured for cutting their flowers, that *R. rugosa's* inutility in that respect excludes it from gardens? It awaits our approval, hardy, healthy, early in leaf, yellow at leaf fall, fragrant, showing flower and hips for successive months.

R. rugosa typica should be expected to have flowers of light rosy lilac. It is still known in some quarters as *R. regeliana;* I recently heard Australian growers using that name. The close set bristly thorns on the pale young growths earned it the name *R. ferox.* Its vernacular names are Rugosa Rose, Japanese Rose and Ramanas Rose. I must have asked a hundred rosarians over the years to tell me what Ramanas means, without finding one who knew. I published the question in a British gardening magazine in vain. Perhaps some reader can enlighten me.

It comes from north China, Korea and Japan, and reached England from Japan about 1796. I have used the term remontant minus, because although Rugosas may be in flower from early summer to autumn, it is not the whole bush which flowers a second time, but later shoots arriving in a haphazard way.

R. rugosa alba *Tall White Remontant* − P6 H7 ***
Five blushing petals open as white as snow, very beautiful with the yellow stamens in the centre. The hips are large and red, of typical Rugosa style, like slightly flattened small tomatoes. The dense leaves cover a handsome, rounded bush. Be warned of inferior forms of this lovely rose, however. All nurserymen who grow it ought to check their stock, to ensure that it has not deteriorated into flowers and hips smaller than they ought to be.

R. rugosa rubra   *Tall   Purple red   Remontant* –   P6   H7   ******
A collection of red forms of Rugosa ought to be made, to purify the present stocks. This variety is set down as *typica* by some authorities and *atropurpurea* by others. It seems to me that *typica* should be paler, *rubra* more purple and *scabrosa* more mauve; this leaves *atropurpurea* as a darker form of *rubra* in theory, but it is another thing to locate it. Some splendid forms of *rubra* exist, with large flowers coloured like claret, with a dash of purple in it; and the contrast of the dusty yellow stamens is astonishing in its effectiveness.

RUGOSA HYBRIDS AND SELECTIONS
'Blanc Double de Coubert'   *Tall   White   Remontant* –   P5   H1
This rose has been praised too much, for the reason that few double Rugosas have appeared to challenge it. The double white flowers are not so handsome as to please a florist, a difficult feat from their stance upon the thin prickly stems of a Rugosa. The petals are thin, easily spoiled by rain; and the bushes are not so well covered in leaves as are most Rugosas. The flowers are fragrant, smelling of Woolworth's cold cream according to a lady named Margaret Folliard in the *Rose Bulletin 1976*. They result in no hips. If one wants a double white rose, I see no point in planting this one for it, far better to have 'Margaret Merril'. Coubert was the village in France where the raiser lived, by name Cochet-Cochet, who introduced the rose in 1892; the parentage stated was *R. rugosa* × 'Sombreuil', the latter a Tea. But we cannot pass that without some comment.

A peculiar difficulty in breeding with *R. rugosa* is that the species and the types similar to it are in great haste to shed their pollen. I had 'Frau Dagmar Hartopp' and 'Scabrosa' in my breeding house for some years, and we rarely intervened sufficiently early to prevent the pollen from falling on the stigmas. By the time the buds were large enough to handle, the pollen was already being ejected. We therefore used Rugosas as pollen parents, not for seed, but obtained little from them, in common with nearly all other breeders. Upon being mated with other roses, their sterling qualities vanished with the first generation, and I never succeeded in recalling their health and vigour subsequently. Yet I am convinced that the Rugosas cannot be a blind alley. We badly need their health, and to know why they resist mildew, blackspot and rust so efficiently. Is the top leaf skin too tough, or the downy underside too impermeable for the disease to grow? Does their sap repel fungi, and if so by what means? Some researcher could make his name by answering those questions, and some breeder could become the Pernet-Ducher of his age by channelling the health of Rugosas into modern roses. Not all Rugosa Hybrids are healthy. The famous 'Conrad Ferdinand Meyer', of lovely large pale pink flowers, is the fastest rose I know to cover its leaves with rust on their undersides.

As to the parentage of 'Blanc Double de Coubert', we have to recognize the possibility that it may have been a seedling of *R. rugosa alba*, with no Tea in it at all.

'F. J. Grootendorst'   *Tall   Red   Remontant* –   P2   H1
In 1891, M. Morlet of Avon in France introduced a Rugosa named 'Fimbriata'. Its petals were frilled, and on that account it was also called 'Dianthiflora' and 'Phoebe's Frilled Pink'. The parentage was supposed to be *R. rugosa* × 'Mme Alfred Carrière'; and whether that was accurate or not, it is certainly a Rugosa. The same tendency to produce frilled petals occurred in the Rugosas again in Holland in 1918, when F. J. Grootendorst & Sons of Boskoop introduced the rose bearing their name, which they had from a Mr de Goey. It is said to be from *R. rugosa rubra* × a Polyantha, probably

'Mme Norbert Levavasseur'; and this is credible, as the flowers are Polyantha size. It is red, with clusters of small flowers, and petal edges indented in a remarkable way. The plants are upright, with foliage akin to the Rugosas, but smaller. It is not a pleasing plant, by reason of its dull red colour according ill with the foliage. But it gave rise to a pink sport which is far more pleasing, and follows shortly as 'Pink Grootendorst'. A darker red sport was introduced in 1936 as 'Grootendorst Supreme'. We note this strange quirk of frilled petals lies within roses, not only the Rugosas, but also in *R. chinensis serratipetala*.

'Frau Dagmar Hartopp' *Medium − Pink Remontant −* P6 H8 ****
One of the most beautiful Rugosas, with wide single flowers of a particularly delicate pink. The hips are deep red and handsome; the growth is unusually short for the class. Very pleasantly fragrant. This is a delightful plant to grow; and it may be propagated by seed, which germinates easily and usually comes true. Known also as 'Fru Dagmar Hastrup.'

'Hollandica' *Taller Lilac pink Remontant −* P5 H4
No garden plant this, except from the accident that it was the rootstock to a dead guest, whose place it has usurped. It is a gaunt plant of many suckers, with light lilac-pink flowers whose colour gives little pleasure. Many people take it for the original wild *R. rugosa,* but the Dutch stock growers disagree. They say it was raised about 1888 by J. Spek of Boskoop from seeds of *R. rugosa,* and is thought to be a hybrid either with *R. cinnamomeae* or 'Manettii'. It is also known in Holland as 'Scherpe Boskoop' and 'Boskoopse Rugosa'. For many years it has been stock in trade to the nurserymen of Boskoop, who root it from cuttings, and then lead the best shoot up a cane for two years, to make standard stems, chiefly for export to British nurseries. One can also use cuttings as rootstocks for bush roses, and it promotes bush growth in the maiden year. Mr Treseder of Cardiff used to grow some roses on it in order to obtain mighty blooms for the summer show; and several nurserymen used it for their 'Mermaid' after finding other stocks incompatible with that temperamental climber.

Having been propagated by cuttings since 1888, it is beset by virus, which the Dutch growers take much pains to eradicate. I have seen many good plants grown on 'Hollandica'; but it is not on my shopping list for rootstocks.

R. × paulii *Trailer White Midsummer* P6 H1
An extraordinary plant, extraordinarily unpleasant in my opinion, which grows outwards upon the ground, and builds up higher at the centre, something like a thicket of brambles. Those who plant it for ground cover receive what they asked for, and will ever after enter its premises with difficulty, for its thorns are fearsome. The foliage is pale and dull; the white single flowers bespangle the plant in summer, and are large enough to make a brave show, disguising briefly the ungainly mass beneath. Personally I would just as soon plant brambles as this, one can at least eat their fruit. From Paul & Son, Cheshunt, some time prior to 1903. It is considered to be a hybrid between *R. arvensis* and *R. rugosa*.

R. × paulii rosea *Trailer Pink Midsummer* P6 H1
A pink version of the foregoing, its flowers much more beautiful; of similar habit to *R. × paulii,* but slightly less vigorous. It is presumably a sport from *R. × paulii.* The sites for these two roses do not exist in the average garden; perhaps in some glade of a wild garden they could be at home.

'Pink Grootendorst' *Tall Pink Remontant* – P2 H1 *
The pink sport referred to under 'F. J. Grootendorst'; the fimbriated flowers are a quaint novelty to those who have not seen them; and this rose, unlike most other Rugosas, is useful for cutting. Introduced by F. J. Grootendorst & Sons in 1923.

'Roseraie de l'Haÿ' *Taller Purple Remontant* – P4 H1**
At first sight the colour is an outrage, purple against bright green leaves; but this variety softens the senses, because it commits the outrage with aplomb, and looks so pleased with itself, as if the double purple flowers have every right to toss in the sun, and are really close confederates of the foliage. A fine upright shrub, pleasantly fragrant, but with no hips to follow the flowers. At the Royal National Rose Society's gardens, a long and triumphant hedge of it overpowers its neighbours in the border. From M. Jules Gravereaux, the Frenchman who did so much to make the Parisian rose gardens at l'Haÿ and Bagatelle. It is probably a hybrid from *R. rugosa rubra,* and not a sport of *R. rugosa rosea* as is usually suggested. Messrs Cochet-Cochet introduced it in 1902.
     Incidentally, there is an uninteresting cherry red Rugosa Hybrid called 'Rose à Parfum de l'Haÿ'; it would be a pity to buy it in error.

'Scabrosa' *Taller Mauve red Remontant* P8 H8 *****
A splendid shrub, the most remontant of the Rugosas, with all their virtues of healthy foliage and fragrance. The plants are bold wide things, early in leaf. I had one in a previous home, which flowered first on Easter Saturday in April, and continued without missing a day in bloom until 29th September; and although I could not vouch for the fortnight we were away in August, I have no doubt it was flowering then. The hips are large and red. I think my plant of 'Scabrosa' was one of the most rewarding plants I ever owned. I felt grieved to leave it when we moved in 1961, but am glad to notice that it is still going strong.
     Rugosas cause one some problems in pruning, because after a few years some of the older shoots, especially to the sides of the plant, become lax as the new growths weigh them down. One hesitates to cut, for fear of making the plant bare at the base; for the lush foliage down to the ground is one of their pleasing features. The only answer is to harden your heart and cut into the old wood, trusting the plant to re-furnish itself in a couple of years.
     The rich colour of 'Scabrosa' is dark in the young flower, lighter upon expansion. The dusty stamens are a ring of light in the young blooms. Having described it as mauve red, I must leave my readers to digest that unknown dish, for I have no power to express it more clearly. Graham Thomas says 'violaceous crimson', The Royal National Rose Society 'mauve pink', Gordon Edwards 'rosy magenta'.
     One of the best rose hedges I have ever seen is made from 'Scabrosa', at the front of the Royal National Rose Society's gardens. The ground is slightly raised, so that motorists, if they dare take their eyes from the road, would look straight to the base of the plants. The requirement was therefore that the chosen variety should clothe itself to the grass, and never get blackspot. 'Scabrosa' proved a perfect choice in both respects.
     Its origin is a mystery, and I fear my firm is guilty of that. We had it for many years, and before the 1939 war, it was confused with a semi-double variety from Paul & Son known as 'Rose Apples'. Having segregated the two, which were so distinct that they should never have been mixed, we eventually discarded 'Rose Apples', and kept this one as being much more beautiful. Of course we did not know its name, and

whenever we had a botanically minded visitor, Bill Harkness would enquire if he could identify it. Somebody eventually came up with the name, but it riles me that I never learned who it was. I have a hazy idea that Thomas Hilling took it away to show to Graham Thomas. I did not much like the name 'Scabrosa'. It means rough to the touch; and I do not know the grounds for the identification. Our name stands under it in *Modern Roses* as introducers, but we do not deserve much credit for it.

'Schneezwerg' *Tall* − *White Remontant* P5 H4

The Snow Dwarf is not so small as he sounds, for he grows chest high quite easily. The leaves betray the fact that here is no true Rugosa, but a hybrid. Unlike most Rugosa hybrids, it has kept its health and hardiness, but at the considerable cost of losing most of the beauty of the leaves, which are dull and pale. The flowers are semi-double, white, helped a good deal by their yellow stamens; they are attractive in form, and very freely borne. The whole ensemble, highly praised by many, is not to my liking. Raised by Peter Lambert of Trier in Germany; the parentage is the subject of much speculation, for while everyone is agreed that some form of *R. rugosa* is one half of it, guesses about the other range from *R. bracteata* to a Polyantha. But what about 'Trier' itself? It was introduced in 1912.

SPECIES & VARIETIES continued

R. salictorum R. saturata R. sertata

R. salictorum comes from Idaho and Nevada; it is pink, something like *R. woodsii*. Its hips seem to be late ripening in Britain, they are still green well into autumn. *R. saturata* is after the style of *R. moyesii,* from China. Its flowers are pink, and its hips coral pink. *R. sertata* is also Chinese; I am not confident of identifying this species; Miss Wilmott says it is white, Graham Thomas pink with a white centre, whilst Roy Shepherd's is rose-purple.

R. setipoda *Taller Pink Midsummer* P6 H9 **

The species which we might call the Chinese Sweet Briar, because its leaves share that pleasant attribute with the European *R. eglanteria,* although not quite so strongly. The name refers to its bristly flower stalks and hips; and it has had an alias, *R. macrophylla crasseaculeata;* the long word at the end describes the bristles as thick needles.

A handsome plant, with beautiful long hips like those of *R. moyesii.* The flowers are light pink, paler at the centre, and well decorated by yellow stamens.

R. sonomensis R. spaldingii R. spithamea R. suffulta R. ultramontana

The first three of these are rare, and are not known to me. *R. sonomensis* is likened to a dwarf form of *R. californica;* which would not surprise me, because it is possible to grow *R. californica* as a dwarf, by pruning it hard and putting it under glass. It responds by flowering profusely before it does much growing. *R. californica* will also yield a number of dwarf plants among its hybrids.

R. spaldingii comes from North America, or rather stays there; it is said to resemble *R. nutkana. R. spithamea* is said to be allied to *R. californica. R. suffulta* is of more interest. It is a short, thorny bush native to a large area in central North America, and bears flowers of bright lilac rose. Roy Shepherd reports that in its native habitat, it blooms both from new and old wood; and it would thus have some promise of remontancy. We have it at the Royal National Rose Society's gardens, and although I have looked for this tendency, it has not been very obvious. *R. ultramontana* is an American species which takes after *R. californica.*

R. sweginzowii *Tallest   Pink   Midsummer*   P4   H10   **

Although obviously named by a botanist, rather than by a nurseryman with the prospect of selling it in his mind, this mouthful when translated into the growing plant is well worth the effort to pronounce it. The hips are red as loganberries polished brightly, of the lovely flagon shape we met in *R. macrophylla* and *R. moyesii*. They are not quite so long, but equally spectacular. The flowers are bright pink, and the bushes have a formidable armoury of thorns and bristles. It came from north-west China about 1909.

R. webbiana *Tall   Pink   Midsummer*   P4   H5   ****

Might be called the Fairy Queen of the wild roses for its sweetness and grace. The plant grows about head high, and trails its older shoots down to the ground, all neatly, in the shape of a graceful lady in lacy crinolines. Lace is the right word too for an impression of the tiny leaves and dark twigs. The little flowers are all delicacy in their pink petals and discreetly attractive perfume. Finally the hips adorn the bush in the autumn, in the shape of ewers held upside-down. They are not large, for nothing about *R. webbiana* is aggressive; their size is sufficient to attract notice and hold admiration.

R. *webbiana* is a Himalayan species, and will not enjoy too much exposure in cold places, therefore plant it where it has some shelter from the wind.

R. willmottiae *Tall   Pink   Midsummer*   P4   H4   **

Like *R. multibracteata* with more of *R. webbiana's* grace. The leaves are small, the twigs thin, the flowers bright pink and small. The plant grows into a wide rounded bush, and can be a splendid feature in the garden, if carefully placed so that its small leaves have something broad and solid nearby. Too many small leafed plants together can look fussy, whereas they should look fresh and dainty, which they best do by contrast. *R. willmottiae* was raised in London from seed collected in south-west China, near Tibet.

R. woodsii fendleri *Tall   Pink   Late spring*   P3   H7   **

The species, *R. woodsii,* is little known in cultivation, this variety being considered superior. Both are natives of North America, approximately from British Columbia to Texas, the species itself being less likely to be found at the southern end of the range. *R. woodsii fendleri* has lilac pink flowers without the harshness sometimes concealed under that description. It makes a rounded bush, well covered in leaves; the hips in the autumn are usually in great abundance, round, bright red and persistent.

Having arrived at the end of my story, I am aware that I could go back to the beginning, which I have done often enough after walking round a rose garden. So many old friends, rosaceous and human, arise as rebukes in my mind upon their omission. I stand to be reviled by the botanists for what I have said about rose names; to be attacked by the exhibitors whose sport I have criticized; to be squashed by the lovers of 'Mme Isaac Pereire'; to be accused of neglect of modern roses; and to be confounded by evidence of error, which I cannot hope to have escaped entirely, for in that case I should be a unique rose author.

The truth is often harsher than one hopes for, and kinder than one fears. What I hope for is that this book may have magnified your love and understanding of the rose.

18. The Heights

The remainder of this book consists of some tables for helpful reference. For a start, one needs some idea of how plants will grow; otherwise the simplest of plans cannot promise success. Not that success is certain in any event, because plants do not come tailor made, but follow their own sweet individual way of growth, often very different from what was expected.

It must therefore be accepted that no matter what heights are given for roses, variations are apt to occur. And it is no use applying a ruler to express their height in inches or centimetres, because they may double or halve it in response to their environment. For that reason I have used comparative terms instead of measurements.

Height alone is insufficient information. Width is even more important, because without some idea of it, we can have no notion of how close the plants should be. I have therefore marked the more upright growers U, and the more spreading ones S. As an approximate guide, expect those marked U to restrict their spread to their own height or less; and those marked S to stretch sideways over an area twice their height or more. The absence of U and S denotes that the variety is midway between them.

The plus and minus signs indicate which roses may be expected the taller or shorter of their various categories. Some of these differences I thought insufficient to record in their descriptions; but as these lists may be a basis for choosing roses, it seems in order to tune in a little more accurately. In the classes shown, the word species covers both species and (supposed) botanical varieties.

The roses in this list are those which bear stars in this book; and before arriving at them, I remind you that a desired height can be assured by growing standard or tree roses; and by training climbers on pillars or other supports.

SHORTEST

'Baby Faurax'			Polyantha
'Baby Masquerade'			Miniature
'Cinderella'			Miniature
'Darling Flame' ('Minuetto')	+		Miniature
'Easter Morning'			Miniature
'Little Flirt'	+		Miniature
'New Penny'			Miniature
'Perla de Alcanada' ('Baby Crimson')	+	S	Miniature
'Perle de Montserrat'			Miniature
'Pour Toi'			Miniature
'Rosina' ('Josephine Wheatcroft')			Miniature
'Starina'			Miniature

SHORTER

'Andrewsii'			Spinosissima Hybrid
'Cécile Brunner'	+		Hybrid China
Hulthemia persica		S	Species
'Katharina Zeimet'			Polyantha
'Marie Pavié'			Polyantha
'Marlena'	−		Floribunda
'Meteor'	−		Floribunda
'Perle d'Or'			Hybrid China
R. stellata mirifica	+		Species
'William III'	−		Spinosissima Hybrid

SHORT

'Dr A. J. Verhage' ('Golden Wave')			Hybrid Tea
'Gruss an Aachen'	+		Floribunda
× *Hulthemosa hardii*			Persica Hybrid
'Josephine Bruce'			Hybrid Tea
'Little White Pet'			Sempervirens Hybrid
'Nathalie Nypels'			Floribunda
'National Trust'			Hybrid Tea
R. carolina plena			Species
R. chinensis viridiflora			Species
R. nitida			Species
'Spong'			Centifolia
'Violinista Costa'	+		Hybrid Tea
'Williams' Double Yellow'			Spinosissima Hybrid
'Yvonne Rabier'			Floribunda

MEDIUM

'Alec's Red'			Hybrid Tea
'Allgold'	−		Floribunda
'Baccara'	+	U	Hybrid Tea
'Ballerina'	+	S	Polyantha
'Belle de Crécy'	+	S	Gallica
'Betty Uprichard'	+	U	Hybrid Tea
'Blue Moon' ('Mainzer Fastnacht')		U	Hybrid Tea
'Buff Beauty'	+	S	Hybrid Musk
'Camaieux'	−	S	Gallica
'Cardinal de Richelieu'	+		Gallica
'Chapeau de Napoleon' ('Crested Moss')			Centifolia
'Charles de Mills'		U	Gallica
'Charlotte Armstrong'			Hybrid Tea
'Dainty Bess'		U	Hybrid Tea
'Dainty Maid'	+		Floribunda
'Double White'			Spinosissima Hybrid
'Elizabeth Harkness'			Hybrid Tea
'Ena Harkness'	−	U	Hybrid Tea
'Escapade'	+		Floribunda
'Felicia'	+		Hybrid Musk
'Félicité Parmentier'	+		Alba

'First Love'		U	Hybrid Tea
'Fragrant Cloud' ('Duftwolke')	–		Hybrid Tea
'Frau Dagmar Hartopp'	–	S	Rugosa Hybrid
'Général Schablikine'			Tea
'Gloire de France'		S	Gallica
'Golden Dawn'		S	Hybrid Tea
'Grandpa Dickson' ('Irish Gold')	–	U	Hybrid Tea
'Honeymoon'		U	Floribunda
'Iceberg' ('Schneewittchen')	+		Floribunda
'John Waterer'	+	U	Hybrid Tea
'Just Joey'	–		Hybrid Tea
'Kaiserin Auguste Viktoria'			Hybrid Tea
'Kordes' Perfecta'			Hybrid Tea
'Laneii'			Moss
'Margaret Merril'			Floribunda
'Marjorie Fair'	+	S	Polyantha
'Masquerade'			Floribunda
'Michèle Meilland'			Hybrid Tea
'Mischief'			Hybrid Tea
'Mojave'		U	Hybrid Tea
'Montezuma'	+		Hybrid Tea
'Mozart'	+	S	Polyantha
'Mrs Colville'	–		Spinosissima Hybrid
'Mrs John Laing'	+	S	Hybrid Perpetual
'Old Blush' ('Monthly Rose')	–		Hybrid China
'Ophelia'		U	Hybrid Tea
'Paddy McGredy'	–		Floribunda
'Pascali'		U	Hybrid Tea
'Penelope'		S	Hybrid Musk
'Petite de Hollande'	+		Centifolia
'Piccadilly'	–		Hybrid Tea
'Pink Favourite'		U	Hybrid Tea
'Pink Parfait'			Floribunda
'Polly'	–		Hybrid Tea
'Precious Platinum'	+		Hybrid Tea
'Président de Sèze'	+		Gallica
'Priscilla Burton'			Floribunda
'Rob Roy'		U	Floribunda
R. chinensis mutabilis ('Tipo Ideale')	+	S	Species
R. foliolosa			Species
R. gallica versicolor ('Rosa Mundi')	–		Species
R. roxburghii (Chestnut Rose)		S	Species
R. roxburghii normalis (Single Chestnut Rose)		S	Species
'Rose Gaujard'			Hybrid Tea
'Rudolph Timm'	+		Floribunda
'Shot Silk'	–		Hybrid Tea
'Silver Jubilee'	–		Hybrid Tea

'Sonia Meilland' ('Sweet Promise')	U	Hybrid Tea
'Southampton'	+	Floribunda
'Souvenir de la Malmaison'		Bourbon
'Spartan'	+	Floribunda
'Stanwell Perpetual'	S	Spinosissima Hybrid
'Super Star' ('Tropicana')	+ U	Hybrid Tea
'Surpasse Tout'	S	Gallica
'Sutter's Gold'		Hybrid Tea
'The Fairy'		Wichuraiana Hybrid
'Wendy Cussons'	+	Hybrid Tea
'Whisky Mac'	– U	Hybrid Tea
'Yesterday'	+ S	Polyantha

TALL

'Alexander'		Hybrid Tea
'Arthur Bell'	U	Floribunda
'Belinda'		Polyantha
'Blanche Moreau'	– U	Moss
'Bloomfield Abundance'	S	Hybrid China
'Boule de Neige'		Bourbon
'Bourbon Queen'		Bourbon
'Bullata'	S	Centifolia
'Canary Bird'	+ S	Xanthina Hybrid
'Celestial'	S	Alba
'Celsiana'	S	Damask
'Common Moss'	– U	Moss
'Doncasterii'	S	Macrophylla Hybrid
'Frensham'	S	Floribunda
'Frühlingsmorgen'	S	Spinosissima Hybrid
'Golden Wings'	– S	Spinosissima Hybrid
'Jacques Cartier'	S	Portland
'Kiese'	+ S	Canina Hybrid
'Königin von Danemarck'		Alba
'Lady Penzance'	S	Eglanteria Hybrid
'Mme Pierre Oger'	U	Bourbon
'Moonlight'	+	Hybrid Musk
'New Dawn'	+ S	Wichuraiana Hybrid
'Peace' ('Mme A. Meilland')	S	Hybrid Tea
'Pink Grootendorst'	U	Rugosa Hybrid
'Pompon Blanc Parfait'	S	Alba
'President Herbert Hoover'	U	Hybrid Tea
'Prosperity'		Hybrid Musk
'Quatre Saisons'	S	Damask
'Quatre Saisons Blanc Mousseux'	S	Damask
'Red Devil'	S	Hybrid Tea
'Roger Lambelin'		Hybrid Perpetual
R. californica		Species
R. × *dupontii*	S	Moschata Hybrid
R. foetida bicolor		
('Austrian Copper')	– S	Species

R × *francofurtana*	–	S	Gallica Hybrid
R. multibracteata		S	Species
R. primula (Incense Rose)	–	S	Species
R. rugosa alba	–	S	Species
R. rugosa rubra		S	Species
R. spinosissima altaica			Species
R. spinosissima hispida	+	S	Species
R. virginiana	–	S	Species
R. webbiana			Species
R. willmottiae		S	Species
R. woodsii fendleri		S	Species
'Rose d'Amour'	–	S	Virginiana Hybrid
'Tuscany'		U	Gallica
'Tuscany Superb'		U	Gallica
'William Lobb'			Moss

TALLER

'Complicata'		S	Macrantha
'Cornelia'	–	S	Hybrid Musk
'Frau Karl Druschki'			Hybrid Perpetual
'Fred Streeter'		S	Moyesii Hybrid
'Fritz Nobis'		S	Eglanteria Hybrid
'Frühlingsgold'	+	S	Spinosissima Hybrid
'Geranium'		S	Moyesii Hybrid
'Golden Chersonese'			Ecae Hybrid
'Janet's Pride'			Eglanteria Hybrid
'Madame Hardy'		S	Damask
'Maiden's Blush'		S	Alba
'Marguerite Hilling'		S	Spinosissima Hybrid
'Maxima'		S	Alba
'Mme Legras de St Germain'		S	Alba
'Nevada'		S	Spinosissima Hybrid
'Queen Elizabeth'		U	Floribunda
R. cantabrigiensis		S	Hugonis Hybrid
R. ecae		U	Species
R. farreri persetosa		S	Species
R. hugonis		S	Species
R. pomifera		S	Species
R. rubrifolia		U	Species
R. sericea pteracantha	+	S	Species
R. setipoda		S	Species
'Roseraie de l'Haÿ'		S	Rugosa Hybrid
'Scabrosa'		S	Rugosa Hybrid
'Semi-plena'		S	Alba

TALLEST

R. caudata		S	Species
R. × *highdownensis*		S	Moyesii Hybrid
R. macrophylla		S	Species
R. macrophylla rubricaulis		S	Species

R. moyesii	S	Species
R. moyesii rosea	S	Species
R. × pruhoniciana	S	Moyesii Hybrid
R. sweginzowii	S	Species
'Scharlachglut' ('Scarlet Fire')	S	Gallica Hybrid
'Sealing Wax'	S	Moyesii Hybrid

CLIMBERS

The plus signs here indicate the comparative size of plant, from a minus sign for a small one, to five plus signs for the largest.

'Albéric Barbier'	+ + + +	Wichuraiana Hybrid
'Albertine'	+ + + +	Wichuraiana Hybrid
'Alister Stella Gray'	+ +	Noisette
'Allen Chandler'	+ + +	Climbing Hybrid Tea
'Allgold, Climbing'	+ + +	Climbing Floribunda
'Aloha'	−	Climbing Hybrid Tea
'Altissimo'	+ +	Climbing Floribunda
'Cécile Brunner, Climbing'	+ + +	Hybrid China
'Christine, Climbing'	+ +	Climbing Hybrid Tea
'Circus, Climbing'	+ +	Climbing Floribunda
'Compassion'	+ + +	Climbing Hybrid Tea
'Crimson Glory, Climbing'	+ +	Climbing Hybrid Tea
'Danse du Feu' ('Spectacular')	+ +	Climbing Floribunda
'Desprez à Fleur Jaune'	+ + +	Noisette
'Dortmund'	+ +	Kordesii Hybrid
'Dr W. van Fleet'	+ + + +	Wichuraiana Hybrid
'Easlea's Golden Rambler'	+ + +	Climbing Hybrid Tea
'Elegance'	+ + + +	Climbing Hybrid Tea
'Emily Gray'	+ + +	Wichuraiana Hybrid
'Ena Harkness, Climbing'	+ +	Climbing Hybrid Tea
'Etoile de Hollande, Climbing'	+ + +	Climbing Hybrid Tea
'Félicité et Perpétue'	+ + +	Sempervirens Hybrid
'Fortune's Double Yellow' ('Beauty of Glazenwood')	−	Hybrid China
'François Juranville'	+ + + +	Wichuraiana Hybrid
'Golden Dawn, Climbing'	+ +	Climbing Hybrid Tea
'Golden Showers'	+	Climbing Floribunda
'Goldfinch'	+	Climbing Polyantha
'Guineé'	+ + +	Climbing Hybrid Tea
'Hamburger Phoenix'	+ + +	Kordesii Hybrid
'Handel'	+ +	Climbing Floribunda
'Iceberg, Climbing'	+ + +	Climbing Floribunda
'Jersey Beauty'	+ + +	Wichuraiana Hybrid
'Lady Hillingdon, Climbing'	+	Tea
'Lawrence Johnston'	+ + +	Foetida Hybrid
'Leverkusen'	+ +	Kordesii Hybrid
'Masquerade, Climbing'	+ +	Climbing Floribunda
'May Queen'	+ +	Wichuraiana Hybrid
'Mermaid'	+ + + + +	Bracteata Hybrid

'Mme Abel Chatenay, Climbing'	+ +	Climbing Hybrid Tea
'Mme Alfred Carrière'	+ +	Noisette
'Mme Caroline Testout, Climbing'	+ + + +	Climbing Hybrid Tea
'Mme Edouard Herriot, Climbing'		
('Daily Mail, Climbing')	+	Climbing Hybrid Tea
'Mme Grégoire Staechelin'		
('Spanish Beauty')	+ + +	Climbing Hybrid Tea
'Morning Jewel'	+	Climbing Floribunda
'Mrs Pierre S. du Pont, Climbing'	+ + +	Climbing Hybrid Tea
'Mrs Sam McGredy, Climbing'	+ + +	Climbing Hybrid Tea
'Parkdirektor Riggers'	+ + +	Kordesii Hybrid
'Paul's Lemon Piller'	+ +	Climbing Hybrid Tea
'Paul's Scarlet Climber'	+ +	Climbing Polyantha
'Perla Rosa, Climbing'	−	Climbing Miniature
'Phyllis Bide'	+	Climbing Polyantha
'Pink Cameo'	−	Climbing Miniature
'Pink Perpetue'	+ +	Climbing Floribunda
'Pompon de Paris, Climbing'	+ + +	Climbing Miniature
'Ritter von Barmstede'	+ +	Kordesii Hybrid
R. banksiae alba-plena		
(Banksian White)	+ + + + +	Species
R. banksiae lutea		
(Banksian Yellow)	+ + + + +	Species
'Shot Silk, Climbing'	+ +	Climbing Hybrid Tea
'The Garland'	+ + +	Climbing Polyantha
'Vanity'	+ +	Hybrid Musk
'Veilchenblau' ('Violet Blue')	+ +	Climbing Polyantha
'Wedding Day'	+ +	Sinowilsonii Hybrid
'William Allen Richardson'	+ +	Noisette
'Zéphirine Drouhin'	+ +	Bourbon

TRAILERS

The plus signs, as for the climbers, indicate the comparative size of the plant, from a minus sign for a small one, to five plus signs for the largest.

'Crimson Shower'	+ +	Wichuraiana Hybrid
'Nozomi'	−	Climbing Miniature
R. filipes	+ + + + +	Species
R. helenae	+ + + +	Species
R. longicuspis	+ + + + +	Species
R. × macrantha	+ +	Macrantha
'Sander's White'	+ +	Wichuraiana Hybrid

19. The Colours

A guide to the roses starred in this book, in groups of similar colours.

WHITE ROSES

WHITE

'Blanche Moreau'	Moss
'Boule de Neige'	Bourbon
'Double White'	Spinosissima Hybrid
'Félicité et Perpétue'	Climber
'Frau Karl Druschki'	Hybrid Perpetual
'Iceberg' ('Schneewittchen')	Floribunda
'Iceberg, Climbing'	Climber
'Kaiserin Auguste Viktoria'	Hybrid Tea
'Katharina Zeimet'	Polyantha
'Little White Pet'	Sempervirens Hybrid
'Madame Hardy'	Damask
'Maxima'	Alba
'Mme Alfred Carrière'	Climber
'Mme Legras de St Germain'	Alba
'Nozomi'	Trailer
'Pascali'	Hybrid Tea
'Pompon Blanc Parfait'	Alba
'Pour Toi'	Miniature
'Quatre Saisons Blanc Mousseux'	Damask
R. banksiae alba-plena (Banksian White)	Climber
R. filipes	Trailer
R. helenae	Trailer
R. longicuspis	Trailer
R. rugosa alba	Species
R. sericea pteracantha	Species
R. spinosissima altaica	Species
'Sander's White'	Trailer
'Semi-plena'	Alba
'Yvonne Rabier'	Floribunda

CREAMY WHITE

'Albéric Barbier'	Climber
'Buff Beauty'	Hybrid Musk
'Desprez à Fleur Jaune'	Climber
'Easter Morning'	Miniature
'Elizabeth Harkness'	Hybrid Tea
'Gruss an Aachen'	Floribunda

'Jersey Beauty'	Climber
'Moonlight'	Hybrid Musk
'Nevada'	Spinosissima Hybrid
'Paul's Lemon Pillar'	Climber
'Prosperity'	Hybrid Musk
R. spinosissima hispida	Species

PEARLY WHITE
'Celestial'	Alba
'Cinderella'	Miniature
'Dr W. van Fleet'	Climber
'Felicia'	Hybrid Musk
'Félicité Parmentier'	Alba
'Maiden's Blush'	Alba
'Margaret Merril'	Floribunda
'New Dawn'	Wichuraiana Hybrid
'Ophelia'	Hybrid Tea
'Penelope'	Hybrid Musk
'Polly'	Hybrid Tea
R. × dupontii	Moschata Hybrid
R. × macrantha	Trailer
'Souvenir de la Malmaison'	Bourbon
'Stanwell Perpetual'	Spinosissima Hybrid
'The Garland'	Climber
'Wedding Day'	Climber

CREAMY YELLOW CHANGING TO RED
R. chinensis mutabilis	Species

GREEN ROSE
R. chinensis viridiflora	China

YELLOW ROSES

PALE YELLOW
'Elegance'	Climber
'Frühlingsgold'	Spinosissima Hybrid
'Golden Wings'	Spinosissima Hybrid
'Goldfinch'	Climber
'Mermaid'	Climber
R. × cantabrigiensis	Hugonis Hybrid
R. hugonis	Species
R. primula (Incense Rose)	Species

DEEP YELLOW
'Alister Stella Gray'	Climber
'Allgold'	Floribunda
'Allgold, Climbing'	Climber
'Arthur Bell'	Floribunda
'Canary Bird'	Xanthina Hybrid

'Christine, Climbing'	Climber
'Dr A. J. Verhage' ('Golden Wave')	Hybrid Tea
'Easlea's Golden Rambler'	Climber
'Emily Gray'	Climber
'Golden Chersonese'	Ecae Hybrid
'Golden Dawn'	Hybrid Tea
'Golden Dawn, Climbing'	Climber
'Golden Showers'	Climber
'Grandpa Dickson' ('Irish Gold')	Hybrid Tea
'Honeymoon'	Floribunda
'Lawrence Johnston'	Climber
'Leverkusen'	Climber
'Mrs Pierre S. du Pont, Climbing'	Climber
R. banksiae lutea ('Banksian Yellow')	Climber
R. ecae	Species
'Rosina' ('Josephine Wheatcroft')	Miniature
'Williams' Double Yellow'	Spinosissima Hybrid

YELLOW WITH RED EYE

Hulthemia persica	Species
× *Hulthemosa hardii*	Persica Hybrid

YELLOW WITH RED FLUSH

'Circus, Climbing'	Climber
'Fortune's Double Yellow' ('Beauty of Glazenwood')	Climber
'William Allen Richardson'	Climber

YELLOW SHADED APRICOT

'Lady Hillingdon, Climbing'	Climber
'Whisky Mac'	Hybrid Tea

YELLOW WITH PINK FLUSH

'Baby Masquerade'	Miniature
'Peace' ('Mme A. Meilland')	Hybrid Tea
'Phyllis Bide'	Climber
'Sutter's Gold'	Hybrid Tea

YELLOW CHANGING TO RED

'Masquerade'	Floribunda
'Masquerade, Climbing'	Climber

PINK ROSES

PALE PINK

'Ballerina'	Polyantha
'Belinda'	Polyantha
'Bloomfield Abundance'	Hybrid China
'Cécile Brunner'	Hybrid China
'Cécile Brunner, Climbing'	Climber
'Celsiana'	Damask
'Dainty Bess'	Hybrid Tea

'Frau Dagmar Hartopp'	Rugosa Hybrid
'Marie Pavié'	Polyantha
'Michèle Meilland'	Hybrid Tea
'Mozart'	Polyantha
'New Penny'	Miniature
'Perla de Montserrat'	Miniature
'Perle d'Or'	Hybrid China
'Quatre Saisons'	Damask
R. rubrifolia	Species
'Rudolph Timm'	Floribunda

DEEP PINK

'Aloha'	Climber
'Andrewsii'	Spinosissima Hybrid
'Bourbon Queen'	Bourbon
'Bullata'	Centifolia
'Chapeau de Napoleon' ('Crested Moss')	Centifolia
'Common Moss'	Moss
'Complicata'	Macrantha
'Cornelia'	Hybrid Musk
'Dainty Maid'	Floribunda
'First Love'	Hybrid Tea
'François Juranville'	Climber
'Fred Streeter'	Moyesii Hybrid
'Fritz Nobis'	Eglanteria Hybrid
'Frühlingsmorgen'	Spinosissima Hybrid
'Jacques Cartier'	Portland
'Königin von Danemarck'	Alba
'May Queen'	Climber
'Mme Caroline Testout, Climbing'	Climber
'Mme Grégoire Staechelin' ('Spanish Beauty')	Climber
'Morning Jewel'	Climber
'Mrs John Laing'	Hybrid Perpetual
'Nathalie Nypels'	Floribunda
'Old Blush' ('Monthly Rose')	Hybrid China
'Perla Rosa, Climbing'	Climber
'Petite de Hollande'	Centifolia
'Pink Cameo'	Climber
'Pink Favourite'	Hybrid Tea
'Pink Grootendorst'	Rugosa Hybrid
'Pink Parfait'	Floribunda
'Pink Perpetue'	Climber
'Pompon de Paris, Climbing'	Climber
'Queen Elizabeth'	Floribunda
'Ritter von Barmstede'	Climber
R. carolina plena	Species
R. farreri persetosa	Species
R. × *francofurtana*	Gallica Hybrid
R. macrophylla	Species

R. macrophylla rubricaulis	Species
R. moyesii rosea	Species
R. multibracteata	Species
R. pomifera	Species
R. roxburghii (Chestnut Rose)	Species
R. roxburghii normalis (Single Chestnut Rose)	Species
R. setipoda	Species
R. sweginzowii	Species
R. webbiana	Species
'Sealing Wax'	Moyesii Hybrid
'Spong'	Centifolia
'The Fairy'	Wichuraiana Hybrid
'Vanity'	Climber
'Zéphirine Drouhin'	Bourbon

ROSY SALMON

'Just Joey'	Hybrid Tea
'Mischief'	Hybrid Tea
'Montezuma'	Hybrid Tea
'Mrs Sam McGredy, Climbing'	Climber
'Sonia Meilland' ('Sweet Promise')	Hybrid Tea
'Spartan'	Floribunda

ROSE RED

'Charlotte Armstrong'	Hybrid Tea
'Paddy McGredy'	Floribunda
R. foliolosa	Species
R. virginiana	Species
'Rose d'Amour'	Virginiana Hybrid
'Wendy Cussons'	Hybrid Tea

ROSY VERMILION

'Super Star' ('Tropicana')	Hybrid Tea

PINK AND WHITE

'Handel'	Climber
'Janet's Pride'	Eglanteria Hybrid
'Kordes' Perfecta'	Hybrid Tea
'Marguerite Hilling'	Spinosissima Hybrid
'Rose Gaujard'	Hybrid Tea

PINK AND YELLOW

'Lady Penzance'	Eglanteria Hybrid
'President Herbert Hoover'	Hybrid Tea

PINK AND ORANGE

'Compassion'	Climber
'Mme Edouard Herriot, Climbing'	Climber
'Mojave'	Hybrid Tea
'Shot Silk'	Hybrid Tea

'Shot Silk, Climbing'	Climber
'Silver Jubilee'	Hybrid Tea
'Southampton'	Floribunda

PINK – TWO TONES

'Albertine'	Climber
'Mme Abel Chatenay, Climbing'	Climber
'Mme Pierre Oger'	Bourbon

PINK AND RED

'Betty Uprichard'	Hybrid Tea
'Violinista Costa'	Hybrid Tea

PURPLE ROSES

ROSY VIOLET

'Escapade'	Floribunda
'Veilchenblau' ('Violet Blue')	Climber

LILAC PINK

'Blue Moon' ('Mainzer Fastnacht')	Hybrid Tea
R. californica	Species
R. woodsii fendleri	Species
'Yesterday'	Polyantha

ROSY PURPLE

'Gloire de France'	Gallica
R. nitida	Species
R. stellata mirifica ('Sacramento Rose')	Species
R. willmottiae	Species

DEEP PURPLE

'Baby Faurax'	Polyantha
'Cardinal de Richelieu'	Gallica
'Charles de Mills'	Gallica
'Laneii'	Moss
'Mrs Colville'	Spinosissima Hybrid
R. rugosa rubra	Species
'Roseraie de l'Haÿ'	Rugosa Hybrid
'William Lobb'	Moss
'William III'	Spinosissima Hybrid

MAUVE

'Belle de Crécy'	Gallica
'Président de Sèze'	Gallica
'Scabrosa'	Rugosa Hybrid

RED ROSES

LIGHT RED

'Doncasterii'	Macrophylla Hybrid
'Général Schablikine'	Tea

'Kiese'	Canina Hybrid
'Marjorie Fair'	Polyantha
'Perla de Alcanada' ('Baby Crimson')	Miniature
'Red Devil'	Hybrid Tea
R. × *highdownensis*	Moyesii Hybrid

VERMILION RED

'Baccara'	Hybrid Tea
'Fragrant Cloud' ('Duftwolke')	Hybrid Tea
'Starina'	Miniature

VERMILION

| 'Alexander' | Hybrid Tea |

SCARLET

'Danse du Feu' ('Spectacular')	Climber
'Meteor'	Floribunda
'Paul's Scarlet Climber'	Climber
'Scharlachglut' ('Scarlet Fire')	Gallica Hybrid

RED AND YELLOW

'Darling Flame' ('Minuetto')	Miniature
'Little Flirt'	Miniature
'Piccadilly'	Hybrid Tea
R. *foetida bicolor* ('Austrian Copper')	Species

RED AND WHITE

'Camaieux'	Gallica
'Dortmund'	Climber
'Priscilla Burton'	Floribunda
'Roger Lambelin'	Hybrid Perpetual
R. *gallica versicolor* ('Rosa Mundi')	Species

CRIMSON

'Alec's Red'	Hybrid Tea
'Allen Chandler'	Climber
'Altissimo'	Climber
'Crimson Shower'	Trailer
'Ena Harkness'	Hybrid Tea
'Ena Harkness, Climbing'	Climber
'Frensham'	Floribunda
'Geranium'	Moyesii Hybrid
'Hamburger Phoenix'	Climber
'Marlena'	Floribunda
'National Trust'	Hybrid Tea
'Parkdirektor Riggers	Climber
'Precious Platinum'	Hybrid Tea
'Rob Roy'	Floribunda
R. *caudata*	Species
R. *moyesii*	Species

R. × pruhoniciana	Moyesii Hybrid
'Surpasse Tout'	Gallica
'Tuscany'	Gallica
'Tuscany Superb'	Gallica

DARKEST CRIMSON

'Crimson Glory, Climbing'	Climber
'Etoile de Hollande, Climbing'	Climber
'Guineé'	Climber
'John Waterer'	Hybrid Tea
'Josephine Bruce'	Hybrid Tea

20. The Flowering Times

Roses which flower only once in the season can with a few exceptions be recognized from the first growth of their lives, whether as seedlings or maiden plants. They spend their first year growing shoots without any flowers upon them. Having gained those bases for future display, they use them to support flowering shoots next season. They always flower from wood made in previous seasons, and never do they initiate in the same season both the new shoot and flowers upon it. What never? Well hardly ever. If they produce new basal shoots, or even suckers, the rule holds good: no flowers until next season. And from that way of growing, it is clearly seen that we must not remove all the old wood at pruning time, for such an action would postpone flowers for another complete year. Their normal period in bloom is usually a few weeks; the earlier varieties in late spring, followed by others through the summer.

Remontant roses grow shoots and flowers in one move, and the rule for them is that every shoot shall have a bloom; it applies even in their nursery year. As their initiation process is longer, they are likely to flower later in the summer than the once flowering roses. It therefore follows that both types are necessary for a long season of roses. In light, temperature and moisture, all conducive to growth, there is nothing to prevent a remontant rose from flowering around the calendar; it is not necessary to live in one of the world's paradises to prove it, a greenhouse will serve. Commercial cut flower growers can make a variety flower five or six times in a year, against the two to three flushes in our gardens.

When choosing your roses, please think of the flowering time. It is a joy to have an early rose or two, as a sign of summer's promise. A variety which looks fresh later on, starting while others are jaded, gives pleasure out of proportion to the small space needed. A garden which relies on one grand riot looks sadly blank before and after it; but a garden where there is nearly always a rose somewhere to be seen is happy and interesting. Do not forget that hips can elevate that interest in the autumn, nor that the flowering time is later (and better) on plants that have been properly pruned; the neglected ones flower earlier, but on thin, short stems.

Here, then, is the flowering programme, with the heights for reference. The seasons will tend to be earlier in warm climates, later in cold ones.

LATE SPRING

'Andrewsii'	Shorter
'Canary Bird'	Tall
'Double White'	Shorter
'Golden Chersonese'	Taller
'Mrs Colville'	Medium −
R. banksiae alba-plena ('Banksian White')	Climber
R. banksiae lutea ('Banksian Yellow')	Climber
R. cantabrigiensis	Taller
R. ecae	Taller

R. hugonis	Taller
R. primula (Incense Rose)	Tall
R. woodsii fendleri	Tall
'Williams' Double Yellow'	Short
'William III'	Shorter

EARLY SUMMER

'Albertine'	Climber
'Fortune's Double Yellow' ('Beauty of Glazenwood')	Climber
'Frühlingsgold'	Taller
'Frühlingsmorgen'	Tall
Hulthemia persica	Shorter
× *Hulthemosa hardii*	Short
'Jersey Beauty'	Climber
'May Queen'	Climber
'Mme Grégoire Staechelin' ('Spanish Beauty')	Climber
'Paul's Lemon Pillar'	Climber
R. hispida	Tall
R. sericea pteracantha	Taller
R. spinosissima altaica	Tall
R. stellata mirifica (Sacramento Rose)	Shorter +
'Spong'	Short

Note: Climbing Hybrid Teas will join this section if grown on a warm wall.

MIDSUMMER

'Belle de Crécy'	Medium +
'Blanche Moreau'	Tall
'Bullata'	Tall
'Camaieux'	Medium −
'Cardinal de Richelieu'	Medium +
'Celsiana'	Tall
'Chapeau de Napoleon' ('Crested Moss')	Medium
'Charles de Mills'	Medium
'Common Moss'	Tall
'Complicata'	Taller
'Doncasterii'	Tall
'François Juranville'	Climber
'Fred Streeter'	Taller
'Fritz Nobis'	Taller
'Geranium'	Taller
'Gloire de France'	Medium
'Janet's Pride'	Taller
'Kiese'	Tall
'Lady Penzance'	Tall
'Laneii'	Medium
'Lawrence Johnston'	Climber
'Madame Hardy'	Taller

'Marguerite Hilling'	Taller
'Nevada'	Taller
'Petite de Hollande'	Medium +
'Président de Sèze'	Medium +
R. caudata	Tallest
R. × dupontii	Tall
R. farreri persetosa	Taller
R. foetida bicolor ('Austrian Copper')	Tall −
R. × francofurtana	Tall −
R. gallica versicolor ('Rosa Mundi')	Medium −
R. × highdownensis	Tallest
R. × macrantha	Trailer
R. macrophylla	Tallest
R. macrophylla rubricaulis	Tallest
R. moyesii	Tallest
R. moyesii rosea	Tallest
R. × pruhoniciana	Tallest
R. roxburghii (Chestnut Rose)	Medium
R. roxburghii normalis (Single Chestnut Rose)	Medium
R. × setipoda	Taller
R. sweginzowii	Tallest
R. webbiana	Tall
R. willmottiae	Tall
'Scharlachglut' ('Scarlet Fire')	Tallest
'Sealing Wax'	Tallest
'Surpasse Tout'	Medium
'Tuscany'	Tall
'Tuscany Superb'	Tall
'William Lobb'	Tall

SUMMER & REMONTANT
It would be a poor compliment to my readers to assume them incapable of choosing, without help, roses to flower in the summer and remontantly. Most of the roses I have marked with a star come under these two categories, and the best aide memoire is Chapter 23.

LATE SUMMER

'Crimson Shower'	Trailer
R. foliolosa	Medium
R. virginiana	Tall −
'Rose d'Amour'	Tall −
'Sander's White'	Trailer
'The Fairy'	Medium

21. The Perfume

Let five people smell a rose, and then endeavour to describe the perfume by likening it to something else; the chances are that five different answers will be received. On fine distinctions of scent, humans have as a rule a poor nasal memory. Many authorities have tried to classify rose perfumes, but again it only needs five to produce five different results. Efforts have been made to analyse rose perfumes, which is an interesting study with some long words in it. But when we come down to it, all that matters to us right now is to know which are the most fragrant roses for our enjoyment. And without invoking anyone else's knowledge and taste, which I own may be superior, I will give you mine by sweetness more than by strength.

The roses have been marked in the foregoing pages with up to ten points for perfume. Only the upper echelon has relevance in our selection, so we will omit those which obtained four points or less. I could have found two or three more deserving ten points, for example 'Papa Meilland', 'Prima Ballerina' and 'Dame Edith Helen'; but alas, they did not pass the test to stand in these pages.

TEN POINTS
'Lady Penzance'   Eglanteria Hybrid

NINE POINTS
'Alec's Red'   Hybrid Tea
'Fragrant Cloud' ('Duftwolke')   Hybrid Tea
'Margaret Merril'   Floribunda
'Polly'   Hybrid Tea

EIGHT POINTS
'Boule de Neige'   Bourbon
'Crimson Glory, Climbing'   Climbing Hybrid Tea
'Königin von Danemarck'   Alba
'Ophelia'   Hybrid Tea
'Scabrosa'   Rugosa Hybrid

SEVEN POINTS
'Belle de Crécy'   Gallica
'Blue Moon' ('Mainzer Fastnacht')   Hybrid Tea
'Compassion'   Climbing Hybrid Tea
'Etoile de Hollande, Climbing'   Climbing Hybrid Tea
'Mme Grégoire Staechelin'   Climbing Hybrid Tea
'Mme Pierre Oger'   Bourbon
'Mrs John Laing'   Hybrid Perpetual
'President Herbert Hoover'   Hybrid Tea
'Sutter's Gold'   Hybrid Tea
'Whisky Mac'   Hybrid Tea

SIX POINTS

'Alister Stella Gray'	Noisette
'Arthur Bell'	Floribunda
'Frau Dagmar Hartopp'	Rugosa Hybrid
'Frühlingsgold'	Spinosissima Hybrid
'Golden Chersonese'	Ecae Hybrid
'Goldfinch, Climbing'	Climbing Polyantha
'Handel'	Climbing Floribunda
'Josephine Bruce'	Hybrid Tea
'Lawrence Johnston'	Foetida Hybrid
'Mme Legras de St Germain'	Alba
'Roger Lambelin'	Hybrid Perpetual
R. *filipes*	Species
R. *helenae*	Species
R. *longicuspis*	Species
R. *primula* (Incense Rose)	Species
R. *rugosa alba*	Species
R. *rugosa rubra*	Species
R. *setipoda*	Species
'Sander's White'	Wichuraiana Hybrid
'Souvenir de la Malmaison'	Bourbon
'Stanwell Perpetual'	Spinosissima Hybrid
'The Garland'	Climbing Polyantha
'Wendy Cussons'	Hybrid Tea
'Williams' Double Yellow'	Spinosissima Hybrid
'Yesterday'	Polyantha

FIVE POINTS

'Bullata'	Centifolia
'Celestial'	Alba
'Celsiana'	Damask
'Double White'	Spinosissima Hybrid
'Dr A. J. Verhage'	Hybrid Tea
'Dr W. van Fleet'	Wichuraiana Hybrid
'Ena Harkness'	Hybrid Tea
'Ena Harkness, Climbing'	Climbing Hybrid Tea
'Escapade'	Floribunda
'Fritz Nobis'	Eglanteria Hybrid
'Frühlingsmorgen'	Spinosissma Hybrid
'Janet's Pride'	Eglanteria Hybrid
'Lady Hillingdon, Climbing'	Tea
'Laneii'	Moss
'Maiden's Blush'	Alba
'Mme Alfred Carrière'	Noisette
'New Dawn'	Wichuraiana Hybrid
'Quatre Saisons'	Damask
'Red Devil'	Hybrid Tea
R. × *dupontii*	Moschata Hybrid
R. × *francofurtana*	Gallica Hybrid
R. *macrophylla*	Species

R. macrophylla rubricaulis	Species
R. spinosissima altaica	Species
R. spinosissima hispida	Species
'Shot Silk'	Hybrid Tea
'Shot Silk, Climbing'	Climbing Hybrid Tea
'Wedding Day'	Sinowilsonii Hybrid
'William Lobb'	Moss
'Yvonne Rabier'	Floribunda
'Zéphirine Drouhin'	Bourbon

22. The Hips

Hips have one advantage over flowers, they last longer; but it would be dishonest to pretend that rose hips are lovely throughout the winter. Some are plundered by birds, others wither; the gorgeous display is for later summer and autumn, and no rosarian should cheat himself of it.

As the purpose of this list is to refer to those roses most beautiful in fruit, we will ignore all the lesser sorts, and mention those with five points or more in their headings. The letters L, M and S are used to indicate whether the hips are Large, Medium or Small.

TEN POINTS

'Doncasterii'	L	Macrophylla Hybrid
'Fred Streeter'	L	Moyesii Hybrid
'Geranium'	L	Moyesii Hybrid
R × highdownensis	L	Moyesii Hybrid
R. macrophylla	L	Species
R. macrophylla rubricaulis	L	Species
R. moyesii	L	Species
R. moyesii rosea	L	Species
R. × pruhoniciana	L	Moyesii Hybrid
R. sweginzowii	L	Species
'Sealing Wax'	L	Moyesii Hybrid

NINE POINTS

R. caudata	L	Species
R. setipoda	L	Species
R. spinosissima hispida	L	Species

EIGHT POINTS

'Frau Dagmar Hartopp'	L	Rugosa Hybrid
R. virginiana	M	Species
'Scabrosa'	L	Rugosa Hybrid

SEVEN POINTS

'Kiese'	L	Canina Hybrid
R. pomifera	L	Species
R. rubrifolia	S	Species
R. rugosa alba	L	Species
R. rugosa rubra	L	Species
R. woodsii fendleri	M	Species
'Scharlachglut' ('Scarlet Fire')	L	Gallica Hybrid

SIX POINTS

'Mme Grégoire Staechelin'	L	Climber
R. helenae	S	Trailer
R. nitida	S	Species
R. roxburghii normalis (Single Chestnut Rose)	M	Species
R. spinosissima altaica	M	Species

FIVE POINTS

'Fritz Nobis'	M	Eglanteria Hybrid
'Mrs Colville'	S	Spinosissima Hybrid
'Penelope'	M	Hybrid Musk
R. filipes	S	Trailer
R. longicuspis	S	Trailer
R. × *macrantha*	M	Trailer
R. webbiana	S	Species
'Semi-plena'	M	Alba
'The Garland'	S	Climber

23. The Stars

Out of the tens of thousands of different roses in the world, I have attempted to distinguish in this book firstly, those of the greatest historic significance, and secondly those of great merit and beauty.

Every age makes a speciality of its own roses, which is a natural expression of confidence in its own work. But we know perfectly well that most roses have a short life, and that the rose catalogues ten years hence will contain a fresh set of names.

I have tried to recognize the enduring and to discard the ephemeral; my selections have been marked with one to five stars. 274 roses are distinguished thus, and in my opinion they are the cream of the genus in this year of writing.

FIVE STARS

'Allgold'	Yellow Floribunda
'Canary Bird'	Yellow Xanthina Hybrid
'Geranium'	Red Moyesii Hybrid
'Golden Chersonese'	Yellow Ecae Hybrid
'Mermaid'	Creamy yellow climber
'Pascali'	White Hybrid Tea
'Queen Elizabeth'	Pink Floribunda
'Red Devil'	Light red Hybrid Tea
'Rob Roy'	Crimson Floribunda
'Scabrosa'	Mauve red Rugosa Hybrid
'Silver Jubilee'	Pink blended Hybrid Tea
'Sonia Meilland' ('Sweet Promise')	Rosy salmon Hybrid Tea
'Wendy Cussons'	Carmine Hybrid Tea

FOUR STARS

'Alexander'	Vermilion Hybrid Tea
'Compassion'	Apricot pink Climber
'Darling Flame' ('Minuetto')	Orange vermilion Miniature
'Elizabeth Harkness'	Ivory Hybrid Tea
'Frau Dagmar Hartopp'	Pink Rugosa Hybrid
'Fritz Nobis'	Pink Eglanteria Hybrid
'Golden Wings'	Cream yellow Spinosissima Hybrid
'Grandpa Dickson' ('Irish Gold')	Yellow Hybrid Tea
'Iceberg' ('Schneewittchen')	White Floribunda
'Little White Pet'	White Sempervirens Hybrid
'Margaret Merril'	White Floribunda
'Marguerite Hilling'	Pink Spinosissima Hybrid
'Mme Grégoire Staechelin' ('Spanish Beauty')	Pink Climber
'Nevada'	White Spinosissima Hybrid

'New Penny'	Pink Miniature
'Pink Parfait'	Pink Floribunda
'Pink Perpetue'	Pink Climber
'Precious Platinum'	Bright crimson Hybrid Tea
'Priscilla Burton'	Red & white Floribunda
R. × *highdownensis*	Light red Moyesii Hybrid
R. *virginiana*	Pink Species
R. *webbiana*	Pink Species
'Rosina' ('Josephine Wheatcroft')	Yellow Miniature
'Southampton'	Apricot orange Floribunda
'Starina'	Vermilion scarlet Miniature
'The Fairy'	Pink Wichuraiana Hybrid

THREE STARS

'Albéric Barbier'	Cream Climber
'Alec's Red'	Red Hybrid Tea
'Allen Chandler'	Crimson Climber
'Aloha'	Pink Climber
'Altissimo'	Crimson Climber
'Arthur Bell'	Yellow Floribunda
'Baby Masquerade'	Yellow & pink Miniature
'Ballerina'	Light pink Polyantha
'Belinda'	Light pink Polyantha
'Cécile Brunner'	Light pink Hybrid China
'Celestial'	Light pink Alba
'Cornelia'	Pink Hybrid Musk
'Crimson Shower'	Red Trailer
'Danse du Feu' ('Spectacular')	Scarlet Climber
'Doncasterii'	Rose red Macrophylla Hybrid
'Dr A. J. Verhage' ('Golden Wave')	Yellow Hybrid Tea
'Easter Morning'	White Miniature
'Ena Harkness, Climbing'	Crimson Climber
'Escapade'	Rosy violet Floribunda
'Etoile de Hollande, Climbing'	Crimson Climber
'Félicité et Perpétue'	White Climber
'Fragrant Cloud' ('Duftwolke')	Red Hybrid Tea
'François Juranville'	Pink Climber
'Fred Streeter'	Pink Moyesii Hybrid
'Golden Showers'	Yellow Climber
'Handel'	Pink & white Climber
'Just Joey'	Coppery buff Hybrid Tea
'Lady Penzance'	Pink & yellow Eglanteria Hybrid
'Madame Hardy'	White Damask
'Marjorie Fair'	Red Polyantha
'Mischief'	Pink Hybrid Tea
'Mme Legras de St Germain'	White Alba
'Mme Pierre Oger'	Pink & white Bourbon
'Morning Jewel'	Pink Climber
'Mozart'	Light pink Polyantha
'Mrs Sam McGredy, Climbing'	Salmon to red Climber

'National Trust' ('Bad Nauheim')	Bright crimson Hybrid Tea
'New Dawn'	Blush white Wichuraiana Hybrid
'Ophelia'	Light pink Hybrid Tea
'Peace' ('Mme A. Meilland')	Yellow & pink Hybrid Tea
'Perla de Montserrat'	Pink Miniature
'Piccadilly'	Red & yellow Hybrid Tea
'Pompon de Paris, Climbing'	Pink Climber
'Pour Toi'	White Miniature
R. banksiae lutea ('Banksian Yellow')	Yellow Climber
R. farreri persetosa	Pink Species
R. macrophylla	Pink Species
R. macrophylla rubricaulis	Pink Species
R. × pruhoniciana	Crimson Moyesii Hybrid
R. rubrifolia	Pink Species
R. rugosa alba	White Species
R. spinosissima hispida	Ivory Species
'Rose Gaujard'	Pink & white Hybrid Tea
'Sander's White'	White Trailer
'Souvenir de la Malmaison'	Blush white Bourbon
'Stanwell Perpetual'	Blush Spinosissima Hybrid
'Sutter's Gold'	Yellow & pink Hybrid Tea
'Williams' Double Yellow'	Yellow Spinosissima Hybrid
'William III'	Purple Spinosissima Hybrid
'Yesterday'	Pink Polyantha
'Yvonne Rabier'	White Floribunda
'Zéphirine Drouhin'	Pink Bourbon

TWO STARS

'Betty Uprichard'	Pink & red Hybrid Tea
'Bloomfield Abundance'	Light pink Hybrid China
'Blue Moon' ('Mainzer Fastnacht')	Lilac pink Hybrid Tea
'Buff Beauty'	Light apricot Hybrid Musk
'Cardinal de Richelieu'	Purple Gallica
'Cécile Brunner, Climbing'	Light pink Climber
'Chapeau de Napoleon' ('Crested Moss')	Pink Centifolia
'Cinderella'	Pale pink Miniature
'Dainty Maid'	Pink Floribunda
'Elegance'	Primrose Climber
'Ena Harkness'	Crimson Hybrid Tea
'Felicia'	Light pink Hybrid Musk
'Félicité Parmentier'	Blush Alba
'First Love'	Pink Hybrid Tea
'Frensham'	Crimson Floribunda
'Gloire de France'	Pink Gallica
'Golden Dawn'	Yellow Hybrid Tea
'Golden Dawn, Climbing'	Yellow Climber
'Honeymoon'	Yellow Floribunda
'Iceberg, Climbing'	White Climber
'Jersey Beauty'	Cream Climber
'John Waterer'	Deep crimson Hybrid Tea

'Josephine Bruce'	Dark red Hybrid Tea
'Kordes' Perfecta'	Cream & pink Hybrid Tea
'Leverkusen'	Yellow Climber
'Little Flirt'	Red & yellow Miniature
'Maiden's Blush'	Blush white Alba
'Marlena'	Crimson Floribunda
'Masquerade, Climbing'	Yellow to red Climber
'Meteor'	Vermilion scarlet Floribunda
'Michèle Meilland'	Light pink Hybrid Tea
'Mme Abel Chatenay, Climbing'	Bicolour pink Climber
'Mme Alfred Carrière'	White Climber
'Mojave'	Orange red Hybrid Tea
'Moonlight'	Cream Hybrid Musk
'Mrs Colville'	Purple Spinosissima Hybrid
'Mrs John Laing'	Pink Hybrid Perpetual
'Nathalie Nypels'	Pink Floribunda
'Nozomi'	White Trailer
'Old Blush' ('Monthly Rose')	Pink Hybrid China
'Paddy McGredy'	Rose red Floribunda
'Penelope'	Light pink Hybrid Musk
'Perla de Alcanada' ('Baby Crimson')	Rose red Miniature
'Petite de Hollande'	Pink Centifolia
'Phyllis Bide'	Yellow & pink Climber
'Pink Favourite'	Bright pink Hybrid Tea
'Ritter von Barmstede'	Pink Climber
R. × cantabrigiensis	Cream Hugonis Hybrid
R. chinensis mutabilis ('Tipo Ideal')	Cream to red Species
R. × dupontii	Blush white Moschata Hybrid
R. filipes	White Trailer
R. foetida bicolor ('Austrian Copper')	Red & yellow Species
R. gallica versicolor ('Rosa Mundi')	Red striped blush Species
R. helenae	White Trailer
R. longicuspis	White Trailer
R. moyesii	Crimson Species
R. moyesii rosea	Pink Species
R. nitida	Pink Species
R. pomifera	Pink Species
R. primula (Incense Rose)	Primrose Species
R. roxburghii normalis (Single Chestnut Rose)	Pink Species
R. rugosa rubra	Purple red Species
R. sericea pteracantha	White Species
R. setipoda	Pink Species
R. sweginzowii	Pink Species
R. willmottiae	Pink Species
R. woodsii fendleri	Pink Species
'Roseraie de l'Haÿ'	Purple Rugosa Hybrid
'Rudolph Timm'	Pale pink Floribunda
'Sealing Wax'	Pink Moyesii Hybrid
'Spong'	Pink Centifolia
'Tuscany Superb'	Maroon Gallica

'Vanity'	Pink Climber
'Violinista Costa'	Coral & rose Hybrid Tea
'Wedding Day'	White to pink Climber

ONE STAR

'Albertine'	Pink Climber
'Alister Stella Gray'	Yellow Climber
'Allgold, Climbing'	Yellow Climber
'Andrewsii'	Pink & cream Spinosissima Hybrid
'Baby Faurax'	Amethyst Polyantha
'Baccara'	Vermilion Hybrid Tea
'Belle de Crécy'	Mauve Gallica
'Blanche Moreau'	White Moss
'Boule de Neige'	White Bourbon
'Bourbon Queen'	Pink Bourbon
'Bullata'	Pink Centifolia
'Camaieux'	Striped Gallica
'Celsiana'	Pink Damask
'Charles de Mills'	Crimson Gallica
'Charlotte Armstrong'	Rose red Hybrid Tea
'Christine, Climbing'	Yellow Climber
'Circus, Climbing'	Yellow & red Climber
'Common Moss'	Pink Moss
'Complicata'	Pink Macrantha Hybrid
'Crimson Glory, Climbing'	Dark red Climber
'Dainty Bess'	Light pink Hybrid Tea
'Desprez à Fleur Jaune'	Pale yellow Climber
'Dortmund'	Red, white eye; Climber
'Double White'	White Spinosissima Hybrid
'Dr W. van Fleet'	Blush white Climber
'Easlea's Golden Rambler'	Yellow Climber
'Emily Gray'	Yellow Climber
'Fortune's Double Yellow' ('Beauty of Glazenwood')	Yellow & red Climber
'Frau Karl Druschki'	White Hybrid Perpetual
'Frühlingsgold'	Cream Spinosissima Hybrid
'Frühlingsmorgen'	Pink Spinosissima Hybrid
'Général Schablikine'	Coppery red Tea
'Goldfinch'	Yellow to white Climber
'Gruss an Aachen'	Creamy pink Floribunda
'Guinée'	Dark red Climber
'Hamburger Phoenix'	Red Climber
Hulthemia persica	Yellow, red eye; Species
× *Hulthemosa hardii*	Yellow, red eye; Persica Hybrid
'Jacques Cartier'	Pink Portland
'Janet's Pride'	Pink & white Eglanteria Hybrid
'Kaiserin Auguste Viktoria'	White Hybrid Tea
'Katharina Zeimet'	White Polyantha
'Kiese'	Light red Canina Hybrid

'Königin von Danemarck' — Pink Alba
'Lady Hillingdon, Climbing' — Apricot yellow Climber
'Laneii' — Purple Moss
'Lawrence Johnston' — Yellow Climber
'Marie Pavié' — Pale pink Polyantha
'Masquerade' — Yellow red Floribunda
'Maxima' — White Alba
'May Queen' — Pink Climber
'Mme Caroline Testout, Climbing' — Pink Climber
'Mme Edouard Herriot, Climbing'
  ('Daily Mail, Climbing') — Coral orange Climber
'Montezuma' — Salmon red Hybrid Tea
'Mrs Pierre S. du Pont, Climbing' — Yellow Climber
'Parkdirektor Riggers' — Crimson Climber
'Paul's Lemon Pillar' — Cream Climber
'Paul's Scarlet Climber' — Scarlet Climber
'Perla Rosa, Climbing' — Pink Climber
'Perle d'Or' — Light pink Hybrid China
'Pink Cameo' — Pink Climber
'Pink Grootendorst' — Pink Rugosa Hybrid
'Polly' — Blush Hybrid Tea
'Pompon Blanc Parfait' — White Alba
'Président de Sèze' — Mauve Gallica
'President Herbert Hoover' — Pink & yellow Hybrid Tea
'Prosperity' — Ivory Hybrid Musk
'Quatre Saisons' — Pink Damask
'Quatre Saisons Blanc Mousseux' — White Damask
'Roger Lambelin' — Red & white Hybrid Perpetual
R. banksiae alba-plena ('Banksian White') — White Climber
R. californica — Lilac pink Species
R. carolina plena — Pink Species
R. caudata — Red Species
R. chinensis viridiflora — Green China
R. ecae — Yellow Species
R. foliolosa — Pink Species
R. × francofurtana — Pink Gallica Hybrid
R. hugonis — Primrose Species
R. × macrantha — Blush Trailer
R. multibracteata — Pink Species
R. roxburghii (Chestnut Rose) — Pink Species
R. spinosissima altaica — White Species
R. stellata mirifica (Sacramento Rose) — Rose purple Species
'Rose d'Amour' — Pink Virginiana Hybrid
'Scharlachglut' ('Scarlet Fire') — Bright red Gallica Hybrid
'Semi-plena' — White Alba
'Shot Silk' — Orange pink Hybrid Tea
'Shot Silk, Climbing' — Orange pink Climber
'Spartan' — Coral pink Floribunda
'Super Star' ('Tropicana') — Coral orange Hybrid Tea
'Surpasse Tout' — Red Gallica

'The Garland'	Blush Climber
'Tuscany'	Maroon Gallica
'Veilchenblau'	Light lilac Climber
'Whisky Mac'	Apricot Hybrid Tea
'William Allen Richardson'	Orange yellow Climber
'William Lobb'	Purple Moss

24. Classification of Species

I hope it is now abundantly clear that there is no clarity about the identification of rose species. Ever since their discovery, they have been subject to changes of name, and no doubt there will be a steady flow of revision in the future. Sometimes the thought occurs to me that one might as well try to map the clouds. The following list is a simplified version of Rehder's classification, and may be a helpful reference. I have included the roses generally recognized as pecies, but have excluded those of hybrid origin.

LEAVES SIMPLE WITHOUT STIPULES
Simplicifoliae
H. persica   Iran

LEAVES PINNATE WITH STIPULES – ALL THE REMAINDER
HIPS PRICKLY, persistent
Hesperrhodos
R. minutifolia   USA
R. stellata   USA
HIPS PRICKLY, soon falling
Platyrhodon
R. roxburghii   China

HIPS SMOOTH OR BRISTLY – ALL THE REMAINDER
Eurosa
STIPULES FREE from leaf stalk, or mostly so; narrow, pointed, soon falling
FLOWERS SMALL, in rounded heads
Banksianae
R. banksiae   China
R. cymosa   China
STIPULES FREE from leaf stalk, or mostly so; toothed
FLOWERS LARGE, solitary
Laevigatae
R. laevigata   China
STIPULES FREE from leaf stalk, or mostly so; deeply toothed
FLOWERS with many leafy bracts
Bracteatae
R. bracteata   China
R. clinophylla   India

STIPULES WELL JOINED TO LEAF STALK – ALL THE REMAINDER
STYLES PROTRUDE from their tube
STYLES SEPARATE
Indicae

R. chinensis	China
R. gigantea	Burma

STYLES PROTRUDE from their tube
STYLES FUSED TOGETHER
Synstylae

R. anemoneflora	China	R. luciae	China
R. arvensis	Europe	R. maximowicziana	Korea
R. cerasocarpa	China	R. moschata	Himalaya
R. crocantha	China	R. mulliganii	China
R. fargesii	China	R. multiflora	Korea
R. filipes	China	R. phoenicia	Turkey
R. gentiliana	China	R. rubus	China
R. glomerata	China	R. sempervirens	Mediterranean
R. helenae	China	R. setigera	USA
R. henryi	China	R. sinowilsonii	China
R. leschenaultii	India	R. soulieana	China
R. longicuspis	China	R. wichuraiana	China

STYLES NOT PROTRUDING MUCH—ALL THE REMAINDER
FLOWERS SOLITARY usually
LEAFLETS FIVE usually
Gallicanae

R. gallica	W. Asia—Europe

FLOWERS SOLITARY usually
LEAFLETS SEVEN or more usually
Pimpinellifoliae

R. ecae	Afghanistan	R. koreana	Korea
R. elasmacantha	Caucasus	R. primula	China
R. farreri	China	R. sericea	Himalaya
R. foetida	Iran	R. spinosissima	Asia—Europe
R. graciliflora	China	R. turkestanica	C. Asia
R. hugonis	China	R. xanthina	China

FLOWERS MANY IN HEADS—ALL THE REMAINDER
THORNS CURVED
Caninae

R. agrestis	Mediterranean	R. hawrana	Hungary
R. billotiana	Europe	R. heckeliana	S. Europe
R. britzensis	C. Asia	R. horrida	W. Asia—S. Europe
R. canina	Europe	R. inodora	Europe
R. chavinii	Europe	R. marginata	W. Asia—Europe
R. coriifolia	W. Asia—Europe	R. micrantha	S. Europe
R. corymbifera	Mediterranean	R. mollis	W. Asia—Europe
R. dumalis	W. Asia—Europe	R. montana	Mediterranean
R. eglanteria	Europe	R. montezumae	New Mexico
R. glutinosa	W. Asia—S. Europe	R. obtusifolia	Europe

R. orientalis	W. Asia—S. Europe	*R. sherardii*	Europe
R. pomifera	W. Asia—Europe	*R. sicula*	Mediterranean
R. pouzinii	Mediterranean	*R. stylosa*	W. Asia—Europe
R. rubrifolia	Europe	*R. tomentosa*	W. Asia—Europe
R. serafinii	S. Europe	*R. tuschetica*	USSR

THORNS STRAIGHT—ALL THE REMAINDER
SEPALS SOON FALL
Carolinae

R. carolina	USA	*R. rudiuscula*	USA
R. foliolosa	USA	*R. subserrulata*	USA
R. nitida	USA	*R. virginiana*	USA
R. palustris	USA		

SEPALS PERSISTENT
Cinnamomeae

R. acicularis	N. America—N. Asia	*R. melina*	USA
R. albertii	C. Asia	*R. mohavensis*	USA
R. amblyotis	N. E. Asia	*R. moyesii*	China
R. arkansana	USA	*R. multibracteata*	China
R. banksiopsis	China	*R. muriculata*	USA
R. beggeriana	C. Asia	*R. murielae*	China
R. bella	China	*R. nanothamnus*	C. Asia
R. blanda	USA	*R. nutkana*	USA
R. californica	USA	*R. pendulina*	Europe
R. caudata	China	*R. persetosa*	China
R. cinnamomea	Asia—Europe	*R. pinetorum*	USA
R. corymbulosa	China	*R. pisocarpa*	USA
R. davidii	China	*R. prattii*	China
R. davurica	China	*R. pyrifera*	USA
R. eglantula	China	*R. rugosa*	E. Asia
R. elymaitica	Iran	*R. salictorum*	USA
R. fedtschenkoana	C. Asia	*R. saturata*	China
R. forrestiana	China	*R. sertata*	China
R. giraldii	China	*R. setipoda*	China
R. gratissima	USA	*R. sonomensis*	USA
R. gymnocarpa	USA	*R. spaldingii*	USA
R. hemsleyana	China	*R. spithamea*	USA
R. holodonta	China	*R. suffulta*	USA
R. laxa	C. Asia	*R. sweginzowii*	China
R. macounii	USA	*R. ultramontana*	USA
R. macrophylla	Himalaya	*R. webbiana*	Himalaya
R. manca	USA	*R. willmottiae*	China
R. marretii	E. Asia	*R. woodsii*	USA

Index

In order not to confuse the eye, the conventions of horticultural typography have been abandoned in this index. Gone are the quotation marks and italics, the Rs and the Xs. Everything is in plain type, and integrated in one A to Z list. And in order not to annoy the mind, a harsh censorship has been exercised. Brief and passing references are not mentioned, to the exclusion of many personal and place names. I hope that every entry leads to a useful and positive fact. Where consecutive pages continue the same subject, the index reference is normally to the first of those pages.

Aalsmeer 109
Abbotswood 216
Aberdeen 73
Achene 219
Acicularis 227
Adam 61, 70
Adelaïde d'Orléans 162
Admiral Rodney 104
Aglaia 160
Agrestis 272
Agrippina 51
Aicardi, Domenico 91
Aimée Vibert 56
Aitchison, Dr J. E. T. 197
Albas 216
Alba maxima 217
—plena 217
—regalis 217
—Rosea 62
—semi-plena 179, 218
—(sempervirens) 162
—suaveolens 218
Albéric Barbier 166
Alberich 159
Albertii 227
Albertine 169
Alec's Red 112
Alexander 113
Alexander of Tunis, Earl 113
Alfred K. Williams 193
Alika 175
Alison Wheatcroft 126
Alister Stella Gray 56
Allen Chandler 140
Allen, E. F. 198
Allgold 125
—Climbing 144
Aloha 140
Alpine Rose 233
Altaica 208

Altissimo 35
Amber 167
Amblyotis 227
American Pillar 163
American Rose Annual 92
——Society 114
American Species 213
Ami Quinard 120
Andersonii 216
Andrewsii 209
Anemoneflora 149
Anemone Rose 42
Anemonoides 42
Angèle Pernet 85
Angiosperms 9
Angle 151
Angle Blush 151
Anna de Diesbach 194
Anna-Maria de Montravel 155
Anna Olivier 64
Anne Elizabeth 98, 130
Anneke Koster 156
Anther 16
Antoine Ducher 75
Antoine Rivoire 71, 73, 80
Apothecary's Rose 173
Apple Rose 222
Archer, W. E. B. & Daughter 85
Arctic Rose 227
Arkansana 227
Armosa 52
Aroma 120
Arthur Bell 128
Arvensis 150
Arvensis Hybrids 150
Atrovirens 162
Attar of roses 177
Auguste Roussel 230
Austrian Briars 79, 198, 211
Austrian Copper 199

Austrian Yellow   198
Autumn Damask   180
Awards to new roses   74
Ayrshires   150
Ayrshire Queen   151

Baby Carnaval   137
Baby Château   120, 124, 127
Baby Crimson   136
Baby Faurax   157
Baby Gold Star   136
Baby Maskerade   137
Baby Masquerade   137
Baby Ramblers   156
Baccara   100
Bad Nauheim   113
Bagatelle   77
Baldwin   159
Balearica   162
Ballerina   159
Baltica   208
Bamboo Rose   154
Bambridge & Harrison   50
Banksiae alba-plena   39
—banksiae   40
—Hybrid   40
—lutea   40
—lutescens   40
—normalis   40
Banksianae   39
Banksian Yellow   40
Banksiopsis   227
Banks, Sir Joseph   39
BARB   108
Barberry Rose   29
Barker, Ernest   61, 108, 190
Baroness Rothschild   193
Baron Girod de l'Ain   195
Baronne Prévost   192
Bashful   159
Beauty of Glazenwood   52
Beauty of Stapleford   69
Beauty of Waltham   193
Bedding Plants   71
Bees of Chester   99
Beggeriana   227
Belinda   159
Bella   227
Belle de Crécy   175
Belle of Portugal   147
Belle Portugaise   147
Belle Siebrecht   74
Bénédict Seguin   85
Bengal Rose   48
Bennett, Henry   67, 69, 71, 72, 194, 221
Bennett's seedling   151
Bentall, J. A.   132
Berberifolia   29

Bertram   159
Betty Prior   120
Betty Uprichard   84
Bicolor   209
Bifera   181
Billotiana   272
Bizarre Triomphant   176
Blackstem Rose   231
Blanc Double de Coubert   236
Blanche Moreau   183
Blanda   228
Blaze   161
Bloomfield Abundance   50
Blue Moon   110
Blue roses   110, 123
Blundell, Dr J. B.   219
Blush Noisette   55, 56
Blush Rambler   160
Boerner, Eugene   117, 122
Bonnie Prince Charlie's Rose   218
Book about Roses, A   25
Book of the Rose, The   25
Books   24
Borboniana   186
Boskoop   135
Boskoopse Rugosa   237
Boule de Neige   188
Bouquet de la Mariée   56
Bouquet d'Or   56
Bourbon Jacques   186
Bourbon Queen   187
Bourbons   185
Boursaults   234
Bract   44
Bracteata   44
Bracteatae   44
Bracteata Hybrids   44
Breeding Roses, Suggestions &
    Examples   15, 17, 34, 36, 40, 45, 55,
    67, 75, 94, 100, 117, 125, 130, 139, 141,
    148, 149, 175, 228, 230, 236
Bréon, M.   185
Bridesmaid   64
Britzensis   272
Brown, Robert   205
Brownell, Dr & Mrs Walter D.   86, 141
Brown's Superb Blush   66
Brunonii   152, 153
Budding   18
Budding Eyes   18
Buff Beauty   132
Bulgaria   179
Bullata   181
Bullate   181
Burkhard   159
Burnet Rose   205
Burr Rose   35
Bush & Shrub   131, 229

Cabbage Roses 180
Calcutta Botanic Garden 35, 48
Californica 155, 228
—plena 228
Calyx 9
Camaieux 175
Camellia Rose 42
Camoëns 70
Canary Bird 213
Candida 150
Canell Rose 228
Canina 127, 214
—Hybrids 216
Caninae 214
Cantabrigiensis 202
Cant, B. R. & Sons 165
Cant, Frank 58
Captain Christy 69
Captain Kidd 163
Capucine Rose 199
Cardinal de Richelieu 176
Carmenetta 222
Carolina 224
—alba 224
—plena 224
—triloba 224
Carolinae 224
Caroline Testout 71
Carolyn Dean 138
Catherine Mermet 63
Catherine Seyton 221
Cathrine Kordes 88, 90
Caudata 228
Cécile Brunner 50, 137
— —Climbing 51
Céleste 216
Celestial 216
Céline Forestier 56
Celsiana 179
Cent-feuilles 180
Centifolia 179, 180
—cristata 182
—muscosa 182, 183
—pomponia 182
Cerasocarpa 171
Cerise Bouquet 233
Champney, John 55
Champney's Pink Cluster 55
Chapeau de Napoleon 182
Chaplin Bros 69
Charles de Mills 176
Charles J. Grahame 75
Charles Lèfebvre 192
Charles Mallerin 98
Charlotte Armstrong 92
Charlotte Elizabeth 98
Charm of Paris 74
Château de Clos Vougeot 78, 120

Chavinii 272
Cherokee Rose 42
Cheshunt Hybrid 69
Chestnut Rose 35
Chimera 51
China Rose 47
China Teas 51
Chinatown 119, 128
Chinensis 47
—Hybrids 50
—longifolia 50
—minima 48, 134
—mutabilis 49, 123
—semperflorens 49, 53, 133
—spontanea 49
—viridiflora 49
Chinese Tree Rose 153
Chinquapin Rose 35
Chlorophyll 101
Christian Curle 167
Christine 83
—Climbing 140
Christopher Stone 90
Chromatella 57
Chromosomes 67, 214
Chrysler Imperial 99
Cinderella 137
Cinnamomea 227, 228
—plena 229
Cinnamomeae 227
Cinnamon Rose 227, 228
Circumpolar Rose 227
Circus 126
—Climbing 144
Circus Parade 126
Claire Jacquier 57
Cläre Grammerstorf 127
Clark, Alister 148
Clarke, John 152
Classification (Table) 271
Clementine 220
Climbing Floribundas 143
—Hybrid Teas 139
—Miniatures 145
—Polyanthas 160
—Roses Old and New 27
Clinophylla 46
Cloth of Gold 57
Clusius 199
Cocker, Alexander M. 31, 108, 112, 116,
117, 129
Coeur d'Amour 111
Colour in roses 110
Colours (Table) 248
Common Blush China 54
Common Moss 183
Communis 183
Compacta Roses 159

Compassion 140
Complete Rosarian, The 28
Complicata 218
Comte de Chambord 185
Comtesse de Labarthe 63
Comtesse de Nadaillac 64
Comtesse du Cayla 51
Comtesse Ouwaroff 63
Conard-Pyle Co 94, 107
Condesa de Sastago 86, 105
Conrad Ferdinand Meyer 236
Cook, John 76
Cooperi 147
Cooper's Burmese Rose 147
Copper Delight 125
Coral Cluster 157
Coriifolia 219
—froebelii 219
Cornelia 132
Corolla 9
Correvon, Henri 135
Coryana 36
Corymbifera 219
Corymbulosa 228
Countess of Gosford 86
Cramoisi Supérieur 51
Crathes Castle 147
Crépin, Professor F. 175
Crested Moss 182
Crested Provence 182
Crimson Ayrshire 151
Crimson Glory 89
— —Climbing 141
Crimson Perpetual 191
Crimson Rambler 160
Crimson Shower 169
Crocantha 171
Cryptogams 9
Cuisse de Nymphe 217
Cultivar 15
Cultivation 19
—Banksians 39
—Cécile Brunner Climbing 51
—Chinensis mutabilis 49
—Climbing Hybrid Teas 139
—H. persica 30
—Iceberg 126
—Miniatures 134
—Moss Roses 183
—Roses in Trees 151
—Standards 126
—Tree Roses 126
—Wichuraiana Hybrids (Climbers &
    Trailers) 165
Curly White 110
Cut flower industry 61, 62, 87, 101
Cuttings 165
Cymédor 192

Cymosa 41

Daily Mail 81
Daily Mail Rose 81
Daily Rose 49, 54
Dainty Bess 85
Dainty Maid 121
Damascena 177
—semperflorens 180
—trigintipetala 177
—versicolor 179
Damask 177
—Perpetuals 185
Dame Edith Helen 98
Danse du Feu 144
Danzille 62
Dark red roses 78
Darling Flame 138
Davidii 229
—elongata 229
Davurica 229
Degenhard 159
De l'Ecluse, Charles 199
De Meaux 182
De Ruiter, Gerrit 157
De Ruiter, Gysbert 157
Desprez 61
Desprez à Fleur Jaune 57
Deterioration 67
De Vink, John 135, 137
Devoniensis 62
Dianthiflora 236
Dick Koster 156
Dickson, Alexander 77
—A.P.C. 74, 108, 111, 116
—Hugh 78
Dicotyledons 9
Dictionary of Gardening (RHS) 28, 133
Diseases 107
Doc 159
Dodonaeus 205
D'ombrain, Rev. H. Honywood 68
Donald Prior 120
Doncaster, E. 230
Doncasterii 230
Dopey 159
Dorothy Dennison 167
Dorothy Perkins 166
D'Orsay Rose 226
Dortmund 170
Dot, Pedro 136
Double Dwarf Pennsylvanian 224
Double White 209
Doubloons 122, 163
Douglas, W. J. A. 165
Dr A. J. Verhage 109
Dr Huey 168
Dr W. van Fleet 167

Dresden Doll   138, 139
Ducher, Antoine   72
Duchesse de Brabant   63
— —Morny   193
—d'Istrie   183
Duchess of Connaught   69
— —Portland   184
— —Westminster   69
Duftwolke   109
Duke of Connaught   69
— —Edinburgh   193
Dumalis   272
Dundee Rambler   150
Duplex   222
Dupont, André   154
Dupontii   153
Dwarf Floribunda   127
Dwarf Polyantha   156

Earldomensis   202
Easlea's Golden Rambler   141
Easlea, Walter   83, 141
Easter Morning   137
Eberwein   159
Ecae   197, 202
—Hybrid   198
Echo   156
Eclipse   90
Edelcaninas   215
Edelrosen   66
Edith Cavell   157
Edland, Harry   74
Edmunds, Fred   112
Edouard   186
Eduardo Toda   136
Eglanteria   219
—duplex   221
Eglanteria Hybrids   220
Eglantula   229
Elasmacantha   213
Elegance   141
Elizabeth Harkness   112
Ellen Poulsen   156
Ellinor Le Grice   125
Else Poulsen   119
— —Climbing   144
Elymajtica   229
Emily Gray   168
Emma Wright   83
Ena Harkness   60, 96
— —Climbing   141
Enzymes   110
Ernest H. Morse   112
Escapade   129
Estrellita de Oro   136
Etoile de Hollande   83
— —Climbing   141
Etoile Luisante   138

Eugénie Jovain   61
Eurosa   38
Eva   132
Everblooming Jack   77
Evergreen Rose   162
Excelsa   167
Exhibitors   64, 89, 104, 190

Fabvier   52
Fairy Moss   138, 139
Fairy Princess   146
Fairy Roses   134
Falkland   210
Fargesii   171
Farreri persetosa   198
Fashion   123
Fa Tee Nurseries   47, 53
Fedtschenkoana   229
Felicia   132
Félicité et Perpétue   162
Félicité Parmentier   217
Fellemberg   52
Ferox   235
Ferruginea   222
Fertilizing   20
Fessel, Henri   95
Field Rose   150
Filament   16
Filipes   151
Filipes Kiftsgate   152
Fimbriata   236
First Love   100
F. J. Grootendorst   236
Floradora   121
Floribundas   117
Floribunda—HT type   128
Flowering Times (Table)   256
Flowering Time: terms used   24
Flowers at home   110
Flower stems   85
Foetida   198
—bicolor   199
—Hybrids   200
—persiana   75, 79, 200, 221
Foliolosa   224
Forrestiana   229
Fortune, Robert   41, 52
Fortune's Double Yellow   52
Fortuniana   41
Forty-Niner   100
For You   136
Foster-Melliar, Rev A.   25
Four Seasons   180
Four Stud Chinas   49, 53, 54
Fragrance   101, 152
Fragrance (Table)   259
Fragrant Cloud   109
Francofurtana   174

François Juranville   167
Franklin Englemann   116
Franz Deegen   118
Frau Dagmar Hartopp   237
Frau Karl Druschki   195
Fräulein Octavia Hesse   221
Fred Streeter   231
French Noisette   55
French Roses   175
Frensham   98, 122
Fritz Nobis   221
Fru Dagmar Hastrup   237
Frühlingsgold   210
Frühlingsmorgen   129, 210
Fryer's Nurseries   159

Gallica complicata   218
—grandiflora   175
—Hybrids   174
—officinalis   173
—pumila   173
—versicolor   173
Gallicanae   172
Gallicas   172, 175
Gamble, James Alexander   71
Gardeners' Chronicle   49
Gardenia   166
Gaujard, Jean   83
Gault, S. Millar   147
Gay Crusader   105
Géant des Batailles   192
Geheimrat Duisberg   88
General Jack   192
Général Jacqueminot   192
General MacArthur   76
Général Schablikine   64
Gentiliana   171
Gentleman's Magazine   53
Genus   11
Genus Rosa, The   26
Georg Arends   76, 103
George Dickson   80
Geranium (Flor)   124
—(Moyesii)   232
Gerard, John   173, 198, 205
Gertrud Westphal   127
Giesebrecht   159
Gigantea   146, 148
—erubescens   146
—Hybrids   146
Gioia   94
Giraldii   229
Glaucophylla   199
Gloire de Dijon   57
——France   176
——Paris   194
Gloire des Lawranceanas   134, 186

——Polyantha   155
——Rosomanes   138, 186
Gloire du Midi   158
Glomerata   171
Gloria Dei   94
—di Roma   91
—Mundi   158
Glutinosa   222
Golden Chersonese   198
—Dawn   86
——Climbing   142
—Delight   125
—Emblem   82, 83
—Glow   137, 171
—Moss   139
—Ophelia   81
—Rambler   56
—Rapture   89
—Rose of China   201
—Salmon   158
——Supérieur   158
—Scepter   98
—Showers   144
—Wave   109
—Wings   210
Goldfinch   160
Goldilocks   122, 125
Goldlachs   158
Goldmoss   139
Gold of Ophir   52
Gooseberry Rose   33
Gottfried Keller   121, 200
Graciliflora   213
Grandiflora   128, 208
Grandpa Dickson   111
Grant, Patrick   86
Gratissima   229
Gravereaux, Jules   77
Gray, Alexander Hill   56, 59
Great Double White   217
Great Dwarf Rose   182
Green Rose   49
Gregory, C. & Son   136
Gregory, C. Walter   105
Greta Kluis   156
Grey Pearl   123
Gronovius   47
Grootendorst Supreme   237
Ground cover roses   146, 164, 168, 170
Grumpy   159
Gruss an Aachen   118
Gruss an Teplitz   52
Guillot   36, 68, 155
Guinée   142
Gustav Piganeau   193
Gustav Régis   73
Gymnocarpa   229
Gymnosperms   9

Hadley 87,
Hamburger Phoenix 170
Handel 144
Hand-painted roses 129
Hanmer, Sir Thomas 173
Happy 159
Hardii 30
Hardy, Eugène 30
Harisonii 210
Harison's Yellow 210
Harkness, John 59, 60
Harkness seedlings 31
Harkness, William Ernest 94, 97, 189
Harmonie 128
Harry Edland 74
Harvey, John H. 207
Hawrana 272
Headleyensis 202
Heather Muir 204
Hebe's Lip 180
Heckeliana 272
Hedges of roses 238
Heights (Table) 241
Height: terms used 23
Heinrich Wendland 88
Helenae 151
Hemisphaerica 199
Hemsleyana 229
Henry, Dr Augustine 49
Henryi 171
Herbstfeuer 235
Her Majesty 194
Hermosa 52
Hesperrhodos 33
Hiawatha 167
Hibernica 216
Hidcote Yellow 201
Highdownensis 232
Hill, E. G. 75, 77, 84
Hill, Joseph H. 84
Hilling, Thomas 174
Himalayan Musk Rose 153
Hinner, Wilhelm 76
Hinrich Gaede 88
Hips 215, 231
Hips: points given 24
Hips (Table) 262
Hispida 209
History of Garden Roses, The 27
— —Roses 27
— —the Rose 27, 35
Hoi-tong-hong 35
Hole, Dean 25, 57, 127
Hollandica 237
Holland Rose 180
Holodonta 229, 231
Holy Rose 174
Honeyglow 125

Honeymoon 127
Hon George Bancroft 69
Honigmond 127
Horace Vernet 193
Horrida 272
Horticultural Society of Lyon 70
Horvath, M. H. 123, 163, 165
Hudson's Bay Rose 228
Hugh Dickson 195
Hugonis 201
—Hybrid 202
Hulthemia berberifolia 29
—persica 29
Hulthemosa guzarica 32
—hardii 30
—kopetdaghensis 32
Hume's Blush Tea-scented China 53
Humilis 224
Humpty-Dumpty 137
Hurst, Dr C. C. 27, 36, 53, 181
Hybrid Austrian Briars 79
—Chinas 50
—Musks 131
—Perpetuals 189, 221
—Polyanthas 117
—Teas 66

Iceberg Climbing 145
—(Flor) 126
—(Wich) 167
Ilona 109
Incarnata 217
Incense Rose 202
Independence 124
Indica 48
—fragrans 53
—humilis 134
—odorata 53
— —hybrida 68
—pumila 134
—sulphurea 54
Indicae 47
Inermis 215
—morlettii 234
Inodora 272
Involucrata 46
Irish Beauty 77
—Brightness 77
—Elegance 77
—Engineer 77
—Fireflame 77
—Gold 111
—Harmony 77
—Modesty 77
—Pride 77
—Star 77

Jackie, Climbing 145
Jackson & Perkins Co 107, 122

Jackson, Dr G. A. D. 219
Jacobite Rose 217
Jacques Cartier 185
Jacques, M. 162, 186
Jäger, August 26
Janet's Pride 220
Japanese Rose 235
Jaune Bicolor 199
—Desprez 57
Jean Lafitte 163
—Sisley 69
Jeans, Rev G. E. 181
Jersey Beauty 166
Joanna Hill 81, 94, 96
John Waterer 113
Joseph Guy 119
Josephine Bruce 99
Joséphine Maltot 62
Josephine Wheatcroft 137
Joseph's Coat 145
Julien Potin 125
Juliet 105
Juno 103
Just Joey 113

Kaiserin Auguste Viktoria 73
Kamchatka Rose 227
Kara 138, 139
Karen Poulsen 120
Karl Herbst 99
Katharina Zeimet 156
Käthe Duvigneau 121
Kathleen 132
Kathleen Harrop 188
Kazanluk 179
Kennedy, John 53
Kerr, William 39
Keynes, Williams & Co 62
Kiese 216
Kiftsgate 152
King Midas 122
Kirsten Poulsen 119
K. of K. 83
Königin von Danemarck 217
Kordes' Harmonie 128
—Perfecta 103
— —Superior 103
—Sondermeldung 124
Kordes, Wilhelm 79, 88, 103, 120, 168, 170
Kordesii 116, 170
—Hybrids 170
Koreana 213
Korp 116

La Belle Marseillaise 52
Labrador Rose 228
Lacharme, François 69

Lady Curzon 218
—Gay 167
—Godiva 167
—Hillingdon 65
— —Climbing 66
—Mary Fitzwilliam 71
—Penzance 221
—Pirrie 78
—Sylvia 81
— —Climbing 140
Laevigata 42
Laevigata Hybrids 42
Laevigatae 42
Lafayette 119
Laffay, M. 67, 191
La Follette 147
La France 68
La Jolla 102
Lamarque 57
Lambert, Peter 119, 195
Lamia 83, 141
Lammerts, Dr W. E. 93, 124
Laneii 183
Lane's Moss 184
La Pâquerette 155
La Reine 191
— —Victoria 188
La Rêve 201
Larman, Herbert 104
La Rosière 195
La Séduisante 217
Lavender Pinocchio 123
La Vie de Bruxelles 180
La Virginal 217
Lawranceana 134
Lawrance, Mary 134
Lawrence Johnston 201
Laxa (rootstock) 219
—(species) 229
Leaf colour 87, 222, 224
Leda 180
Le Grice, E. B. 28, 125
Lens, Louis 110
Leonida 45
Léontine Gervais 167
Leroy, André 27
Leschenaultii 171
Leverkusen 171
L'heritierana 234
Liberty 75
L'Idéal 57
Lilac Charm 123
Lilian 125
Lindleyana 46
Lindley, John 133
Lindsay, Nancy 32
Little Flirt 138
—Showoff 145

—White Pet 164
L'Obscurité 69
Longicuspis 151
Long John Silver 163
Lord Penzance 221
Lorraine Lee 148
— —Climbing 148
Los Angeles 82
Loudon, Earl of 150
Lovely Rambler 151
Lowea berberifolia 29
Lucas, E. V. 58
Luciae 164
Lucida 44, 226
—plena 226
Lucy Ashton 221
Lutea (Foetida) 79, 198
—maxima 211
—plena 213
—(Spin) 211
Lutescens 209
Lyellii 46
Lyon Rose 78

Mabel Morse 84
Macartnea 44
Macartney Rose 44
Macounii 229
Macrantha 218
Macranthas 218
Macrophylla 230
—crasseaculeata 239
—Hybrids 230
—rubricaulis 230
Madame Hardy 179
Magnifica 124, 127, 221
Magnolia Rose 62
Maiden's Blush 217
Mainzer Fastnacht 111
Majalis 229
Mallerin, Charles 93, 98, 142
Maman Cochet 65
Manca 231
Manda, W. A. 165
Manettii 57
Ma Pâquerette 155
Marbled 206
Maréchal Niel 58
Margaret McGredy 85
—Merril 131
Marginata 272
Margo Koster 156
Marguerite Brassac 193
—Hilling 211
Marie Baumann 193
—Leonida 44
—Louise 180
—Pavié 155

—van Houtte 64
Marjorie Fair 159
Mark Sullivan 139
Marlena 127
Marquise de Sinéty 77
Marrettii 231
Martin, Mr 151
Mary Hart 87
Mary Queen of Scots 211
Mary Wheatcroft 91
Masquerade 123
—Climbing 145
Ma Surprise 36
Matangi 129
Mattock, John 109
Max Graf 168, 170
Maxima 217
Maximowicziana 171
May Queen 166
McFarland, Dr J. Horace 26, 36
McGredy, Sam (2nd) 45, 84, 86, 108
— —(3rd) 86
— —(4th) 79, 86, 103, 129
McGredy's Yellow 89
Meg Merrilies 221
Meilland, Alain 114, 115
—Antoine 93
—Francis 79, 93, 98, 101
Meipuma 116
Mélanie Cornu 192
Mélanie Lamaire 52
Melina 231
Memorial Rose 164
Mermaid 45, 63
Meteor 127
Mev G. A. van Rossem 85
Mev Nathalie Nypels 119
Michael Saunders 69
Michèle Meilland 96
Micrantha 272
Microcarpa 41
Microphylla 36
—coryana 37
Microphyllae 35
Micrugosa 37
Midnight Sun 86
Midnite Sun 86
Mignon 51
Mignonette 155
Miniatures 133
Minna 221
Minna Kordes 122
Minnehaha 167
Minuetto 138
Minutifolia 33
Minutifoliae 33
Mirandy 99
Mirifica 34

Mischief 109
Miss Edith Cavell 157
—Lawrance's Rose 134
—Lowe's Variety 53
Mlle Bertha Ludi 118
Mme Abel Chatenay 73
— — —Climbing 142
—Alfred Carrière 58
—A. Meilland 94
—Bérard 201
—Bravy 62, 70
—Butterfly 81
—Caroline Testout 71
— — —Climbing 142
—Denis 62
—de Sancy de Parabère 234
—de Sertot 62
—de St. Joseph 70
—de Tartas 63
—Edouard Herriot 81
— — —Climbing 142
—Ernst Calvat 188
—Eugène Résal 53
—Fabvier 52
—Falcot 63
—Gabriel Luiset 193
—Grégoire Staechelin 143
—Hardy 179
—Henri Guillot 68
—Isaac Pereire 188
—Jules Bouché 80
—Laurette Messimy 53
—Legras de St. Germain 217
—Neumann 52
—Norbert Levavasseur 156
—Pierre Oger 188
—Ravary 75
—Roussel 61
—Victor Verdier 69
Modern Roses 26, 36
Mohavensis 231
Mojave 102
Mollis 222
Monocotyledons 9
Monstrous 220
Montana 272
Montezuma 102
Montezumae 223
Montgomery Co 87
Monthly Rose 49, 54
Moonlight 132
Moore, Ralph S. 137
Morlettii 234
Morning Jewel 145
Moschata 55, 152
—Hybrid 153
—hybrida 55
—nepalensis 153

Moss Roses 182
— —Miniature 138
Mossy 220
Moulin Rouge 74
Moyessii 231
—fargesii 231
—Hybrids 231
—rosea 231
Mozart 159
Mrs Beatty 125
—Beckwith 125
—Colville 208, 212
—Foley Hobbs 65
—G. A. van Rossem 85
—Herbert Stevens 65
— — —Climbing 66
—John Laing 194
—Pierre S. du Pont 93
— — —Climbing 143
—Sam McGredy 86
—Sam McGredy Climbing 143
—Wakefield Christie-Miller 71
—Wemyss Quin 82
—W. J. Grant 73
Mu-hsiang 40
Müller, Dr Franz 200
Mulliganii 171
Multibracteata 106, 233
Multiflora 117, 154, 155
—carnea 154
—cathayensis 154
—Hybrids 155
—nana 134, 154
—platyphylla 154
—watsoniana 154
Muriculata 233
Murielae 233
Muriel Wilson 66
Murrells 136
Musk Rose 152
Mutation 51

Nabonnand 64
Names, criticism of 35, 114
Nancy Lee 69
Nanothamnus 233
Nathalie Nypels 119
National Rose Society 74, 79, 128, 190
National Society of Horticulture 79
National Trust 113
National Trust (The) 174
Naylor, Major-General R. F. B. 109, 113, 124
Nevada 212
New Dawn 169
New Penny 138
News 123
Nicolas, Dr J. H. 122

Niphetos 62
—Climbing 62
Nitida 225
Nivea 56
Noisette Desprez 57
—Louis 55, 134
—Philippe 55
Noisettes 55
Noisettiana 55
—manettii 57
Nordia 119
Norman, Albert 97
Normandica 182
Nozomi 146
Nuage Parfumé 109
Nur Mahal 178
Nursery crop yield 88
Nutkana 233

Obtusifolia 272
O'Dell, Michael 109
Odorata 53, 59
—gigantea 146
—ochroleuca 54, 59
—pseudindica 52
Old Blush 54, 55
Old Noisette 55
Old Glory 57
Old Master 129
Old Pink Moss 183
Old Shrub Roses, The 27, 174
Old Yellow Scotch 213
Omeiensis 204
Ophelia 80
Orientalis 273
Origin & Evolution (Notes on) 27
Orléans Rose 156
Ormiston Roy 210
Osbeck, Peter 54
Otto of roses 178
Otto von Bismarck 195
Ovary 16
Over-abundance 107
Over the Rainbow, Climbing 145

Paddy McGredy 128
Paestana 184, 191
Paestum 184
Page, Courtenay 45, 142
Paintbrush 138, 139
Painted Damask 180
—Lady 207
Palustris 225
Papa Meilland 93
Papillae 101
Papoose 145
Pâquerette 155

Para Ti 136
Parentage, Expression of 36, 75, 129
Parkdirektor Riggers 117, 171
Parks, John 40, 54
Parks' Yellow Tea-Scented China 54, 56
Parsons, Alfred 26
Parson's Pink China 54, 55
Parviflora 224
Pascali 110
Pasture Rose 224
Patio roses 127
Paul & Son 69
Paul, Arthur 45
Paul Crampel 158
Paul, Jamain 193
Paul Neyron 194
Paul William 25
Paul William & Son 69, 80
Paulii 237
—rosea 237
Paul's Himalayan Musk 153
—Lemon Pillar 143
—Scarlet Climber 160
Pawsey, Roger 109, 113
Peace 93
Peace, Climbing 140
Pearl 69
—of Canada 136
Pedicel necrosis 16
Pemberton, Rev Joseph H. 26, 56, 57, 131, 190
Pendulina 233
—Hybrids 234
Penelope 133
Pennsylvanica 224
Penzanceana 221
Penzance Hybrids 220
—Lord 220
Peon 135
Perfecta 103
—Superior 103
Perfect flowers 9
Perfume 101, 152, 177
—points given 24
—(Table) 259
Périchon, M. 185
Perla de Alcanada 136
— —Montserrat 136
—Rosa 146
— —Climbing 146
Perle des Jardins 64
— —Rouges 155
Perle d'Or 54
Pernet-Ducher, Claudius 80, 83
— —Gabrielle 83
— —Georges 80, 83
— —Joseph 72, 75, 79, 81, 83, 84, 93
Pernetiana 79

Perpetuals 189
Perpetual White Moss 180
Persetosa 234
Persian Rose 29
—Yellow 75, 79, 200, 221
Persica 29
—Hybrids 30
Petite de Hollande 182
—Junon de Hollande 182
Petworth 232
Pfänder 215
Phanerogams 9
Pharisäer 76
Phoebe's Frilled Pink 236
Phoenicia 171, 177
Photosynthesis 101
Phyllis Bide 161
—Gold 90
Picasso 129
Piccadilly 105
Picture 88
Pigmy roses 134
Pimpernel Rose 205
Pimpinellifoliae 195
Pinetorum 234
Pink Cameo 146
—Cherokee 42
—Favourite 102
—Grootendorst 237, 238
—Moss 183
—Parfait 128
—Perpetue 145
—Radiance 76
—Roamer 165
Pinnate 30
Pinocchio 121, 123
Pisocarpa 234
Pistils 9, 16
Plant Breeders' Rights 92, 114
Planting 19
Plant Patents 92, 169
Platyrhodon 35
Pliny 181
Pollen 16
Pollmeriana 155
Polly 86
Polyantha 117, 120, 131, 155
—grandiflora 171
—(multiflora) 154
—Pompon 156
Pomifera 222
Pompon Blanc Parfait 218
—Jaune 199
—Parfait 218
—Rose 182
—de Paris 135
— — —Climbing 146
—des Dames 182

Portland, Oregon 73
Portlands 184
Poulsen, Dines 118
—Dorus Theus 119
—Niels Dines 119
—Svend 117, 119
Poulsen's Yellow 121
Pour Toi 136
Pouzinii 273
Powell, Margaret 112
Prairie Rose 163
Pratensis 224
Prattii 234
Precious Platinum 116
Président Chaussé 139
President Coolidge 163
Président de Sèze 176
President Herbert Hoover 87
Primula 202
Prince Camille de Rohan 195
—Charlie's Rose 213
Princesse Hélène 191
Priscilla Burton 129
Prominent 116
Proof of the Pudding 92
Propagation 18, 157
—Budding 18
—Cuttings 165
Prosperity 133
Provence Rose 179, 180
Province Rose 180
Provins Rose 173
Pruhoniciana 232
Pruning 19
—Banksians 39
—Fortune's Double Yellow 52
—Gallicas 175
—Queen Elizabeth 124
—Rugosas 238
—Wichuraiana Hybrids 165
—yellow sp. of Pimpinellifoliae 197
Pteragonis cantabrigiensis 202
Punjab Regiment 113
Pyle, Robert 94, 136
Pyrifera 234

Quatre Saisons 180, 181
— —Blanc Mousseux 180
Queen Alexandra Rose, The 105
Queen Elizabeth 103, 124
Queen Mother, Her Majesty the 117
Queen of Beauty and Fragrance 187
Queen of Bourbons 187
— —Perpetuals 177

Raban, H. Nigel 200
Radiance 76
Ragged Robin 138, 186

Ramanas Rose 235
Rambler & Trailer 150
Ramona 43
Rapa 226
Rapture 89
Rayon d'Or 79
Recommendation stars 24
Recommended roses (Table) 264
Red Baby Rambler 156
—Cherokee 43
—Damask 173
—Devil 111
—Dorothy Perkins 167
—Ensign 97
—Letter Day 83
—Pet 155
—Planet 116
—Spider 20
—Star 119
Redouté, Pierre Joseph 53
Regeliana 235
Regular flowers 10
Rehder, A. 15
Reina Elisenda 124
Reine des Français 191
— —Îles Bourbon 187
— —Neiges 195
—Victoria 188
Religion & the Rose 202
Remontant 24, 48
Repens 150
Rêve d'Or 58
Réveil Dijonnais 201
Richardii 174
Richmond 77
Ritter von Barmstede 171
Rivers, Thomas 25, 58, 126, 153, 185
Roberts, Dr Andrew 197, 198, 233
Robin Hood 120, 158
Robinson, Harold 91
—Herbert 90
—Thomas 136
Rob Roy 130
Rödhätte 118, 119
Roger Lambelin 194
Rome Glory 91
Roosevelt, Theodore 63
Rootstocks 18, 103, 168, 215, 219, 220
Rosaceae 9, 11
Rosa Mundi 173
Rose Amateur's Guide, The 25
Rose Annuals 28
—à Parfum de l'Hay 238
—Apples 238
—Bradwardine 221
—Capucine 199
—Châtaigne 35
—d'Amour 226

—de la Reine 191
—de Mai 229
—de Meaux 182
—de Pâques 229
—du Roi 191
—du Saint-Sacrament 229
—Edouard 186
—Elf 121
—Garden, The 25
—Gaujard 103
—Growing Complete 28
Roselandia 81
Rose Marie Viaud 161
—Mosaic 102, 123
Rosenelfe 120
Rosenlexikon 26
Rosenmärchen 121
Rose Oeillet de Saint Arquey 55
—of the Tombs 175
Roseraie de l'Haÿ 238
Roses, definition 11
Rose Societies 21
Roses, Their History etc. 26, 132
Rose Van Sian 176
Rosier Camellia 42
—de Philippe Noisette 55
—de Thionville 180
Rosiers tiges 126, 233
Rosina 137
Roulet, Colonel 135
Rouletii 135
Roussel, A. 192
Rowley, Gordon 71, 205
Roxburghii 35, 106
—hirtula 36
—Hybrids 36
—normalis 36
—plena 36
Royal Dane 119
—Horticultural Society 40, 54
—National Rose Society 74, 79, 128, 190
Rubiginosa 220
Rubra 173
Rubrifolia 222
Rubus 171
Rudiuscula 225
Rudolph Timm 124, 131
Ruga 151
Rugosa 235
—alba 235
—atropurpurea 236
—Hybrids 236
—rubra 236
—scabrosa 238
—typica 235
Rumsey, Roy 145
Russian Hybrids 31
Rust 107

Sabine, Joseph 150, 205
Sacramento Rose 34
Safrano 61
Saga 124
Salictorum 239
Salmon Spray 86
Sancta 174
Sander's White 167
Sanguinea 53
San Rafael Rose 52
Saturata 239
Scabrosa 238
Scarlet Fire 175
—Four Seasons 184
Scent 101, 152
—(Table) 259
Scharlachglut 175
Scherpe Boskoop 237
Scherzo 116
Schneekönigin 195
Schneewittchen 127
Schneezwerg 239
Schwartz, Joseph 70
Scotch Roses 204
—Yellow 213
Sea Foam 45
Sealing Wax 232
Seed 11, 219, 222
Seedlings 17
Semi-double 11
Semi-plena 218
Semperflorens minima 133
Sempervirens 56, 162
—anemoniflora 149
—Hybrids 162
Sénateur Amic 148
Seneca 184
Sensation 84
Sepal 9
Serafinii 222
Sericea 202
—pteracantha 203
Serpens 150
Serratipetala 54
Sertata 239
Setigera 123, 163
—Hybrids 163
Setina 52
Setipoda 239
Seven Sisters Rose 154
Shafter 168
Shailer's White Moss 183
Shakespeare's musk-rose 150
Shea, Charles E. 79
Shepherd, Roy E. 27, 35, 40, 210
Sherardii 222
Shot Silk 84
Shot Silk, Climbing 143

Shreeves, Eric 99
Shrub & bush 131
Shrub Roses of Today 27
Sibirica 208
Sicula 273
Sierra Snowstorm 138
Signora (Piero Puricelli) 91
Silver Jubilee 116
—Moon 43
Silvestris 150
Simplicifolia 29
Simplicifoliae 29
Sims, J. 133
Single 11, 77
Sinica Anemone 42
—(China) 48
—(Laev) 42
Sinowilsonii 164
—Hybrid 164
Sisley, Jean 67
Sissi 111
Skyrocket 133
Slater's Crimson China 49
Sleepy 159
Slingeri 213
Slinger, William 189
Sneezy 159
Snow Queen 195
Socrates 68
Soleil d'Or 75
Sonia 114
—Meilland 114
Sonomensis 239
Soulieana 164
Southampton 130
South Orange Perfection 165
Southport 97
Souvenir de Claudius Pernet 83
— —Georges Pernet 83
— —la Malmaison 187
— —Princesse de Lamballe 187
—d'Elise Vardon 63
—S.A. Prince 63
— —St Ann's 187
—d'un Ami 63
Spaldingii 239
Spanbauer, Frank 110
Spanish Beauty 143
Spartan 125
Species, classification 15, 271
—definition 12
—identification 12
Spectacular 144
Spek, Jan 99
Spek's Yellow 98
Spinosissima 204
—altaica 208
—bicolor 209

—dunwichensis 208
—hispida 208
—Hybrids 209
—myriacantha 209
—nana 209
Spithamea 239
Splendens 151
Spong 182
Sport 51, 81, 87
Stamen 9, 16
Standard roses 126, 233
Stanwell Perpetual 207, 212
Starina 138
Stars for Recommendation 24, 264
Stellata 33
—mirifica 33
Sterling Silver 111
Stern, Sir Frederick 164, 232
Stevens Rose 229
Stigmas 16
Stipule 11, 228
St John's Rose 174
St Mark's Rose 226
Stocks 18, 103, 168, 215, 219, 220
—canina 68
—Dog Rose Cuttings 60
—Manettii 57
—Rugosa 237
Streeter, Fred 231
Styles 16, 47, 149
Stylosa 273
Subserrulata 224
Suffulta 239
Sugar Sweet 118
Sulphurea 199
Sulphur Rose 199
Superb 157
Superba 158
Super Star 106
Surpasse Tout 176
Susan Louise 148
Sutter's Gold 99
Sutton, Gordon 219
Swamp Rose 225
Sweet Fairy 137
Sweetheart Rose 51
Sweet Promise 114
Sweet, Robert 133
Sweginzowii 240
Swim, Herbert C. 100
Synstylae 149

Talisman 87
Tantau, Mathias 106
Tausendschön 161
Teas 59
Temple Bells 170
—Rose 186

Ten Sisters 160
Ternata 42
Testout, Caroline 72
The Bride 64
The Doctor 91, 122
The Fairy 169
The Garland 161
The Mouse 123
Theophrastus 181
Thomas, G. S. 27, 153, 174
Thoresbyana 151
Thornless Rose 188
Threepenny Bit Rose 198
Tipo Ideale 49
Titania 136
Tomentosa 222
Tom Thumb 136
Tour de Malakoff 182
Tree Roses 126, 233
Trial Grounds, Bagatelle 77
— —Haywards Heath 74
— —St. Albans 74
Tricolore de Flandre 176
Triomphe de la Guillotière 36
Triphylla 149
Troika 119
Tropicana 107
Turbinata 174
Turkestanica 213
Turner, L. G. 22
Turner's Crimson Rambler 160
Tuscany 176
Tuscany Superb 177
Tuschetica 273
Tzigane 105, 128

Ulrich Brunner (Fils) 194
Ultramontana 239
Understocks 18, 103, 168, 215, 219, 220

Valerie 167
Valley of Roses 179
Van Fleet, Dr Walter 43, 167
Vanity 133
Variety 15
Veilchenblau 161
Velvet Rose 176
Vera Dalton 98
Verbeek, G. & Zn 109
Vernonii 33
Victor Verdier 69, 192
Villosa 222
Violet Blue 161
Violinista Costa 92
Virginiana 225
—humilis 224
—Hybrid 226
—plena 226
Virginian Lass 234

Virginia Red   225
Virus   67, 102, 154
Viscountess Falmouth   69
Viviand-Morel, Ernest   76

Webbiana   240
Wedding Day   164
Weeks, O. L.   100
Wendy   136
Wendy Cussons   105
Western Roses   33
Westminster   106
Wheatcroft Bros   90, 95
Wheatcroft, Harry   90, 106, 125
Wheatcroft's Baby Crimson   136
Whisky Mac   111
White American Beauty   195
—Baby Rambler   156
—Bath   183
—Butterfly   110
—Dog Rose   150
—Dorothy   167
—Maman Cochet   65
—Pet   163
Wichuraiana   164
—Hybrids   164
Width of plants (Table)   241
Wilhelm   133
William Allen Richardson   58, 161
—Francis Bennett   70
—Harvey   97
—Lobb   139, 183
William's Double Yellow   213
Williams, Dr A. H.   168

William the Fourth   210
William III   212
Willmott, Ellen   26
Willmottiae   240
Willock, Sir Henry   200
Windsor, Duke of   94
Wine   215
Wintoniensis   232
Wolley-Dod's Rose   222
Woodsii fendleri   240
World's Fair   122
Wyatt, L. A.   28, 53, 61
Wylie, Ann P.   27, 214

Xanthina   213
—spontanea   213
Xavier Olibo   70
Xerophyte   29

Yellow Banksian   40
—Cécile Brunner   54
Yellowcrest   125
Yellow Kaiserin Auguste Viktoria   118
—Provence   199
—Sweet Briar   198
—Sweetheart   137
Yesterday   159
York and Lancaster   179
Young, W. Cdr. N.   28, 153
Yvonne Rabier   118

Zee   138, 145
Zéphirine Drouhin   188
Zorina   122

U